AF703292

5G Technology

Kruger Brentt
Publishers

5G Technology

Ava Wilson
Ethan O'Ryan

Kruger Brentt
Publishers

2025

Kruger Brentt Publishers UK. LTD.
Company Number 9728962

Regd. Office: 68 St Margarets Road, Edgware, Middlesex HA8 9UU

© 2025 AUTHORS

ISBN: 978-1-78715-303-5

Disclaimer:

Every possible effort has been made to ensure that the information contained in this book is accurate at the time of going to press, and the publisher and author cannot accept responsibility for any errors or omissions, however caused. No responsibility for loss or damage occasioned to any person acting, or refraining from action, as a result of the material in this publication can be accepted by the editor, the publisher or the author. The Publisher is not associated with any product or vendor mentioned in the book. The contents of this work are intended to further general scientific research, understanding and discussion only. Readers should consult with a specialist where appropriate.

Every effort has been made to trace the owners of copyright material used in this book, if any. The author and the publisher will be grateful for any omission brought to their notice for acknowledgement in the future editions of the book.

All Rights reserved under International Copyright Conventions. No part of this publication may be reproduced, stored in a retrieval system, or transmitted in any form or by any means, electronic, mechanical, photocopying, recording or otherwise without the prior written consent of the publisher and the copyright owner.

For information on all our publications visit our website at http://krugerbrentt.com/

PREFACE

"5G Technology" embarks on an exploration of the transformative potential of fifth-generation (5G) wireless technology, offering readers a comprehensive understanding of its technical foundations, applications, and implications for various industries and society at large. This book serves as an essential resource for professionals, policymakers, researchers, and enthusiasts seeking insights into the unprecedented opportunities and challenges presented by the advent of 5G.

The emergence of 5G technology represents a significant milestone in the evolution of wireless communication, promising ultra-fast speeds, low latency, high reliability, and massive connectivity that will revolutionize how we connect, communicate, and interact with the world around us. From enhanced mobile broadband to mission-critical applications in healthcare, transportation, manufacturing, and beyond, 5G has the potential to unleash a new era of innovation and economic growth.

The primary objective of this book is to provide readers with a comprehensive overview of 5G technology, covering key topics such as the technical specifications of 5G networks, deployment strategies, spectrum allocation, infrastructure requirements, and use cases across different industry sectors. Each chapter offers insights, case studies, and expert perspectives to help readers navigate the complexities of 5G and understand its implications for their respective fields.

Contributions from leading experts in the field delve into various aspects of 5G technology, including its impact on mobile communications, Internet of Things (IoT) applications, smart cities, autonomous vehicles, augmented reality, virtual reality, healthcare delivery, and digital transformation. Special emphasis is placed on the opportunities for innovation, entrepreneurship, and social impact that 5G technology presents, as well as the challenges related to security, privacy, and digital divide.

As we stand on the brink of the 5G revolution, it is essential to foster collaboration, dialogue, and informed decision-making among stakeholders to realize the full potential of this transformative technology. By embracing a multidisciplinary and inclusive approach to 5G innovation and deployment, we can harness its power to create a more connected, sustainable, and resilient future for all.

We extend our sincere gratitude to the contributors whose expertise and dedication have enriched this book. It is our hope that "5G Technology" will serve as a valuable resource and catalyst for dialogue, innovation, and progress in the dynamic landscape of wireless communication and digital connectivity.

Ava Wilson

Ethan O'Ryan

CONTENTS

CHAPTER 1

INTRODUCTION TO 5G TECHNOLOGY

1.1 EVOLUTION OF MOBILE COMMUNICATION TECHNOLOGIES

Mobile communication technologies have undergone a remarkable evolution since their inception, revolutionizing the way people communicate, access information, and interact with the world around them. From the early days of analog communication to the advent of 5G networks, this evolution has been marked by significant advancements in technology, infrastructure, and user experiences. The evolution of mobile communication technologies has been driven by a relentless pursuit of innovation and a growing demand for connectivity, mobility, and digital experiences. From the early days of analog cellular networks to the advent of 5G and beyond, each generation of mobile technology has brought about profound changes in how we communicate, collaborate, and conduct business. As we stand on the brink of a new era of connectivity, the possibilities for mobile innovation are limitless, shaping the future of technology and society in profound ways.

1.1.1 Analog Era

The journey of mobile communication technologies began in the 1980s with the introduction of analog cellular networks. These networks relied on analog signals to transmit voice calls, offering limited coverage and capacity. The first-generation (1G) mobile systems, such as Advanced Mobile Phone Service (AMPS) in the United States and Nordic Mobile Telephone (NMT) in Europe, laid the foundation for wireless communication but were characterized by poor sound quality and susceptibility to interference.

1.1.2 Digital Revolution

The transition from analog to digital communication marked a significant turning point in the evolution of mobile technologies. Second-generation (2G) systems, introduced in the early 1990s, brought about digital voice encoding, enabling clearer calls and improved spectral efficiency. The Global System for Mobile Communications (GSM) emerged as the dominant 2G standard, facilitating international roaming and interoperability between networks.

1.1.3 Mobile Internet and Multimedia

The advent of third-generation (3G) networks in the early 2000s ushered in the era of mobile internet and multimedia services. 3G technologies, such as Universal Mobile Telecommunications System (UMTS) and Code Division Multiple Access (CDMA2000), enabled high-speed data transmission, paving the way for services like mobile web browsing, video streaming, and multimedia messaging. These advancements transformed mobile devices into powerful tools for accessing information and entertainment on the go.

1.1.4 Rise of Smartphones

The proliferation of smartphones in the late 2000s further accelerated the evolution of mobile communication technologies. Combining advanced computing capabilities with cellular connectivity, smartphones revolutionized the way people communicate, work, and socialize. The introduction of Apple's iPhone in 2007 and Google's Android operating system in 2008 marked the beginning of the smartphone era, driving innovation in hardware, software, and user interfaces.

1.1.5 4G LTE and Mobile Broadband

Fourth-generation (4G) Long-Term Evolution (LTE) networks emerged as the standard for high-speed mobile broadband in the 2010s. Offering significantly faster data rates and lower latency than 3G technologies, 4G LTE enabled seamless streaming of HD video, online gaming, and cloud-based applications. The widespread adoption of 4G transformed the way people consume digital content and spurred the growth of the app economy.

1.1.6 Internet of Things (IoT) and Connected Devices

The evolution of mobile communication technologies has extended beyond smartphones to encompass a diverse ecosystem of connected devices and applications. The Internet of Things (IoT) has emerged as a key driver of innovation, enabling the connectivity of everyday objects and appliances to the internet. From smart thermostats and wearables to connected cars and industrial sensors, IoT devices leverage mobile networks to collect data, automate processes, and enhance efficiency.

1.1.7 5G and Beyond

The fifth-generation (5G) of mobile communication represents the next frontier in wireless connectivity, promising unprecedented speed, capacity, and reliability. With peak data rates surpassing 10 gigabits per second and latency reduced to milliseconds, 5G networks will enable transformative applications such as augmented reality, autonomous vehicles, and remote surgery. Beyond 5G, emerging technologies like satellite communication, edge computing, and artificial intelligence are poised to further revolutionize the mobile landscape, ushering in an era of ubiquitous connectivity and digital innovation.

1.2 NEED FOR 5G: CURRENT CHALLENGES AND OPPORTUNITIES

The advent of 5G technology heralds a new era of connectivity, promising lightning-fast speeds, ultra-low latency, and unparalleled reliability. As the world becomes increasingly interconnected, the demand for seamless communication and data transfer has surged. However, the deployment of 5G networks comes with its own set of challenges and opportunities, shaping the future of telecommunications and beyond.

The need for 5G technology is undeniable, driven by the growing demand for faster, more reliable connectivity and the proliferation of IoT devices and digital applications. However, realizing the full potential of 5G requires overcoming various challenges, including infrastructure upgrades, spectrum allocation, regulatory hurdles, security concerns, and bridging the digital divide. Nevertheless, the opportunities presented by 5G are immense, from enhanced connectivity and IoT innovation to economic growth and sustainable development. By addressing these challenges and seizing the opportunities, we can unlock the transformative power of 5G and shape a more connected, efficient, and prosperous future.

1.2.1 Challenges

Transitioning to 5G requires significant infrastructure upgrades. Existing networks may not be equipped to handle the demands of 5G technology, necessitating extensive investments in infrastructure development. This includes the deployment of small cells, fiber-optic cables, and advanced antennae to support the high-frequency bands used by 5G.

Spectrum allocation is crucial for the effective deployment of 5G networks. While higher frequency bands offer faster speeds and greater bandwidth, they have limited range and penetration capabilities. Finding the right balance between high and low-frequency bands is essential to ensure optimal coverage and performance.

Regulatory hurdles pose a significant challenge to the rollout of 5G networks. Obtaining permits for infrastructure deployment, navigating spectrum auctions, and addressing concerns about privacy and security require coordination between governments, regulatory bodies, and industry stakeholders.

The increased connectivity and data transmission capabilities of 5G networks also raise security concerns. As more devices become interconnected, the risk of cyberattacks and data breaches escalates. Ensuring robust security measures, such as encryption protocols and network segmentation, is essential to safeguarding sensitive information.

Bridging the digital divide remains a significant challenge, particularly in rural and underserved areas. While urban centers may see rapid deployment of 5G networks, rural communities often lack the infrastructure and resources to access high-speed internet. Addressing this disparity requires innovative solutions and targeted investment in rural connectivity initiatives.

1.2.2 Opportunities

5G technology promises to revolutionize connectivity, offering speeds up to 100 times faster than 4G networks. This opens up new possibilities for streaming high-definition content, immersive gaming experiences, and real-time communication applications.

The Internet of Things (IoT) and Industry 4.0 stand to benefit significantly from the capabilities of 5G technology. With its low latency and high reliability, 5G enables seamless connectivity between smart devices, autonomous vehicles, and industrial equipment, paving the way for more efficient and automated processes.

The widespread adoption of 5G is expected to spur innovation and drive economic growth. From augmented reality and virtual reality applications to autonomous vehicles and remote healthcare services, 5G technology fuels a new wave of technological advancement, creating opportunities for businesses and entrepreneurs alike.

5G plays a crucial role in the development of smart cities and sustainable urban environments. By enabling connected infrastructure, smart grid systems, and efficient transportation networks, 5G facilitates resource optimization, reduces carbon emissions, and enhances quality of life for urban residents.

The COVID-19 pandemic highlighted the importance of remote healthcare and online education. 5G technology offers the bandwidth and reliability needed to support telemedicine platforms, remote monitoring devices, and virtual classrooms, bridging the gap between patients, students, and healthcare providers.

1.3 KEY FEATURES AND GOALS OF 5G TECHNOLOGY

In telecommunications, 5G is the fifth-generation technology standard for cellular networks, which cellular phone companies began deploying worldwide in 2019, and is the successor to 4G technology that provides connectivity to most current mobile phones.

Like its predecessors, 5G networks are cellular networks, in which the service area is divided into small geographical areas called cells.

All 5G wireless devices in a cell are connected to the Internet and the telephone network by radio waves through a basestation and antennae in the cell. The new networks have higher download speeds, with a peak speed of 10 gigabits per second (Gbit/s) when there is only one user in the network. 5G has higher bandwidth to deliver faster speeds than 4G and can connect more devices, improving the quality of Internet services in crowded areas. Due to the increased bandwidth, it is expected the 5G networks will increasingly be used as general internet service providers (ISPs), competing with existing ISPs such as cable internet, and also will make possible new applications in internet-of-things (IoT) and machine-to-machine areas. Cellphones with 4G capability alone are not able to use the 5G networks.

5G networks are cellular networks, in which the service area is divided into small geographical areas called cells. All 5G wireless devices in a cell communicate by radio waves with a cellular base station via fixed antennas, over frequencies assigned by the base station. The base stations, termed nodes, are connected to switching centers in the telephone network and routers for Internet access by high-bandwidth optical fiber or wireless backhaul connections. As in other cellular networks, a mobile device moving from one cell to another is automatically handed off seamlessly.

The industry consortium setting standards for 5G, the 3rd Generation Partnership Project (3GPP), defines "5G" as any system using 5G NR (5G New Radio) software — a definition that came into general use by late 2018.

Several network operators use millimeter waves called FR2 in 5G terminology, for additional capacity and higher throughputs. Millimeter waves have a shorter range than the lower frequency microwaves, therefore the cells are of a smaller size. Millimeter waves also have more trouble passing through building walls and humans. Millimeter-wave antennas are smaller than the large antennas used in previous cellular networks.

The increased data rate is achieved partly by using additional higher-frequency radio waves in addition to the low- and medium-band frequencies used in previous cellular networks. For providing a wide range of services, 5G networks can operate in three frequency bands — low, medium, and high.

5G can be implemented in low-band, mid-band or high-band millimeter-wave. Low-band 5G uses a similar frequency range to 4G cellphones, 600–900 MHz, which can potentially offer higher download speeds than 4G: 5–250 megabits per second (Mbit/s). Low-band cell towers have a range and coverage area similar to 4G towers. Mid-band 5G uses microwaves of 1.7–4.7 GHz, allowing speeds of 100–900 Mbit/s, with each cell tower providing service up to several kilometers in radius. This level of service is the most widely deployed, and was deployed in many metropolitan areas in 2020. Some regions are not implementing the low band, making Mid-band the minimum service level. High-band 5G uses frequencies of 24–47 GHz, near the bottom of the millimeter wave band, although higher frequencies may be used in the future. It often achieves download speeds in the gigabit-per-second (Gbit/s) range, comparable to co-axial cable Internet service. However, millimeter waves (mmWave or mmW) have a more limited range, requiring many small cells. They can be impeded or blocked by materials in walls or windows or pedestrians. Due to their higher cost, plans are to deploy these cells only in dense urban environments and areas where crowds of people congregate such as sports stadiums and convention centers. The above speeds are those achieved in actual tests in 2020, and speeds are expected to increase during rollout. The spectrum ranging from 24.25 to 29.5 GHz has been the most licensed and deployed 5G mmWave spectrum range in the world.

Rollout of 5G technology has led to debate over its security and relationship with Chinese vendors. It has also been the subject of health concerns and misinformation, including discredited conspiracy theories linking it to the COVID-19 pandemic.

1.3.1 The Backdrop

In April 2008, NASA partnered with Geoff Brown and Machine-to-Machine Intelligence (M2Mi) Corp to develop a fifth generation communications technology approach, though largely concerned with working with nanosats. That same year, the South Korean IT R&D program of "5G mobile communication systems based on beam-division multiple access and relays with group cooperation" was formed.

In August 2012, New York University founded NYU Wireless, a multi-disciplinary academic research centre that has conducted pioneering work in 5G wireless communications. On October 8, 2012, the UK's University of Surrey secured £35M for a new 5G research centre, jointly funded by the British government's UK Research Partnership Investment Fund (UKRPIF) and a consortium of key international mobile operators and infrastructure providers, including Huawei, Samsung, Telefónica Europe, Fujitsu Laboratories Europe, Rohde & Schwarz, and Aircom International. It will offer testing facilities to mobile operators keen to develop a mobile standard that uses less energy and less radio spectrum, while delivering speeds higher than current 4G with aspirations for the new technology to be ready within a decade. On November 1, 2012, the EU project "Mobile and wireless communications Enablers for the Twenty-twenty Information Society" (METIS) starts its activity toward the definition of 5G. METIS achieved an early global consensus on these systems. In this sense, METIS played an important role of building consensus among other external major stakeholders prior to global standardization activities. This was done by initiating and addressing work in relevant global fora (e.g. ITU-R), as well as in national and regional regulatory bodies. That same month, the iJOIN EU project was launched, focusing on "small cell" technology, which is of key importance for taking advantage of limited and strategic resources, such as the radio wave spectrum. According to Günther Oettinger, the European Commissioner for Digital Economy and Society (2014–2019), "an innovative utilization of spectrum" is one of the key factors at the heart of 5G success. Oettinger further described it as "the essential resource for the wireless connectivity of which 5G will be the main driver". iJOIN was selected by the European Commission as one of the pioneering 5G research projects to showcase early results on this technology at the Mobile World Congress 2015 (Barcelona, Spain).

In February 2013, ITU-R Working Party 5D (WP 5D) started two study items: (1) Study on IMT Vision for 2020 and beyond, and; (2) Study on future technology trends for terrestrial IMT systems. Both aiming at having a better understanding of future technical aspects of mobile communications toward the definition of the next generation mobile. On May 12, 2013, Samsung Electronics stated that they had developed a "5G" system. The core technology has a maximum speed of tens of Gbit/s (gigabits per second). In testing, the transfer speeds for the "5G" network sent data at 1.056 Gbit/s to a distance of up to 2 kilometers with the use of an 8*8 MIMO. In July 2013, India and Israel agreed to work jointly on development of fifth generation (5G) telecom technologies. On October 1, 2013, NTT (Nippon Telegraph and Telephone), the same company to launch world's first 5G network in Japan, wins Minister of Internal Affairs and Communications Award at CEATEC for 5G R&D efforts. On November 6, 2013, Huawei announced plans to invest a minimum of $600 million into R&D for next generation 5G networks capable of speeds 100 times higher than modern LTE networks.

On April 3, 2019, South Korea became the first country to adopt 5G. Just hours later, Verizon launched its 5G services in the United States, and disputed South Korea's claim of becoming the world's first country with a 5G network, because allegedly, South Korea's 5G service was launched initially for just six South Korean celebrities so that South Korea could claim the title of having the world's first 5G network. In fact, the three main South Korean telecommunication companies (SK Telecom, KT, and LG Uplus) added more than 40,000 users to their 5G network on the launch day. In June 2019, the Philippines became the first country in Southeast Asia to roll out a 5G broadband network after Globe Telecom commercially launched its 5G data plans to customers. AT&T brings 5G service to consumers and businesses in December 2019 ahead of plans to offer 5G throughout the United States in the first half of 2020.

In 2020, AIS and TrueMove H launched 5G services in Thailand, making it the first country in Southeast Asia to have commercial 5G. A functional mockup of a Russian 5G base station, developed by domestic specialists as part of Rostec's digital division Rostec.digital, was presented in Nizhny Novgorod at the annual conference "Digital Industry of Industrial Russia".

1.3.2 Application Areas

The ITU-R has defined three main application areas for the enhanced capabilities of 5G. They are Enhanced Mobile Broadband (eMBB), Ultra Reliable Low Latency Communications (URLLC), and Massive Machine Type Communications (mMTC). Only eMBB is deployed in 2020; URLLC and mMTC are several years away in most locations.

Enhanced Mobile Broadband (eMBB) uses 5G as a progression from 4G LTE mobile broadband services, with faster connections, higher throughput, and more capacity. This will benefit areas of higher traffic such as stadiums, cities, and concert venues.

'Ultra-Reliable Low-Latency Communications' (URLLC) refers to using the network for mission-critical applications that require uninterrupted and robust data exchange. Short-packet data transmission is used to meet both reliability and latency requirements of the wireless communication networks.

Massive Machine-Type Communications (mMTC) would be used to connect to a large number of devices. 5G technology will connect some of the 50 billion connected IoT devices. Most will use the less expensive Wi-Fi. Drones, transmitting via 4G or 5G, will aid in disaster recovery efforts, providing real-time data for emergency responders. Most cars will have a 4G or 5G cellular connection for many services. Autonomous cars do not require 5G, as they have to be able to operate where they do not have a network connection. However, most autonomous vehicles also feature tele-operations for mission accomplishment, and these greatly benefit from 5G technology.

1.3.3 Performance

Speed

5G is capable of delivering significantly faster data rates than 4G, with peak data rates of up to 20 gigabits per second (Gbps). Furthermore, average 5G download speeds have been recorded at 186.3 Mbit/s in the U.S. by T-Mobile, while South Korea leads globally with average speeds of 432 megabits per second (Mbps). 5G networks are also designed to provide significantly more capacity than 4G networks, with a projected 100-fold increase in network capacity and efficiency.

The most widely used form of 5G, sub-6 GHz 5G (mid-band), is capable of delivering data rates ranging from 10 to 1,000 megabits per second (Mbps), with a much greater reach than mmWave bands. C-Band (n77/n78) was deployed by various U.S. operators in 2022 in the sub-6 bands, although its deployment by Verizon and AT&T was delayed until early January 2022 due to safety concerns raised by the Federal Aviation Administration.

Low-band frequencies (such as n5) offer a greater coverage area for a given cell, but their data rates are lower than those of mid and high bands in the range of 5–250 megabits per second (Mbps).

Latency

In 5G, the ideal "air latency" is of the order of 8 to 12 milliseconds i.e., excluding delays due to HARQ retransmissions, handovers, etc. Retransmission latency and backhaul latency to the server must be added to the "air latency" for correct comparisons. Verizon reported the latency on its 5G early deployment is 30 ms. Edge Servers close to the towers can probably reduce latency to between 10 and 15 milliseconds.

Latency is much higher during handovers; ranging from 50 to 500 milliseconds depending on the type of handover. Reducing handover interruption time is an ongoing area of research and development; options include modifying the handover margin (offset) and the time-to-trigger (TTT).

Error Rate

5G uses an adaptive modulation and coding scheme (MCS) to keep the block error rate (BLER) extremely low. Whenever the error rate crosses a (very low) threshold the transmitter will switch to a lower MCS, which will be less error-prone. This way speed is sacrificed to ensure an almost zero error rate.

Range

The range of 5G depends on many factors: transmit power, frequency, and interference. For example, mmWave (e.g., :band n258) will have a lower range than mid-band (e.g.: band n78) which will have a lower range than low-band (e.g.: band n5) Given the marketing hype on what 5G can offer, simulators and drive tests are used by cellular service providers for the precise measurement of 5G performance.

1.3.4 Standards

Initially, the term was associated with the International Telecommunication Union's IMT-2020 standard, which required a theoretical peak download speed of 20 gigabits per second and 10 gigabits per second upload speed, along with other requirements. Then, the industry standards group 3GPP chose the 5G NR (New Radio) standard together with LTE as their proposal for submission to the IMT-2020 standard.

5G NR can include lower frequencies (FR1), below 6 GHz, and higher frequencies (FR2), above 24 GHz. However, the speed and latency in early FR1 deployments, using 5G NR software on 4G hardware (non-standalone), are only slightly better than new 4G systems, estimated at 15 to 50% better.

The standard documents are organized by 3rd Generation Partnership Project (3GPP), with its system architecture defined in TS 23.501. The packet protocol for mobility management (establishing connection and moving between base stations) and session management (connecting to networks and network slices) is described in TS 24.501. Specifications of key data structures are found in TS 23.003.

Fronthaul Network

IEEE covers several areas of 5G with a core focus on wireline sections between the Remote Radio Head (RRH) and Base Band Unit (BBU). The 1914.1 standards focus on network architecture and dividing the connection between the RRU and BBU into two key sections. Radio Unit (RU) to the Distributor Unit (DU) being the NGFI-I (Next Generation Fronthaul Interface) and the DU to the Central Unit (CU) being the NGFI-II interface allowing a more diverse and cost-effective network. NGFI-I and NGFI-II have defined performance values which should be compiled to ensure different traffic types defined by the ITU are capable of being carried. The IEEE 1914.3 standard is creating a new Ethernet frame format capable of carrying IQ data in a much more efficient way depending on the functional split utilized. This is based on the 3GPP definition of functional splits.

5G NR

5G NR (New Radio) is the de facto air interface developed for 5G networks. It is the global standard for 3GPP 5G networks. The study of NR within 3GPP started in 2015, and the first specification was made available by the end of 2017. While the 3GPP standardization process was ongoing, the industry had already begun efforts to implement infrastructure compliant with the draft standard, with the first large-scale commercial launch of 5G NR having occurred at the end of 2018. Since 2019, many operators have deployed 5G NR networks and handset manufacturers have developed 5G NR enabled handsets.

5Gi

5Gi is an alternative 5G variant developed in India. It was developed in a joint collaboration between IIT Madras, IIT Hyderabad, TSDSI, and the Centre of Excellence in Wireless Technology (CEWiT). 5Gi is designed to improve 5G coverage in rural and remote areas over varying geographical terrains. 5Gi uses Low Mobility Large Cell (LMLC) to extend 5G connectivity and the range of a base station. In April 2022, 5Gi was merged with the global 5G NR standard in the 3GPP Release 17 specifications.

Pre-standard Implementations

- 5G TF: American carrier Verizon used a pre-standard variation of 5G known as 5G TF (Verizon 5G Technical Forum) for Fixed Wireless Access in 2018. The 5G service provided to customers in this standard is incompatible with 5G NR. Verizon has since migrated to 5G NR.
- 5G-SIG: KT Corporation had a pre-standard variation of 5G developed called 5G-SIG. This was deployed at the Pyeongchang 2018 Winter Olympics.

Internet of Things

In the Internet of things (IoT), 3GPP is going to submit the evolution of NB-IoT and eMTC (LTE-M) as 5G technologies for the LPWA (Low Power Wide Area) use case.

Non-Terrestrial Network

Standards are being developed by 3GPP to provide access to end devices via non-terrestrial networks (NTN), i.e., satellite or airborne telecommunication equipment to allow for better coverage outside of populated or otherwise hard to reach locations. The enhanced communication quality relies on the unique properties of Air to Ground channel.

Several manufacturers have announced and released hardware that integrates 5G with satellite networks:

- Samsung Electronics introduced a standardized 5G NTN modem technology in Korea in February 2023, simulated on their Exynos Modem 5300, facilitating smartphone-satellite communication.
- MediaTek launched the world's first commercially available 5G IoT-NTN chipset, MT6825, capable of automatic satellite message receipt and extensive power efficiency.
- Qualcomm, in collaboration with Skylo, announced new satellite IoT solutions on June 22, 2023, including the Qualcomm 212S and 9205S modems, supporting the Qualcomm Aware platform for real-time asset tracking and device management.
- Motorola's Defy Satellite Link hotspot, powered by MediaTek's MT6825, became available in June 2023, providing a portable satellite messaging solution with robust battery life and built-in GPS.
- Rakuten Symphony, in collaboration with Supermicro, announced high-performing Open RAN technologies and storage systems for operators of cloud-based mobile services.

1.3.5 Deployment

Beyond mobile operator networks, 5G is also expected to be used for private networks with applications in industrial IoT, enterprise networking, and critical communications, in what being described as NR-U (5G NR in Unlicensed Spectrum) and Non-Public Networks (NPNs) operating in licensed spectrum. By the mid-to-late 2020s, standalone private 5G networks are expected to become the predominant wireless communications medium to support the ongoing Industry 4.0 revolution for the digitization and automation of manufacturing and process industries.

Initial 5G NR launches depended on pairing with existing LTE (4G) infrastructure in non-standalone (NSA) mode (5G NR radio with 4G core), before maturation of the standalone (SA) mode with the 5G core network.

As of April 2019, the Global Mobile Suppliers Association had identified 224 operators in 88 countries that have demonstrated, are testing or trialing, or have been licensed to conduct field trials of 5G technologies, are deploying 5G networks or have announced service launches. The equivalent numbers in November 2018 were 192 operators in 81 countries. The first country to adopt 5G on a large scale was South Korea, in April 2019. Swedish telecoms giant Ericsson predicted that 5G internet will cover up to 65% of the world's population by the end of 2025. Also, it plans to invest 1 billion reals ($238.30 million) in Brazil to add a new assembly line dedicated to fifth-generation technology (5G) for its Latin American operations.

When South Korea launched its 5G network, all carriers used Samsung, Ericsson, and Nokia base stations and equipment, except for LG U Plus, who also used Huawei equipment. Samsung was the largest supplier for 5G base stations in South Korea at launch, having shipped 53,000 base stations at the time, out of 86,000 base stations installed across the country at the time.

The first fairly substantial deployments were in April 2019. In South Korea, SK Telecom claimed 38,000 base stations, KT Corporation 30,000 and LG U Plus 18,000; of which 85% are in six major cities. They are using 3.5 GHz (sub-6) spectrum in non-standalone (NSA) mode and tested speeds were from 193 to 430 Mbit/s down. 260,000 signed up in the first month and 4.7 million by the end of 2019. T-Mobile US was the first company in the world to launch a commercially available 5G NR Standalone network. Nine companies sell 5G radio hardware and 5G systems for carriers: Altiostar, Cisco Systems, Datang Telecom/Fiberhome, Ericsson, Huawei, Nokia, Qualcomm, Samsung, and ZTE. As of 2023, Huawei is the leading 5G equipment manufacturer and has the greatest market share of 5G equipment and has built approximately 70% of worldwide 5G base stations.

Spectrum

Large quantities of new radio spectrum (5G NR frequency bands) have been allocated to 5G. For example, in July 2016, the U.S. Federal Communications Commission (FCC) freed up vast amounts of bandwidth in underused high-band spectrum for 5G. The Spectrum Frontiers Proposal (SFP) doubled the amount of millimeter-wave unlicensed spectrum to 14 GHz and created four times the amount of flexible, mobile-use spectrum the FCC had licensed to date. In March 2018, European Union lawmakers agreed to open up the 3.6 and 26 GHz bands by 2020.

As of March 2019, there are reportedly 52 countries, territories, special administrative regions, disputed territories and dependencies that are formally considering introducing certain spectrum bands for terrestrial 5G services, are holding consultations regarding suitable spectrum allocations for 5G, have reserved spectrum for 5G, have announced plans to auction frequencies or have already allocated spectrum for 5G use.

1.3.6 5G Devices

In March 2019, the Global Mobile Suppliers Association released the industry's first database tracking worldwide 5G device launches. In it, the GSA identified 23 vendors who have confirmed the availability of forthcoming 5G devices with 33 different devices including regional variants. There were seven announced 5G device form factors: (telephones (×12 devices), hotspots (×4), indoor and outdoor customer-premises equipment (×8), modules (×5), Snap-on dongles and adapters

(×2), and USB terminals (×1)). By October 2019, the number of announced 5G devices had risen to 129, across 15 form factors, from 56 vendors.

In the 5G IoT chipset arena, as of April 2019 there were four commercial 5G modem chipsets and one commercial processor/platform, with more launches expected in the near future. On March 4, 2019, the first-ever all-5G smartphone Samsung Galaxy S10 5G was released. According to Business Insider, the 5G feature was showcased as more expensive in comparison with the 4G Samsung Galaxy S10e. On March 19, 2020, HMD Global, the current maker of Nokia-branded phones, announced the Nokia 8.3 5G, which it claimed as having a wider range of 5G compatibility than any other phone released to that time. The mid-range model is claimed to support all 5G bands from 600 MHz to 3.8 GHz. Many phone manufacturers support 5G. Google Pixel devices support 5G, starting with the 4a 5G and Pixel 5. Apple devices also support 5G, starting with the iPhone 12 and later models.

1.3.7 Technology

New Radio Frequencies

The air interface defined by 3GPP for 5G is known as New Radio (NR), and the specification is subdivided into two frequency bands, FR1 (below 6 GHz) and FR2 (24–54 GHz).

Frequency Range 1 (< 6 GHz)

Otherwise known as sub-6, the maximum channel bandwidth defined for FR1 is 100 MHz, due to the scarcity of continuous spectrum in this crowded frequency range. The band most widely being used for 5G in this range is 3.3–4.2 GHz. The Korean carriers use the n78 band at 3.5 GHz. Some parties used the term "mid-band" frequency to refer to higher part of this frequency range that was not used in previous generations of mobile communication.

Frequency Range 2 (24–71 GHz)

The minimum channel bandwidth defined for FR2 is 50 MHz and the maximum is 400 MHz, with two-channel aggregation supported in 3GPP Release 15. Signals in this frequency range with wavelengths between 4 and 12 mm are called millimeter waves. The higher the carrier frequency, the greater the ability to support high data-transfer speeds. This is because a given channel bandwidth takes up a lower fraction of the carrier frequency, so high-bandwidth channels are easier to realize at higher carrier frequencies.

Massive MIMO

MIMO systems use multiple antennas at the transmitter and receiver ends of a wireless communication system. Multiple antennas use the spatial dimension for multiplexing in addition to the time and frequency ones, without changing the bandwidth requirements of the system. Massive MIMO (multiple-input and multiple-output) antennas increases sector throughput and capacity density using large numbers of antennas. This includes Single User MIMO and Multi-user MIMO (MU-MIMO). Each antenna is individually-controlled and may embed radio transceiver components.

In general, more antennas equal better performance. But more antennas also require bigger arrays that draw more power. Some of the places service providers deploy radio links have very tight constraints, so finding the right solution means weighing tradeoffs. For in-building coverage, the performance gain is often worth it. For outdoor or street-level coverage, maybe not.

Edge Computing

Edge computing is delivered by computing servers closer to the ultimate user. It reduces latency, data traffic congestion and can improve service availability.

Small Cell

Small cells are low-powered cellular radio access nodes that operate in licensed and unlicensed spectrum that have a range of 10 meters to a few kilometers. Small cells are critical to 5G networks, as 5G's radio waves can't travel long distances, because of 5G's higher frequencies.

Beamforming

There are two kinds of beamforming (BF): digital and analog. Digital beamforming involves sending the data across multiple streams (layers), while analog beamforming shaping the radio waves to point in a specific direction. The analog BF technique combines the power from elements of the antenna array in such a way that signals at particular angles experience constructive interference, while other signals pointing to other angles experience destructive interference. This improves signal quality in the specific direction, as well as data transfer speeds. 5G uses both digital and analog beamforming to improve the system capacity.

Convergence of Wi-Fi and Cellular

One expected benefit of the transition to 5G is the convergence of multiple networking functions to achieve cost, power, and complexity reductions. LTE has targeted convergence with Wi-Fi band/technology via various efforts, such as License Assisted Access (LAA; 5G signal in unlicensed frequency bands that are also used by Wi-Fi) and LTE-WLAN Aggregation (LWA; convergence with Wi-Fi Radio), but the differing capabilities of cellular and Wi-Fi have limited the scope of convergence. However, significant improvement in cellular performance specifications in 5G, combined with migration from Distributed Radio Access Network (D-RAN) to Cloud- or Centralized-RAN (C-RAN) and rollout of cellular small cells can potentially narrow the gap between Wi-Fi and cellular networks in dense and indoor deployments. Radio convergence could result in sharing ranging from the aggregation of cellular and Wi-Fi channels to the use of a single silicon device for multiple radio access technologies.

NOMA (Non-orthogonal Multiple Access)

NOMA (non-orthogonal multiple access) is a proposed multiple-access technique for future cellular systems via allocation of power.

SDN/NFV

Initially, cellular mobile communications technologies were designed in the context of providing voice services and Internet access. Today a new era of innovative tools and technologies is inclined towards developing a new pool of applications. This pool of applications consists of different domains such as the Internet of Things (IoT), web of connected autonomous vehicles, remotely controlled robots, and heterogeneous sensors connected to serve versatile applications. In this context, network slicing has emerged as a key technology to efficiently embrace this new market model.

Service-Based Architecture

Table 1.1: 5G Network Functions

NF Name	NF Acronym	Analogous EPC element
Authentication Server Function	AUSF	MME / HSS (Authentication)
Access and Mobility Management Function	AMF	MME
Unstructured Data Storage Function	UDSF	N/A
Network Exposure Function	NEF	N/A
Network Slice Specific Authentication and	NSSAAF	N/A Authorization Function
Network Slice Selection Function	NSSF	N/A
Policy Control Function	PCF	PCRF
Session Management Function	SMF	MME / PGW-C
Unified Data Management	UDM	HSS (DB Front End)
Unified Data Repository	UDR	HSS (User Database)
User Plane Function	UPF	SGW-U / PGW-U
UE radio Capability Management Function	UCMF	N/A
Application Function	AF	AF (IMS)
Network Data Analytics Function	NWDAF	N/A
Charging Function	CHF	CSCF

The 5G Service-Based architecture replaces the referenced-based architecture of the Evolved Packet Core that is used in 4G. The SBA breaks up the core functionality of the network into interconnected network functions (NFs), which are typically implemented as Cloud-Native Network Functions. These NFs register with the Network Repository Function (NRF) which maintains their state, and communicate with each other using the Service Communication Proxy (SCP). The interfaces between the elements all utilize RESTful APIs. By breaking functionality down this way, mobile operators are able to utilize different infrastructure vendors for different functions, and the flexibility to scale each function independently as needed.

In addition, the standard describes network entities for roaming and inter-network connectivity, including the Security Edge Protection Proxy (SEPP), the Non-3GPP InterWorking Function (N3IWF), the Trusted Non-3GPP Gateway Function (TNGF), the Wireline Access Gateway Function (W-AGF), and the Trusted WLAN Interworking Function (TWIF). These can be deployed by operators as needed depending on their deployment.

Channel Coding

The channel coding techniques for 5G NR have changed from Turbo codes in 4G to polar codes for the control channels and LDPC (low-density parity check codes) for the data channels.

Operation in Unlicensed Spectrum

In December 2018, 3GPP began working on unlicensed spectrum specifications known as 5G NR-U, targeting 3GPP Release 16. Qualcomm has made a similar proposal for LTE in unlicensed spectrum.

1.3.8 Future Evolution

5G-Advanced

5G-Advanced (also known as 5.5G) is a name for 3GPP release 18, which as of 2021 is under conceptual development. 5G-Advanced is expected to appear in commercial products in 2024.

1.3.9 Concerns

Security Concerns

A report published by the European Commission and European Agency for Cybersecurity details the security issues surrounding 5G. The report warns against using a single supplier for a carrier's 5G infrastructure, especially those based outside the European Union. (Nokia and Ericsson are the only European manufacturers of 5G equipment.)

On October 18, 2018, a team of researchers from ETH Zurich, the University of Lorraine and the University of Dundee released a paper entitled, "A Formal Analysis of 5G Authentication". It alerted that 5G technology could open ground for a new era of security threats. The paper described the technology as "immature and insufficiently tested," and one that "enables the movement and access of vastly higher quantities of data, and thus broadens attack surfaces". Simultaneously, network security companies such as Fortinet, Arbor Networks, A10 Networks, and Voxility advised on personalized and mixed security deployments against massive DDoS attacks foreseen after 5G deployment.

IoT Analytics estimated an increase in the number of IoT devices, enabled by 5G technology, from 7 billion in 2018 to 21.5 billion by 2025. This can raise the attack surface for these devices to a substantial scale, and the capacity for DDoS attacks, cryptojacking, and other cyberattacks could boost proportionally. In addition, the EPS solution for 5G networks has identified a design vulnerability. The vulnerability affects the operation of the device during cellular network switching.

Due to fears of potential espionage of users of Chinese equipment vendors, several countries (including the United States, Australia and the United Kingdom as of early 2019) have taken actions to restrict or eliminate the use of Chinese equipment in their respective 5G networks. A 2012 U.S. House Permanent Select Committee on Intelligence report concluded that using equipment made by Huawei and ZTE, another Chinese telecommunications company, could "undermine core U.S. national security interests". In 2018, six U.S. intelligence chiefs, including the directors of the CIA and FBI, cautioned Americans against using Huawei products, warning that the company could conduct "undetected espionage". Further, a 2017 investigation by the FBI/ determined that Chinese-made Huawei equipment could disrupt U.S. nuclear arsenal communications. Chinese vendors and the Chinese government have denied claims of espionage, but experts have pointed out that Huawei would have no choice but to hand over network data to the Chinese government if Beijing asked for it because of Chinese National Security Law.

In August, 2020, the U.S. State Department launched "The Clean Network" as a U.S. government-led, bi-partisan effort to address what it described as "the long-term threat to data privacy, security, human rights and principled collaboration posed to the free world from authoritarian malign actors". Promoters of the initiative have stated that it has resulted in an "alliance of democracies and companies", "based on democratic values". On October 7, 2020, the UK Parliament's Defence Committee released a report claiming that there was clear evidence of collusion between Huawei and Chinese state and the Chinese Communist Party. The UK Parliament's Defence Committee said that the government should consider removal of all Huawei equipment from its 5G networks earlier than planned. In December 2020, the United States announced that more than 60 nations, representing more than two thirds of the world's gross domestic product, and 200 telecom companies, had publicly committed to the principles of The Clean Network. This alliance of democracies included 27 of the 30 NATO members; 26 of the 27 EU members, 31 of the 37 OECD nations, 11 of the 12 Three Seas nations as well as Japan, Israel, Australia, Singapore, Taiwan, Canada, Vietnam, and India.

Electromagnetic Interference

Weather Forecasting

The spectrum used by various 5G proposals, especially the n258 band centered at 26 GHz, will be near that of passive remote sensing such as by weather and Earth observation satellites, particularly for water vapor monitoring at 23.8 GHz. Interference is expected to occur due to such proximity and its effect could be significant without effective controls. An increase in interference already occurred with some other prior proximate band usages. Interference to satellite operations impairs numerical weather prediction performance with substantially deleterious economic and public safety impacts in areas such as commercial aviation.

The concerns prompted U.S. Secretary of Commerce Wilbur Ross and NASA Administrator Jim Bridenstine in February 2019 to urge the FCC to delay some spectrum auction proposals, which was rejected. Acting NOAA director Neil Jacobs testified before the House Committee in May 2019 that 5G out-of-band emissions could produce a 30% reduction in weather forecast accuracy and that the resulting degradation in ECMWF model performance would have resulted in failure to predict the track and thus the impact of Superstorm Sandy in 2012. The United States Navy in March 2019 wrote a memorandum warning of deterioration and made technical suggestions to control band bleed-over limits, for testing and fielding, and for coordination of the wireless industry and regulators with weather forecasting organizations.

At the 2019 quadrennial World Radiocommunication Conference (WRC), atmospheric scientists advocated for a strong buffer of "55 dBW, European regulators agreed on a recommendation of "42 dBW, and US regulators (the FCC) recommended a restriction of "20 dBW, which would permit signals 150 times stronger than the European proposal. The ITU decided on an intermediate "33 dBW until September 1, 2027, and after that a standard of "39 dBW. This is closer to the European recommendation but even the delayed higher standard is much weaker than that requested by atmospheric scientists, triggering warnings from the World Meteorological Organization (WMO) that the ITU standard, at 10 times less stringent than its recommendation, brings the "potential to significantly degrade the accuracy of data collected". A representative of the American Meteorological Society (AMS) also warned of interference, and the European Centre for Medium-Range Weather Forecasts (ECMWF), sternly warned, saying that society risks "history repeat[ing] itself" by ignoring atmospheric scientists' warnings (referencing global warming, monitoring of which could be imperiled). In December 2019, a bipartisan request was sent from the US House Science Committee to the Government Accountability Office (GAO) to investigate why there is such a discrepancy between recommendations of US civilian and military science agencies and the regulator, the FCC.

Aviation

The United States FAA has warned that radar altimeters on aircraft, which operate between 4.2 and 4.4 GHz, might be affected by 5G operations between 3.7 and 3.98 GHz. This is particularly an issue with older altimeters using RF filters which lack protection from neighboring bands. This is not as much of an issue in Europe, where 5G uses lower frequencies between 3.4 and 3.8 GHz. Nonetheless, the DGAC in France has also expressed similar worries and recommended 5G phones be turned off or be put in airplane mode during flights.

On December 31, 2021, U.S. Transportation Secretary Pete Buttigieg and Steve Dickinson, administrator of the Federal Aviation Administration asked the chief executives of AT&T and Verizon to delay 5G implementation over aviation concerns. The government officials asked for a two-week delay starting on January 5, 2022, while investigations are conducted on the effects on radar altimeters. The government transportation officials also asked the cellular providers to hold off their new 5G service near 50 priority airports, to minimize disruption to air traffic that would be caused by some planes being disallowed from landing in poor visibility. After coming to an agreement with government officials the day before, Verizon and AT&T activated their 5G networks on January 19, 2022, except for certain towers near 50 airports. AT&T scaled back its deployment even further than its agreement with the FAA required.

The FAA rushed to test and certify radar altimeters for interference so that planes could be allowed to perform instrument landings (e.g., at night and in low visibility) at affected airports. By January 16, it had certified equipment on 45% of the U.S. fleet, and 78% by January 20. Airlines complained about the avoidable impact on their operations, and commentators said the affair called into question the competence of the FAA. Several international airlines substituted different planes so they could avoid problems landing at scheduled airports, and about 2% of flights (320) were cancelled by the evening of January 19.

Satellite

A number of 5G networks deployed on the radio frequency band of 3.3–3.6 GHz are expected to cause interference with C-Band satellite stations, which operate by receiving satellite signals at 3.4–4.2 GHz frequency. This interference can be mitigated with low-noise block downconverters and waveguide filters.

Wi-Fi

In regions like the US and EU, the 6 GHz band is to be opened up for unlicensed applications, which would permit the deployment of 5G-NR Unlicensed, 5G version of LTE in unlicensed spectrum, as well as Wi-Fi 6e. However, interference could occur with the co-existence of different standards in the frequency band.

Overhype

There have been concerns surrounding the promotion of 5G, questioning whether the technology is overhyped. There are questions on whether 5G will truly change the customer experience, ability for 5G's mmWave signal to provide significant coverage, overstating what 5G can achieve or misattributing continuous technological improvement to "5G", lack of new use case for carriers to profit from, wrong focus on emphasizing direct benefits on individual consumers instead of for internet of things devices or solving the last mile problem, and overshadowing the possibility that in some aspects there might be other more appropriate technologies. Such sort of concerns have also led to consumers not trusting information provided by cellular providers on the topic.

1.3.10 Misinformation

Health

There is a long history of fear and anxiety surrounding wireless signals that predates 5G technology. The fears about 5G are similar to those that have persisted throughout the 1990s and 2000s. They center on fringe claims that non-ionizing radiation poses dangers to human health. Unlike ionizing radiation, non-ionizing radiation cannot remove electrons from atoms. According to the US Centers for Disease Control and Prevention (CDC) "exposure to intense, direct amounts of non-ionizing radiation may result in damage to tissue due to heat. This is not common and mainly of concern in the workplace for those who work on large sources of non-ionizing radiation devices and instruments." Some advocates of fringe health claim the regulatory standards are too low and influenced by lobbying groups.

There have been rumors that 5G mobile phone use can cause cancer, but this is a myth. Many popular books of dubious merit have been published on the subject including one by Joseph Mercola alleging that wireless technologies caused numerous conditions from ADHD to heart diseases and brain cancer. Mercola has drawn sharp criticism for his anti-vaccinationism during the COVID-19 pandemic and was warned by the Food and Drug Administration to stop selling fake COVID-19 cures through his online alternative medicine business.

According to the New York Times, one origin of the 5G health controversy was an erroneous unpublished study that physicist Bill P. Curry did for the Broward County School Board in 2000 which indicated that the absorption of external microwaves by brain tissue increased with frequency. According to experts this was wrong, the millimeter waves used in 5G are safer than lower frequency microwaves because they cannot penetrate the skin and reach internal organs. Curry had confused in vitro and in vivo research. However Curry's study was widely distributed on the internet. Writing in The New York Times in 2019, William Broad reported that RT America began airing programming linking 5G to harmful health effects which "lack scientific support", such as "brain cancer, infertility, autism, heart tumors, and Alzheimer's disease". Broad asserted that the claims had increased. RT America had run seven programs on this theme by mid-April 2019 but only one in the whole of 2018. The network's coverage had spread to hundreds of blogs and websites.

In April 2019, the city of Brussels in Belgium blocked a 5G trial because of radiation rules. In Geneva, Switzerland, a planned upgrade to 5G was stopped for the same reason. The Swiss Telecommunications Association (ASUT) has said that studies have been unable to show that 5G frequencies have any health impact.

According to CNET, "Members of Parliament in the Netherlands are also calling on the government to take a closer look at 5G. Several leaders in the United States Congress have written to the Federal Communications Commission expressing concern about potential health risks. In Mill Valley, California, the city council blocked the deployment of new 5G wireless cells." Similar concerns were raised in Vermont and New Hampshire. The US FDA is quoted saying that it "continues to believe that the current safety limits for cellphone radiofrequency energy exposure remain acceptable for protecting the public health." After campaigning by activist groups, a series of small localities in the UK, including Totnes, Brighton and Hove, Glastonbury, and Frome, passed resolutions against the implementation of further 5G infrastructure, though these resolutions have no impact on rollout plans.

Low-level EMF does have some effects on other organisms. Vian et al., 2006 finds an effect of microwave on gene expression in plants. A meta-analysis of 95 in vitro and in vivo studies showed that an average of 80% of the in vivo research showed effects of such radiation, as did 58% of the in vitro research, but that the results were inconclusive as to whether any of these effects pose a health risk.

COVID-19 Conspiracy Theories and Arson Attacks

As the introduction of 5G technology coincided with the time of COVID-19 pandemic, several conspiracy theories circulating online posited a link between COVID-19 and 5G. This has led to dozens of arson attacks being made on telecom masts in the Netherlands (Amsterdam, Rotterdam, etc.), Ireland (Cork, etc.), Cyprus, the United Kingdom (Dagenham, Huddersfield, Birmingham, Belfast and Liverpool), Belgium (Pelt), Italy (Maddaloni), Croatia (Bibinje) and Sweden. It led to at least 61 suspected arson attacks against telephone masts in the United Kingdom alone and over twenty in The Netherlands.

In the early months of the pandemic, anti-lockdown protesters at protests over responses to the COVID-19 pandemic in Australia were seen with anti-5G signs, an early sign of what became a wider campaign by conspiracy theorists to link the pandemic with 5G technology. There are two versions of the 5G-COVID-19 conspiracy theory:

1. The first version claims that radiation weakens the immune system, making the body more vulnerable to SARS-CoV-2 (the virus that causes COVID-19).
2. The second version claims that 5G causes COVID-19. There are different variations on this. Some claim that the pandemic is coverup of illness caused by 5G radiation or that COVID-19 originated in Wuhan because that city was "the guinea-pig city for 5G".

1.3.11 Marketing of Non-5G Services

In various parts of the world, carriers have launched numerous differently branded technologies, such as "5G Evolution", which advertise improving existing networks with the use of "5G technology". However, these pre-5G networks are an improvement on specifications of existing LTE networks that are not exclusive to 5G. While the technology promises to deliver higher speeds, and is described by AT&T as a "foundation for our evolution to 5G while the 5G standards are being finalized", it cannot be considered to be true 5G. When AT&T announced 5G Evolution, 4x4 MIMO, the technology that AT&T is using to deliver the higher speeds, had already been put in place by T-Mobile without being branded with the 5G moniker. It is claimed that such branding is a marketing move that will cause confusion with consumers, as it is not made clear that such improvements are not true 5G.

1.3.12 Other Applications

Automobiles

5G Automotive Association have been promoting the C-V2X communication technology that will first be deployed in 4G. It provides for communication between vehicles and infrastructures.

Digital Twins

A real time digital twin of the real object such as a turbine engine, aircraft, wind turbines, offshore platform and pipelines. 5G networks helps in building it due to the latency and throughput to capture near real-time IoT data and support digital twins.

Public Safety

Mission-critical push-to-talk (MCPTT) and mission-critical video and data are expected to be furthered in 5G.

Fixed Wireless

Fixed wireless connections will offer an alternative to fixed line broadband (ADSL, VDSL, Fiber optic, and DOCSIS connections) in some locations.

Wireless Video Transmission for Broadcast Applications

Sony has tested the possibility of using local 5G networks to replace the SDI cables currently used in broadcast camcorders. The 5G Broadcast tests started around 2020 (Orkneys, Bavaria, Austria, Central Bohemia) based on FeMBMS (Further evolved multimedia broadcast multicast service). The aim is to serve unlimited number of mobile or fixed devices with video (TV) and audio (radio) streams without these consuming any data flow or even being authenticated in a network.

1.4 COMPARISON WITH PREVIOUS GENERATIONS (1G TO 4G)

1.4.1 1G

1G refers to the first generation of cellular network (wireless) technology. These are mobile telecommunications standards that were introduced in the 1980s and were superseded by 2G. The main difference between these two mobile cellular generations is that the audio transmissions of 1G networks were analog, while 2G networks were entirely digital.

There were many different 1G cellular standards developed and used in different countries, but the most widely adopted globally were the Nordic Mobile Telephone (NMT) and Advanced Mobile Phone System (AMPS) systems. The inherent advantages of digital technology over that of analog meant that 2G networks went on to eventually completely replace them. Many 1G networks were switched off in developed economies by 2000, but in some places networks continued to operate into the 2010s.

The antecedent to 1G technology is the mobile radio telephone (i.e. “0G”), where portable phones would connect to a centralised operator. 1G refers to the very first generation of cellular networks. Cellular technology employ a network of cells throughout a geographical area using low-power radio transmitters.

History

The first commercial cellular network was launched in Japan by Nippon Telegraph and Telephone (NTT) in 1979, initially in the metropolitan area of Tokyo. The first phone that used this network was called TZ-801 built by Panasonic. Within five years, the NTT network had been expanded to cover the whole population of Japan and became the first nationwide 1G/cellular network. Before the network in Japan, Bell Laboratories built the first cellular network around Chicago in 1977 and trialled it in 1978.

As in the pre-cellular era, the Nordic countries were among the pioneers in wireless technologies. These countries together designed the NMT standard which first launched in Sweden in 1981. NMT was the first mobile phone network to feature international roaming. In 1983, the first 1G cellular network launched in the United States, which was Chicago-based Ameritech using the Motorola DynaTAC mobile phone.

In the early to mid 1990s, 1G was superseded by newer 2G (second generation) cellular technologies such as GSM and cdmaOne. Although 1G also used digital signaling to connect the radio towers (which listen to the handsets) to the rest of the telephone system, the voice itself during a call is encoded to digital signals in 2G whereas 1G uses analog FM modulation for the voice transmission, much like a 2-way land mobile radio. Most 1G networks had been discontinued by the early 2000s. Some regions especially Eastern Europe continued running these networks for much longer. The last operating 1G network was closed down in Russia in 2017.

Adoption

After Japan, the earliest commercial cellular networks launched in 1981 in Sweden, Norway and Saudi Arabia, followed by Denmark, Finland and Spain in 1982, the U.S. in 1983 and Hong Kong, South Korea, Austria and Canada in 1984. By 1986 networks had also launched in Tunisia, Malaysia, Oman, Ireland, Italy, Luxembourg, Netherlands, United Kingdom, West Germany, France, South Africa, Israel, Thailand, Indonesia, Iceland, Turkey, the Virgin Islands and Australia. Generally, African countries were slower to take up 1G networks, while Eastern European were among the last due to the political situation.

In Europe, the United Kingdom had the largest number of cellular subscribers as of 1990 numbering 1.1 million, while the second largest market was Sweden with 482 thousand. Although Japan was the first country with a nationwide cellular network, the number of users was significantly lower than other developed economies with a penetration rate of only 0.15 percent in 1989. As of January 1991, the highest penetration rates were in Sweden and Finland with both countries above 50 percent closely followed by Norway and Iceland. The United States had a rate of 21.2 percent. In most other European countries it was below 10 percent.

1G Standards

Analog cellular technologies that were used were:

- Advanced Mobile Phone System (AMPS)
- Nordic Mobile Telephone (NMT)
- Total Access Communication System (TACS) developed in the United Kingdom and also some other parts of the world
- C-450 developed in West Germany and also adopted in Portugal and South Africa
- Radiocom 2000 in France (France Telecom only)
- RTMI in Italy
- MCS-L1 and MCS-L2 (developed by NTT) in Japan
- JTACS (a variant of TACS operated by Daini Denden Planning, Inc. (DDI)) in Japan

1.4.2 2G

2G is a short notation for second-generation cellular network, a group of technology standards employed for cellular networks. 2G was commercially launched on the GSM standard in Finland by Radiolinja (now part of Elisa Oyj) in 1991. After 2G was launched, the previous mobile wireless network systems were retroactively dubbed 1G. While radio signals on 1G networks are analog, radio signals on 2G networks are digital, though both systems use digital signaling to connect cellular radio towers to the rest of the mobile network system. 2G was superseded by 3G technology.

The most common 2G technology was the time-division multiple access (TDMA)-based GSM standard, used in most of the world outside Japan. In North America, Digital AMPS (IS-54 and IS-136) and cdmaOne (IS-95) were dominant, but GSM was also used. In Japan the ubiquitous system was Personal Digital Cellular (PDC) though another, Personal Handy-phone System (PHS), also existed.

Three primary benefits of 2G networks over their 1G predecessors were:

1. Digitally encrypted phone conversations, at least between the mobile phone and the cellular base station but not necessarily in the rest of the network.
2. Significantly more efficient use of the radio frequency spectrum enabling more users per frequency band.
3. Data services for mobile, starting with SMS text messages then expanding to Multimedia Messaging Service (MMS).

With General Packet Radio Service (GPRS), 2G offers a theoretical maximum transfer speed of 40 kbit/s (5 kB/s). With EDGE (Enhanced Data Rates for GSM Evolution), there is a theoretical maximum transfer speed of 384 kbit/s (48 kB/s).

Evolution

2.5G (GPRS)

2.5G ("second and a half generation") is used to describe 2G-systems that have implemented a packet-switched domain in addition to the circuit-switched domain. It does not necessarily provide faster service because bundling of timeslots is used for circuit-switched data services (HSCSD) as well.

2.75G (EDGE)

GPRS networks evolved to EDGE networks with the introduction of 8PSK encoding. While the symbol rate remained the same at 270.833 samples per second, each symbol carried three bits instead of one. Enhanced Data rates for GSM Evolution (EDGE), Enhanced GPRS (EGPRS), or IMT Single Carrier (IMT-SC) is a backward-compatible digital mobile phone technology that allows improved data transmission rates, as an extension on top of standard GSM. EDGE was deployed on GSM networks beginning in 2003, initially by AT&T in the United States.

Phase-out

2G, understood as GSM and CdmaOne, has been superseded by newer technologies such as 3G (UMTS / CDMA2000), 4G (LTE / WiMAX) and 5G (5G NR). However, 2G networks were still available as of 2023 in most parts of the world, while notably excluding the majority of carriers in North America, East Asia, and Australasia.

Many modern LTE-enabled devices have the ability to fall back to 2G for phone calls, necessary especially in rural areas where later generations have not yet been implemented. In some places, its successor 3G is being shut down rather than 2G – Vodafone previously announced that it had switched off 3G across Europe in 2020 but still retains 2G as a fallback service. In the US T-Mobile shut down their 3G services while retaining their 2G GSM network.

Various carriers have made announcements that 2G technology in the United States, Japan, Australia, and other countries are in the process of being shut down, or have already shut down 2G services so that carriers can re-use the frequencies for newer technologies (e.g., 4G, 5G).

In 2022, Android 12 introduced a system setting to disable 2G connectivity for the device, as 2G is considered to be insecure. Specifically, there exist well known methods to attack weaknesses in GSM since 2009 with practical use in crime. Attack routes on 2G CdmaOne were found later and remain less publicized.

Criticism

In some parts of the world, including the United Kingdom, 2G remains widely used for older feature phones and for internet of things (IoT) devices such as smart meters, eCall systems and vehicle trackers to avoid the high patent licensing cost of newer technologies. Terminating 2G services could leave vulnerable people who rely on 2G infrastructure unable to communicate even with emergency contacts, causing harm and possibly deaths.

1.4.3 3G

3G is the third generation of wireless mobile telecommunications technology. It is the upgrade over 2G, 2.5G, GPRS and 2.75G Enhanced Data Rates for GSM Evolution networks, offering faster data transfer, and better voice quality. This network was superseded by 4G, and later on by 5G. This network is based on a set of standards used for mobile devices and mobile telecommunications use services and networks that comply with the International Mobile Telecommunications-2000 (IMT-2000) specifications by the International Telecommunication Union. 3G finds application in wireless voice telephony, mobile Internet access, fixed wireless Internet access, video calls and mobile TV.

3G telecommunication networks support services that provide an information transfer rate of at least 144 kbit/s. Later 3G releases, often denoted 3.5G and 3.75G, also provide mobile broadband access of several Mbit/s to smartphones and mobile modems in laptop computers. This ensures it can be applied to wireless voice calls, mobile Internet access, fixed wireless Internet access, video calls and mobile TV technologies.

A new generation of cellular standards has appeared approximately every tenth year since 1G systems were introduced in 1979 and the early to mid-1980s. Each generation is characterized by new frequency bands, higher data rates and non-backward-compatible transmission technology. The first commercial 3G networks were introduced in mid-2001.

Several telecommunications companies marketed wireless mobile Internet services as 3G, indicating that the advertised service was provided over a 3G wireless network. However, 3G services have largely been supplanted in marketing by 4G and 5G services in most areas of the world. Services advertised as 3G are required to meet IMT-2000 technical standards, including standards for reliability and speed (data transfer rates).

To meet the IMT-2000 standards, a system must provide peak data rates of at least 144 kbit/s. However, many services advertised as 3G provide higher speed than the minimum technical requirements for a 3G service. Subsequent 3G releases, denoted 3.5G and 3.75G, provided mobile broadband access of several Mbit/s for smartphones and mobile modems in laptop computers.

3G branded standards:

- The UMTS (Universal Mobile Telecommunications System) system, standardized by 3GPP in 2001, was used in Europe, Japan, China (with a different radio interface) and other regions predominated by GSM (Global Systems for Mobile) 2G system infrastructure. The cell phones are typically UMTS and GSM hybrids. Several radio interfaces are offered, sharing the same infrastructure:
    - The original and most widespread radio interface is called W-CDMA (Wideband Code Division Multiple Access).
    - The TD-SCDMA radio interface was commercialized in 2009 and only offered in China.
    - The latest UMTS release, HSPA+, can provide peak data rates up to 56 Mbit/s in the downlink in theory (28 Mbit/s in existing services) and 22 Mbit/s in the uplink.
- The CDMA2000 system, first offered in 2002, standardized by 3GPP2, used especially in North America and South Korea, sharing infrastructure with the IS-95 2G standard. The cell phones are typically CDMA2000 and IS-95

hybrids. The latest release EVDO Rev. B offers peak rates of 14.7 Mbit/s downstream.

The 3G systems and radio interfaces are based on spread spectrum radio transmission technology. While the GSM EDGE standard ("2.9G"), DECT cordless phones and Mobile WiMAX standards formally also fulfill the IMT-2000 requirements and are approved as 3G standards by ITU, these are typically not branded as 3G and are based on completely different technologies.

The common standards complying with the IMT2000/3G standard are:

- EDGE, a revision by the 3GPP organization to the older 2G GSM based transmission methods, which utilizes the same switching nodes, base station sites, and frequencies as GPRS, but includes a new base station and cellphone RF circuits. It is based on the three times as efficient 8PSK modulation scheme as a supplement to the original GMSK modulation scheme. EDGE is still used extensively due to its ease of upgrade from existing 2G GSM infrastructure and cell phones.
    - EDGE combined with the GPRS 2.5G technology is called EGPRS, and allows peak data rates in the order of 200 kbit/s, just like the original UMTS WCDMA versions and thus formally fulfill the IMT2000 requirements on 3G systems. However, in practice, EDGE is seldom marketed as a 3G system, but a 2.9G system. EDGE shows slightly better system spectral efficiency than the original UMTS and CDMA2000 systems, but it is difficult to reach much higher peak data rates due to the limited GSM spectral bandwidth of 200 kHz, and it is thus a dead end.
    - EDGE was also a mode in the IS-136 TDMA system, no longer used.
    - Evolved EDGE, the latest revision, has peaks of 1 Mbit/s downstream and 400 kbit/s upstream but is not commercially used.
- The Universal Mobile Telecommunications System, created and revised by the 3GPP. The family is a full revision from GSM in terms of encoding methods and hardware, although some GSM sites can be retrofitted to broadcast in the UMTS/W-CDMA format.
    - W-CDMA is the most common deployment, commonly operated on the 2,100 MHz band. A few others use the 850, 900, and 1,900 MHz bands.
        * HSPA is an amalgamation of several upgrades to the original W-CDMA standard and offers speeds of 14.4 Mbit/s down and 5.76 Mbit/s up. HSPA is backward-compatible and uses the same frequencies as W-CDMA.
        * HSPA+, a further revision and upgrade of HSPA, can provide theoretical peak data rates up to 168 Mbit/s in the downlink and 22 Mbit/s in the uplink, using a combination of air interface improvements as well as multi-carrier HSPA and MIMO. Technically

though, MIMO and DC-HSPA can be used without the "+" enhancements of HSPA+.

- The CDMA2000 system, or IS-2000, including CDMA2000 1x and CDMA2000 High Rate Packet Data (or EVDO), standardized by 3GPP2 (differing from the 3GPP), evolving from the original IS-95 CDMA system, is used especially in North America, China, India, Pakistan, Japan, South Korea, Southeast Asia, Europe, and Africa.
  - CDMA2000 1x Rev. E has an increased voice capacity (by three times the original amount) compared to Rev. 0 EVDO Rev. B offers downstream peak rates of 14.7 Mbit/s while Rev. C enhanced existing and new terminal user experience.

While DECT cordless phones and Mobile WiMAX standards formally also fulfill the IMT-2000 requirements, they are not usually considered due to their rarity and unsuitability for usage with mobile phones.

Break-up of 3G Systems

The 3G (UMTS and CDMA2000) research and development projects started in 1992. In 1999, ITU approved five radio interfaces for IMT-2000 as a part of the ITU-R M.1457 Recommendation; WiMAX was added in 2007.

There are evolutionary standards (EDGE and CDMA) that are backward-compatible extensions to pre-existing 2G networks as well as revolutionary standards that require all-new network hardware and frequency allocations. The cell phones use UMTS in combination with 2G GSM standards and bandwidths, but do not support EDGE. The latter group is the UMTS family, which consists of standards developed for IMT-2000, as well as the independently developed standards DECT and WiMAX, which were included because they fit the IMT-2000 definition.

While EDGE fulfills the 3G specifications, most GSM/UMTS phones report EDGE ("2.75G") and UMTS ("3G") functionality.

History

3G technology was the result of research and development work carried out by the International Telecommunication Union (ITU) in the early 1980s. 3G specifications and standards were developed in fifteen years. The technical specifications were made available to the public under the name IMT-2000. The communication spectrum between 400 MHz to 3 GHz was allocated for 3G. Both the government and communication companies approved the 3G standard. The first pre-commercial 3G network was launched by NTT DoCoMo in Japan in 1998, branded as FOMA. It was first available in May 2001 as a pre-release (test) of W-CDMA technology. The first commercial launch of 3G was also by NTT DoCoMo in Japan on 1 October 2001, although it was initially somewhat limited in scope; broader availability of the system was delayed by apparent concerns over its reliability.

The first European pre-commercial network was an UMTS network on the Isle of Man by Manx Telecom, the operator then owned by British Telecom, and the first commercial network (also UMTS based W-CDMA) in Europe was opened for business by Telenor in December 2001 with no commercial handsets and thus no paying customers.

The first network to go commercially live was by SK Telecom in South Korea on the CDMA-based 1xEV-DO technology in January 2002. By May 2002, the second South Korean 3G network was by KT on EV-DO and thus the South Koreans were the first to see competition among 3G operators.

The first commercial United States 3G network was by Monet Mobile Networks, on CDMA2000 1x EV-DO technology, but the network provider later shut down operations. The second 3G network operator in the US was Verizon Wireless in July 2002, also on CDMA2000 1x EV-DO. AT&T Mobility was also a true 3G UMTS network, having completed its upgrade of the 3G network to HSUPA.

The first commercial United Kingdom 3G network was started by Hutchison Telecom which was originally behind Orange S.A. In 2003, it announced first commercial third generation or 3G mobile phone network in the UK.

The first pre-commercial demonstration network in the southern hemisphere was built in Adelaide, South Australia, by m.Net Corporation in February 2002 using UMTS on 2100 MHz. This was a demonstration network for the 2002 IT World Congress. The first commercial 3G network was launched by Hutchison Telecommunications branded as Three or “3” in June 2003.

In India, on 11 December 2008, the first 3G mobile and internet services were launched by a state-owned company, Mahanagar Telecom Nigam Limited (MTNL), within the metropolitan cities of Delhi and Mumbai. After MTNL, another state-owned company, Bharat Sanchar Nigam Limited (BSNL), began deploying the 3G networks country-wide. Emtel launched the first 3G network in Africa.

Adoption

Japan was one of the first countries to adopt 3G, the reason being the process of 3G spectrum allocation, which in Japan was awarded without much upfront cost. The frequency spectrum was allocated in the US and Europe based on auctioning, thereby requiring a huge initial investment for any company wishing to provide 3G services. European companies collectively paid over 100 billion dollars in their spectrum auctions.

Nepal Telecom adopted 3G Service for the first time in southern Asia. However, its 3G was relatively slow to be adopted in Nepal. In some instances, 3G networks do not use the same radio frequencies as 2G, so mobile operators must build entirely new networks and license entirely new frequencies, especially to achieve high data transmission rates. Other countries' delays were due to the expenses of upgrading transmission hardware, especially for UMTS, whose deployment required the replacement of most broadcast towers. Due to these issues and difficulties with deployment, many carriers could not or delayed the acquisition of these updated capabilities.

In December 2007, 190 3G networks were operating in 40 countries and 154 HSDPA networks were operating in 71 countries, according to the Global Mobile Suppliers Association (GSA). In Asia, Europe, Canada, and the US, telecommunication companies use W-CDMA technology with the support of around 100 terminal designs to operate 3G mobile networks.

The roll-out of 3G networks was delayed by the enormous costs of additional spectrum licensing fees in some countries. The license fees in some European countries were particularly high, bolstered by government auctions of a limited number of licenses and sealed bid auctions, and initial excitement over 3G's potential. This led to a telecoms crash that ran concurrently with similar crashes in the fibre-optic and dot.com fields.

The 3G standard is perhaps well known because of a massive expansion of the mobile communications market post-2G and advances of the consumer mobile phone. An especially notable development during this time is the smartphone (for example, the iPhone, and the Android family), combining the abilities of a PDA with a mobile phone, leading to widespread demand for mobile internet connectivity. 3G has also introduced the term "mobile broadband" because its speed and capability made it a viable alternative for internet browsing, and USB Modems connecting to 3G networks, and now 4G became increasingly common.

Market Penetration

By June 2007, the 200 millionth 3G subscriber had been connected of which 10 million were in Nepal and 8.2 million in India. This 200 millionth is only 6.7% of the 3 billion mobile phone subscriptions worldwide. (When counting CDMA2000 1x RTT customers—max bitrate 72% of the 200 kbit/s which defines 3G—the total size of the nearly-3G subscriber base was 475 million as of June 2007, which was 15.8% of all subscribers worldwide.) In the countries where 3G was launched first - Japan and South Korea - 3G penetration is over 70%. In Europe the leading country for 3G penetration is Italy with a third of its subscribers migrated to 3G. Other leading countries for 3G use include Nepal, UK, Austria, Australia and Singapore at the 32% migration level.

According to ITU estimates, as of Q4 2012 there were 2096 million active mobile-broadband subscribers worldwide out of a total of 6835 million subscribers—this is just over 30%. About half the mobile-broadband subscriptions are for subscribers in developed nations, 934 million out of 1600 million total, well over 50%. Note however that there is a distinction between a phone with mobile-broadband connectivity and a smart phone with a large display and so on—although according to the ITU and informatandm.com the US has 321 million mobile subscriptions, including 256 million that are 3G or 4G, which is both 80% of the subscriber base and 80% of the US population, according to ComScore just a year earlier in Q4 2011 only about 42% of people surveyed in the US reported they owned a smart phone. In Japan, 3G penetration was similar at about 81%, but smart phone ownership was lower at about 17%. In China, there were 486.5 million 3G subscribers in June 2014, in a population of 1,385,566,537 (2013 UN estimate).

Decline and Decommissions

Since the increasing adoption of 4G networks across the globe, 3G use has been in decline. Several operators around the world have already or are in the process of shutting down their 3G networks. In several places, 3G is being shut down while its older predecessor 2G is being kept in operation; Vodafone Europe is doing this, citing 2G's usefulness as a low-power fallback. EE in the UK, plans to switch off their 3G networks in early 2024. In the US, Verizon shutdown their 3G services on 31 December 2022, T-Mobile shut down Sprint's networks on 31 March 2022 and shutdown their main networks on 1 July 2022, and AT&T has done so on 22 February 2022.

Currently 3G around the world is declining in availability and support. Technology that depends on 3G for usage are becoming inoperable in many places. For example, the European Union plans to ensure that member countries maintain 2G networks as a fallback, so 3G devices that are backwards compatible with 2G frequencies can continue to be used. However, in countries that plan to decommission 2G networks or have already done so as well, such as the United States and Singapore, devices supporting only 3G and backwards compatible with 2G are becoming inoperable. As of February 2022, less than 1% of cell phone customers in the United States used 3G; AT&T offered free replacement devices to some customers in the run-up to its shutdown.

Patents

It has been estimated that there are almost 8,000 patents declared essential (FRAND) related to the 483 technical specifications which form the 3GPP and 3GPP2 standards. Twelve companies accounted in 2004 for 90% of the patents (Qualcomm, Ericsson, Nokia, Motorola, Philips, NTT DoCoMo, Siemens, Mitsubishi, Fujitsu, Hitachi, InterDigital, and Matsushita).

Even then, some patents essential to 3G might not have been declared by their patent holders. It is believed that Nortel and Lucent have undisclosed patents essential to these standards.

Furthermore, the existing 3G Patent Platform Partnership Patent pool has little impact on FRAND protection because it excludes the four largest patent owners for 3G.

Features

Data Rates

ITU has not provided a clear definition of the data rate that users can expect from 3G equipment or providers. Thus users sold 3G service may not be able to point to a standard and say that the rates it specifies are not being met. While stating in commentary that "it is expected that IMT-2000 will provide higher transmission rates: a minimum data rate of 2 Mbit/s for stationary or walking users, and 348 kbit/s in a moving vehicle," the ITU does not actually clearly specify minimum required rates, nor required average rates, nor what modes of the interfaces qualify as 3G, so various data rates are sold as '3G' in the market.

In a market implementation, 3G downlink data speeds defined by telecom service providers vary depending on the underlying technology deployed; up to 384kbit/s for UMTS (WCDMA), up to 7.2Mbit/sec for HSPA, and a theoretical maximum of 21.1 Mbit/s for HSPA+ and 42.2 Mbit/s for DC-HSPA+ (technically 3.5G, but usually clubbed under the tradename of 3G). Compare data speeds with 3.5G and 4G.

Security

3G networks offer greater security than their 2G predecessors. By allowing the UE (User Equipment) to authenticate the network it is attaching to, the user can be sure the network is the intended one and not an impersonator. 3G networks use the KASUMI block cipher instead of the older A5/1 stream cipher. However, a number of serious weaknesses in the KASUMI cipher have been identified. In addition to the 3G network infrastructure security, end-to-end security is offered when application frameworks such as IMS are accessed, although this is not strictly a 3G property.

Applications of 3G

The bandwidth and location information available to 3G devices gives rise to applications not previously available to mobile phone users. It became possible to conveniently surf the internet on a 3G network on the go with minimum hassle, and do many other tasks previously a slow and difficult hassle on 2G. Medical devices, fire alarms, ankle monitors use this network for accomplishing their designated tasks alongside mobile phone users. This network marked the first for a cellular communications network to be used in such a wide variety of tasks, kick-starting the beginning of widespread usage of cellular networks.

Evolution

Both 3GPP and 3GPP2 are working on the extensions to 3G standards that are based on an all-IP network infrastructure and using advanced wireless technologies such as MIMO. These specifications already display features characteristic for IMT-Advanced (4G), the successor of 3G. However, falling short of the bandwidth requirements for 4G (which is 1 Gbit/s for stationary and 100 Mbit/s for mobile operation), these standards are classified as 3.9G or Pre-4G. 3GPP plans to meet the 4G goals with LTE Advanced, whereas Qualcomm has halted UMB development in favour of the LTE family. On 14 December 2009, TeliaSonera announced in an official press release that "We are very proud to be the first operator in the world to offer our customers 4G services." With the launch of their LTE network, initially they are offering pre-4G (or beyond 3G) services in Stockholm, Sweden and Oslo, Norway.

1.4.4 4G

4G is the fourth generation of broadband cellular network technology, succeeding 3G and preceding 5G. A 4G system must provide capabilities defined by ITU in IMT Advanced. Potential and current applications include amended mobile web access, IP telephony, gaming services, high-definition mobile TV, video conferencing, and 3D television.

However, in December 2010, the ITU expanded its definition of 4G to include Long Term Evolution (LTE), Worldwide Interoperability for Microwave Access (WiMAX), and Evolved High Speed Packet Access (HSPA+).

The first-release WiMAX standard was commercially deployed in South Korea in 2006 and has since been deployed in most parts of the world.

The first-release LTE standard was commercially deployed in Oslo, Norway, and Stockholm, Sweden in 2009, and has since been deployed throughout most parts of the world. However, it has been debated whether the first-release versions should be considered 4G. The 4G wireless cellular standard was defined by the International Telecommunication Union (ITU) and specifies the key characteristics of the standard, including transmission technology and data speeds.

Each generation of wireless cellular technology has introduced increased bandwidth speeds and network capacity. 4G has speeds of up to 150 Mbit/s download and 50 Mbit/s upload, whereas 3G had a peak speed of 7.2 Mbit/s download and 2 Mbit/s upload. As of 2022, 4G technology accounted for 60 percent of all mobile connections worldwide.

History of 4G and Pre-4G Technologies

The 4G system was originally envisioned by the DARPA, the US Defense Advanced Research Projects Agency. DARPA selected the distributed architecture and end-to-end Internet protocol (IP), and believed at an early stage in peer-to-peer networking in which every mobile device would be both a transceiver and a router for other devices in the network, eliminating the spoke-and-hub weakness of 2G and 3G cellular systems. Since the 2.5G GPRS system, cellular systems have provided dual infrastructures: packet switched nodes for data services, and circuit switched nodes for voice calls. In 4G systems, the circuit-switched infrastructure is abandoned and only a packet-switched network is provided, while 2.5G and 3G systems require both packet-switched and circuit-switched network nodes, i.e., two infrastructures in parallel. This means that in 4G traditional voice calls are replaced by IP telephony.

- In 2002, the strategic vision for 4G—which ITU designated as IMT Advanced—was laid out.
- In 2004, LTE was first proposed by NTT DoCoMo of Japan.
- In 2005, OFDMA transmission technology is chosen as candidate for the HSOPA downlink, later renamed 3GPP Long Term Evolution (LTE) air interface E-UTRA.
- In November 2005, KT Corporation demonstrated mobile WiMAX service in Busan, South Korea.
- In April 2006, KT Corporation started the world's first commercial mobile WiMAX service in Seoul, South Korea.
- In mid-2006, Sprint announced that it would invest about US$5 billion in a WiMAX technology buildout over the next few years ($7.26 billion in real terms). Since that time Sprint has faced many setbacks that have resulted in steep quarterly losses. On 7 May 2008, Sprint, Imagine, Google, Intel, Comcast, Bright House, and Time Warner announced a pooling of an average of 120 MHz of spectrum; Sprint merged its Xohm WiMAX division with Clearwire to form a company which will take the name "Clear".
- In February 2007, the Japanese company NTT DoCoMo tested a 4G communication system prototype with 4×4 MIMO called VSF-OFCDM at 100 Mbit/s while moving, and 1 Gbit/s while stationary. NTT DoCoMo completed a trial in which they reached a maximum packet transmission rate of approximately 5 Gbit/s in the downlink with 12×12 MIMO using a 100 MHz frequency bandwidth while moving at 10 km/h, and is planning on releasing the first commercial network in 2010.
- In September 2007, NTT Docomo demonstrated e-UTRA data rates of 200 Mbit/s with power consumption below 100 mW during the test.
- In January 2008, a U.S. Federal Communications Commission (FCC) spectrum auction for the 700 MHz former analog TV frequencies began. As a result, the biggest share of the spectrum went to Verizon Wireless and the next biggest to AT&T. Both of these companies have stated their intention of supporting LTE.
- In January 2008, EU commissioner Viviane Reding suggested re-allocation of 500–800 MHz spectrum for wireless communication, including WiMAX.
- On 15 February 2008, Skyworks Solutions released a front-end module for e-UTRAN.

- In November 2008, ITU-R established the detailed performance requirements of IMT-Advanced, by issuing a Circular Letter calling for candidate Radio Access Technologies (RATs) for IMT-Advanced.
- In April 2008, just after receiving the circular letter, the 3GPP organized a workshop on IMT-Advanced where it was decided that LTE Advanced, an evolution of current LTE standard, will meet or even exceed IMT-Advanced requirements following the ITU-R agenda.
- In April 2008, LG and Nortel demonstrated e-UTRA data rates of 50 Mbit/s while travelling at 110 km/h.
- On 12 November 2008, HTC announced the first WiMAX-enabled mobile phone, the Max 4G
- On 15 December 2008, San Miguel Corporation, the largest food and beverage conglomerate in southeast Asia, has signed a memorandum of understanding with Qatar Telecom QSC (Qtel) to build wireless broadband and mobile communications projects in the Philippines. The joint-venture formed wi-tribe Philippines, which offers 4G in the country. Around the same time Globe Telecom rolled out the first WiMAX service in the Philippines.
- On 3 March 2009, Lithuania's LRTC announcing the first operational "4G" mobile WiMAX network in Baltic states.
- In December 2009, Sprint began advertising "4G" service in selected cities in the United States, despite average download speeds of only 3–6 Mbit/s with peak speeds of 10 Mbit/s (not available in all markets).
- On 14 December 2009, the first commercial LTE deployment was in the Scandinavian capitals Stockholm and Oslo by the Swedish-Finnish network operator TeliaSonera and its Norwegian brandname NetCom (Norway). TeliaSonera branded the network "4G". The modem devices on offer were manufactured by Samsung (dongle GT-B3710), and the network infrastructure created by Huawei (in Oslo) and Ericsson (in Stockholm). TeliaSonera plans to roll out nationwide LTE across Sweden, Norway and Finland. TeliaSonera used spectral bandwidth of 10 MHz, and single-in-single-out, which should provide physical layer net bit rates of up to 50 Mbit/s downlink and 25 Mbit/s in the uplink. Introductory tests showed a TCP throughput of 42.8 Mbit/s downlink and 5.3 Mbit/s uplink in Stockholm.
- On 4 June 2010, Sprint released the first WiMAX smartphone in the US, the HTC Evo 4G.
- On November 4, 2010, the Samsung Craft offered by MetroPCS is the first commercially available LTE smartphone

- On 6 December 2010, at the ITU World Radiocommunication Seminar 2010, the ITU stated that LTE, WiMAX and similar "evolved 3G technologies" could be considered "4G".
- In 2011, Argentina's Claro launched a pre-4G HSPA+ network in the country.
- In 2011, Thailand's Truemove-H launched a pre-4G HSPA+ network with nationwide availability.
- On March 17, 2011, the HTC Thunderbolt offered by Verizon in the U.S. was the second LTE smartphone to be sold commercially.
- In February 2012, Ericsson demonstrated mobile-TV over LTE, utilizing the new eMBMS service (enhanced Multimedia Broadcast Multicast Service).

Since 2009, the LTE-Standard has strongly evolved over the years, resulting in many deployments by various operators across the globe. Among the vast range of deployments, many operators are considering the deployment and operation of LTE networks. A compilation of planned LTE deployments can be found at: List of planned LTE networks.

Key Features and Advancements

- Speed: 4G networks offer faster data download and upload speeds compared to 3G. Theoretically, 4G can achieve speeds of up to 100 megabits per second (Mbit/s) for high mobility communication and 1 gigabit per second (Gbit/s) for stationary users.
- Latency: Reduced latency, resulting in more responsive user experiences.
- Capacity: Enhanced network capacity allowing more simultaneous connections.
- Advanced Antenna Techniques: Use of MIMO (Multiple Input Multiple Output) and beamforming for better signal quality and improved spectral efficiency.

Technical Overview

In November 2008, the International Telecommunication Union-Radio communications sector (ITU-R) specified a set of requirements for 4G standards, named the International Mobile Telecommunications Advanced (IMT-Advanced) specification, setting peak speed requirements for 4G service at 100 megabits per second (Mbit/s)(=12.5 megabytes per second) for high mobility communication (such as from trains and cars) and 1 gigabit per second (Gbit/s) for low mobility communication (such as pedestrians and stationary users).

Since the first-release versions of Mobile WiMAX and LTE support much less than 1 Gbit/s peak bit rate, they are not fully IMT-Advanced compliant, but are often branded

4G by service providers. According to operators, a generation of the network refers to the deployment of a new non-backward-compatible technology. On December 6, 2010, ITU-R recognized that these two technologies, as well as other beyond-3G technologies that do not fulfill the IMT-Advanced requirements, could nevertheless be considered "4G", provided they represent forerunners to IMT-Advanced compliant versions and "a substantial level of improvement in performance and capabilities with respect to the initial third generation systems now deployed".

Mobile WiMAX Release 2 (also known as WirelessMAN-Advanced or IEEE 802.16m) and LTE Advanced (LTE-A) are IMT-Advanced compliant backwards compatible versions of the above two systems, standardized during the spring 2011, and promising speeds in the order of 1 Gbit/s. Services were expected in 2013.

As opposed to earlier generations, a 4G system does not support traditional circuit-switched telephony service, but instead relies on all-Internet Protocol (IP) based communication such as IP telephony. The spread spectrum radio technology used in 3G systems is abandoned in all 4G candidate systems and replaced by OFDMA multi-carrier transmission and other frequency-domain equalization (FDE) schemes, making it possible to transfer very high bit rates despite extensive multi-path radio propagation (echoes). The peak bit rate is further improved by smart antenna arrays for multiple-input multiple-output (MIMO) communications.

Background

In the field of mobile communications, a "generation" generally refers to a change in the fundamental nature of the service, non-backwards-compatible transmission technology, higher peak bit rates, new frequency bands, wider channel frequency bandwidth in Hertz, and higher capacity for many simultaneous data transfers (higher system spectral efficiency in bit/second/Hertz/site).

New mobile generations have appeared about every ten years since the first move from 1981 analog (1G) to digital (2G) transmission in 1992. This was followed, in 2001, by 3G multi-media support, spread spectrum transmission and a minimum peak bit rate of 200 kbit/s, in 2011/2012 to be followed by "real" 4G, which refers to all-IP packet-switched networks giving mobile ultra-broadband (gigabit speed) access.

While the ITU has adopted recommendations for technologies that would be used for future global communications, they do not actually perform the standardization or development work themselves, instead relying on the work of other standard bodies such as IEEE, WiMAX Forum, and 3GPP.

In the mid-1990s, the ITU-R standardization organization released the IMT-2000 requirements as a framework for what standards should be considered 3G systems, requiring 2000 kbit/s peak bit rate. In 2008, ITU-R specified the IMT Advanced (International Mobile Telecommunications Advanced) requirements for 4G systems.

The fastest 3G-based standard in the UMTS family is the HSPA+ standard, which has been commercially available since 2009 and offers 21 Mbit/s downstream (11 Mbit/s upstream) without MIMO, i.e., with only one antenna, and in 2011 accelerated up to 42 Mbit/s peak bit rate downstream using either DC-HSPA+ (simultaneous use of two 5 MHz UMTS carriers) or 2x2 MIMO. In theory speeds up to 672 Mbit/s are possible, but have not been deployed yet. The fastest 3G-based standard in the CDMA2000 family is the EV-DO Rev. B, which is available since 2010 and offers 15.67 Mbit/s downstream.

IMT-Advanced Requirements

- Be based on an all-IP packet switched network.
- Have peak data rates of up to approximately 100 Mbit/s for high mobility such as mobile access and up to approximately 1 Gbit/s for low mobility such as nomadic/local wireless access.
- Be able to dynamically share and use the network resources to support more simultaneous users per cell.
- Use scalable channel bandwidths of 5–20 MHz, optionally up to 40 MHz.
- Have peak link spectral efficiency of 15 bit/s·Hz in the downlink, and 6.75 bit/s·Hz in the up link (meaning that 1 Gbit/s in the downlink should be possible over less than 67 MHz bandwidth).
- System spectral efficiency is, in indoor cases, 3 bit/s·Hz·cell for downlink and 2.25 bit/s·Hz·cell for up link.
- Smooth handovers across heterogeneous networks.

In September 2009, the technology proposals were submitted to the International Telecommunication Union (ITU) as 4G candidates. Basically all proposals are based on two technologies:

- LTE Advanced standardized by the 3GPP
- 802.16m standardized by the IEEE

Implementations of Mobile WiMAX and first-release LTE were largely considered a stopgap solution that would offer a considerable boost until WiMAX 2 (based on the 802.16m specification) and LTE Advanced was deployed. The latter's standard versions were ratified in spring 2011.

The first set of 3GPP requirements on LTE Advanced was approved in June 2008. LTE Advanced was standardized in 2010 as part of Release 10 of the 3GPP specification.

Some sources consider first-release LTE and Mobile WiMAX implementations as pre-4G or near-4G, as they do not fully comply with the planned requirements of 1 Gbit/s for stationary reception and 100 Mbit/s for mobile.

Confusion has been caused by some mobile carriers who have launched products advertised as 4G but which according to some sources are pre-4G versions, commonly referred to as 3.9G, which do not follow the ITU-R defined principles for 4G standards, but today can be called 4G according to ITU-R. Vodafone Netherlands for example, advertised LTE as 4G, while advertising LTE Advanced as their '4G+' service. A common argument for branding 3.9G systems as new-generation is that they use different frequency bands from 3G technologies; that they are based on a new radio-interface paradigm; and that the standards are not backwards compatible with 3G, whilst some of the standards are forwards compatible with IMT-2000 compliant versions of the same standards.

System Standards

IMT-2000 Compliant 4G Standards

As of October 2010, ITU-R Working Party 5D approved two industry-developed technologies (LTE Advanced and WirelessMAN-Advanced) for inclusion in the ITU's International Mobile Telecommunications Advanced program (IMT-Advanced program), which is focused on global communication systems that will be available several years from now.

LTE Advanced

LTE Advanced (Long Term Evolution Advanced) is a candidate for IMT-Advanced standard, formally submitted by the 3GPP organization to ITU-T in the fall 2009, and expected to be released in 2013. The target of 3GPP LTE Advanced is to reach and surpass the ITU requirements. LTE Advanced is essentially an enhancement to LTE. It is not a new technology, but rather an improvement on the existing LTE network. This upgrade path makes it more cost effective for vendors to offer LTE and then upgrade to LTE Advanced which is similar to the upgrade from WCDMA to HSPA. LTE and LTE Advanced will also make use of additional spectrums and multiplexing to allow it to achieve higher data speeds. Coordinated Multi-point Transmission will also allow more system capacity to help handle the enhanced data speeds.

Table 1.2: Data Speeds of LTE-Advanced

	LTE Advanced
Peak download	1000 Mbit/s
Peak upload	500 Mbit/s

IEEE 802.16m or WirelessMAN-Advanced

The IEEE 802.16m or WirelessMAN-Advanced (WiMAX 2) evolution of 802.16e is under development, with the objective to fulfill the IMT-Advanced criteria of 1 Gbit/s for stationary reception and 100 Mbit/s for mobile reception.

Forerunner Versions

Long Term Evolution (LTE)

The pre-4G 3GPP Long Term Evolution (LTE) technology is often branded "4G – LTE", but the first LTE release does not fully comply with the IMT-Advanced requireents. LTE has a theoretical net bit rate capcity of up to 100 Mbit/s in the downlink and 50 Mbit/s in the uplink if a 20 MHz channel is used — and more if multiple-input multiple-output (MIMO), i.e., antenna arrays, are used.

The physical radio interface was at an early stage named High Speed OFDM Packet Access (HSOPA), now named Evolved UMTS Terrestrial Radio Access (E-UTRA). The first LTE USB dongles do not support any other radio interface.

The world's first publicly available LTE service was opened in the two Scandinavian capitals, Stockholm (Ericsson and Nokia Siemens Networks systems) and Oslo (a Huawei system) on December 14, 2009, and branded 4G. The user terminals were manufactured by Samsung. As of November 2012, the five publicly available LTE services in the United States are provided by MetroPCS, Verizon Wireless, AT&T Mobility, U.S. Cellular, Sprint, and T-Mobile US.

Fig. 1.1: Telia-branded Samsung LTE Modem

Fig. 1.2: Huawei 4G+ Dual Band Modem

T-Mobile Hungary launched a public beta test (called friendly user test) on 7 October 2011, and has offered commercial 4G LTE services since 1 January 2012.

In South Korea, SK Telecom and LG U+ have enabled access to LTE service since 1 July 2011 for data devices, slated to go nationwide by 2012. KT Telecom closed its 2G service by March 2012 and completed nationwide LTE service in the same frequency around 1.8 GHz by June 2012.

In the United Kingdom, LTE services were launched by EE in October 2012, by O2 and Vodafone in August 2013, and by Three in December 2013.

Table 1.3: Data speeds of LTE

	LTE
Peak download	150 Mbit/s
Peak upload	50 Mbit/s

Mobile WiMAX (IEEE 802.16e)

The Mobile WiMAX (IEEE 802.16e-2005) mobile wireless broadband access (MWBA) standard (also known as WiBro in South Korea) is sometimes branded 4G, and offers peak data rates of 128 Mbit/s downlink and 56 Mbit/s uplink over 20 MHz wide channels.

In June 2006, the world's first commercial mobile WiMAX service was opened by KT in Seoul, South Korea.

Sprint has begun using Mobile WiMAX, as of 29 September 2008, branding it as a "4G" network even though the current version does not fulfill the IMT Advanced requirements on 4G systems.

In Russia, Belarus and Nicaragua WiMax broadband internet access were offered by a Russian company Scartel, and was also branded 4G, Yota.

Table 1.4: Data Speeds of WiMAX

WiMAX	
Peak download	128 Mbit/s
Peak upload	56 Mbit/s

In the latest version of the standard, WiMax 2.1, the standard has been updated to be not compatible with earlier WiMax standard, and is instead interchangeable with LTE-TDD system, effectively merging WiMax standard with LTE.

TD-LTE for China Market

Just as Long-Term Evolution (LTE) and WiMAX are being vigorously promoted in the global telecommunications industry, the former (LTE) is also the most powerful 4G mobile communications leading technology and has quickly occupied the Chinese market. TD-LTE, one of the two variants of the LTE air interface technologies, is not yet mature, but many domestic and international wireless carriers are, one after the other turning to TD-LTE.

IBM's data shows that 67% of the operators are considering LTE because this is the main source of their future market. The above news also confirms IBM's statement that while only 8% of the operators are considering the use of WiMAX, WiMAX can provide the fastest network transmission to its customers on the market and could challenge LTE.

TD-LTE is not the first 4G wireless mobile broadband network data standard, but it is China's 4G standard that was amended and published by China's largest telecom operator – China Mobile. After a series of field trials, is expected to be released into the commercial phase in the next two years. Ulf Ewaldsson, Ericsson's vice president said: "the Chinese Ministry of Industry and China Mobile in the fourth quarter of this year will hold a large-scale field test, by then, Ericsson will help the hand." But viewing from the current development trend, whether this standard advocated by China Mobile will be widely recognized by the international market is still debatable.

Discontinued Candidate Systems

UMB (Formerly EV-DO Rev. C)

UMB (Ultra Mobile Broadband) was the brand name for a discontinued 4G project within the 3GPP2 standardization group to improve the CDMA2000 mobile phone standard for next generation applications and requirements. In November 2008, Qualcomm, UMB's lead sponsor, announced it was ending development of the technology, favoring LTE instead. The objective was to achieve data speeds over 275 Mbit/s downstream and over 75 Mbit/s upstream.

Flash-OFDM

At an early stage the Flash-OFDM system was expected to be further developed into a 4G standard.

iBurst and MBWA (IEEE 802.20) Systems

The iBurst system (or HC-SDMA, High Capacity Spatial Division Multiple Access) was at an early stage considered to be a 4G predecessor. It was later further developed into the Mobile Broadband Wireless Access (MBWA) system, also known as IEEE 802.20.

Principal Technologies in all Candidate Systems

Key Features

The following key features can be observed in all suggested 4G technologies:

- Physical layer transmission techniques are as follows:
  - MIMO: To attain ultra high spectral efficiency by means of spatial processing including multi-antenna and multi-user MIMO
  - Frequency-domain-equalization, for example multi-carrier modulation (OFDM) in the downlink or single-carrier frequency-domain-equalization (SC-FDE) in the uplink: To exploit the frequency selective channel property without complex equalization
  - Frequency-domain statistical multiplexing, for example (OFDMA) or (single-carrier FDMA) (SC-FDMA, a.k.a. linearly precoded OFDMA, LP-OFDMA) in the uplink: Variable bit rate by assigning different sub-channels to different users based on the channel conditions
  - Turbo principle error-correcting codes: To minimize the required SNR at the reception side
- Channel-dependent scheduling: To use the time-varying channel
- Link adaptation: Adaptive modulation and error-correcting codes
- Mobile IP utilized for mobility
- IP-based femtocells (home nodes connected to fixed Internet broadband infrastructure)

As opposed to earlier generations, 4G systems do not support circuit switched telephony. IEEE 802.20, UMB and OFDM standards lack soft-handover support, also known as cooperative relaying.

Multiplexing and Access Schemes

Recently, new access schemes like Orthogonal FDMA (OFDMA), Single Carrier FDMA (SC-FDMA), Interleaved FDMA, and Multi-carrier CDMA (MC-CDMA) are gaining more importance for the next generation systems. These are based on efficient FFT algorithms and frequency domain equalization, resulting in a lower number of multiplications per second. They also make it possible to control the bandwidth and form the spectrum in a flexible way. However, they require advanced dynamic channel allocation and adaptive traffic scheduling.

WiMax is using OFDMA in the downlink and in the uplink. For the LTE (telecommunication), OFDMA is used for the downlink; by contrast, Single-carrier FDMA is used for the uplink since OFDMA contributes more to the PAPR related issues and results in nonlinear operation of amplifiers. IFDMA provides less power fluctuation and thus requires energy-inefficient linear amplifiers. Similarly, MC-CDMA is in the proposal for the IEEE 802.20 standard. These access schemes offer the same efficiencies as older technologies like CDMA. Apart from this, scalability and higher data rates can be achieved.

This is an added advantage especially in the MIMO environments since the spatial multiplexing transmission of MIMO systems inherently require high complexity equalization at the receiver.

In addition to improvements in these multiplexing systems, improved modulation techniques are being used. Whereas earlier standards largely used Phase-shift keying, more efficient systems such as 64QAM are being proposed for use with the 3GPP Long Term Evolution standards.

IPv6 Support

Unlike 3G, which is based on two parallel infrastructures consisting of circuit switched and packet switched network nodes, 4G is based on packet switching only. This requires low-latency data transmission. As IPv4 addresses are (nearly) exhausted, IPv6 is essential to support the large number of wireless-enabled devices that communicate using IP. By increasing the number of IP addresses available, IPv6 removes the need for network address translation (NAT), a method of sharing a limited number of addresses among a larger group of devices, which has a number of problems and limitations. When using IPv6, some kind of NAT is still required for communication with legacy IPv4 devices that are not also IPv6-connected.

As of June 2009, Verizon has posted Specifications Archived March 6, 2018, at the Wayback Machine that require any 4G devices on its network to support IPv6.

Advanced Antenna Systems

The performance of radio communications depends on an antenna system, termed smart or intelligent antenna. Recently, multiple antenna technologies are emerging to achieve the goal of 4G systems such as high rate, high reliability, and long range communications. In the early 1990s, to cater for the growing data rate needs of data communication, many transmission schemes were proposed. One technology, spatial multiplexing, gained importance for its bandwidth conservation and power efficiency. Spatial multiplexing involves deploying multiple antennas at the transmitter and at the receiver. Independent streams can then be transmitted simultaneously from all the antennas. This technology, called MIMO (as a branch of intelligent antenna), multiplies the base data rate by (the smaller of) the number of transmit antennas or the number of receive antennas. Apart from this, the reliability in transmitting high speed data in the fading channel can be improved by using more antennas at the transmitter or at the receiver. This is called transmit or receive diversity. Both transmit/receive diversity and transmit spatial multiplexing are categorized into the space-time coding techniques, which does not necessarily require the channel knowledge at the transmitter. The other category is closed-loop multiple antenna technologies, which require channel knowledge at the transmitter.

Open-wireless Architecture and Software-defined Radio (SDR)

One of the key technologies for 4G and beyond is called Open Wireless Architecture (OWA), supporting multiple wireless air interfaces in an open architecture platform. SDR is one form of open wireless architecture (OWA). Since 4G is a collection of wireless standards, the final form of a 4G device will constitute various standards. This can be efficiently realized using SDR technology, which is categorized to the area of the radio convergence.

Disadvantages

4G introduces a potential inconvenience for those who travel internationally or wish to switch carriers. In order to make and receive 4G voice calls (VoLTE), the subscriber handset must not only have a matching frequency band (and in some cases require unlocking), it must also have the matching enablement settings for the local carrier and/or country. While a phone purchased from a given carrier can be expected to work with that carrier, making 4G voice calls on another carrier's network (including international roaming) may be impossible without a software update specific to the local carrier and the phone model in question, which may or may not be available (although fallback to 2G/3G for voice calling may still be possible if a 2G/3G network is available with a matching frequency band).

Beyond 4G Research

A major issue in 4G systems is to make the high bit rates available in a larger portion of the cell, especially to users in an exposed position in between several base stations. In current research, this issue is addressed by macro-diversity techniques, also known as group cooperative relay, and also by Beam-Division Multiple Access (BDMA).

Pervasive networks are an amorphous and at present entirely hypothetical concept where the user can be simultaneously connected to several wireless access technologies and can seamlessly move between them. These access technologies can be Wi-Fi, UMTS, EDGE, or any other future access technology. Included in this concept is also smart-radio (also known as cognitive radio) technology to efficiently manage spectrum use and transmission power as well as the use of mesh routing protocols to create a pervasive network.

The Future of 4G

As of 2023, many countries and regions have started the transition from 4G to 5G, the next generation of cellular technology. 5G promises even faster speeds, lower latency, and the ability to connect a vast number of devices simultaneously. 4G networks are expected to coexist with 5G networks for several years, providing coverage in areas where 5G is not available.

CHAPTER 2

FUNDAMENTALS OF WIRELESS COMMUNICATION

2.1 BASICS OF RADIO FREQUENCY AND SPECTRUM

2.1.1 Radio Frequency

Carrier Signal

- It's a high-frequency signal that "carries" the lower bandwidth of "real" information signals such voice and data
- The reason is that due to the miniaturization of consumer electronics, a high RF carrier signal is needed for efficient electromagnetic radiation using small antenna in transmission and reception of wireless networks.

Baseband Signal

It's a low bandwidth analog signal containing data such as voice and data typically found after downconverting from RF to DC before analog to digital converter (ADC) in radio receiver or right after digital to analog converter (DAC) in radio transmitter.

Two main reasons for using a low BW baseband signal are:

- Come within sampling range of ADC/DAC: Sampling rates are limited on ADC/DAC mixed-signal hardware which is needed for pre/post-digital signal processing.
- Improved selectivity: An easier filter design with sharper rolloff can be constructed at lower frequencies.

Orthogonal relationship (i.e. 90 degrees) between two vectors. Two components I (in-phase signal) and Q (out-of-phase signal) are 90 degrees out of phase. IQ signals are the building block of modern digital modulation and demodulation schemes.

Modulation

Modulation means encoding a message. In the context of RF, one can think of it in two ways:

- Encoding a baseband message on a carrier frequency signal.

- Frequency shifts the baseband signal to a radio frequency signal.

Analog Modulation

It is used to encode analog baseband signal onto an RF carrier signal for long-range transmission with low data bandwidth such as voice, and small data packets.

Typical analog modulations are:

- Amplitude Modulation (AM): Analog baseband signal is encoded on an RF carrier signal in the form of varying RF carrier signal amplitude.
- Frequency Modulation (FM): Analog baseband signal is encoded on an RF carrier signal in the form of varying RF carrier signal frequency

Digital Modulation

It is used to encode digital baseband signal (i.e., binary bits 0 and 1) onto an RF carrier signal for short to mid-range transmission with high data bandwidth such as large file download and video streaming.

Typical digital modulations are:

- Amplitude Shift Keying: 1-bit binary signal modulation scheme where 1 and 0 are represented by turning on and off RF carrier transmission.
- Frequency Shift Keying: 1-bit binary signal modulation scheme where 1 and 0 are represented by changing RF carrier signal from high to low frequency.
- Phase Shift keying: 1-bit symbol binary signal modulation scheme where 1 and 0 are represented by change RF carrier signal phase relationship.
- Quadrature Amplitude modulation (QAM): a baseband signal is encoded by summing two carrier signals 90 degrees out of phase (i.e. I & Q components) resulting in a single signal that is controlled by phase and amplitude variation of two I/Q carriers.
- Digital symbols are reconstructed by a combination of amplitude and phase relationship of the I & Q components. This is very clever and powerful because by varying amplitude and phase relationships of I & Q carriers, a range of unique symbols can be creatd resulting in an increase of bits/symbol; Hence higher data throughput is achieved.
- This technique increases spectral efficiency (i.e., more bits/symbols transmitted per fixed channel bandwidth).
- Quadrature Phase shift Keying (QPSK): It's a 2-bit modulation technique with 4 unique symbols, 00, 01, 10, and 11 are represented by phase change (45,135, 225, or 315 degrees) of the carrier signal using I and Q components in quadrature amplitude modulation (QAM).

Analog/Digital Demodulation

Demodulation is analogous to decoding an RF signal which involves removing carrier frequency component from the RF signal leaving the baseband signal behind for further processing.

Basic Principles of Operations

RF system is responsible for the transmission and reception of wireless signals.

- RF transmission: An RF signal is created by upshifting a low bandwidth (DC-like) signal to radio frequency by a radio transmitter.
- RF reception: An RF signal is picked up by the antenna and downshifted to a low bandwidth (DC-like) signal by a radio receiver.

Basic RF System Building Blocks

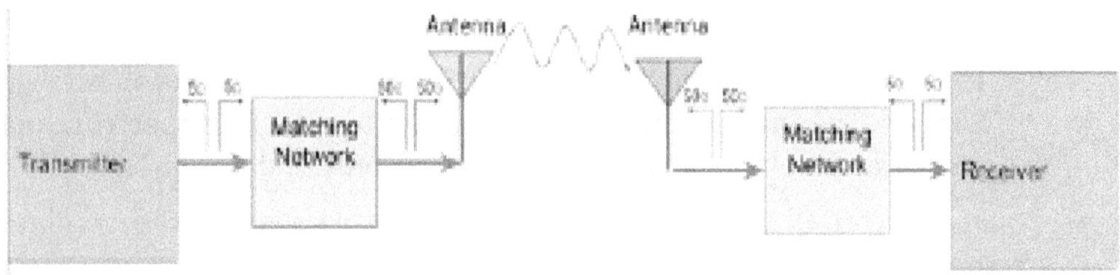

Fig: 2.1: RF Communication Block Diagram

2.1.2 Block Descriptions

- Transmitter: It is an integrated RF hardware containing DAC for generating analog baseband signal, mixer for modulation, and power amplifier for over the air transmission. Its main job is to up-shift baseband signal to RF signal and increases RF output power for transmission.
- Receiver: It is an integrated RF hardware containing low noise amplifier (LNA), mixer for demodulation, and ADC for converting analog baseband signal to digital domain for digital signal processing. Its main job is to amplify received RF signal before down-shift to baseband signal.
- Matching Network: Matching network is made up of inductors and capacitors that is used to match source output impedance (Transmitter Power Amplifier/ Receiver) to the load impedance (Antenna Impedance). Its main job is to maximize power transfer.

In practice, matching to 50 ohm is used due to characteristic impedance of transmission line in RF system in designed as 50 ohms.

Types of Matching Network:

- Two element matching: L matching network

- No flexibility of quality factor Q: Highly dependent on input and load impedance
  - Forbidden region exists on the smith chart for load impedance
  - This means that 2 element matching network is limited to certain load impedance type.
- Application: Antenna uses L network because it covers a wider range/broadband signals (i.e., higher bandwidth and lower quality factor of the matching network)
- Three element matching: PI and T matching network
  - More flexibility on quality factor for Q
  - No forbidden region on the smith chart for load impedance
  - This means that any arbitrary source and load impedance can be matched using 3-element matching network.
  - In practice, 3-element is used for RF system design due to stringent wireless channel bandwidth and roll offs to meet the spectrum mask and adjacent channel leakage of RF emission standards.
- Quality factor Q: Q value of a matching network reports the oscillatory resonance performance of the matching network.
- A high Q matching means that the equivalent lossy component of the network is low. This means that the resonance peak of the circuit (assuming matching network is modeled as series RLC) is higher because series R is smaller due to lower equivalent lossy element.
- Note: Resonance curve is a current vs. frequency response where current is measured as the series current going through the RLC matching network model.
- Another important relationship between Q to signal bandwidth is that Q = Fo/(3dB bandwidth), which means that higher Q means narrower 3-dB bandwidth which is needed for limited and fixed bandwidth standards used today such as 20 MHz bandwidth for Wi-Fi channels.

RF Performance Characterization

- Smith Chart: It's an impedance visualization tool that is used to characterize impedance of a lumped passive circuit.
  - For two element matching network, two circles are used, constant conductance circuit and resistance circle, to move the load impedance ZL to the origin of the smith chart (i.e 50 ohms).
  - For 3 element matching network, 3 circles are used to the move load impedance ZL to the origin of the smith chart (i.e 50 ohms).

- Transmitter:
  - Efficiency, output dynamic range.
  - Gain compression: it's a measures of nonlinearity usually characterized by input power level that reaches 1 dB compression (i.e 1 dB point away from the perfect straight linear line).
- Receiver:
  - Sensitivity: minimal power level needed for required SNR
  - Selectivity: only select desired signal (i.e specify attenuation of out of band signals)

System Level

Link Budget

It is used to estimate line of sight range of wireless communication link by calculate received power at receiver.

- Received Power (dBm) = Transmitted Power (dBm) + Gains (dB) – Losses (dB)
- Gains are amplifers and antenna.
- Losses are free-space path loss, pcb path and component loss.

Link Margin

It is used to calculate much margin is needed for a communication system accounting signal attenuation due to multi-path fading during the transmission channel.

- Link Margin = Received Power – Receive Sensitivity

Adjacent Channels Power Ratio (ACPR)

It is a measurement of the amount of interference in the adjacent frequency channel usually as the ratio of average power adjacent outband channel to the average power in the in-band channel,

Phase Noise

Random frequency fluctuations of the main RF carrier frequency cause by imperfect clock generator source such as the local oscillator used for generating RF carrier frequency.

Noise Figure

A measure of degradation of signal SNR caused by RF hardware placed in the transmission and reception path.

- The reason for the added noise is due to intrinsic RF component noise that is added to the signal path.

Component Level

- S parameter: It is used to measure traveling waves for RF signals on printed circuit boards.
  - insertion loss (S21/S12)
  - It measures the loss of signal power by an insertion element such as a RF filter measured in dB.
- Application: Lower insertion loss of an RF element means lower power loss in the RF element resulting in high power available power transfer to the load.
  - Return loss (S11/S22)
  - It measures the loss of signal power reflected by the transmission medium such as impedance discontinuity measured in dB.
- Application: Antenna radiation power is generally characterized by return loss (S11). A -10 dB S11 means that power return is 10% of the original signal, which infers that 90% of signal is radiated.

Measurements

Digital Modulation Scheme Representation

- Constellation Diagram: It plots each signal symbol after demodulation on a complex plane represented by I (lies on real horizontal axis) and Q (lies in imaginary Y axis) components.
- Application: Due to noise such as Gaussian noise and phase noise introduced by the communication channel, the received symbols does not lie exactly on the ideal reference points on the chart, hence constellation aggregates a period of multiple received signals as a visual indicator for engineers to evaluate amount of signal deviation error also known as error vector magnitude (EVM)
- Carrier to Noise Ratio (C/N) and Signal to Noise Ratio (SNR): They used to characterize RF signal quality in an noisy environment. C/N is analogous to SNR with the difference that digital modulation is used for C/N analysis and analog modulation is used for SNR analysis. In digital modulation and transmission,RF signal quality is entirely depended on carrier signal (constant frequency and amplitude) with respect to noisy environment.,
- Bit Error Rate (BER)/ Packet Error Rate (PER): As constellation points packed more closely used in digital modulation scheme such as QAM for higher data throughput, lowering C/N increases bit error rate. BER/PER is an important test metric to evaluate communication system robustness against noise environment.

Common Wireless System Level Test items

Transmitter:

- Average power: It measures the radio transmitter output power performance.
- Spectrum Mask: Wireless standards limits transmitter spectrum shape from exceeding certain limits.
- Error Vector Magnitude: It measures how far the received symbol points away from ideal location on the constellation Diagram.
- Frequency error/offset: It's the frequency error of the carrier frequency from its ideal carrier frequency measured in HZ PPM.

Receiver:

- Minimum Detectable Signal (Sensitivity), Selectivity (ability to reject out-of band signals), Linearity, Bit error rate (BER).

Practical Design Overview

- The main goal of RF system design is to maximize power transfer within allowed radiation limit and acceptable signal integrity.
- Lowering the insertion loss of the matching network increases amount of power available to the Antenna.
- RF testing covers generally lowest, mid, and highest channel withing an RF band (e.g 2.4 GHz and 5.0 GHz WLAN band).
- Limiting power amplifier output on lowest and highest RF channel are typical configuration of WLAN transmiter to limit adjacent channel interference as required by wireless standards and regulatory communication compliance.

2.1.3 Spectrum

The radio spectrum is the part of the electromagnetic spectrum with frequencies from 3 Hz to 3,000 GHz (3 THz). Electromagnetic waves in this frequency range, called radio waves, are widely used in modern technology, particularly in telecommunication. To prevent interference between different users, the generation and transmission of radio waves is strictly regulated by national laws, coordinated by an international body, the International Telecommunication Union (ITU).

Different parts of the radio spectrum are allocated by the ITU for different radio transmission technologies and applications; some 40 radiocommunication services are defined in the ITU's Radio Regulations (RR).

In some cases, parts of the radio spectrum are sold or licensed to operators of private radio transmission services (for example, cellular telephone operators or broadcast television stations). Ranges of allocated frequencies are often referred to by their provisioned use (for example, cellular spectrum or television spectrum).

Because it is a fixed resource which is in demand by an increasing number of users, the radio spectrum has become increasingly congested in recent decades, and the need to utilize it more effectively is driving modern telecommunications innovations such as trunked radio systems, spread spectrum, ultra-wideband, frequency reuse, dynamic spectrum management, frequency pooling, and cognitive radio.

Limits

The frequency boundaries of the radio spectrum are a matter of convention in physics and are somewhat arbitrary. Since radio waves are the lowest frequency category of electromagnetic waves, there is no lower limit to the frequency of radio waves. Radio waves are defined by the ITU as: "electromagnetic waves of frequencies arbitrarily lower than 3000 GHz, propagated in space without artificial guide".

At the high frequency end the radio spectrum is bounded by the infrared band. The boundary between radio waves and infrared waves is defined at different frequencies in different scientific fields. The terahertz band, from 300 gigahertz to 3 terahertz, can be considered either as microwaves or infrared. It is the highest band categorized as radio waves by the International Telecommunication Union. but spectroscopic scientists consider these frequencies part of the far infrared and mid infrared bands.

Because it is a fixed resource, the practical limits and basic physical considerations of the radio spectrum, the frequencies which are useful for radio communication, are determined by technological limitations which are impossible to overcome. So although the radio spectrum is becoming increasingly congested, there is no possible way to add additional frequency bandwidth outside of that currently in use. The lowest frequencies used for radio communication are limited by the increasing size of transmitting antennas required.

The size of antenna required to radiate radio power efficiently increases in proportion to wavelength or inversely with frequency. Below about 10 kHz (a wavelength of 30 km), elevated wire antennas kilometers in diameter are required, so very few radio systems use frequencies below this.

A second limit is the decreasing bandwidth available at low frequencies, which limits the data rate that can be transmitted. Below about 30 kHz, audio modulation is impractical and only slow baud rate data communication is used. The lowest frequencies that have been used for radio communication are around 80 Hz, in ELF submarine communications systems built by a few nations' navies to communicate with their submerged submarines hundreds of meters underwater. These employ huge ground dipole antennas 20–60 km long excited by megawatts of transmitter power, and transmit data at an extremely slow rate of about 1 bit per minute (17 millibits per second, or about 5 minutes per character).

The highest frequencies useful for radio communication are limited by the absorption of microwave energy by the atmosphere.

As frequency increases above 30 GHz (the beginning of the millimeter wave band), atmospheric gases absorb increasing amounts of power, so the power in a beam of radio waves decreases exponentially with distance from the transmitting antenna.

At 30 GHz, useful communication is limited to about 1 km, but as frequency increases the range at which the waves can be received decreases. In the terahertz band above 300 GHz, the radio waves are attenuated to zero within a few meters due to the absorption of electromagnetic radiation by the atmosphere (mainly due to ozone, water vapor and carbon dioxide), which is so great that it is essentially opaque to electromagnetic emissions, until it becomes transparent again near the infrared and in the visible light ranges.

Bands

A radio band is a small frequency band (a contiguous section of the range of the radio spectrum) in which channels are usually used or set aside for the same purpose. To prevent interference and allow for efficient use of the radio spectrum, similar services are allocated in bands. For example, broadcasting, mobile radio, or navigation devices, will be allocated in non-overlapping ranges of frequencies.

Band Plan

For each radio band, the ITU has a band plan (or frequency plan) which dictates how it is to be used and shared, to avoid interference and to set protocol for the compatibility of transmitters and receivers.

Each frequency plan defines the frequency range to be included, how channels are to be defined, and what will be carried on those channels. Typical definitions set forth in a frequency plan are:

- numbering scheme – which channel numbers or letters (if any) will be assigned
- center frequencies – how far apart the carrier wave for each channel will be
- bandwidth and/or deviation – how wide each channel will be
- spectral mask – how extraneous signals will be attenuated by frequency
- modulation – what type will be used or are permissible
- content – what types of information are allowed, such as audio or video, analog or digital
- licensing – what the procedure will be to obtain a broadcast license

ITU

The actual authorized frequency bands are defined by the ITU and the local regulating agencies like the US Federal Communications Commission (FCC) and voluntary best practices help avoid interference. As a matter of convention, the ITU divides the radio spectrum into 12 bands, each beginning at a wavelength which is a power of ten (10) metres, with corresponding frequency of 3×10 hertz, and each covering a decade of frequency or wavelength.

Each of these bands has a traditional name. For example, the term high frequency (HF) designates the wavelength range from 100 to 10 metres, corresponding to a frequency range of 3 to 30 MHz. This is just a symbol and is not related to allocation; the ITU further divides each band into subbands allocated to different services. Above 300 GHz, the absorption of electromagnetic radiation by Earth's atmosphere is so great that the atmosphere is effectively opaque, until it becomes transparent again in the near-infrared and optical window frequency ranges.

These ITU radio bands are defined in the ITU Radio Regulations. Article 2, provision No. 2.1 states that "the radio spectrum shall be subdivided into nine frequency bands, which shall be designated by progressive whole numbers in accordance with the following table". The table originated with a recommendation of the fourth CCIR meeting, held in Bucharest in 1937, and was approved by the International Radio Conference held at Atlantic City, NJ in 1947.

The idea to give each band a number, in which the number is the logarithm of the approximate geometric mean of the upper and lower band limits in Hz, originated with B. C. Fleming-Williams, who suggested it in a letter to the editor of Wireless Engineer in 1942. For example, the approximate geometric mean of band 7 is 10 MHz, or 10 Hz.

IEEE Radar Bands

Frequency bands in the microwave range are designated by letters. This convention began around World War II with military designations for frequencies used in radar, which was the first application of microwaves. Unfortunately, there are several incompatible naming systems for microwave bands, and even within a given system the exact frequency range designated by a letter may vary somewhat between different application areas. One widely used standard is the IEEE radar bands established by the US Institute of Electrical and Electronics Engineers.

Table 2.1: Radar-frequency Bands according to IEEE Standard

Banddesignation	Frequency Range	Explanation of meaning of letters
HF	0.003 to 0.03 GHz	High frequency
VHF	0.03 to 0.3 GHz	Very high frequency
UHF	0.3 to 1 GHz	Ultra-high frequency

L	1 to 2 GHz	Long wave
S	2 to 4 GHz	Short wave
C	4 to 8 GHz	Compromise between S and X
X	8 to 12 GHz	Used in World War II for fire control, X for cross (as in crosshair). Exotic.
Ku	12 to 18 GHz	Kurz-under
K	18 to 27 GHz	German: Kurz (short)
Ka	27 to 40 GHz	Kurz-above
V	40 to 75 GHz	
W	75 to 110 GHz	W follows V in the alphabet
mm or G	110 to 300 GHz	Millimeter

Table 2.2: Waveguide Frequency Bands

Band	Frequency Range
R band	1.70 to 2.60 GHz
D band	2.20 to 3.30 GHz
S band	2.60 to 3.95 GHz
E band	3.30 to 4.90 GHz
G band	3.95 to 5.85 GHz
F band	4.90 to 7.05 GHz
C band	5.85 to 8.20 GHz
H band	7.05 to 10.10 GHz
X band	8.2 to 12.4 GHz
Ku band	12.4 to 18.0 GHz
K band	18.0 to 26.5 GHz
Ka band	26.5 to 40.0 GHz
Q band	33 to 50 GHz
U band	40 to 60 GHz
V band	50 to 75 GHz
E band	60 to 90 GHz
W band	75 to 110 GHz
F band	90 to 140 GHz
D band	110 to 170 GHz
Y band	325 to 500 GHz

Applications

Broadcasting

Broadcast frequencies:

- Longwave AM Radio = 148.5 kHz – 283.5 kHz (LF)
- Mediumwave AM Radio = 520 kHz – 1700 kHz (MF)
- Shortwave AM Radio = 3 MHz – 30 MHz (HF)

Designations for television and FM radio broadcast frequencies vary between countries. Since VHF and UHF frequencies are desirable for many uses in urban areas, in North America some parts of the former television broadcasting band have been reassigned to cellular phone and various land mobile communications systems. Even within the allocation still dedicated to television, TV-band devices use channels without local broadcasters. The Apex band in the United States was a pre-WWII allocation for VHF audio broadcasting; it was made obsolete after the introduction of FM broadcasting.

Air Band

Airband refers to VHF frequencies 108 to 137 MHz, used for navigation and voice communication with aircraft. Trans-oceanic aircraft also carry HF radio and satellite transceivers.

Marine Band

The greatest incentive for development of radio was the need to communicate with ships out of visual range of shore. From the very early days of radio, large oceangoing vessels carried powerful long-wave and medium-wave transmitters. High-frequency allocations are still designated for ships, although satellite systems have taken over some of the safety applications previously served by 500 kHz and other frequencies. 2182 kHz is a medium-wave frequency still used for marine emergency communication. Marine VHF radio is used in coastal waters and relatively short-range communication between vessels and to shore stations. Radios are channelized, with different channels used for different purposes; marine Channel 16 is used for calling and emergencies.

Amateur Radio Frequencies

Amateur radio frequency allocations vary around the world. Several bands are common for amateurs worldwide, usually in the HF part of the spectrum. Other bands are national or regional allocations only due to differing allocations for other services, especially in the VHF and UHF parts of the radio spectrum.

Citizens' Band and Personal Radio Services

Citizens' band radio is allocated in many countries, using channelized radios in the upper HF part of the spectrum (around 27 MHz). It is used for personal, small business and hobby purposes. Other frequency allocations are used for similar services in different jurisdictions, for example UHF CB is allocated in Australia. A wide range of personal radio services exist around the world, usually emphasizing short-range communication between individuals or for small businesses, simplified license requirements or in some countries covered by a class license, and usually FM transceivers using around 1 watt or less.

Industrial, Scientific and Medical

The ISM bands were initially reserved for non-communications uses of RF energy, such as microwave ovens, radio-frequency heating, and similar purposes. However, in recent years the largest use of these bands has been by short-range low-power communications systems, since users do not have to hold a radio operator's license. Cordless telephones, wireless computer networks, Bluetooth devices, and garage door openers all use the ISM bands. ISM devices do not have regulatory protection against interference from other users of the band.

Land Mobile Bands

Bands of frequencies, especially in the VHF and UHF parts of the spectrum, are allocated for communication between fixed base stations and land mobile vehicle-mounted or portable transceivers. In the United States these services are informally known as business band radio. Trunking systems are often used to make most efficient use of the limited number of frequencies available. The demand for mobile telephone service has led to large blocks of radio spectrum allocated to cellular frequencies.

Radio Control

Reliable radio control uses bands dedicated to the purpose. Radio-controlled toys may use portions of unlicensed spectrum in the 27 MHz or 49 MHz bands, but more costly aircraft, boat, or land vehicle models use dedicated radio control frequencies near 72 MHz to avoid interference by unlicensed uses. The 21st century has seen a move to 2.4 GHz spread spectrum RC control systems. Licensed amateur radio operators use portions of the 6-meter band in North America. Industrial remote control of cranes or railway locomotives use assigned frequencies that vary by area.

Radar

Radar applications use relatively high power pulse transmitters and sensitive receivers, so radar is operated on bands not used for other purposes. Most radar bands are in the microwave part of the spectrum, although certain important applications for meteorology make use of powerful transmitters in the UHF band.

2.2 MODULATION AND MULTIPLE ACCESS SCHEMES

In the realm of wireless communication, modulation and multiple access schemes serve as the backbone of efficient data transmission. Modulation techniques shape the characteristics of electromagnetic waves to encode digital information, while multiple access schemes enable multiple users to share the limited spectrum resources effectively. Understanding these fundamental concepts is essential for optimizing spectral efficiency, minimizing interference, and supporting the growing demand for wireless connectivity. Modulation and multiple access schemes are foundational elements of wireless communication, enabling efficient data transmission in diverse environments. From analog modulation techniques like AM and FM to advanced multiple access schemes like CDMA and OFDMA, these technologies have evolved to meet the growing demands of modern wireless networks. As we look towards the future, continued innovation in modulation and multiple access schemes will be essential for unlocking the full potential of wireless communication and supporting the proliferation of connected devices and applications.

2.2.1 Modulation Techniques

Modulation techniques modify one or more properties of a carrier signal to encode digital information. These techniques enable the transmission of data over wireless channels by altering parameters such as amplitude, frequency, or phase. Common modulation schemes include:

1. Amplitude Modulation (AM): AM involves varying the amplitude of the carrier signal in proportion to the amplitude of the input signal. It is widely used in broadcasting and simple communication systems, although it is susceptible to noise and interference.
2. Frequency Modulation (FM): FM alters the frequency of the carrier signal based on the variations in the input signal. FM is known for its resilience to amplitude variations and noise, making it suitable for high-fidelity audio transmission and radio broadcasting.
3. Phase Modulation (PM): PM modifies the phase of the carrier signal in response to changes in the input signal. PM is commonly used in digital communication systems and satellite links, offering robustness against amplitude variations and noise.
4. Quadrature Amplitude Modulation (QAM): QAM combines both amplitude and phase modulation to achieve higher spectral efficiency. By varying both the amplitude and phase of the carrier signal, QAM can transmit

multiple bits per symbol, making it suitable for digital communication systems with limited bandwidth.

2.2.2 Multiple Access Schemes

Multiple access schemes enable multiple users to share the available spectrum resources efficiently. These schemes allocate the spectrum in both time and frequency domains, allowing multiple users to transmit simultaneously without causing interference. Common multiple access schemes include:

1. Frequency Division Multiple Access (FDMA): FDMA divides the available spectrum into multiple frequency bands, with each user allocated a separate frequency band for communication. FDMA is commonly used in analog communication systems and satellite links but is less efficient in handling bursty traffic.
2. Time Division Multiple Access (TDMA): TDMA divides the available time slots within a given frequency band among multiple users, enabling each user to transmit data during their allocated time slot. TDMA is widely used in cellular networks, where users share the same frequency but communicate at different times.
3. Code Division Multiple Access (CDMA): CDMA assigns a unique code sequence to each user, allowing multiple users to transmit simultaneously over the same frequency band. By spreading the signals across a wide bandwidth, CDMA enables robust communication and efficient spectrum utilization. CDMA is a cornerstone technology in modern cellular networks, including 3G and 4G LTE.
4. Orthogonal Frequency Division Multiple Access (OFDMA): OFDMA combines the principles of FDMA and orthogonal frequency-division multiplexing (OFDM) to allocate subcarriers in both frequency and time domains. OFDMA is the foundation of 4G LTE and 5G NR networks, offering high spectral efficiency, low latency, and improved coverage.

2.2.3 Challenges and Future Directions

While modulation and multiple access schemes have revolutionized wireless communication, several challenges remain. Interference mitigation, spectrum scarcity, and the ever-increasing demand for higher data rates pose significant hurdles for future wireless networks. Advanced signal processing techniques, such as beamforming, interference cancellation, and dynamic spectrum sharing, hold promise for addressing these challenges and enhancing the efficiency of wireless communication systems.

Moreover, the evolution of modulation and multiple access schemes continues with the emergence of 5G and beyond. Massive MIMO (Multiple Input Multiple Output), millimeter-wave communication, and non-orthogonal multiple access (NOMA) are among the key technologies shaping the future of wireless networks. These advancements aim to further improve spectral efficiency, increase network capacity, and enable new applications, such as ultra-reliable low-latency communication (URLLC) and massive IoT (Internet of Things).

2.3 ANTENNA SYSTEMS AND PROPAGATION

Antenna systems and propagation play a pivotal role in modern communication, enabling the transmission and reception of signals across vast distances. From wireless communication to satellite broadcasting, antennas serve as the gateway for information exchange. Conclusion: Antenna systems and propagation are foundational elements of modern communication infrastructure, enabling connectivity across diverse applications and environments. By understanding the principles of antenna design, propagation mechanisms, and optimization techniques, engineers can develop innovative solutions to address current and future communication challenges. As technology continues to advance, antenna systems will play a critical role in shaping the future of wireless communication, enabling seamless connectivity and empowering societies worldwide.

2.3.1 Fundamentals of Antenna Systems

Antennas are devices designed to transmit or receive electromagnetic waves. They convert electrical signals into electromagnetic waves for transmission or vice versa for reception. The key components of an antenna system include the radiating element, feed mechanism, and supporting structure. The radiating element, often a metal conductor, is responsible for emitting or capturing electromagnetic waves. The feed mechanism supplies electrical signals to the radiating element, facilitating the transmission or reception process. Meanwhile, the supporting structure provides mechanical stability and determines the antenna's physical configuration.

2.3.2 Propagation Mechanisms

Propagation refers to the behavior of electromagnetic waves as they travel through different mediums. Understanding propagation mechanisms is essential for optimizing antenna performance and ensuring reliable communication. The propagation of electromagnetic waves is influenced by various factors, including frequency, distance, terrain, and atmospheric conditions.

One of the primary propagation mechanisms is line-of-sight propagation, where electromagnetic waves travel directly from the transmitting antenna to the receiving antenna without significant obstacles. Line-of-sight communication is commonly used in point-to-point wireless links, such as microwave communication and satellite communication.

Another propagation mechanism is tropospheric propagation, which involves the bending of electromagnetic waves due to atmospheric conditions. Tropospheric propagation enables long-distance communication beyond the line of sight, making it crucial for terrestrial microwave links and over-the-horizon radar systems.

Additionally, ionospheric propagation occurs in the ionosphere, a region of the Earth's atmosphere that ionizes due to solar radiation. Ionospheric propagation enables long-distance radio communication by reflecting radio waves back to the Earth's surface. This phenomenon is exploited in shortwave radio broadcasting and skywave communication.

2.3.3 Antenna Design and Optimization

The design of an antenna significantly impacts its performance and efficiency. Antenna engineers utilize various design techniques to optimize antenna characteristics such as gain, bandwidth, radiation pattern, and polarization. One common approach is to use computer-aided design (CAD) software to simulate antenna behavior and fine-tune design parameters.

Antenna optimization involves balancing trade-offs between conflicting requirements. For example, increasing antenna gain typically results in a narrower beamwidth, which may reduce coverage area but enhance signal strength in a specific direction. Similarly, widening the antenna's bandwidth may compromise its efficiency or increase its size and complexity.

Furthermore, antenna diversity techniques are employed to mitigate the effects of multipath propagation and fading in wireless communication systems. Diversity techniques involve using multiple antennas at the transmitter or receiver to improve signal reliability by exploiting spatial diversity.

2.3.4 Applications of Antenna Systems

Antenna systems find applications across a wide range of industries and technologies, contributing to the advancement of telecommunications, broadcasting, navigation, and remote sensing.

In telecommunications, antennas enable wireless connectivity for mobile phones, Wi-Fi networks, and other wireless communication devices. The proliferation of smartphones and mobile broadband services has driven the demand for compact, high-performance antennas capable of operating across multiple frequency bands.

In broadcasting, antennas are used for terrestrial television and radio transmission, satellite broadcasting, and digital audio broadcasting (DAB). Broadcast antennas are designed to cover large geographical areas while ensuring signal quality and reliability for millions of viewers and listeners.

In navigation and positioning systems, antennas play a crucial role in global navigation satellite systems (GNSS) such as GPS, Galileo, and GLONASS. GNSS antennas receive signals from satellites orbiting the Earth, allowing users to determine their precise location and navigate accurately.

In remote sensing applications, antennas are deployed on satellites and aircraft to collect data for weather forecasting, environmental monitoring, and disaster management. Remote sensing antennas capture electromagnetic signals reflected or emitted by the Earth's surface, atmosphere, and oceans, providing valuable information for scientific research and decision-making.

2.3.5 Future Trends and Challenges

The field of antenna systems and propagation continues to evolve rapidly, driven by advancements in wireless communication, sensor networks, and Internet of Things (IoT) technologies. Emerging trends include the development of smart antennas, millimeter-wave communication, massive MIMO (Multiple-Input Multiple-Output), and mmWave beamforming techniques.

However, several challenges must be addressed to realize the full potential of these technologies. These challenges include spectrum congestion, interference, power consumption, and regulatory constraints. Additionally, the integration of antennas into compact and complex devices such as wearables, drones, and IoT sensors requires innovative design solutions and manufacturing techniques.

2.4 SIGNAL PROCESSING IN WIRELESS COMMUNICATION

Signal processing lies at the heart of wireless communication systems, where it plays a vital role in transmitting, receiving, and manipulating electromagnetic signals to convey information across vast distances. From mobile networks to satellite communications, signal processing techniques are essential for optimizing data transmission, enhancing signal quality, and mitigating the effects of noise and interference. Conclusion: Signal processing is a cornerstone of wireless communication systems, enabling the efficient transmission, reception, and manipulation of electromagnetic signals to support diverse applications and communication requirements. By understanding the principles of signal processing and leveraging advanced techniques and algorithms, engineers can develop innovative solutions to address current and future challenges in wireless communication, paving the way for enhanced connectivity and ubiquitous access to information.

2.4.1 Fundamentals of Signal Processing

Signal processing encompasses a broad range of techniques for analyzing, modifying, and synthesizing signals to extract useful information or achieve specific objectives. In the context of wireless communication, signal processing involves the manipulation of electromagnetic signals, including modulation, demodulation, coding, decoding, equalization, and synchronization.

Modulation is the process of encoding information onto a carrier signal by varying one or more of its properties, such as amplitude, frequency, or phase. Common modulation techniques include amplitude modulation (AM), frequency modulation

(FM), and phase modulation (PM). Modulation schemes are selected based on factors such as bandwidth efficiency, spectral efficiency, and resilience to noise and interference.

Demodulation is the inverse process of modulation, where the encoded information is extracted from the modulated carrier signal. Demodulation techniques include coherent and non-coherent detection methods, each suited to different modulation schemes and communication environments.

Coding and decoding involve the use of error-correcting codes to add redundancy to transmitted data, enabling the receiver to detect and correct errors caused by noise, interference, or channel impairments. Forward error correction (FEC) and convolutional coding are commonly used coding techniques in wireless communication systems.

Equalization is a signal processing technique used to compensate for distortion and intersymbol interference (ISI) caused by multipath propagation in wireless channels. Equalizers adjust the amplitude, phase, and timing of received signals to improve signal quality and recover transmitted data accurately.

Synchronization involves aligning the timing and phase of transmitted and received signals to ensure accurate signal detection and demodulation. Timing synchronization and carrier synchronization are essential for maintaining signal coherence and minimizing transmission errors.

2.4.2 Applications

Signal processing techniques are integral to a wide range of wireless communication systems, spanning cellular networks, satellite communication, wireless LANs, and IoT devices.

In cellular networks, signal processing enables efficient allocation of radio resources, adaptive modulation and coding, and interference mitigation techniques such as beamforming and spatial multiplexing. Advanced signal processing algorithms are employed in 5G and beyond-5G (B5G) systems to achieve higher data rates, lower latency, and improved reliability.

In satellite communication, signal processing is essential for uplink and downlink signal conditioning, frequency and timing synchronization, and Doppler compensation. Adaptive coding and modulation (ACM) techniques optimize satellite link performance under varying atmospheric conditions and user demand.

In wireless LANs (WLANs), signal processing facilitates channel estimation, beamforming, and spatial diversity techniques to improve coverage, throughput, and reliability in indoor and outdoor environments. Multiple antenna systems, such as MIMO (Multiple-Input Multiple-Output) and MU-MIMO (Multi-User MIMO), leverage signal processing to exploit spatial diversity and increase network capacity.

In IoT devices, signal processing enables low-power communication, spectrum sensing, and cognitive radio techniques to accommodate diverse applications and communication requirements. Energy-efficient signal processing algorithms are essential for prolonging battery life and enabling ubiquitous connectivity in IoT ecosystems.

2.4.3 Future Trends and Challenges

The field of signal processing in wireless communication is continuously evolving, driven by emerging technologies such as massive MIMO, mmWave communication, and artificial intelligence (AI)-based signal processing.

Massive MIMO systems employ large antenna arrays to serve multiple users simultaneously, exploiting spatial diversity and interference suppression techniques to enhance spectral efficiency and network capacity. However, massive MIMO requires advanced signal processing algorithms for channel estimation, precoding, and beamforming to realize its full potential.

Millimeter-wave (mmWave) communication promises ultra-high-speed wireless links for 5G and beyond, but it poses challenges such as severe path loss, atmospheric absorption, and beam alignment. Signal processing techniques such as beam steering, beam tracking, and hybrid beamforming are essential for overcoming these challenges and enabling reliable mmWave communication.

Artificial intelligence (AI) and machine learning (ML) are increasingly being applied to signal processing tasks in wireless communication, including channel estimation, interference mitigation, and resource allocation. AI-based signal processing algorithms offer the potential for adaptive, self-optimizing wireless networks capable of autonomously adapting to changing conditions and user requirements.

CHAPTER 3

5G ARCHITECTURE AND NETWORK COMPONENTS

3.1 CORE NETWORK AND RADIO ACCESS NETWORK (RAN)

Core Network and Radio Access Network (RAN) are integral components of modern mobile communication systems, providing the infrastructure and functionality necessary for the operation of cellular networks. Together, they form the backbone of wireless communication, enabling the seamless transmission of voice, data, and multimedia services to millions of users worldwide.

Core Network and Radio Access Network (RAN) are fundamental components of mobile communication systems, providing the infrastructure and functionality necessary for the operation of cellular networks. By understanding the architecture, functionalities, and interplay between Core Network and RAN, we can appreciate their role in enabling seamless connectivity, mobility management, and service provisioning for millions of mobile users worldwide. As mobile communication continues to evolve, Core Network and RAN technologies will play a critical role in driving innovation, enabling new applications, and shaping the future of wireless connectivity.

3.1.1 Core Network

The Core Network serves as the central hub of a cellular network, responsible for routing and managing communications between mobile devices, external networks, and service platforms. It comprises various network elements and protocols designed to facilitate the delivery of voice, data, and multimedia services with high reliability, scalability, and efficiency.

One of the key components of the Core Network is the Mobile Switching Center (MSC), which funcions as the central point for call control and mobility management. The MSC coordinates the establishment, routing, and termination of voice calls, as well as the handover of mobile devices between different base stations.

Another essential element is the Home Location Register (HLR) and Visitor Location Register (VLR), which store subscriber information and manage user mobility within the network. The HLR maintains permanent subscriber data, while the VLR temporarily stores information about subscribers visiting a particular location area.

The Serving GPRS Support Node (SGSN) and Gateway GPRS Support Node (GGSN) are responsible for packet-switched data transmission in cellular networks, supporting services such as mobile internet browsing, email, and multimedia messaging. The SGSN handles mobility management and packet routing within the radio access network, while the GGSN serves as the interface between the cellular network and external IP networks, such as the internet.

In addition to these components, the Core Network includes various other elements such as the Mobile Management Entity (MME), Packet Data Network Gateway (PDN-GW), and Authentication, Authorization, and Accounting (AAA) server, each performing specific functions to ensure the efficient operation of the network.

3.1.2 Radio Access Network (RAN)

A radio access network (RAN) is part of a mobile telecommunication system implementing a radio access technology (RAT). Conceptually, it resides between a device such as a mobile phone, a computer, or any remotely controlled machine and provides connection with its core network (CN). Depending on the standard, mobile phones and other wireless connected devices are varyingly known as user equipment (UE), terminal equipment, mobile station (MS), etc. RAN functionality is typically provided by a silicon chip residing in both the core network as well as the user equipment.

```
        CN
       /  \
      /    \
    RAN    RAN
    / \    / \
  UE  UE  UE  UE
```

Examples of RAN types are:

- GRAN: GSM
- GERAN: Essentially the same as GRAN but specifying the inclusion of EDGE packet radio services
- UTRAN: UMTS
- E-UTRAN: The Long Term Evolution (LTE) high speed and low latency

It is also possible for a single handset/phone to be simultaneously connected to multiple RANs. Handsets capable of this are sometimes called dual-mode handsets. For instance it is common for handsets to support both GSM and UMTS (a.k.a. "3G") RATs. Such devices seamlessly transfer an ongoing call between different radio access networks without the user noticing any disruption in service.

RAN in the United States

According to research company New Street, mobile providers T-Mobile US and AT&T use Swedish communication company Ericsson as their primary RAN provider, while Verizon primarily uses South Korean provider Samsung. Nokia is the minority vendor for all major US wireless providers. According to EJL Wireless Research, Verizon is also using Ericsson.

3.1.3 Interplay between Core Network and RAN

The Core Network and RAN are interconnected through various interfaces and protocols, enabling the exchange of signaling and user data between network elements. Signaling protocols such as Signaling System 7 (SS7) and Diameter facilitate communication between the Core Network elements, while radio protocols such as Radio Resource Control (RRC) and Medium Access Control (MAC) govern interactions within the RAN.

The interaction between the Core Network and RAN is essential for mobility management, handover control, and service provisioning in cellular networks. When a mobile device moves between different cells or switches between different radio access technologies (e.g., from 4G to 5G), the Core Network and RAN collaborate to ensure uninterrupted connectivity and seamless service continuity.

Moreover, the Core Network and RAN work together to optimize network performance, allocate radio resources efficiently, and provide quality of service (QoS) guarantees for different types of traffic. Through mechanisms such as load balancing, traffic shaping, and congestion control, the Core Network and RAN dynamically adapt to changing network conditions and user demand, ensuring a high level of service availability and reliability.

3.1.4 Applications and Future Developments

Core Network and RAN technologies are continuously evolving to meet the growing demands of mobile communication, driven by advancements in wireless standards, network architecture, and communication protocols. Emerging trends such as network virtualization, software-defined networking (SDN), and cloud-native architectures are reshaping the Core Network and RAN landscape, enabling greater flexibility, scalability, and agility in network deployment and management.

In the era of 5G and beyond, Core Network and RAN technologies are poised to enable transformative applications and services such as ultra-reliable low-latency communication (URLLC), massive machine-type communication (mMTC), and network slicing. These capabilities will support diverse use cases ranging from autonomous vehicles and industrial automation to augmented reality and remote healthcare, revolutionizing the way we live, work, and interact in an increasingly connected world.

3.2 SMALL CELLS AND MASSIVE MIMO

Small Cells and Massive MIMO (Multiple-Input Multiple-Output) are two key technologies that are revolutionizing wireless communication networks, particularly in the context of 5G deployment and beyond. Small Cells offer a decentralized approach to network coverage and capacity enhancement, while Massive MIMO enables significant improvements in spectral efficiency and network performance. Small Cells and Massive MIMO are two key technologies that are reshaping the landscape of wireless communication networks, particularly in the context of 5G deployment and beyond. By leveraging the advantages of Small Cells and Massive MIMO, operators can enhance network capacity, coverage, and performance, while enabling new services and applications that were previously not possible. As these technologies continue to evolve, we can expect further advancements in wireless communication networks, driving innovation and transforming the way we connect and communicate in an increasingly connected world.

3.2.1 Small Cells

Small cells are low-powered cellular radio access nodes that operate in spectrum that have a range of 10 meters to a few kilometers. They are base stations with low power consumption and cheap cost. They can provide high data rates by being deployed densely to achieve high spatial spectrum efficiency.

Recent FCC orders have provided size and elevation guidelines to help more clearly define small cell equipment. They are "small" compared to a mobile macrocell, partly because they have a shorter range and partly because they typically handle fewer concurrent calls or sessions. As wireless carriers seek to 'densify' existing wireless networks to provide for the data capacity demands of 5G, small cells are currently viewed as a solution to allow re-using the same frequencies, and as an important method of increasing cellular network capacity, quality, and resilience with a growing focus using LTE Advanced.

Types of Small Cells

Small cells may encompass femtocells, picocells, and microcells. Small-cell networks can also be realized by means of distributed radio technology using centralized baseband units and remote radio heads. Beamforming technology (focusing a radio signal on a very specific area) can further enhance or focus small cell coverage. These approaches to small cells all feature central management by mobile network operators.

Small cells provide a small radio footprint, which can range from 10 meters within urban and in-building locations to 2 km for a rural location. Picocells and microcells can also have a range of a few hundred meters to a few kilometers, but they differ from femtocells in that they do not always have self-organising and self-management capabilities.

Small cells are available for a wide range of air interfaces including GSM, CDMA2000, TD-SCDMA, W-CDMA, LTE and 5G. In 3GPP terminology, a Home Node B (HNB) is a 3G femtocell. A Home eNode B (HeNB) is an LTE femtocell. Wi-Fi is a small cell but does not operate in licensed spectrum and therefore cannot be managed as effectively as small cells utilising licensed spectrum. Small cell deployments vary according to the use case and radio technology employed.

Umbrella Term

The most common form of small cells are femtocells. They were initially designed for residential and small business use, with a short range and a limited number of channels. Femtocells with increased range and capacity spawned a proliferation of terms: metrocells, metro femtocells, public access femtocells, enterprise femtocells, super femtos, Class 3 femto, greater femtos and microcells. The term "small cells" is frequently used by analysts and the industry as an umbrella to describe the different implementations of femtocells, and to clear up any confusion that femtocells are limited to residential uses. Small cells are sometimes, incorrectly, also used to describe distributed-antenna systems (DAS) which are not low-powered access nodes.

Purpose

Small cells can be used to provide in-building and outdoor wireless service. Mobile operators use them to extend their service coverage and/or increase network capacity.

ABI Research argues that small cells also help service providers discover new revenue opportunities through their location and presence information. If a registered user enters a femtozone, the network is notified of their location. The service provider, with the user's permission, could share this location information to update user's social media status, for instance. Opening up small-cell APIs to the wider mobile ecosystem could enable a long-tail effect.

Rural coverage is also a key market that has developed as mobile operators have started to install public access metrocells in remote and rural areas that either have only 2G coverage or no coverage at all. The cost advantages of small cells compared with macro cells make it economically feasible to provide coverage of much smaller communities – from a few ten to a few hundred. The Small Cell Forum have published a white paper outlining the technology and business case aspects. Mobile operators in both developing and developed countries are either trialing or installing such systems. The pioneer in providing rural coverage using small cells was SoftBank Mobile – the Japanese mobile operator – who have installed more than 3000 public access 3G small cells on post offices throughout rural Japan. In the UK, Vodafone's Rural Open Sure Signal program and EE's rural 3G/4G scheme increase geographic coverage.

Future Mobile Networks

Small cells are an integral part of LTE networks. In 3G networks, small cells are viewed as an offload technique. In 4G networks, the principle of heterogeneous network (HetNet) is introduced where the mobile network is constructed with layers of small and large cells. In LTE, all cells will be self-organizing, drawing upon the principles laid down in current Home NodeB (HNB), the 3GPP term for residential femtocells.

Future innovations in radio access design introduce the idea of an almost flat architecture where the difference between a small cell and a macrocell depends on how many cubes are stacked together.

The transmitting signal from Macro Base Station (MBS) weakens quickly once the MBS signal reaches indoors. Femtocells provide a solution to the difficulties present in macrocell-based system. Thus, Femto Base Station (FBS) network coverage is one of the prime concerns in indoor environment to get good quality of service (QoS).

Market Deployments to Date

By December 2017 a total of over 12 million small cells have been deployed worldwide, with forecasts as high as 70 million by 2025.

Small Cell Backhaul

Backhaul is needed to connect the small cells to the core network, internet and other services. For in-building use, existing broadband internet can be used. In urban outdoors, mobile operators consider this more challenging than macrocell backhaul because a) small cells are typically in hard-to-reach, near-street-level locations rather than in more open, above-rooftop locations and b) carrier grade connectivity must be provided at much lower cost per bit. Many different wireless and wired technologies have been proposed as solutions, and it is agreed that a toolbox of these will be needed to address a range of deployment scenarios. An industry consensus view of how the different solution characteristics match with requirements is published by the Small Cell Forum. The backhaul solution is influenced by a number of factors, including the operator's original motivation to deploy small cells, which could be for targeted capacity, indoor or outdoor coverage.

3.2.2 Massive MIMO

In radio, multiple-input and multiple-output (MIMO) is a method for multiplying the capacity of a radio link using multiple transmission and receiving antennas to exploit multipath propagation. MIMO has become an essential element of wireless communication standards including IEEE 802.11n (Wi-Fi 4), IEEE 802.11ac (Wi-Fi 5), HSPA+ (3G), WiMAX, and Long Term Evolution (LTE). More recently, MIMO has been applied to power-line communication for three-wire installations as part of the ITU G.hn standard and of the HomePlug AV2 specification.

At one time, in wireless the term "MIMO" referred to the use of multiple antennas at the transmitter and the receiver. In modern usage, "MIMO" specifically refers to a class of techniques for sending and receiving more than one data signal simultaneously over the same radio channel by exploiting the difference in signal propagation between different antennas (e.g., due to multipath propagation). Additionally, modern MIMO usage often refers to multiple data signals sent to different receivers (with one or more receive antennas) though this is more accurately termed multi-user multiple-input single-output (MU-MISO).

Early Research

MIMO is often traced back to 1970s research papers concerning multi-channel digital transmission systems and interference (crosstalk) between wire pairs in a cable bundle: AR Kaye and DA George (1970), Branderburg and Wyner (1974), and W. van Etten (1975, 1976). Although these are not examples of exploiting multipath propagation to send multiple information streams, some of the mathematical techniques for dealing with mutual interference proved useful to MIMO development. In the mid-1980s Jack Salz at Bell Laboratories took this research a step further, investigating multi-user systems operating over "mutually cross-coupled linear networks with additive noise sources" such as time-division multiplexing and dually-polarized radio systems.

Methods were developed to improve the performance of cellular radio networks and enable more aggressive frequency reuse in the early 1990s. Space-division multiple access (SDMA) uses directional or smart antennas to communicate on the same frequency with users in different locations within range of the same base station. An SDMA system was proposed by Richard Roy and Björn Ottersten, researchers at ArrayComm, in 1991. Their US patent (No. 5515378 issued in 1996) describes a method for increasing capacity using "an array of receiving antennas at the base station" with a "plurality of remote users."

Invention

Arogyaswami Paulraj and Thomas Kailath proposed an SDMA-based inverse multiplexing technique in 1993. Their US patent (No. 5,345,599 issued in 1994) described a method of broadcasting at high data rates by splitting a high-rate signal "into several low-rate signals" to be transmitted from "spatially separated transmitters" and recovered by the receive antenna array based on differences in "directions-of-arrival." Paulraj was awarded the prestigious Marconi Prize in 2014 for "his pioneering contributions to developing the theory and applications of MIMO antennas.... His idea for using multiple antennas at both the transmitting and receiving stations – which is at the heart of the current high speed WiFi and 4G mobile systems – has revolutionized high speed wireless."

In an April 1996 paper and subsequent patent, Greg Raleigh proposed that natural multipath propagation can be exploited to transmit multiple, independent information streams using co-located antennas and multi-dimensional signal processing. The paper also identified practical solutions for modulation (MIMO-OFDM), coding, synchronization, and channel estimation. Later that year (September 1996) Gerard J. Foschini submitted a paper that also suggested it is possible to multiply the capacity of a wireless link using what the author described as "layered space-time architecture."

Greg Raleigh, V. K. Jones, and Michael Pollack founded Clarity Wireless in 1996, and built and field-tested a prototype MIMO system. Cisco Systems acquired Clarity Wireless in 1998. Bell Labs built a laboratory prototype demonstrating its V-BLAST (Vertical-Bell Laboratories Layered Space-Time) technology in 1998. Arogyaswami Paulraj founded Iospan Wireless in late 1998 to develop MIMO-OFDM products. Iospan was acquired by Intel in 2003. Neither Clarity Wireless nor Iospan Wireless shipped MIMO-OFDM products before being acquired.

Standards and Commercialization

MIMO technology has been standardized for wireless LANs, 3G mobile phone networks, and 4G mobile phone networks and is now in widespread commercial use. Greg Raleigh and V. K. Jones founded Airgo Networks in 2001 to develop MIMO-OFDM chipsets for wireless LANs. The Institute of Electrical and Electronics Engineers (IEEE) created a task group in late 2003 to develop a wireless LAN standard delivering at least 100 Mbit/s of user data throughput. There were two major competing proposals: TGn Sync was backed by companies including Intel and Philips, and WWiSE was supported by companies including Airgo Networks, Broadcom, and Texas Instruments. Both groups agreed that the 802.11n standard would be based on MIMO-OFDM with 20 MHz and 40 MHz channel options. TGn Sync, WWiSE, and a third proposal (MITMOT, backed by Motorola and Mitsubishi) were merged to create what was called the Joint Proposal. In 2004, Airgo became the first company to ship MIMO-OFDM products. Qualcomm acquired Airgo Networks in late 2006. The final 802.11n standard supported speeds up to 600 Mbit/s (using four simultaneous data streams) and was published in late 2009.

Surendra Babu Mandava and Arogyaswami Paulraj founded Beceem Communications in 2004 to produce MIMO-OFDM chipsets for WiMAX. The company was acquired by Broadcom in 2010. WiMAX was developed as an alternative to cellular standards, is based on the 802.16e standard, and uses MIMO-OFDM to deliver speeds up to 138 Mbit/s. The more advanced 802.16m standard enables download speeds up to 1 Gbit/s. A nationwide WiMAX network was built in the United States by Clearwire, a subsidiary of Sprint-Nextel, covering 130 million points of presence (PoPs) by mid-2012. Sprint subsequently announced plans to deploy LTE (the cellular 4G standard) covering 31 cities by mid-2013 and to shut down its WiMAX network by the end of 2015.

The first 4G cellular standard was proposed by NTT DoCoMo in 2004. Long term evolution (LTE) is based on MIMO-OFDM and continues to be developed by the

3rd Generation Partnership Project (3GPP). LTE specifies downlink rates up to 300 Mbit/s, uplink rates up to 75 Mbit/s, and quality of service parameters such as low latency. LTE Advanced adds support for picocells, femtocells, and multi-carrier channels up to 100 MHz wide. LTE has been embraced by both GSM/UMTS and CDMA operators.

The first LTE services were launched in Oslo and Stockholm by TeliaSonera in 2009. As of 2015, there were more than 360 LTE networks in 123 countries operational with approximately 373 million connections (devices).

Functions

MIMO can be sub-divided into three main categories: precoding, spatial multiplexing (SM), and diversity coding.

Precoding

Precoding is multi-stream beamforming, in the narrowest definition. In more general terms, it is considered to be all spatial processing that occurs at the transmitter. In (single-stream) beamforming, the same signal is emitted from each of the transmit antennas with appropriate phase and gain weighting such that the signal power is maximized at the receiver input. The benefits of beamforming are to increase the received signal gain – by making signals emitted from different antennas add up constructively – and to reduce the multipath fading effect. In line-of-sight propagation, beamforming results in a well-defined directional pattern. However, conventional beams are not a good analogy in cellular networks, which are mainly characterized by multipath propagation. When the receiver has multiple antennas, the transmit beamforming cannot simultaneously maximize the signal level at all of the receive antennas, and precoding with multiple streams is often beneficial. Precoding requires knowledge of channel state information (CSI) at the transmitter and the receiver.

Spatial Multiplexing

Spatial multiplexing requires MIMO antenna configuration. In spatial multiplexing, a high-rate signal is split into multiple lower-rate streams and each stream is transmitted from a different transmit antenna in the same frequency channel. If these signals arrive at the receiver antenna array with sufficiently different spatial signatures and the receiver has accurate CSI, it can separate these streams into (almost) parallel channels. Spatial multiplexing is a very powerful technique for increasing channel capacity at higher signal-to-noise ratios (SNR). The maximum number of spatial streams is limited by the lesser of the number of antennas at the transmitter or receiver. Spatial multiplexing can be used without CSI at the transmitter, but can be combined with precoding if CSI is available. Spatial multiplexing can also be used for simultaneous transmission to multiple receivers, known as space–division multiple access or multi-user MIMO, in which case CSI is required at the transmitter. The scheduling of receivers with different spatial signatures allows good separability.

Diversity Coding

Diversity coding techniques are used when there is no channel knowledge at the transmitter. In diversity methods, a single stream (unlike multiple streams in spatial multiplexing) is transmitted, but the signal is coded using techniques called space-time coding. The signal is emitted from each of the transmit antennas with full or near orthogonal coding. Diversity coding exploits the independent fading in the multiple antenna links to enhance signal diversity. Because there is no channel knowledge, there is no beamforming or array gain from diversity coding. Diversity coding can be combined with spatial multiplexing when some channel knowledge is available at the receiver.

Forms

Multi-antenna Types

Multi-antenna MIMO (or single-user MIMO) technology has been developed and implemented in some standards, e.g., 802.11n products.

- SISO/SIMO/MISO are special cases of MIMO:
  - Multiple-input single-output (MISO) is a special case when the receiver has a single antenna.
  - Single-input multiple-output (SIMO) is a special case when the transmitter has a single antenna.
  - Single-input single-output (SISO) is a conventional radio system where neither transmitter nor receiver has multiple antennas.
- Principal single-user MIMO techniques:
  - Bell Laboratories Layered Space-Time (BLAST), Gerard. J. Foschini (1996)
  - Per Antenna Rate Control (PARC), Varanasi, Guess (1998), Chung, Huang, Lozano (2001)
  - Selective Per Antenna Rate Control (SPARC), Ericsson (2004)
- Some limitations:
  - The physical antenna spacing is selected to be large; multiple wavelengths at the base station. The antenna separation at the receiver is heavily space-constrained in handsets, though advanced antenna design and algorithm techniques are under discussion. Refer to: multi-user MIMO

Multi-user Types

- Multi-user MIMO (MU-MIMO):
  - In recent 3GPP and WiMAX standards, MU-MIMO is being treated as one of the candidate technologies adoptable in the specification by a number of companies, including Samsung, Intel, Qualcomm, Ericsson, TI, Huawei, Philips, Nokia, and Freescale. For these and other firms active in the mobile hardware market, MU-MIMO is more feasible for low-complexity cell phones with a small number of reception antennas, whereas single-user SU-MIMO's higher per-user throughput is better suited to more complex user devices with more antennas.
  - Enhanced multiuser MIMO: 1) Employs advanced decoding techniques, 2) Employs advanced precoding techniques
  - SDMA represents either space-division multiple access or super-division multiple access where super emphasises that orthogonal division such as frequency- and time-division is not used but non-orthogonal approaches such as superposition coding are used.
- Cooperative MIMO (CO-MIMO):
  - Uses multiple neighboring base stations to jointly transmit/receive data to/from users. As a result, neighboring base stations don't cause intercell interference as in the conventional MIMO systems.
- Macrodiversity MIMO:
  - A form of space diversity scheme which uses multiple transmit or receive base stations for communicating coherently with single or multiple users which are possibly distributed in the coverage area, in the same time and frequency resource.
  - The transmitters are far apart in contrast to traditional microdiversity MIMO schemes such as single-user MIMO. In a multi-user macrodiversity MIMO scenario, users may also be far apart. Therefore, every constituent link in the virtual MIMO link has distinct average link SNR. This difference is mainly due to the different long-term channel impairments such as path loss and shadow fading which are experienced by different links.
  - Macrodiversity MIMO schemes pose unprecedented theoretical and practical challenges. Among many theoretical challenges, perhaps the most fundamental challenge is to understand how the different average link SNRs affect the overall system capacity and individual user performance in fading environments.
- MIMO routing:
  - Routing a cluster by a cluster in each hop, where the number of nodes

in each cluster is larger or equal to one. MIMO routing is different from conventional (SISO) routing since conventional routing protocols route node-by-node in each hop.

- Massive MIMO:
  - A technology where the number of terminals is much less than the number of base station (mobile station) antennas. In a rich scattering environment, the full advantages of the massive MIMO system can be exploited using simple beamforming strategies such as maximum ratio transmission (MRT), maximum ratio-combining (MRC) or zero forcing (ZF). To achieve these benefits of massive MIMO, accurate CSI must be available perfectly. However, in practice, the channel between the transmitter and receiver is estimated from orthogonal pilot sequences which are limited by the coherence time of the channel. Most importantly, in a multicell setup, the reuse of pilot sequences of several co-channel cells will create pilot contamination. When there is pilot contamination, the performance of massive MIMO degrades quite drastically. To alleviate the effect of pilot contamination, Tadilo E. Bogale and Long B. Le propose a simple pilot assignment and channel estimation method from limited training sequences. However, in 2018, research by Emil Björnson, Jakob Hoydis, and Luca Sanguinetti was published which shows that pilot contamination is solvable and that the capacity of a channel can always be increased, both in theory and in practice, by increasing the number of antennas.
- Holographic MIMO:
  - Another recent technology is holographic MIMO to realize high energy and spectral efficiency with very high spatial resolution. Holographic MIMO is a key conceptual key enabler that is recently gaining increasing popularity, because of its low-cost transformative wireless structure consisting of sub-wavelength metallic or dielectric scattering particles, which is capable of deforming electromagnetic wave properties, according to some desirable objectives.

Applications

Third Generation (3G) (CDMA and UMTS) allows for implementing space-time transmit diversity schemes, in combination with transmit beamforming at base stations. Fourth Generation (4G) LTE And LTE Advanced define very advanced air interfaces extensively relying on MIMO techniques. LTE primarily focuses on single-link MIMO relying on Spatial Multiplexing and space-time coding while LTE-Advanced further extends the design to multi-user MIMO. In wireless local area networks (WLAN), the IEEE 802.11n (Wi-Fi), MIMO technology is implemented in the standard using three different techniques: antenna selection, space-time coding and possibly beamforming.

Spatial multiplexing techniques make the receivers very complex, and therefore they are typically combined with orthogonal frequency-division multiplexing (OFDM) or with orthogonal frequency-division multiple access (OFDMA) modulation, where the problems created by a multi-path channel are handled efficiently. The IEEE 802.16e standard incorporates MIMO-OFDMA. The IEEE 802.11n standard, released in October 2009, recommends MIMO-OFDM.

MIMO is also planned to be used in mobile radio telephone standards such as recent 3GPP and 3GPP2. In 3GPP, High-Speed Packet Access plus (HSPA+) and Long Term Evolution (LTE) standards take MIMO into account. Moreover, to fully support cellular environments, MIMO research consortia including IST-MASCOT propose to develop advanced MIMO techniques, e.g., multi-user MIMO (MU-MIMO).

MIMO wireless communications architectures and processing techniques can be applied to sensing problems. This is studied in a sub-discipline called MIMO radar.

MIMO technology can be used in non-wireless communications systems. One example is the home networking standard ITU-T G.9963, which defines a powerline communications system that uses MIMO techniques to transmit multiple signals over multiple AC wires (phase, neutral and ground).

MIMO Detection

A fundamental problem in MIMO communication is estimating the transmit vector, x, given the received vector, y. This can be posed as a statistical detection problem, and addressed using a variety of techniques including zero-forcing, successive interference cancellation a.k.a. V-blast, Maximum likelihood estimation and recently, neural network MIMO detection. Such techniques commonly assume that the channel matrix H is known at the receiver. In practice, in communication systems, the transmitter sends a Pilot signal and the receiver learns the state of the channel (i.e., H) from the received signal Y and the Pilot signal X. Recently, there are works on MIMO detection using Deep learning tools which have shown to work better than other methods such as zero-forcing.

Testing

MIMO signal testing focuses first on the transmitter/receiver system. The random phases of the sub-carrier signals can produce instantaneous power levels that cause the amplifier to compress, momentarily causing distortion and ultimately symbol errors. Signals with a high PAR (peak-to-average ratio) can cause amplifiers to compress unpredictably during transmission. OFDM signals are very dynamic and compression problems can be hard to detect because of their noise-like nature.

Knowing the quality of the signal channel is also critical. A channel emulator can simulate how a device performs at the cell edge, can add noise or can simulate what the channel looks like at speed. To fully qualify the performance of a receiver, a calibrated transmitter, such as a vector signal generator (VSG), and channel emulator can be used to test the receiver under a variety of different conditions. Conversely, the transmitter's performance under a number of different conditions can be verified using a channel emulator and a calibrated receiver, such as a vector signal analyzer (VSA).

Understanding the channel allows for manipulation of the phase and amplitude of each transmitter in order to form a beam. To correctly form a beam, the transmitter needs to understand the characteristics of the channel. This process is called channel sounding or channel estimation. A known signal is sent to the mobile device that enables it to build a picture of the channel environment. The mobile device sends back the channel characteristics to the transmitter. The transmitter can then apply the correct phase and amplitude adjustments to form a beam directed at the mobile device. This is called a closed-loop MIMO system. For beamforming, it is required to adjust the phases and amplitude of each transmitter. In a beamformer optimized for spatial diversity or spatial multiplexing, each antenna element simultaneously transmits a weighted combination of two data symbols.

3.2.3 Applications and Future Developments

Small Cells and Massive MIMO are driving significant advancements in wireless communication networks, enabling new applications and services that were previously not feasible. In addition to enhancing network capacity and coverage, these technologies are paving the way for innovative use cases such as augmented reality (AR), virtual reality (VR), autonomous vehicles, and industrial automation.

In the future, we can expect further advancements in Small Cells and Massive MIMO technology, driven by ongoing research and development efforts in academia and industry. Emerging trends such as millimeter-wave communication, network slicing, and artificial intelligence (AI)-based optimization are expected to further enhance the capabilities of Small Cells and Massive MIMO, enabling new levels of performance, flexibility, and scalability in wireless networks.

3.3 CLOUD RAN AND NETWORK FUNCTION VIRTUALIZATION (NFN)

Cloud RAN (Radio Access Network) and Network Function Virtualization (NFV) are transformative technologies that are reshaping the architecture and operation of mobile networks. By centralizing network functions and virtualizing network resources, Cloud RAN and NFV enable operators to achieve greater flexibility, scalability, and efficiency in the deployment and management of wireless infrastructure. Cloud RAN and Network Function Virtualization (NFV) are transformative technologies that are revolutionizing the architecture and operation of mobile networks. By centralizing baseband processing functions and virtualizing network resources, Cloud RAN and NFV enable operators to achieve greater flexibility, scalability, and efficiency in the deployment and management of wireless infrastructure. As these technologies continue to evolve, we can expect further advancements in mobile network architecture, service delivery, and user experience, driving innovation and transforming the way we connect and communicate in an increasingly connected world.

3.3.1 Cloud RAN

C-RAN (Cloud-RAN), also referred to as Centralized-RAN, is an architecture for cellular networks. C-RAN is a centralized, cloud computing-based architecture for radio access networks that supports 2G, 3G, 4G and future wireless communication standards. Its name comes from the four 'C's in the main characteristics of C-RAN system, "Clean, Centralized processing, Collaborative radio, and a real-time Cloud Radio Access Network".

Background

Traditional cellular, or Radio Access Networks (RAN), consist of many stand-alone base stations (BTS). Each BTS covers a small area, whereas a group BTS provides coverage over a continuous area. Each BTS processes and transmits its own signal to and from the mobile terminal, and forwards the data payload to and from the mobile terminal and out to the core network via the backhaul. Each BTS has its own cooling, back haul transportation, backup battery, monitoring system, and so on. Because of limited spectral resources, network operators 'reuse' the frequency among different base stations, which can cause interference between neighboring cells.

There are several limitations in the traditional cellular architecture. First, each BTS is costly to build and operate. Moore's law helps reduce the size and power of an electrical system, but the supporting facilities of the BTS are not improved quite as well. Second, when more BTS are added to a system to improve its capacity, interference among BTS is more severe as BTS are closer to each other and more of them are using the same frequency. Third, because users are mobile, the traffic of each BTS fluctuates (called 'tide effect'), and as a result, the average utilization rate of individual BTS is pretty low. However, these processing resources cannot be shared with other BTS. Therefore, all BTS are designed to handle the maximum traffic, not average traffic, resulting in a waste of processing resources and power at idle times.

Evolution of Base Station Architecture

All-in-one Macro Base Station

In the 1G and 2G cellular networks, base stations had an all-in-one architecture. Analog, digital, and power functions were housed in a single cabinet as large as a refrigerator. Usually the base station cabinet was placed in a dedicated room along with all necessary supporting facilitates such as power, backup battery, air conditioning, environment surveillance, and backhaul transmission equipment.

The RF signal is generated by the base station RF unit and propagates through pairs of RF cables up to the antennas on the top of a base station tower or other mounting points. This all-in-one architecture was mostly found in macro cell deployments.

Distributed Base Station

For 3G, a distributed base station architecture was introduced by Ericsson, Nokia, Huawei, and other leading telecom equipment vendors. In this architecture the radio function unit, also known as the remote radio head (RRH), is separated from the digital function unit, or baseband unit (BBU) by fiber. Digital baseband signals are carried over fiber, using the Open Base Station Architecture Initiative (OBSAI) or Common Public Radio Interface (CPRI) standard. The RRH can be installed on the top of tower close to the antenna, reducing the loss compared to the traditional base station where the RF signal has to travel through a long cable from the base station cabinet to the antenna at the top of the tower. The fiber link between RRH and BBU also allows more flexibility in network planning and deployment as they can be placed a few hundred meters or a few kilometers away. Most modern base stations now use this decoupled architecture.

C-RAN/Cloud-RAN

C-RAN may be viewed as an architectural evolution of the above distributed base station system. It takes advantage of many technological advances in wireless, optical and IT communications systems. For example, it uses the latest CPRI standard, low cost Coarse or Dense Wavelength Division Multiplexing (CWDM/ DWDM) technology, and mmWave to allow transmission of baseband signal over long distance thus achieving large scale centralised base station deployment. It applies recent Data Centre Network technology to allow a low cost, high reliability, low latency and high bandwidth interconnect network in the BBU pool. It utilizes open platforms and real-time virtualization technology rooted in cloud computing to achieve dynamic shared resource allocation and support multi-vendor, multi-technology environments.

Architecture

C-RAN architecture has the following characteristics that are distinct from other cellular architectures:

1. Large scale centralized deployment: Allows many RRHs to connect to a centralized BBU pool. The maximum distance can be 20km in fiber link for 4G (LTE/LTE-A) systems, and even longer distances (40~80km) for 3G (WCDMA/TD-SCDMA) and 2G (GSM/CDMA) systems.
2. Native support to Collaborative Radio technologies: Any BBU can talk with any other BBU within the BBU pool with very high bandwidth (10 Gbit/s and above) and low latency (10 ìs level). This is enabled by the interconnection of BBUs in the pool. This is one major difference from BBU

Hotelling, or base station Hotelling; in the latter case, the BBUs of different base stations are simply stacked together and have no direct link between them to allow physical layer co-ordination.

3. Real-time virtualization capability based on open platform: This is different from traditional base stations built on proprietary hardware, where the software and hardware are close-sourced and provided by single vendors. In contrast, a C-RAN BBU pool is built on open hardware, like x86/ARM CPU based servers, and interface cards that handle fiber links to RRHs and inter-connections in the pool. Real-time virtualization ensures that resources in the pool can be allocated dynamically to base station software stacks, say 4G/3G/2G function modules from different vendors, according to network load. However, to satisfy the strict timing requirements of wireless communication systems, the real-time performance for C-RAN is at the level of tens of microseconds, which is two orders of magnitude better than the millisecond level 'real-time' performance usually seen in Cloud Computing environments.

Similar Architecture and Systems

KT, a telecom operator in the Republic of Korea, introduced a Cloud Computing Center (CCC) system in their 3G (WCDMA/HSPA) and 4G (LTE/LTE-A) network in 2011 and 2012. The concept of CCC is basically the same as C-RAN.

SK Telecom has also deployed Smart Cloud Access Network (SCAN) and Advanced-SCAN in their 4G (LTE/LTE-A) network in Korea no later than 2012.

In 2014, Airvana (now CommScope) introduced OneCell, a C-RAN-based small cell system designed for enterprises and public spaces.

Competing Architectures in Cellular Network Evolution

All-in-one BTS

One major alternative solution that is addressing similar challenges of RAN, is the small size, all-in-one outdoor BTS. Thanks to the achievements in the semiconductor industry, all the functionality of a BTS, including RF, baseband processing, MAC processing and package level processing, can now be implemented in a volume of <50 liters. This makes the system small and weatherproof, reduces the difficulty of BTS site choice and construction, eliminates the air conditioning requirement, and thus reduces operational costs.

However, because each BTS is still working on its own, it cannot readily make use of the collaboration algorithms to reduce the interference between neighboring BTSs. It is also relatively hard to upgrade or repair because the all-in-one BTS units are usually mounted near the antenna. More processing units in less-protected environments also implies a higher failure rate compared to C-RAN, which only has the RRU deployed outdoors.

The advantage of Cloud RAN lies in its ability to implement LTE-Advanced features such as Coordinated MultiPoint (CoMP) with very low latency between multiple radio heads. However, the economic benefit of improvements such as CoMP can be negated by the higher backhaul costs for some operators.

Small Cell

The main competition between small cell and C-RAN occurs in two deployment scenarios: outdoor hotspot coverage and indoor coverage.

3.3.2 Network Function Virtualization (NFV)

Network functions virtualization (NFV) is a network architecture concept that leverages IT virtualization technologies to virtualize entire classes of network node functions into building blocks that may connect, or chain together, to create and deliver communication services.

NFV relies upon traditional server-virtualization techniques such as those used in enterprise IT. A virtualized network function, or VNF, is implemented within one or more virtual machines or containers running different software and processes, on top of commercial off the shelf (COTS) high-volume servers, switches and storage devices, or even cloud computing infrastructure, instead of having custom hardware appliances for each network function thereby avoiding vendor lock-in.

For example, a virtual session border controller could be deployed to protect a network without the typical cost and complexity of obtaining and installing physical network protection units. Other examples of NFV include virtualized load balancers, firewalls, intrusion detection devices and WAN accelerators to name a few.

The decoupling of the network function software from the customized hardware platform realizes a flexible network architecture that enables agile network management, fast new service roll outs with significant reduction in CAPEX and OPEX.

Background

Product development within the telecommunication industry has traditionally followed rigorous standards for stability, protocol adherence and quality, reflected by the use of the term carrier grade to designate equipment demonstrating this high reliability and performance factor. While this model worked well in the past, it inevitably led to long product cycles, a slow pace of development and reliance on proprietary or specific hardware, e.g., bespoke application-specific integrated circuits (ASICs). This development model resulted in significant delays when rolling out new services, posed complex interoperability challenges and significant increase in CAPEX/OPEX when scaling network systems & infrastructure and enhancing network service capabilities to meet increasing network load and performance demands. Moreover, the rise of significant competition in communication service offerings from agile organizations operating at large scale on the public Internet (such as Google Talk, Skype, Netflix) has spurred service providers to look for innovative ways to disrupt the status quo and increase revenue streams.

Framework

The NFV framework consists of three main components:

1. Virtualized network functions (VNFs) are software implementations of network functions that can be deployed on a network functions virtualization infrastructure (NFVI).
2. Network functions virtualization infrastructure (NFVI) is the totality of all hardware and software components that build the environment where NFVs are deployed. The NFV infrastructure can span several locations. The network providing connectivity between these locations is considered as part of the NFV infrastructure.
3. Network functions virtualization management and orchestration architectural framework (NFV-MANO Architectural Framework) is the collection of all functional blocks, data repositories used by these blocks, and reference points and interfaces through which these functional blocks exchange information for the purpose of managing and orchestrating NFVI and VNFs.

The building block for both the NFVI and the NFV-MANO is the NFV platform. In the NFVI role, it consists of both virtual and physical processing and storage resources, and virtualization software. In its NFV-MANO role it consists of VNF and NFVI managers and virtualization software operating on a hardware controller. The NFV platform implements carrier-grade features used to manage and monitor the platform components, recover from failures and provide effective security – all required for the public carrier network.

Practical Aspects

A service provider that follows the NFV design implements one or more virtualized network functions, or VNFs. A VNF by itself does not automatically provide a usable product or service to the provider's customers. To build more complex services, the notion of service chaining is used, where multiple VNFs are used in sequence to deliver a service.

Another aspect of implementing NFV is the orchestration process. To build highly reliable and scalable services, NFV requires that the network be able to instantiate VNF instances, monitor them, repair them, and (most important for a service provider business) bill for the services rendered. These attributes, referred to as carrier-grade features, are allocated to an orchestration layer in order to provide high availability and security, and low operation and maintenance costs.

Importantly, the orchestration layer must be able to manage VNFs irrespective of the underlying technology within the VNF. For example, an orchestration layer must be able to manage an SBC VNF from vendor X running on VMware vSphere just as well as an IMS VNF from vendor Y running on KVM.

Distributed NFV

The initial perception of NFV was that virtualized capability should be implemented in data centers. This approach works in many – but not all – cases. NFV presumes and emphasizes the widest possible flexibility as to the physical location of the virtualized functions.

Ideally, therefore, virtualized functions should be located where they are the most effective and least expensive. That means a service provider should be free to locate NFV in all possible locations, from the data center to the network node to the customer premises. This approach, known as distributed NFV, has been emphasized from the beginning as NFV was being developed and standardized, and is prominent in the recently released NFV ISG documents.

For some cases there are clear advantages for a service provider to locate this virtualized functionality at the customer premises. These advantages range from economics to performance to the feasibility of the functions being virtualized.

The first ETSI NFV ISG-approved public multi-vendor proof of concept (PoC) of D-NFV was conducted by Cyan, Inc., RAD, Fortinet and Certes Networks in Chicago in June, 2014, and was sponsored by CenturyLink. It was based on RAD's dedicated customer-edge D-NFV equipment running Fortinet's Next Generation Firewall (NGFW) and Certes Networks' virtual encryption/decryption engine as Virtual Network Functions (VNFs) with Cyan's Blue Planet system orchestrating the entire ecosystem. RAD's D-NFV solution, a Layer 2/Layer 3 network termination unit (NTU) equipped with a D-NFV X86 server module that functions as a virtualization engine at the customer edge, became commercially available by the end of that month. During 2014 RAD also had organized a D-NFV Alliance, an ecosystem of vendors and international systems integrators specializing in new NFV applications.

NFV Modularity Benefits

When designing and developing the software that provides the VNFs, vendors may structure that software into software components (implementation view of a software architecture) and package those components into one or more images (deployment view of a software architecture). These vendor-defined software components are called VNF Components (VNFCs). VNFs are implemented with one or more VNFCs and it is assumed, without loss of generality, that VNFC instances map 1:1 to VM Images.

VNFCs should in general be able to scale up and/or scale out. By being able to allocate flexible (virtual) CPUs to each of the VNFC instances, the network management layer can scale up (i.e., scale vertically) the VNFC to provide the throughput/performance and scalability expectations over a single system or a single platform. Similarly, the network management layer can scale out (i.e., scale horizontally) a VNFC by activating multiple instances of such VNFC over multiple platforms and therefore reach out to the performance and architecture specifications whilst not compromising the other VNFC function stabilities.

Early adopters of such architecture blueprints have already implemented the NFV modularity principles.

Relationship to SDN

Network Functions Virtualisation is highly complementary to SDN. In essence, SDN is an approach to building data networking equipment and software that separates and abstracts elements of these systems. It does this by decoupling the control plane and data plane from each other, such that the control plane resides centrally and the forwarding components remain distributed. The control plane interacts with both northbound and southbound. In the northbound direction the control plane provides a common abstracted view of the network to higher-level applications and programs using high-level APIs and novel management paradigms, such as Intent-based networking. In the southbound direction the control plane programs the forwarding behavior of the data plane, using device level APIs of the physical network equipment distributed around the network.

Thus, NFV is not dependent on SDN or SDN concepts, but NFV and SDN can cooperate to enhance the management of a NFV infrastructure and to create a more dynamic network environment. It is entirely possible to implement a virtualized network function (VNF) as a standalone entity using existing networking and orchestration paradigms. However, there are inherent benefits in leveraging SDN concepts to implement and manage an NFV infrastructure, particularly when looking at the management and orchestration of Network Services (NS), composed of different type of Network Functions (NF), such as Physical Network Functions (PNF) and VNFs, and placed between different geo-located NFV infrastructures, and that's why multivendor platforms are being defined that incorporate SDN and NFV in concerted ecosystems.

An NFV system needs a central orchestration and management system that takes operator requests associated with an NS or a VNF, translates them into the appropriate processing, storage and network configuration needed to bring the NS or VNF into operation. Once in operation, the VNF and the networks it is connected to potentially must be monitored for capacity and utilization, and adapted if necessary.

All network control functions in an NFV infrastructure can be accomplished using SDN concepts and NFV could be considered one of the primary SDN use cases in service provider environments. For example, within each NFV infrastructure site, a VIM could rely upon an SDN controller to set up and configure the overlay networks interconnecting (e.g., VXLAN) the VNFs and PNFs composing an NS. The SDN controller would then configure the NFV infrastructure switches and routers, as well as the network gateways, as needed. Similarly, a Wide Area Infrastructure Manager (WIM) could rely upon an SDN controller to set up overlay networks to interconnect NSs that are deployed to different geo-located NFV infrastructures. It is also apparent that many SDN use-cases could incorporate concepts introduced in the NFV initiative. Examples include where the centralized controller is controlling a distributed forwarding function that could in fact be also virtualized on existing processing or routing equipment.

Industry Impact

NFV has proven a popular standard even in its infancy. Its immediate applications are numerous, such as virtualization of mobile base stations, platform as a service (PaaS), content delivery networks (CDN), fixed access and home environments. The potential benefits of NFV is anticipated to be significant. Virtualization of network functions deployed on general purpose standardized hardware is expected to reduce capital and operational expenditures, and service and product introduction times. Many major network equipment vendors have announced support for NFV. This has coincided with NFV announcements from major software suppliers who provide the NFV platforms used by equipment suppliers to build their NFV products.

However, to realize the anticipated benefits of virtualization, network equipment vendors are improving IT virtualization technology to incorporate carrier-grade attributes required to achieve high availability, scalability, performance, and effective network management capabilities. To minimize the total cost of ownership (TCO), carrier-grade features must be implemented as efficiently as possible. This requires that NFV solutions make efficient use of redundant resources to achieve five-nines availability (99.999%), and of computing resource without compromising performance predictability.

The NFV platform is the foundation for achieving efficient carrier-grade NFV solutions. It is a software platform running on standard multi-core hardware and built using open source software that incorporates carrier-grade features. The NFV platform software is responsible for dynamically reassigning VNFs due to failures and changes in traffic load, and therefore plays an important role in achieving high availability. There are numerous initiatives underway to specify, align and promote NFV carrier-grade capabilities such as ETSI NFV Proof of Concept, ATIS Open Platform for NFV Project, Carrier Network Virtualization Awards and various supplier ecosystems.

The vSwitch, a key component of NFV platforms, is responsible for providing connectivity both VM-to-VM (between VMs) and between VMs and the outside network. Its performance determines both the bandwidth of the VNFs and the cost-efficiency of NFV solutions. The standard Open vSwitch's (OVS) performance has shortcomings that must be resolved to meet the needs of NFVI solutions. Significant performance improvements are being reported by NFV suppliers for both OVS and Accelerated Open vSwitch (AVS) versions.

Virtualization is also changing the way availability is specified, measured and achieved in NFV solutions. As VNFs replace traditional function-dedicated equipment, there is a shift from equipment-based availability to a service-based, end-to-end, layered approach. Virtualizing network functions breaks the explicit coupling with specific equipment, therefore availability is defined by the availability of VNF services. Because NFV technology can virtualize a wide range of network function types, each with their own service availability expectations, NFV platforms should support a wide range of fault tolerance options. This flexibility enables CSPs to optimize their NFV solutions to meet any VNF availability requirement.

Management and Orchestration (MANO)

ETSI has already indicated that an important part of controlling the NFV environment be done through automated orchestration. NFV Management and Orchestration (NFV-MANO) refers to a set of functions within an NFV system to manage and orchestrate the allocation of virtual infrastructure resources to virtualized network functions (VNFs) and network services (NSs). They are the brains of the NFV system and a key automation enabler.

The main functional blocks within the NFV-MANO architectural framework (ETSI GS NFV-006) are:

- Network Functions Virtualisation Orchestrator (NFVO);
- Virtualised Network Function Manager (VNFM); and
- Virtualised Infrastructure Manager (VIM).

The entry point in NFV-MANO for external operations support systems (OSS) and business support systems (BSS) is the NFVO, which is in charge of managing the lifecycle of NS instances. The management of the lifecycle of VNF instances constituting an NS instance is delegated by the NFVO to one more or VNFMs. Both the NFVO and the VNFMs uses the services exposed by one or more VIMs for allocating virtual infrastructure resources to the objects they manage. Additional functions are used for managing containerized VNFs: the Container Infrastructure Service Management (CISM) and the Container Image Registry (CIR) functions. The CISM is responsible for maintaining the containerized workloads while the CIR is responsible for storing and maintaining information of OS container software images The behavior of the NFVO and VNFM is driven by the contents of deployment templates (a.k.a. NFV descriptors) such as a Network Service Descriptor (NSD) and a VNF Descriptor (VNFD).

ETSI delivers a full set of standards enabling an open ecosystem where Virtualized Network Functions (VNFs) can be interoperable with independently developed management and orchestration systems, and where the components of a management and orchestration system are themselves interoperable. This includes a set of Restful API specifications as well as the specifications of a packaging format for delivering VNFs to service providers and of the deployment templates to be packaged with the software images to enable managing the lifecycle of VNFs. Deployment templates can be based on TOSCA or YANG.

An OpenAPI (a.k.a. Swagger) representation of the API specifications is available and maintained on the ETSI forge server, along with TOSCA and YANG definition files to be used when creating deployment templates.

Performance Study

Recent performance study on NFV focused on the throughput, latency and jitter of virtualized network functions (VNFs), as well as NFV scalability in terms of the number of VNFs a single physical server can support. Open source NFV platforms are available, one representative is openNetVM. openNetVM is a high performance NFV platform based on DPDK and Docker containers. openNetVM provides a flexible framework for deploying network functions and interconnecting them to build service chains. openNetVM is an open source version of the NetVM platform described in NSDI 2014 and HotMiddlebox 2016 papers, released under the BSD license. The source code can be found at GitHub:openNetVM

Cloud-native Network Functions

From 2018, many VNF providers began to migrate many of their VNFs to a container-based architecture. Such VNFs also known as Cloud-Native Network Functions (CNF) utilize many innovations deployed commonly on internet infrastructure. These include auto-scaling, supporting a continuous delivery / DevOps deployment model, and efficiency gains by sharing common services across platforms. Through service discovery and orchestration, a network based on CNFs will be more resilient to infrastructure resource failures. Utilizing containers, and thus dispensing with the overhead inherent in traditional virtualization through the elimination of the guest OS can greatly increase infrastructure resource efficiency.

3.3.3 Applications and Future Developments

Cloud RAN and NFV are driving significant advancements in the architecture and operation of mobile networks, enabling new applications and services that were previously not feasible. In addition to enhancing network capacity, coverage, and performance, these technologies are paving the way for innovative use cases such as network slicing, edge computing, and Internet of Things (IoT) connectivity.

In the future, we can expect further advancements in Cloud RAN and NFV technology, driven by ongoing research and development efforts in academia and industry. Emerging trends such as network slicing, edge intelligence, and artificial intelligence (AI)-based optimization are expected to further enhance the capabilities of Cloud RAN and NFV, enabling new levels of performance, flexibility, and scalability in mobile networks.

3.4 SOFTWARE-DEFINED NETWORKING (SDN) IN 5G

Software-Defined Networking (SDN) has emerged as a transformative technology in the field of telecommunications, revolutionizing the way networks are designed, deployed, and managed. In the context of 5G, SDN plays a crucial role in enabling flexible, scalable, and intelligent networks capable of supporting a diverse range of applications and services. Software-Defined Networking (SDN) is a transformative technology that is revolutionizing the architecture and operation of telecommunications networks, particularly in the context of 5G. By decoupling the control plane from the data plane and centralizing network intelligence in software-defined controllers, SDN enables greater flexibility, scalability, and intelligence in the deployment and management of 5G networks. As SDN continues to evolve, we can expect further advancements in network architecture, service delivery, and user experience, driving innovation and shaping the future of telecommunications.

3.4.1 Fundamentals of Software-Defined Networking (SDN)

Software-defined networking (SDN) technology is an approach to network management that enables dynamic, programmatically efficient network configuration to improve network performance and monitoring, in a manner more akin to cloud computing than to traditional network management. SDN is meant to address the static architecture of traditional networks and may be employed to centralize network intelligence in one network component by disassociating the forwarding process of network packets (data plane) from the routing process (control plane). The control plane consists of one or more controllers, which are considered the brains of the SDN network, where the whole intelligence is incorporated. However, centralization has certain drawbacks related to security, scalability and elasticity.

SDN was commonly associated with the OpenFlow protocol (for remote communication with network plane elements to determine the path of network packets across network switches) since OpenFlow's emergence in 2011. However, since 2012, proprietary systems have also used the term. These include Cisco Systems' Open Network Environment and Nicira's network virtualization platform. SD-WAN applies similar technology to a wide area network (WAN).

History

The history of SDN principles can be traced back to the separation of the control and data plane first used in public switched telephone networks. This provided a manner of simplifying provisioning and management years before the architecture was used in data networks.

The Internet Engineering Task Force (IETF) began considering various ways to decouple the control and forwarding functions in a proposed interface standard published in 2004 named Forwarding and Control Element Separation (ForCES). The ForCES Working Group also proposed a companion SoftRouter architecture. Additional early standards from the IETF that pursued separating control from data include the Linux Netlink as an IP services protocol and a path computation element (PCE)-based architecture.

These early attempts failed to gain traction. One reason is that many in the Internet community viewed separating control from data to be risky, especially given the potential for failure in the control plane. Another reason is that vendors were concerned that creating standard application programming interfaces (APIs) between the control and data planes would result in increased competition. The use of open-source software in split control/data plane architectures traces its roots to the Ethane project at Stanford's computer-science department. Ethane's simple switch design led to the creation of OpenFlow, and an API for OpenFlow was first created in 2008. In that same year, NOX, an operating system for networks, was created.

Several patent applications were filed by independent researchers in 2007 describing practical applications for SDN, operating system for networks, network infrastructure compute units as a multi-core CPU and a method for virtual-network segmentation based on functionality. These applications became public in 2009 and have since been abandoned.

SDN research included emulators such as vSDNEmul, EstiNet, and Mininet. Work on OpenFlow continued at Stanford, including with the creation of testbeds to evaluate the use of the protocol in a single campus network, as well as across the WAN as a backbone for connecting multiple campuses. In academic settings, there were several research and production networks based on OpenFlow switches from NEC and Hewlett-Packard, as well as those based on Quanta Computer whiteboxes starting in about 2009.

Beyond academia, the first deployments were by Nicira in 2010 to control OVS from Onix, codeveloped with NTT and Google. A notable deployment was Google's B4 in 2012. Later, Google announced the first OpenFlow/Onix deployments in is datacenters. Another large deployment exists at China Mobile.

The Open Networking Foundation was founded in 2011 to promote SDN and OpenFlow. At the 2014 Interop and Tech Field Day, software-defined networking was demonstrated by Avaya using shortest-path bridging (IEEE 802.1aq) and OpenStack as an automated campus, extending automation from the data center to the end device and removing manual provisioning from service delivery.

Concept

SDN architectures decouple network control and forwarding functions, enabling the network control to become directly programmable and the underlying infrastructure to be abstracted from applications and network services. The OpenFlow protocol can be used in SDN technologies. The SDN architecture is:

- Directly programmable: Network control is directly programmable because it is decoupled from forwarding functions.
- Agile: Abstracting control from forwarding lets administrators dynamically adjust network-wide traffic flow to meet changing needs.
- Centrally managed: Network intelligence is (logically) centralized in software-based SDN controllers that maintain a global view of the network, which appears to applications and policy engines as a single, logical switch.
- Programmatically configured: SDN lets network managers configure, manage, secure, and optimize network resources very quickly via dynamic, automated SDN programs, which they can write themselves because the programs do not depend on proprietary software.
- Open standards-based and vendor-neutral: When implemented through open standards, SDN simplifies network design and operation because instructions are provided by SDN controllers instead of multiple, vendor-specific devices and protocols.

New Network Architecture

The explosion of mobile devices and content, server virtualization, and the advent of cloud services are among the trends driving the networking industry to re-examine traditional network architectures. Many conventional networks are hierarchical, built with tiers of Ethernet switches arranged in a tree structure. This design made sense when client-server computing was dominant, but such a static architecture is ill-suited to the dynamic computing and storage needs of today's enterprise data centers, campuses, and carrier environments. Some of the key computing trends driving the need for a new network paradigm include:

- Changing traffic patterns: Within the enterprise data center, traffic patterns have changed significantly. In contrast to client-server applications where the bulk of the communication occurs between one client and one server, today's applications access different databases and servers, creating a flurry of "east-west" machine-to-machine traffic before returning data to the end user device in the classic "north-south" traffic pattern. At the same time, users are changing network traffic patterns as they push for access to corporate content and applications from any type of device (including their own), connecting from anywhere, at any time. Finally, many enterprise data centers managers are contemplating a utility computing model, which might include a private cloud, public cloud, or some mix of both, resulting in additional traffic across the wide area network.

- The "consumerization of IT": Users are increasingly employing mobile personal devices such as smartphones, tablets, and notebooks to access the corporate network. IT is under pressure to accommodate these personal devices in a fine-grained manner while protecting corporate data and intellectual property and meeting compliance mandates.
- The rise of cloud services: Enterprises have enthusiastically embraced both public and private cloud services, resulting in unprecedented growth of these services. Many enterprise business want the agility to access applications, infrastructure and other IT resources on demand and discretely. IT planning for cloud services must be performed in an environment of increased security, compliance and auditing requirements, along with business reorganizations, consolidations and mergers that can rapidly change assumptions. Providing self-service provisioning, whether in a private or public cloud, requires elastic scaling of computing, storage and network resources, ideally from a common viewpoint and with a common suite of tools.
- "Big data" means more bandwidth: Handling today's "big data" or mega datasets requires massive parallel processing on thousands of servers, all of which need direct connections to each other. The rise of mega datasets is fueling a constant demand for additional network capacity in the data center. Operators of hyperscale data center networks face the daunting task of scaling the network to previously unimaginable size, maintaining any-to-any connectivity without going broke.
- Energy use on large datacenters: As Internet of Things, cloud computing and SaaS emerged, the need for larger datacenters has increased the energy consumption of those facilities. Many researchers have improved SDN's energy efficiency applying existing routing techniques to dynamically adjust the network data plane to save energy. Also techniques to improve control plane energy efficiency are being researched.

Architectural Components

- SDN Application: SDN Applications are programs that explicitly, directly, and programmatically communicate their network requirements and desired network behavior to the SDN Controller via a northbound interface (NBI). In addition, they may consume an abstracted view of the network for their internal decision-making purposes. An SDN Application consists of one SDN Application Logic and one or more NBI Drivers. SDN Applications may themselves expose another layer of abstracted network control, thus offering one or more higher-level NBIs through respective NBI agents.

- SDN Controller: The SDN Controller is a logically centralized entity in charge of (i) translating the requirements from the SDN Application layer down to the SDN Datapaths and (ii) providing the SDN Applications with an abstract view of the network (which may include statistics and events). An SDN Controller consists of one or more NBI Agents, the SDN Control Logic, and the Control to Data-Plane Interface (CDPI) driver. Definition as a logically centralized entity neither prescribes nor precludes implementation details such as the federation of multiple controllers, the hierarchical connection of controllers, communication interfaces between controllers, nor virtualization or slicing of network resources.
- SDN Datapath: The SDN Datapath is a logical network device that exposes visibility and uncontested control over its advertised forwarding and data processing capabilities. The logical representation may encompass all or a subset of the physical substrate resources. An SDN Datapath comprises a CDPI agent and a set of one or more traffic forwarding engines and zero or more traffic processing functions. These engines and functions may include simple forwarding between the datapath's external interfaces or internal traffic processing or termination functions. One or more SDN Datapaths may be contained in a single (physical) network element—an integrated physical combination of communications resources, managed as a unit. An SDN Datapath may also be defined across multiple physical network elements. This logical definition neither prescribes nor precludes implementation details such as the logical to physical mapping, management of shared physical resources, virtualization or slicing of the SDN Datapath, interoperability with non-SDN networking, nor the data processing functionality, which can include OSI layer 4-7 functions.
- SDN Control to Data-Plane Interface (CDPI): The SDN CDPI is the interface defined between an SDN Controller and an SDN Datapath, which provides at least (i) programmatic control of all forwarding operations, (ii) capabilities advertisement, (iii) statistics reporting, and (iv) event notification. One value of SDN lies in the expectation that the CDPI is implemented in an open, vendor-neutral and interoperable way.
- SDN Northbound Interfaces (NBI): SDN NBIs are interfaces between SDN Applications and SDN Controllers and typically provide abstract network views and enable direct expression of network behavior and requirements. This may occur at any level of abstraction (latitude) and across different sets of functionality (longitude). One value of SDN lies in the expectation that these interfaces are implemented in an open, vendor-neutral and interoperable way.

SDN Control Plane

- Centralized-Hierarchical–Distributed: The implementation of the SDN control plane can follow a centralized, hierarchical, or decentralized design. Initial SDN control plane proposals focused on a centralized solution, where a single control entity has a global view of the network. While this simplifies the implementation of the control logic, it has scalability limitations as the size and dynamics of the network increase. To overcome these limitations, several approaches have been proposed in the literature that fall into two categories, hierarchical and fully distributed approaches. In hierarchical solutions, distributed controllers operate on a partitioned network view, while decisions that require network-wide knowledge are taken by a logically centralized root controller. In distributed approaches, controllers operate on their local view or they may exchange synchronization messages to enhance their knowledge. Distributed solutions are more suitable for supporting adaptive SDN applications.
- Controller Placement: A key issue when designing a distributed SDN control plane is to decide on the number and placement of control entities. An important parameter to consider while doing so is the propagation delay between the controllers and the network devices, especially in the context of large networks. Other objectives that have been considered involve control path reliability, fault tolerance, and application requirements.

SDN Data Plane

In SDN, the data plane is responsible for processing data-carrying packets using a set of rules specified by the control plane. The data plane may be implemented in physical hardware switches or in software implementations, such as Open vSwitch. The memory capacity of hardware switches may limit the number of rules that can be stored where as software implementations may have higher capacity.

The location of the SDN data plane and agent can be used to classify SDN implementations:

- Hardware Switch-based SDNs: This approach implements the data plane processing inside a physical device. OpenFlow switches may use TCAM tables to route packet sequences (flows). These switches may use an ASIC for its implementation.
- Software Switch-Based SDNs: Some physical switches may implement SDN support using software on the device, such as Open vSwitch, to populate flow tables and to act as the SDN agent when communicating with the controller. Hypervisors may likewise use software implementations to support SDN protocols in the virtual switches used to support their virtual machines.

- Host-Based SDNs: Rather than deploying the data plane and SDN agent in network infrastructure, host-based SDNs deploy the SDN agent inside the operating system of the communicating endpoints. Such implementations can provide additional context about the application, user, and activity associated with network flows. To achieve the same traffic engineering capabilities of switch-based SDNs, host-based SDNs may require the use of carefully designed VLAN and spanning tree assignments.

Flow table entries may be populated in a proactive, reactive, or hybrid fashion. In the proactive mode, the controller populates flow table entries for all possible traffic matches possible for this switch in advance. This mode can be compared with typical routing table entries today, where all static entries are installed ahead of time. Following this, no request is sent to the controller since all incoming flows will find a matching entry. A major advantage in proactive mode is that all packets are forwarded in line rate (considering all flow table entries in TCAM) and no delay is added. In the reactive mode, entries are populated on demand. If a packet arrives without a corresponding match rule in the flow table, the SDN agent sends a request to the controller for further instruction it the reactive mode. The controller examines the SDN agent requests and provides instructions, installing a rule in the flow table for the corresponding packet if necessary. The hybrid mode uses the low-latency proactive forwarding mode for a portion of traffic while relying on the flexibility of reactive mode processing for the remaining traffic.

Applications

SDMN

Software-defined mobile networking (SDMN) is an approach to the design of mobile networks where all protocol-specific features are implemented in software, maximizing the use of generic and commodity hardware and software in both the core network and radio access network. It is proposed as an extension of SDN paradigm to incorporate mobile network specific functionalities. Since 3GPP Rel.14, a Control User Plane Separation was introduced in the Mobile Core Network architectures with the PFCP protocol.

SD-WAN

An SD-WAN is a WAN managed using the principles of software-defined networking. The main driver of SD-WAN is to lower WAN costs using more affordable and commercially available leased lines, as an alternative or partial replacement of more expensive MPLS lines. Control and management is administered separately from the hardware with central controllers allowing for easier configuration and administration.

SD-LAN

An SD-LAN is a Local area network (LAN) built around the principles of software-defined networking, though there are key differences in topology, network security, application visibility and control, management and quality of service. SD-LAN decouples control management, and data planes to enable a policy driven architecture for wired and wireless LANs. SD-LANs are characterized by their use of a cloud management system and wireless connectivity without the presence of a physical controller.

Security using the SDN paradigm

SDN architecture may enable, facilitate or enhance network-related security applications due to the controller's central view of the network, and its capacity to reprogram the data plane at any time. While the security of SDN architecture itself remains an open question that has already been studied a couple of times in the research community, the following paragraphs only focus on the security applications made possible or revisited using SDN.

Several research works on SDN have already investigated security applications built upon the SDN controller, with different aims in mind. Distributed Denial of Service (DDoS) detection and mitigation, as well as botnet and worm propagation, are some concrete use-cases of such applications: basically, the idea consists in periodically collecting network statistics from the forwarding plane of the network in a standardized manner (e.g., using Openflow), and then apply classification algorithms on those statistics in order to detect any network anomalies. If an anomaly is detected, the application instructs the controller how to reprogram the data plane in order to mitigate it.

Another kind of security application leverages the SDN controller by implementing some moving target defense (MTD) algorithms. MTD algorithms are typically used to make any attack on a given system or network more difficult than usual by periodically hiding or changing key properties of that system or network. In traditional networks, implementing MTD algorithms is not a trivial task since it is difficult to build a central authority able of determining - for each part of the system to be protected - which key properties are hidden or changed. In an SDN network, such tasks become more straightforward thanks to the centrality of the controller. One application can for example periodically assign virtual IPs to hosts within the network, and the mapping virtual IP/real IP is then performed by the controller. Another application can simulate some fake opened/closed/filtered ports on random hosts in the network in order to add significant noise during reconnaissance phase (e.g., scanning) performed by an attacker.

Additional value regarding security in SDN enabled networks can also be gained using FlowVisor and FlowChecker respectively. The former tries to use a single hardware forwarding plane sharing multiple separated logical networks. Following this approach the same hardware resources can be used for production and development purposes as well as separating monitoring, configuration and internet traffic, where each scenario can have its own logical topology which is called slice. In conjunction with this approach FlowChecker realizes the validation of new OpenFlow rules that are deployed by users using their own slice.

SDN controller applications are mostly deployed in large-scale scenarios, which requires comprehensive checks of possible programming errors. A system to do this called NICE was described in 2012. Introducing an overarching security architecture requires a comprehensive and protracted approach to SDN. Since it was introduced, designers are looking at possible ways to secure SDN that do not compromise scalability. One architecture called SN-SECA (SDN+NFV) Security Architecture.

Group Data Delivery Using SDN

Distributed applications that run across datacenters usually replicate data for the purpose of synchronization, fault resiliency, load balancing and getting data closer to users (which reduces latency to users and increases their perceived throughput). Also, many applications, such as Hadoop, replicate data within a datacenter across multiple racks to increase fault tolerance and make data recovery easier. All of these operations require data delivery from one machine or datacenter to multiple machines or datacenters. The process of reliably delivering data from one machine to multiple machines is referred to as Reliable Group Data Delivery (RGDD).

SDN switches can be used for RGDD via installation of rules that allow forwarding to multiple outgoing ports. For example, OpenFlow provides support for Group Tables since version 1.1 which makes this possible. Using SDN, a central controller can carefully and intelligently setup forwarding trees for RGDD. Such trees can be built while paying attention to network congestion/load status to improve performance. For example, MCTCP is a scheme for delivery to many nodes inside datacenters that relies on regular and structured topologies of datacenter networks while DCCast and QuickCast are approaches for fast and efficient data and content replication across datacenters over private WANs.

Relationship to NFV

Network Function Virtualization, or NFV for short, is a concept that complements SDN. Thus, NFV is not dependent on SDN or SDN concepts. NFV separates software from hardware to enable flexible network deployment and dynamic operation. NFV deployments typically use commodity servers to run network services software versions that previously were hardware-based. These software-based services that run in an NFV environment are called Virtual Network Functions (VNF). SDN-NFV hybrid program was provided for high efficiency, elastic and scalable capabilities NFV aimed at accelerating service innovation and provisioning using standard IT virtualization technologies. SDN provides the agility of controlling the generic forwarding devices such as the routers and switches by using SDN controllers. On the other hand, NFV agility is provided for the network applications by using virtualized servers. It is entirely possible to implement a virtualized network function (VNF) as a standalone entity using existing networking and orchestration paradigms. However, there are inherent benefits in leveraging SDN concepts to implement and manage an NFV infrastructure, particularly when looking at the management and orchestration of VNFs, and that's why multivendor platforms are being defined that incorporate SDN and NFV in concerted ecosystems.

Relationship to DPI

DPI Deep Packet Inspection provides network with application-awareness, while SDN provides applications with network-awareness. Although SDN will radically change the generic network architectures, it should cope with working with traditional network architectures to offer high interoperability. The new SDN based network architecture should consider all the capabilities that are currently provided in separate devices or software other than the main forwarding devices (routers and switches) such as the DPI, security appliances

Quality of Experience (QoE) Estimation using SDN

When using an SDN based model for transmitting multimedia traffic, an important aspect to take account is the QoE estimation. To estimate the QoE, first we have to be able to classify the traffic and then, it's recommended that the system can solve critical problems on its own by analyzing the traffic.

3.4.2 Software-Defined Networking (SDN) in 5G

In the context of 5G, Software-Defined Networking (SDN) plays a crucial role in enabling the flexibility, scalability, and intelligence required to support the diverse range of applications and services envisioned for the next generation of mobile networks. SDN enables dynamic network slicing, service chaining, and traffic steering, allowing operators to efficiently allocate network resources and optimize network performance for different use cases and service requirements.

One of the key benefits of SDN in 5G is its ability to enable dynamic network slicing, where a single physical network infrastructure is partitioned into multiple virtual networks, each tailored to specific applications, industries, or customer segments. By dynamically allocating network resources and configuring network policies through software-defined controllers, operators can create and manage network slices with different performance characteristics (e.g., latency, throughput, reliability) to meet the diverse requirements of 5G use cases such as enhanced mobile broadband (eMBB), ultra-reliable low-latency communication (URLLC), and massive machine-type communication (mMTC).

Moreover, SDN enables intelligent traffic steering and optimization, allowing operators to dynamically route traffic based on application requirements, network conditions, and user preferences. By leveraging real-time network telemetry data and machine learning algorithms, SDN controllers can optimize traffic flows, mitigate congestion, and improve Quality of Service (QoS) for critical applications and services, such as autonomous vehicles, remote surgery, and industrial automation.

Furthermore, SDN enables the orchestration of network functions and services through service chaining, where multiple network functions (e.g., firewall, load balancer, intrusion detection) are dynamically chained together to create end-to-end service paths. By programmatically configuring service chains and traffic policies, operators can deliver customized services, implement security policies, and enforce compliance requirements, thereby enhancing the overall security, reliability, and agility of 5G networks.

3.4.3 Applications and Future Developments

Software-Defined Networking (SDN) in 5G enables a wide range of applications and use cases across various industries and sectors, including telecommunications, healthcare, transportation, and manufacturing. By providing centralized control, programmability, and automation of network resources, SDN facilitates the deployment of innovative services and applications that leverage the capabilities of 5G networks, such as augmented reality (AR), virtual reality (VR), smart cities, and IoT connectivity.

In the future, we can expect further advancements in SDN technology, driven by ongoing research and development efforts in academia and industry. Emerging trends such as intent-based networking, network automation, and AI-driven optimization are expected to further enhance the capabilities of SDN in 5G, enabling operators to build and manage intelligent, self-optimizing networks that can adapt to changing conditions and user demands.

CHAPTER 4

NEW RADIO (NR) INTERFACE

4.1 OVERVIEW OF 5G NEW RADIO

5G NR (New Radio) is a radio access technology (RAT) developed by the 3rd Generation Partnership Project (3GPP) for the 5G (fifth generation) mobile network. It was designed to be the global standard for the air interface of 5G networks. It is based on orthogonal frequency-division multiplexing (OFDM), as is the 4G (fourth generation) long-term evolution (LTE) standard. The 3GPP specification 38 series provides the technical details behind 5G NR, the successor of LTE. The study of NR within 3GPP started in 2015, and the first specification was made available by the end of 2017. While the 3GPP standardization process was ongoing, the industry had already begun efforts to implement infrastructure compliant with the draft standard, with the first large-scale commercial launch of 5G NR having occurred in the end of 2018. Since 2019, many operators have deployed 5G NR networks and handset manufacturers have developed 5G NR enabled handsets.

4.2 FREQUENCY BANDS AND SPECTRUM ALLOCATION

Frequency allocation (or spectrum allocation) is the part of spectrum management dealing with the designation and regulation of the electromagnetic spectrum into frequency bands, normally done by governments in most countries. Because radio propagation does not stop at national boundaries, governments have sought to harmonise the allocation of RF bands and their standardization.

4.2.1 ITU Definition

The International Telecommunication Union defines frequency allocation as being of "a given frequency band for the purpose of its use by one or more terrestrial or space radiocommunication services or the radio astronomy service under specified conditions".

4.2.2 Bodies

Several bodies set standards for frequency allocation, including:

- International Telecommunication Union (ITU)
- European Conference of Postal and Telecommunications Administrations (CEPT)
- Inter-American Telecommunication Commission (CITEL)

To improve harmonisation in spectrum utilisation, most service allocations are incorporated in national Tables of Frequency Allocations and Utilisations within the responsibility of the appropriate national administration. Allocations are:

- primary;
- secondary; and
- exclusive or shared utilization, within the responsibility of national administrations.

Allocations of military usage will be in accordance with the ITU Radio Regulations. In NATO countries, military mobile utilizations are made in accordance with the NATO Joint Civil/Military Frequency Agreement (NJFA).

4.2.3 5G NR Frequency Bands

Frequency bands for 5G New Radio (5G NR), which is the air interface or radio access technology of the 5G mobile networks, are separated into two different frequency ranges. First there is Frequency Range 1 (FR1), which includes sub-6 GHz frequency bands, some of which are traditionally used by previous standards, but has been extended to cover potential new spectrum offerings from 410 MHz to 7125 MHz. The other is Frequency Range 2 (FR2), which includes frequency bands from 24.25 GHz to 71.0 GHz. Frequency bands are also available for non-terrestrial networks (NTN) in the sub-6 GHz range.

4.3 MODULATION AND WAVEFORMS IN NR

Modulation and waveforms are fundamental aspects of wireless communication systems, determining how information is encoded and transmitted over the air. In the context of 5G New Radio (NR), modulation and waveform technologies play a critical role in achieving high data rates, low latency, and reliable connectivity for a wide range of applications and use cases. Modulation and waveforms are essential components of 5G NR, enabling high-speed, low-latency, and reliable wireless communication for a wide range of applications and use cases. By leveraging advanced modulation schemes, adaptive modulation and coding techniques, and flexible waveform formats, 5G NR can achieve unprecedented levels of spectral efficiency, coverage, and capacity, paving the way for the future of wireless connectivity and innovation. As 5G NR continues to evolve, modulation and waveform technologies will play a critical role in shaping the performance, efficiency, and capabilities of next-generation wireless networks, driving the continued advancement of mobile communication and enabling new possibilities for the connected world.

4.3.1 Fundamentals of Modulation

In electronics and telecommunications, modulation is the process of varying one or more properties of a periodic waveform, called the carrier signal, with a separate signal called the modulation signal that typically contains information to be transmitted. For example, the modulation signal might be an audio signal representing sound from a microphone, a video signal representing moving images from a video camera, or a digital signal representing a sequence of binary digits, a bitstream from a computer.

This carrier wave usually has a much higher frequency than the message signal does. This is because it is impractical to transmit signals with low frequencies. Generally, to receive a radio wave one needs a radio antenna with length of one fourth of wavelength. For low frequency radio waves, Wavelength is in kilometers and building such a large antenna is not practical. In radio communication, the modulated carrier is transmitted through space as a radio wave to a radio receiver.

Another purpose of modulation is to transmit multiple channels of information through a single communication medium, using frequency-division multiplexing (FDM). For example, in cable television (which uses FDM), many carrier signals, each modulated with a different television channel, are transported through a single cable to customers. Since each carrier occupies a different frequency, the channels do not interfere with each other. At the destination end, the carrier signal is demodulated to extract the information bearing modulation signal.

A modulator is a device or circuit that performs modulation. A demodulator (sometimes detector) is a circuit that performs demodulation, the inverse of modulation. A modem (from modulator–demdulator), used in bidirectional communication, can perform both operations. The lower frequency band occupied by the modulation signal is called the baseband, while the higher frequency band occupied by the modulated carrier is called the passband.

In analog modulation, an analog modulation signal is "impressed" on the carrier. Examples are amplitude modulation (AM) in which the amplitude (strength) of the carrier wave is varied by the modulation signal, and frequency modulation (FM) in which the frequency of the carrier wave is varied by the modulation signal. These were the earliest types of modulation, and are used to transmit an audio signal representing sound in AM and FM radio broadcasting. More recent systems use digital modulation, which impresses a digital signal consisting of a sequence of binary digits (bits), a bitstream, on the carrier, by means of mapping bits to elements from a discrete alphabet to be transmitted. This alphabet can consist of a set of real or complex numbers, or sequences, like oscillations of different frequencies, so-called frequency-shift keying (FSK) modulation. A more complicated digital modulation method that employs multiple carriers, orthogonal frequency-division multiplexing (OFDM), is used in WiFi networks, digital radio stations and digital cable television transmission.

Analog Modulation Methods

In analog modulation, the modulation is applied continuously in response to the analog information signal. Common analog modulation techniques include:

- Amplitude modulation (AM) (here the amplitude of the carrier signal is varied in accordance with the instantaneous amplitude of the modulating signal)
  - Double-sideband modulation (DSB)
    - Double-sideband modulation with carrier (DSB-WC) (used on the AM radio broadcasting band)
    - Double-sideband suppressed-carrier transmission (DSB-SC)
    - Double-sideband reduced carrier transmission (DSB-RC)
  - Single-sideband modulation (SSB, or SSB-AM)
    - Single-sideband modulation with carrier (SSB-WC)
    - Single-sideband modulation suppressed carrier modulation (SSB-SC)
  - Vestigial sideband modulation (VSB, or VSB-AM)
  - Quadrature amplitude modulation (QAM)
- Angle modulation, which is approximately constant envelope
  - Frequency modulation (FM) (here the frequency of the carrier signal is varied in accordance with the instantaneous amplitude of the modulating signal)
  - Phase modulation (PM) (here the phase shift of the carrier signal is varied in accordance with the instantaneous amplitude of the modulating signal)
  - Transpositional Modulation (TM), in which the waveform inflection is modified resulting in a signal where each quarter cycle is transposed in the modulation process. TM is a pseudo-analog modulation (AM). Where an AM carrier also carries a phase variable phase.

Digital Modulation Methods

In digital modulation, an analog carrier signal is modulated by a discrete signal. Digital modulation methods can be considered as digital-to-analog conversion and the corresponding demodulation or detection as analog-to-digital conversion. The changes in the carrier signal are chosen from a finite number of M alternative symbols (the modulation alphabet).

- A simple example: A telephone line is designed for transferring audible sounds, for example, tones, and not digital bits (zeros and ones). Computers may, however, communicate over a telephone line by means of modems, which are representing the digital bits by tones, called symbols. If there are four alternative symbols (corresponding to a musical instrument that can generate four different tones, one at a time), the first symbol may represent the bit sequence 00, the second 01, the third 10 and the fourth

11. If the modem plays a melody consisting of 1000 tones per second, the symbol rate is 1000 symbols/second, or 1000 baud. Since each tone (i.e., symbol) represents a message consisting of two digital bits in this example, the bit rate is twice the symbol rate, i.e., 2000 bits per second.

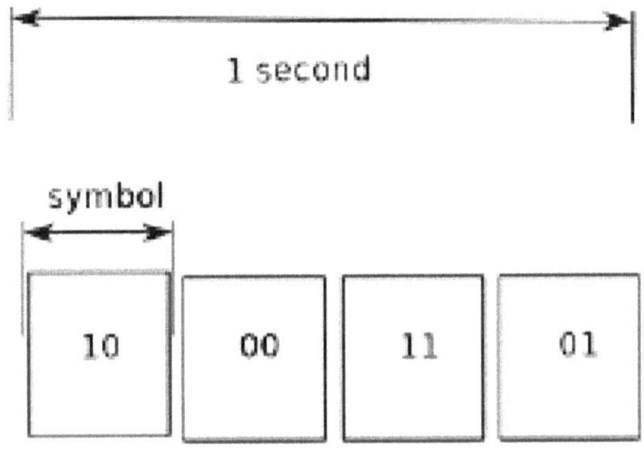

Fig. 4.1: Schematic of 4 Baud, 8 Bit/s Data Link Containing Arbitrarily Chosen Values

According to one definition of digital signal, the modulated signal is a digital signal. According to another definition, the modulation is a form of digital-to-analog conversion. Most textbooks would consider digital modulation schemes as a form of digital transmission, synonymous to data transmission; very few would consider it as analog transmission.

Fundamental Digital Modulation Methods

The most fundamental digital modulation techniques are based on keying:

- PSK (phase-shift keying): A finite number of phases are used.
- FSK (frequency-shift keying): A finite number of frequencies are used.
- ASK (amplitude-shift keying): A finite number of amplitudes are used.
- QAM (quadrature amplitude modulation): A finite number of at least two phases and at least two amplitudes are used.

In QAM, an in-phase signal (or I, with one example being a cosine waveform) and a quadrature phase signal (or Q, with an example being a sine wave) are amplitude modulated with a finite number of amplitudes and then summed. It can be seen as a two-channel system, each channel using ASK. The resulting signal is equivalent to a combination of PSK and ASK.

Each of these phases, frequencies or amplitudes are assigned a unique pattern of binary bits. Usually, each phase, frequency or amplitude encodes an equal number of bits. This number of bits comprises the symbol that is represented by the particular phase, frequency or amplitude.

If the alphabet consists of M = 2 N M = 2alternative symbols, each symbol represents a message consisting of N bits. If the symbol rate (also known as the baud rate) is f S fs symbols/second (or baud), the data rate is NN f S fs bit/second.

For example, with an alphabet consisting of 16 alternative symbols, each symbol represents 4 bits. Thus, the data rate is four times the baud rate.

In the case of PSK, ASK or QAM, where the carrier frequency of the modulated signal is constant, the modulation alphabet is often conveniently represented on a constellation diagram, showing the amplitude of the I signal at the x-axis, and the amplitude of the Q signal at the y-axis, for each symbol.

Modulator and Detector Principles of Operation

PSK and ASK, and sometimes also FSK, are often generated and detected using the principle of QAM. The I and Q signals can be combined into a complex-valued signal I+jQ (where j is the imaginary unit). The resulting so called equivalent lowpass signal or equivalent baseband signal is a complex-valued representation of the real-valued modulated physical signal (the so-called passband signal or RF signal).

These are the general steps used by the modulator to transmit data:

1. Group the incoming data bits into codewords, one for each symbol that will be transmitted.
2. Map the codewords to attributes, for example, amplitudes of the I and Q signals (the equivalent low pass signal), or frequency or phase values.
3. Adapt pulse shaping or some other filtering to limit the bandwidth and form the spectrum of the equivalent low pass signal, typically using digital signal processing.
4. Perform digital to analog conversion (DAC) of the I and Q signals (since today all of the above is normally achieved using digital signal processing, DSP).
5. Generate a high-frequency sine carrier waveform, and perhaps also a cosine quadrature component. Carry out the modulation, for example by multiplying the sine and cosine waveform with the I and Q signals, resulting in the equivalent low pass signal being frequency shifted to the modulated passband signal or RF signal. Sometimes this is achieved using DSP technology, for example direct digital synthesis using a waveform table, instead of analog signal processing. In that case, the above DAC step should be done after this step.
6. Amplification and analog bandpass filtering to avoid harmonic distortion and periodic spectrum.

At the receiver side, the demodulator typically performs:

1. Bandpass filtering.

2. Automatic gain control, AGC (to compensate for attenuation, for example fading).
3. Frequency shifting of the RF signal to the equivalent baseband I and Q signals, or to an intermediate frequency (IF) signal, by multiplying the RF signal with a local oscillator sine wave and cosine wave frequency.
4. Sampling and analog-to-digital conversion (ADC) (sometimes before or instead of the above point, for example by means of undersampling).
5. Equalization filtering, for example, a matched filter, compensation for multipath propagation, time spreading, phase distortion and frequency selective fading, to avoid intersymbol interference and symbol distortion.
6. Detection of the amplitudes of the I and Q signals, or the frequency or phase of the IF signal.
7. Quantization of the amplitudes, frequencies or phases to the nearest allowed symbol values.
8. Mapping of the quantized amplitudes, frequencies or phases to codewords (bit groups).
9. Parallel-to-serial conversion of the codewords into a bit stream.
10. Pass the resultant bit stream on for further processing such as removal of any error-correcting codes.

As is common to all digital communication systems, the design of both the modulator and demodulator must be done simultaneously. Digital modulation schemes are possible because the transmitter-receiver pair has prior knowledge of how data is encoded and represented in the communications system. In all digital communication systems, both the modulator at the transmitter and the demodulator at the receiver are structured so that they perform inverse operations.

Asynchronous methods do not require a receiver reference clock signal that is phase synchronized with the sender carrier signal. In this case, modulation symbols (rather than bits, characters, or data packets) are asynchronously transferred. The opposite is synchronous modulation.

Common Digital Modulation Techniques

The most common digital modulation techniques are:

- Phase-shift keying (PSK)
  - Binary PSK (BPSK), using M=2 symbols
  - Quadrature PSK (QPSK), using M=4 symbols
  - 8PSK, using M=8 symbols
  - 16PSK, using M=16 symbols

  - Differential PSK (DPSK)
  - Differential QPSK (DQPSK)
  - Offset QPSK (OQPSK)
  - $\pi/4$–QPSK
- Frequency-shift keying (FSK)
  - Audio frequency-shift keying (AFSK)
  - Multi-frequency shift keying (M-ary FSK or MFSK)
  - Dual-tone multi-frequency (DTMF)
- Amplitude-shift keying (ASK)
- On-off keying (OOK), the most common ASK form
  - M-ary vestigial sideband modulation, for example 8VSB
- Quadrature amplitude modulation (QAM), a combination of PSK and ASK
  - Polar modulation like QAM a combination of PSK and ASK
- Continuous phase modulation (CPM) methods
  - Minimum-shift keying (MSK)
  - Gaussian minimum-shift keying (GMSK)
  - Continuous-phase frequency-shift keying (CPFSK)
- Orthogonal frequency-division multiplexing (OFDM) modulation
  - Discrete multitone (DMT), including adaptive modulation and bit-loading
- Wavelet modulation
- Trellis coded modulation (TCM), also known as Trellis modulation
- Spread spectrum techniques
  - Direct-sequence spread spectrum (DSSS)
  - Chirp spread spectrum (CSS) according to IEEE 802.15.4a CSS uses pseudo-stochastic coding
  - Frequency-hopping spread spectrum (FHSS) applies a special scheme for channel release

MSK and GMSK are particular cases of continuous phase modulation. Indeed, MSK is a particular case of the sub-family of CPM known as continuous-phase frequency-shift keying (CPFSK) which is defined by a rectangular frequency pulse (i.e., a linearly increasing phase pulse) of one-symbol-time duration (total response signaling).

OFDM is based on the idea of frequency-division multiplexing (FDM), but the multiplexed streams are all parts of a single original stream. The bit stream is split into several parallel data streams, each transferred over its own sub-carrier using some conventional digital modulation scheme. The modulated sub-carriers are summed to form an OFDM signal. This dividing and recombining help with handling channel impairments. OFDM is considered as a modulation technique rather than a multiplex technique since it transfers one bit stream over one communication channel using one sequence of so-called OFDM symbols. OFDM can be extended to multi-user channel access method in the orthogonal frequency-division multiple access (OFDMA) and multi-carrier code-division multiple access (MC-CDMA) schemes, allowing several users to share the same physical medium by giving different sub-carriers or spreading codes to different users.

Of the two kinds of RF power amplifier, switching amplifiers (Class D amplifiers) cost less and use less battery power than linear amplifiers of the same output power. However, they only work with relatively constant-amplitude-modulation signals such as angle modulation (FSK or PSK) and CDMA, but not with QAM and OFDM. Nevertheless, even though switching amplifiers are completely unsuitable for normal QAM constellations, often the QAM modulation principle are used to drive switching amplifiers with these FM and other waveforms, and sometimes QAM demodulators are used to receive the signals put out by these switching amplifiers.

Automatic Digital Modulation Recognition (ADMR)

Automatic digital modulation recognition in intelligent communication systems is one of the most important issues in software-defined radio and cognitive radio. According to incremental expanse of intelligent receivers, automatic modulation recognition becomes a challenging topic in telecommunication systems and computer engineering. Such systems have many civil and military applications. Moreover, blind recognition of modulation type is an important problem in commercial systems, especially in software-defined radio. Usually in such systems, there are some extra information for system configuration, but considering blind approaches in intelligent receivers, we can reduce information overload and increase transmission performance. Obviously, with no knowledge of the transmitted data and many unknown parameters at the receiver, such as the signal power, carrier frequency and phase offsets, timing information, etc., blind identification of the modulation is made fairly difficult. This becomes even more challenging in real-world scenarios with multipath fading, frequency-selective and time-varying channels.

There are two main approaches to automatic modulation recognition. The first approach uses likelihood-based methods to assign an input signal to a proper class. Another recent approach is based on feature extraction.

Digital Baseband Modulation

Digital baseband modulation changes the characteristics of a baseband signal, i.e., one without a carrier at a higher frequency. This can be used as equivalent signal to be later frequency-converted to a carrier frequency, or for direct communication in baseband. The latter methods both involve relatively simple line codes, as often used in local buses, and complicated baseband signalling schemes such as used in DSL.

Pulse Modulation Methods

Pulse modulation schemes aim at transferring a narrowband analog signal over an analog baseband channel as a two-level signal by modulating a pulse wave. Some pulse modulation schemes also allow the narrowband analog signal to be transferred as a digital signal (i.e., as a quantized discrete-time signal) with a fixed bit rate, which can be transferred over an underlying digital transmission system, for example, some line code. These are not modulation schemes in the conventional sense since they are not channel coding schemes, but should be considered as source coding schemes, and in some cases analog-to-digital conversion techniques.

Miscellaneous Modulation Techniques

- The use of on-off keying to transmit Morse code at radio frequencies is known as continuous wave (CW) operation.
- Adaptive modulation.
- Space modulation is a method whereby signals are modulated within airspace such as that used in instrument landing systems.
- The microwave auditory effect has been pulse modulated with audio waveforms to evoke understandable spoken numbers.

4.3.2 Fundamentals of Waveforms

In addition to modulation schemes, 5G NR introduces new waveform technologies designed to enhance spectral efficiency, support diverse deployment scenarios, and enable new features and capabilities. One of the key waveform technologies introduced in 5G NR is the CP-OFDM (Cyclic Prefix Orthogonal Frequency Division Multiplexing) waveform, which builds upon the success of OFDM technology used in previous wireless standards such as LTE.

CP-OFDM divides the available spectrum into multiple subcarriers, each carrying a portion of the transmitted data. By spacing subcarriers closely together and using guard intervals to mitigate intersymbol interference, CP-OFDM achieves high spectral efficiency and robustness to frequency-selective fading and multipath propagation.

In addition to CP-OFDM, 5G NR introduces new waveform formats such as FBMC (Filter Bank Multicarrier) and UFMC (Universal Filtered Multicarrier), which offer enhanced spectral efficiency and flexibility compared to traditional OFDM waveforms. These waveforms use advanced filtering techniques to reduce out-of-band emissions and improve spectral containment, allowing more efficient use of available spectrum resources and better coexistence with adjacent channels.

Furthermore, 5G NR introduces waveform flexibility through the use of numerology parameters such as subcarrier spacing, cyclic prefix length, and slot duration. By selecting appropriate numerology parameters based on deployment scenario and service requirements, operators can optimize spectral efficiency, latency, and coverage for different use cases such as enhanced mobile broadband (eMBB), ultra-reliable low-latency communication (URLLC), and massive machine-type communication (mMTC).

4.3.3 Implications for 5G NR

Modulation and waveforms are fundamental building blocks of 5G NR, shaping the performance, efficiency, and capabilities of next-generation wireless communication systems. By leveraging advanced modulation schemes, adaptive modulation and coding techniques, and flexible waveform formats, 5G NR can achieve higher data rates, lower latency, and better coverage compared to previous wireless standards.

Moreover, modulation and waveform technologies enable new features and use cases in 5G NR, such as beamforming, massive MIMO (Multiple-Input Multiple-Output), and network slicing. These technologies enable operators to deliver customized services and applications with varying requirements for throughput, latency, reliability, and coverage, thereby unlocking new revenue streams and business opportunities in the 5G ecosystem.

4.4 BEAMFORMING AND MASSIVE MIMO IN NR

Beamforming and Massive MIMO are advanced antenna technologies that play a pivotal role in enhancing the performance, capacity, and coverage of 5G New Radio (NR) systems. By exploiting spatial diversity and multipath propagation, beamforming and Massive MIMO enable operators to achieve higher data rates, lower latency, and better spectral efficiency, thereby supporting a wide range of applications and use cases. Beamforming and Massive MIMO are transformative antenna technologies that are driving the evolution of wireless communication in 5G NR. By exploiting spatial diversity and multipath propagation, beamforming and Massive MIMO enable operators to achieve higher spectral efficiency, better coverage, and improved capacity, supporting a wide range of applications and use cases in 5G networks. As 5G NR continues to evolve, beamforming and Massive MIMO will play a critical role in shaping the performance, efficiency, and capabilities of next-generation wireless networks, driving innovation and enabling new possibilities for the connected world.

4.4.1 Fundamentals of Beamforming

Beamforming or spatial filtering is a signal processing technique used in sensor arrays for directional signal transmission or reception. This is achieved by combining elements in an antenna array in such a way that signals at particular angles experience constructive interference while others experience destructive interference. Beamforming can be used at both the transmitting and receiving ends in order to achieve spatial selectivity. The improvement compared with omnidirectional reception/transmission is known as the directivity of the array.

Beamforming can be used for radio or sound waves. It has found numerous applications in radar, sonar, seismology, wireless communications, radio astronomy, acoustics and biomedicine. Adaptive beamforming is used to detect and estimate the signal of interest at the output of a sensor array by means of optimal (e.g., least-squares) spatial filtering and interference rejection.

Techniques

To change the directionality of the array when transmitting, a beamformer controls the phase and relative amplitude of the signal at each transmitter, in order to create a pattern of constructive and destructive interference in the wavefront. When receiving, information from different sensors is combined in a way where the expected pattern of radiation is preferentially observed.

For example, in sonar, to send a sharp pulse of underwater sound towards a ship in the distance, simply simultaneously transmitting that sharp pulse from every sonar projector in an array fails because the ship will first hear the pulse from the speaker that happens to be nearest the ship, then later pulses from speakers that happen to be further from the ship. The beamforming technique involves sending the pulse from each projector at slightly different times (the projector closest to the ship last), so that every pulse hits the ship at exactly the same time, producing the effect of a single strong pulse from a single powerful projector. The same technique can be carried out in air using loudspeakers, or in radar/radio using antennas.

In passive sonar, and in reception in active sonar, the beamforming technique involves combining delayed signals from each hydrophone at slightly different times (the hydrophone closest to the target will be combined after the longest delay), so that every signal reaches the output at exactly the same time, making one loud signal, as if the signal came from a single, very sensitive hydrophone. Receive beamforming can also be used with microphones or radar antennas.

With narrowband systems the time delay is equivalent to a "phase shift", so in this case the array of antennas, each one shifted a slightly different amount, is called a phased array. A narrow band system, typical of radars, is one where the bandwidth is only a small fraction of the center frequency. With wideband systems this approximation no longer holds, which is typical in sonars.

In the receive beamformer the signal from each antenna may be amplified by a different "weight." Different weighting patterns (e.g., Dolph–Chebyshev) can be used to achieve the desired sensitivity patterns. A main lobe is produced together with nulls and sidelobes. As well as controlling the main lobe width (beamwidth) and the sidelobe levels, the position of a null can be controlled. This is useful to ignore noise or jammers in one particular direction, while listening for events in other directions. A similar result can be obtained on transmission.

Beamforming techniques can be broadly divided into two categories:

- conventional (fixed or switched beam) beamformers
- adaptive beamformers or phased array
  - Desired signal maximization mode
  - Interference signal minimization or cancellation mode

Conventional beamformers, such as the Butler matrix, use a fixed set of weightings and time-delays (or phasings) to combine the signals from the sensors in the array, primarily using only information about the location of the sensors in space and the wave directions of interest. In contrast, adaptive beamforming techniques (e.g., MUSIC, SAMV) generally combine this information with properties of the signals actually received by the array, typically to improve rejection of unwanted signals from other directions. This process may be carried out in either the time or the frequency domain.

As the name indicates, an adaptive beamformer is able to automatically adapt its response to different situations. Some criterion has to be set up to allow the adaptation to proceed such as minimizing the total noise output. Because of the variation of noise with frequency, in wide band systems it may be desirable to carry out the process in the frequency domain.

Beamforming can be computationally intensive. Sonar phased array has a data rate low enough that it can be processed in real time in software, which is flexible enough to transmit or receive in several directions at once. In contrast, radar phased array has a data rate so high that it usually requires dedicated hardware processing, which is hard-wired to transmit or receive in only one direction at a time. However, newer field programmable gate arrays are fast enough to handle radar data in real time, and can be quickly re-programmed like software, blurring the hardware/software distinction.

Sonar Beamforming Requirements

Sonar beamforming utilizes a similar technique to electromagnetic beamforming, but varies considerably in implementation details. Sonar applications vary from 1 Hz to as high as 2 MHz, and array elements may be few and large, or number in the hundreds yet very small. This will shift sonar beamforming design efforts significantly between demands of such system components as the "front end" (transducers, pre-amplifiers and digitizers) and the actual beamformer computational hardware downstream. High frequency, focused beam, multi-element imaging-search sonars and acoustic cameras often implement fifth-order spatial processing that places strains equivalent to Aegis radar demands on the processors.

Many sonar systems, such as on torpedoes, are made up of arrays of up to 100 elements that must accomplish beam steering over a 100 degree field of view and work in both active and passive modes.

Sonar arrays are used both actively and passively in 1-, 2-, and 3-dimensional arrays.

- 1-dimensional "line" arrays are usually in multi-element passive systems towed behind ships and in single- or multi-element side-scan sonar.
- 2-dimensional "planar" arrays are common in active/passive ship hull mounted sonars and some side-scan sonar.
- 3-dimensional spherical and cylindrical arrays are used in 'sonar domes' in the modern submarine and ships.

Sonar differs from radar in that in some applications such as wide-area-search all directions often need to be listened to, and in some applications broadcast to, simultaneously. Thus a multibeam system is needed. In a narrowband sonar receiver, the phases for each beam can be manipulated entirely by signal processing software, as compared to present radar systems that use hardware to 'listen' in a single direction at a time.

Sonar also uses beamforming to compensate for the significant problem of the slower propagation speed of sound as compared to that of electromagnetic radiation. In side-look-sonars, the speed of the towing system or vehicle carrying the sonar is moving at sufficient speed to move the sonar out of the field of the returning sound "ping". In addition to focusing algorithms intended to improve reception, many side scan sonars also employ beam steering to look forward and backward to "catch" incoming pulses that would have been missed by a single sidelooking beam.

Evolved Beamformer

The delay-and-sum beamforming technique uses multiple microphones to localize sound sources. One disadvantage of this technique is that adjustments of the position or of the number of microphones changes the performance of the beamformer nonlinearly. Additionally, due to the number of combinations possible, it is computationally hard to find the best configuration. One of the techniques to solve this problem is the use of genetic algorithms. Such algorithm searches for the microphone array configuration that provides the highest signal-to-noise ratio for each steered orientation. Experiments showed that such algorithm could find the best configuration of a constrained search space comprising ~33 million solutions in a matter of seconds instead of days.

History in Wireless Communication Standards

Beamforming techniques used in cellular phone standards have advanced through the generations to make use of more complex systems to achieve higher density cells, with higher throughput.

- Passive mode: (Almost) non-standardized solutions
  - Wideband code division multiple access (WCDMA) supports direction of arrival (DOA) based beamforming
- Active mode: Mandatory standardized solutions
  - 2G – Transmit antenna selection as an elementary beamforming
  - 3G – WCDMA: transmit antenna array (TxAA) beamforming
  - 3G evolution – LTE/UMB: multiple-input multiple-output (MIMO) precoding based beamforming with partial space-division multiple access (SDMA)
  - Beyond 3G (4G, 5G...) – More advanced beamforming solutions to support SDMA such as closed-loop beamforming and multi-dimensional beamforming are expected

An increasing number of consumer 802.11ac Wi-Fi devices with MIMO capability can support beamforming to boost data communication rates.

Digital, Analog, and Hybrid

To receive (but not transmit), there is a distinction between analog and digital beamforming. For example, if there are 100 sensor elements, the "digital beamforming" approach entails that each of the 100 signals passes through an analog-to-digital converter to create 100 digital data streams. Then these data streams are added up digitally, with appropriate scale-factors or phase-shifts, to get the composite signals. By contrast, the "analog beamforming" approach entails taking the 100 analog signals, scaling or phase-shifting them using analog methods, summing them, and then usually digitizing the single output data stream.

Digital beamforming has the advantage that the digital data streams (100 in this example) can be manipulated and combined in many possible ways in parallel, to get many different output signals in parallel. The signals from every direction can be measured simultaneously, and the signals can be integrated for a longer time when studying far-off objects and simultaneously integrated for a shorter time to study fast-moving close objects, and so on. This cannot be done as effectively for analog beamforming, not only because each parallel signal combination requires its own circuitry, but more fundamentally because digital data can be copied perfectly but analog data cannot. (There is only so much analog power available, and amplification adds noise.) Therefore, if the received analog signal is split up and sent into a large number of different signal combination circuits, it can reduce the signal-to-noise ratio of each.

In MIMO communication systems with large number of antennas, so called massive MIMO systems, the beamforming algorithms executed at the digital baseband can get very complex. In addition, if all beamforming is done at baseband, each antenna needs its own RF feed. At high frequencies and with large number of antenna elements, this can be very costly, and increase loss and complexity in the system. To remedy these issues, hybrid beamforming has been suggested where some of the beamforming is done using analog components and not digital.

There are many possible different functions that can be performed using analog components instead of at the digital baseband.

Beamforming, whether done digitally, or by means of analog architecture, has recently been applied in integrated sensing and communication technology. For instance, a beamformer was suggested, in imperfect channel state information situations to perform communication tasks, while at the same time performing target detection to sense targets in the scene.

For Speech Audio

Beamforming can be used to try to extract sound sources in a room, such as multiple speakers in the cocktail party problem. This requires the locations of the speakers to be known in advance, for example by using the time of arrival from the sources to mics in the array, and inferring the locations from the distances.

Compared to carrier-wave telecommunications, natural audio contains a variety of frequencies. It is advantageous to separate frequency bands prior to beamforming because different frequencies have different optimal beamform filters (and hence can be treated as separate problems, in parallel, and then recombined afterward). Properly isolating these bands involves specialized non-standard filter banks. In contrast, for example, the standard fast Fourier transform (FFT) band-filters implicitly assume that the only frequencies present in the signal are exact harmonics; frequencies which lie between these harmonics will typically activate all of the FFT channels (which is not what is wanted in a beamform analysis). Instead, filters can be designed in which only local frequencies are detected by each channel (while retaining the recombination property to be able to reconstruct the original signal), and these are typically non-orthogonal unlike the FFT basis.

4.4.2 Beamforming techniques in 5G NR include

1. Analog Beamforming: Analog beamforming uses phase shifters to adjust the phase of signals transmitted by each antenna element, enabling the formation of narrow beams in specific directions. Analog beamforming is simple and efficient but lacks the flexibility and adaptability of digital beamforming.
2. Digital Beamforming: Digital beamforming involves processing baseband signals digitally to adjust the phase and amplitude of signals transmitted by each antenna element. Digital beamforming offers greater flexibility and adaptability compared to analog beamforming, enabling dynamic beam steering and beamforming optimization.

3. Hybrid Beamforming: Hybrid beamforming combines the advantages of analog and digital beamforming, using a combination of analog phase shifters and digital signal processing to steer transmit beams efficiently. Hybrid beamforming strikes a balance between performance and complexity, making it suitable for practical implementation in 5G NR systems.

4.4.3 Benefits of Beamforming

Beamforming offers several benefits in 5G NR, including:

1. Improved Coverage: By focusing transmit energy towards specific users or areas, beamforming improves signal strength and coverage, particularly in areas with high user density or challenging propagation conditions.
2. Increased Capacity: Beamforming enables spatial multiplexing, allowing multiple users to share the same frequency resources without interfering with each other. This increases network capacity and throughput, supporting higher data rates and more simultaneous connections.
3. Reduced Interference: By directing transmit energy away from unwanted directions, beamforming reduces interference and improves signal-to-interference-plus-noise ratio (SINR), resulting in higher data rates and better quality of service for users.
4. Energy Efficiency: Beamforming enables more efficient use of transmit power by focusing energy towards desired users or areas, reducing wasted energy and improving spectral efficiency.

4.4.4 Fundamentals of Massive MIMO

Massive MIMO is an advanced antenna technology that uses large antenna arrays to serve multiple users simultaneously, exploiting spatial diversity and multipath propagation to improve spectral efficiency and network capacity. Unlike traditional MIMO systems, which typically use a few antennas (e.g., 2x2 or 4x4), Massive MIMO systems can have hundreds or even thousands of antennas, enabling unprecedented levels of spatial multiplexing and interference suppression.

In 5G NR, Massive MIMO is employed in both the downlink (transmit) and uplink (receive) directions, enabling efficient transmission and reception of data between base stations and mobile devices. Massive MIMO systems use techniques such as precoding, spatial multiplexing, and channel state information (CSI) feedback to optimize signal transmission and reception, maximizing throughput and minimizing interference.

4.4.5 Benefits of Massive MIMO

Massive MIMO offers several benefits in 5G NR, including:

1. Higher Spectral Efficiency: By serving multiple users simultaneously with spatially orthogonal beams, Massive MIMO increases spectral efficiency and network capacity, supporting higher data rates and more simultaneous connections.
2. Improved Coverage: Massive MIMO improves coverage and signal quality by exploiting spatial diversity and multipath propagation, particularly in areas with challenging propagation conditions or high user density.
3. Better Energy Efficiency: Massive MIMO enables more efficient use of transmit power by focusing energy towards desired users and directions, reducing wasted energy and improving spectral efficiency.
4. Enhanced Interference Suppression: Massive MIMO suppresses interference through spatial nulling and interference cancellation techniques, improving signal-to-interference-plus-noise ratio (SINR) and enabling higher data rates and better quality of service for users.

4.4.6 Implications for 5G NR

Beamforming and Massive MIMO are key enablers of 5G NR, providing the foundation for high-speed, low-latency, and reliable wireless communication. By leveraging spatial diversity and multipath propagation, beamforming and Massive MIMO enable operators to achieve higher spectral efficiency, better coverage, and improved capacity, supporting a wide range of applications and use cases in 5G networks.

Moreover, beamforming and Massive MIMO enable new features and capabilities in 5G NR, such as dynamic beamforming, coordinated multipoint (CoMP) transmission, and multi-user MIMO (MU-MIMO). These technologies enable operators to deliver customized services and applications with varying requirements for throughput, latency, reliability, and coverage, thereby unlocking new revenue streams and business opportunities in the 5G ecosystem.

CHAPTER 5

5G SERVICES AND USE CASES

5.1 ENHANCED MOBILE BROADBAND (EMBB)

Enhanced Mobile Broadband (eMBB) stands as one of the cornerstone use cases of 5G technology, promising to revolutionize wireless connectivity by delivering unprecedented levels of data throughput, low latency, and reliability. eMBB aims to provide users with seamless access to high-speed internet services, immersive multimedia experiences, and real-time applications, shaping the way people communicate, work, and interact in an increasingly connected world. Enhanced Mobile Broadband (eMBB) stands as a transformative use case of 5G technology, promising to revolutionize wireless connectivity by delivering higher data rates, lower latency, and improved reliability. eMBB enables users to access high-speed internet services, immersive multimedia experiences, and real-time applications, shaping the way people communicate, work, and interact in an increasingly connected world. As eMBB continues to evolve, we can expect further advancements in wireless technology and the emergence of new applications and use cases that will drive innovation, economic growth, and societal development in the years to come.

Fundamentals of eMBB: eMBB is one of the three primary use cases defined by the International Telecommunication Union (ITU) for 5G technology, alongside massive machine-type communication (mMTC) and ultra-reliable low-latency communication (URLLC). Unlike its counterparts, which target specific vertical industries and applications, eMBB aims to enhance the overall broadband experience for mobile users by providing higher data rates, increased network capacity, and improved user experience across a wide range of services and applications.

5.1.1 The Key Features of eMBB

1. Higher Data Throughput: eMBB promises to deliver significantly higher data rates compared to previous generations of wireless technology, enabling users to download and upload large files, stream high-definition videos, and engage in bandwidth-intensive applications with minimal latency and buffering.
2. Lower Latency: eMBB aims to reduce latency to milliseconds or even microseconds, enabling real-time communication and interactive applications such as online gaming, virtual reality (VR), augmented reality (AR), and remote control of connected devices.

3. Improved Spectral Efficiency: eMBB utilizes advanced modulation schemes, waveform technologies, and antenna techniques such as beamforming and massive MIMO to increase spectral efficiency, allowing more data to be transmitted over the same bandwidth.
4. Enhanced Mobility: eMBB supports seamless mobility and handover between cells, enabling users to maintain connectivity while moving at high speeds, such as in vehicles or trains. This ensures a consistent user experience across different scenarios and environments.

5.1.2 Benefits of eMBB

eMBB offers several benefits over previous generations of wireless technology, including:

1. High-Speed Internet Access: eMBB enables users to access high-speed internet services on the go, allowing them to download and upload content, stream multimedia, and browse the web with ease and convenience.
2. Immersive Multimedia Experiences: eMBB supports immersive multimedia experiences such as high-definition video streaming, virtual reality (VR), and augmented reality (AR), enabling users to engage with content in new and interactive ways.
3. Enhanced Productivity: eMBB enables users to access cloud-based applications and services, collaborate in real time, and work remotely with the same level of connectivity and performance as in the office, improving productivity and flexibility for businesses and individuals alike.
4. Innovative Applications: eMBB opens up new possibilities for innovative applications and services across various industries, including healthcare, education, transportation, and entertainment. These applications leverage high-speed connectivity, low latency, and reliability to deliver transformative experiences and solutions.

5.1.3 pplications of embb

eMBB enables a wide range of applications and services across various industries and sectors, including:

1. Video Streaming and Gaming: eMBB allows users to stream high-definition videos, play online games, and engage in real-time multiplayer gaming experiences without buffering or lag.
2. Virtual Reality (VR) and Augmented Reality (AR): eMBB supports immersive VR and AR applications, allowing users to experience virtual environments, interact with digital objects, and access contextual information in real time.

3. Cloud Computing and Remote Work: eMBB enables users to access cloud-based applications and services, collaborate with colleagues, and work remotely from anywhere with high-speed internet connectivity.
4. Smart Cities and IoT: eMBB facilitates the deployment of smart city initiatives and IoT (Internet of Things) solutions, enabling real-time monitoring, control, and optimization of urban infrastructure and services.

5.1.4 Implications for the Future

eMBB is poised to transform the way people communicate, work, and interact in the digital age, unlocking new opportunities for innovation, economic growth, and societal development. As eMBB continues to evolve, we can expect further advancements in wireless technology, including higher data rates, lower latency, and improved reliability, enabling new applications and use cases that were previously not possible.

Moreover, eMBB will play a crucial role in enabling emerging technologies such as autonomous vehicles, remote healthcare, and smart manufacturing, which rely on high-speed, low-latency connectivity to function effectively. By providing ubiquitous access to high-speed internet services, eMBB will bridge the digital divide, empower underserved communities, and foster inclusive growth and development.

5.2 ULTRA-RELIABLE LOW LATENCY COMMUNICATION (URLLC)

Ultra-Reliable Low Latency Communication (URLLC) stands as one of the key pillars of 5G technology, offering unprecedented levels of reliability and responsiveness for critical applications that demand real-time communication and mission-critical reliability. From autonomous vehicles to industrial automation and remote surgery, URLLC promises to enable a wide range of innovative use cases that rely on ultra-low latency, high reliability, and stringent quality of service (QoS) requirements. Ultra-Reliable Low Latency Communication (URLLC) stands as a critical enabler of 5G technology, offering unprecedented levels of reliability and responsiveness for critical applications that demand real-time communication and mission-critical reliability. By providing ultra-low latency, high reliability, and stringent QoS requirements, URLLC unlocks new possibilities for innovation, safety, and efficiency across various industries and sectors, shaping the future of communication and technology. As URLLC continues to evolve, addressing challenges and considerations, we can expect further advancements in wireless technology and the emergence of new applications and use cases that will drive innovation, economic growth, and societal development in the years to come.

5.2.1 Fundamentals of URLLC

URLLC is defined as a communication service in which data transmission is characterized by ultra-low latency, high reliability, and stringent QoS requirements.

Unlike other use cases of 5G technology, which may prioritize high data rates or massive connectivity, URLLC focuses on ensuring that data is delivered with minimal delay and maximum reliability, even in the most demanding and challenging environments.

The key features of URLLC include:

1. Ultra-Low Latency: URLLC aims to minimize end-to-end latency to milliseconds or even microseconds, enabling real-time communication and control for applications that require instantaneous response and feedback. This is essential for applications such as autonomous vehicles, industrial automation, and remote surgery, where even the slightest delay can have serious consequences.
2. High Reliability: URLLC guarantees a high level of reliability for data transmission, with error rates as low as one error in 10^9 bits (10^-9) or better. This ensures that critical data is delivered accurately and reliably, even in harsh and challenging environments with high levels of noise, interference, and packet loss.
3. Stringent QoS Requirements: URLLC imposes stringent requirements on key performance indicators (KPIs) such as latency, reliability, and jitter, which must be met consistently to ensure the quality of service for critical applications. This requires efficient resource allocation, prioritization, and scheduling mechanisms to meet the demanding needs of URLLC traffic.

5.2.2 Benefits of URLLC

URLLC offers several benefits over traditional communication technologies, including:

1. Real-Time Communication: URLLC enables real-time communication and control for critical applications such as autonomous vehicles, industrial automation, and remote surgery, allowing for instantaneous response and feedback.
2. Mission-Critical Reliability: URLLC guarantees a high level of reliability for data transmission, ensuring that critical data is delivered accurately and reliably, even in challenging and dynamic environments.
3. Improved Safety and Efficiency: URLLC enhances safety and efficiency in various industries and sectors by enabling real-time monitoring, control, and optimization of processes and systems, reducing the risk of accidents, errors, and downtime.
4. Innovative Use Cases: URLLC unlocks new possibilities for innovative applications and services across various industries, including healthcare, transportation, manufacturing, and public safety, which rely on ultra-low latency and high reliability to function effectively.

5.2.3 Applications of URLLC

URLLC enables a wide range of critical applications and use cases across various industries and sectors, including:

1. Autonomous Vehicles: URLLC enables real-time communication between autonomous vehicles and infrastructure, allowing for coordinated maneuvering, collision avoidance, and traffic management in dynamic and congested environments.
2. Industrial Automation: URLLC supports real-time monitoring, control, and optimization of industrial processes and systems, enabling factories and manufacturing plants to operate more efficiently, safely, and productively.
3. Remote Surgery: URLLC enables surgeons to perform remote surgeries and procedures with minimal latency and maximum precision, allowing for real-time feedback and control over robotic surgical instruments and devices.
4. Public Safety and Emergency Services: URLLC enables first responders and emergency services to communicate and coordinate more effectively in crisis situations, ensuring timely response and assistance to those in need.

5.2.4 Challenges and Implications for the Future

Despite its promising benefits and applications, URLLC poses several challenges and considerations that must be addressed to realize its full potential:

1. Resource Allocation and Scheduling: URLLC requires efficient resource allocation and scheduling mechanisms to meet the stringent latency and reliability requirements of critical applications, which may compete with other traffic types for limited network resources.
2. Interference and Congestion: URLLC traffic may be susceptible to interference and congestion, particularly in dense urban environments and high-traffic areas, which can degrade performance and reliability.
3. Security and Privacy: URLLC applications and services may be vulnerable to security threats and privacy breaches, which can compromise the integrity, confidentiality, and availability of critical data and systems.
4. Regulatory and Compliance: URLLC applications and services may be subject to regulatory requirements and compliance standards, particularly in highly regulated industries such as healthcare, transportation, and public safety, which may impose additional constraints and considerations on deployment and operation.

5.3 MASSIVE MACHINE TYPE COMMUNICATION (MMTC)

Massive Machine Type Communication (mMTC) is a fundamental aspect of 5G technology, designed to facilitate communication between a vast number of devices, sensors, and machines in the Internet of Things (IoT) ecosystem. mMTC promises to enable a wide range of applications and services, from smart cities and industrial automation to environmental monitoring and healthcare, by providing scalable, efficient, and reliable connectivity for billions of connected devices.

Massive Machine Type Communication (mMTC) stands as a critical enabler of 5G technology, offering scalable, efficient, and reliable connectivity for billions of devices and sensors in the Internet of Things (IoT) ecosystem. By providing connectivity for a wide range of applications and industries, mMTC promises to unlock new possibilities for innovation, efficiency, and sustainability, shaping the future of connectivity and technology. As mMTC continues to evolve, addressing challenges and considerations, we can expect further advancements in wireless technology and the emergence of new applications and use cases that will drive innovation, economic growth, and societal development in the years to come.

5.3.1 Fundamentals of mMTC

mMTC is defined as a communication service in which a large number of devices and sensors transmit small amounts of data sporadically or periodically, typically with low power consumption and low data rates. Unlike traditional communication services, which prioritize high data rates and low latency, mMTC focuses on supporting massive scale and density of devices, enabling connectivity for billions of devices and sensors in diverse environments and applications.

The key features of mMTC include:

1. Scalability: mMTC is designed to scale to support a massive number of devices and sensors, ranging from hundreds of thousands to billions, without compromising performance or reliability. This scalability is essential for IoT applications such as smart cities, industrial automation, and environmental monitoring, which involve a large number of interconnected devices and sensors.
2. Efficiency: mMTC optimizes resource utilization and energy consumption to ensure efficient communication between devices and sensors. This includes techniques such as power saving modes, efficient signaling protocols, and lightweight data formats, which minimize overhead and maximize battery life for battery-powered devices.
3. Reliability: mMTC guarantees reliable communication for devices and sensors, even in challenging and dynamic environments with high levels of interference, congestion, and mobility. This reliability is essential for critical applications such as healthcare, transportation, and public safety, which rely on real-time data transmission and decision-making.
4. Flexibility: mMTC supports diverse deployment scenarios and use cases, ranging from indoor environments with dense device deployments to

outdoor environments with wide area coverage requirements. This flexibility enables mMTC to address a wide range of applications and industries, including smart homes, smart buildings, smart agriculture, and smart manufacturing.

5.3.2 Benefits

mMTC offers several benefits over traditional communication technologies, including:

1. Connectivity for Billions of Devices: mMTC enables connectivity for billions of devices and sensors, allowing them to exchange data, communicate with each other, and interact with cloud-based applications and services in real time.
2. Scalable Deployment: mMTC supports scalable deployment of IoT solutions across various industries and sectors, allowing organizations to deploy and manage large-scale IoT networks with ease and efficiency.
3. Efficient Resource Utilization: mMTC optimizes resource utilization and energy consumption, minimizing overhead and maximizing battery life for battery-powered devices, which is essential for IoT deployments in remote or inaccessible locations.
4. Real-Time Data Insights: mMTC enables real-time data collection, analysis, and decision-making, providing organizations with valuable insights and intelligence to optimize operations, improve efficiency, and enhance user experience.

5.3.3 Applications

mMTC enables a wide range of applications and services across various industries and sectors, including:

1. Smart Cities: mMTC enables smart city initiatives such as intelligent transportation systems, environmental monitoring, smart lighting, and waste management, allowing cities to become more efficient, sustainable, and livable.
2. Industrial Automation: mMTC supports industrial automation and smart manufacturing applications such as asset tracking, predictive maintenance, and remote monitoring and control of machinery and equipment, improving productivity, safety, and efficiency in factories and manufacturing plants.
3. Healthcare: mMTC enables remote patient monitoring, telemedicine, and personalized healthcare applications, allowing healthcare providers to deliver better care, improve patient outcomes, and reduce healthcare costs.

4. Agriculture: mMTC supports precision agriculture and smart farming applications such as soil monitoring, crop monitoring, and livestock tracking, enabling farmers to optimize crop yields, reduce resource consumption, and improve sustainability.

5.3.4 Challenges and Implications for the Future

Despite its promising benefits and applications, mMTC poses several challenges and considerations that must be addressed to realize its full potential:

1. Interference and Congestion: mMTC traffic may be susceptible to interference and congestion, particularly in dense urban environments and high-traffic areas, which can degrade performance and reliability.
2. Security and Privacy: mMTC devices and sensors may be vulnerable to security threats and privacy breaches, which can compromise the integrity, confidentiality, and availability of critical data and systems.
3. Standardization and Interoperability: mMTC deployments may require standardization and interoperability across different devices, networks, and platforms, to ensure seamless integration and compatibility.
4. Regulatory and Compliance: mMTC applications and services may be subject to regulatory requirements and compliance standards, particularly in highly regulated industries such as healthcare, transportation, and public safety, which may impose additional constraints and considerations on deployment and operation.

5.4 INTERNET OF THINGS (IOT) IN 5G

5.4.1 Internet of Things

The Internet of things (IoT) describes devices with sensors, processing ability, software and other technologies that connect and exchange data with other devices and systems over the Internet or other communications networks. The Internet of things encompasses electronics, communication, and computer science engineering. "Internet of things" has been considered a misnomer because devices do not need to be connected to the public internet; they only need to be connected to a network and be individually addressable.

The field has evolved due to the convergence of multiple technologies, including ubiquitous computing, commodity sensors, and increasingly powerful embedded systems, as well as machine learning. Older fields of embedded systems, wireless sensor networks, control systems, automation (including home and building automation), independently and collectively enable the Internet of things. In the consumer market, IoT technology is most synonymous with "smart home" products, including devices and appliances (lighting fixtures, thermostats, home security systems, cameras, and other home appliances) that support one or more common ecosystems and can be controlled via devices associated with that ecosystem, such as smartphones and smart speakers. IoT is also used in healthcare systems.

There are a number of concerns about the risks in the growth of IoT technologies and products, especially in the areas of privacy and security, and consequently there have been industry and government moves to address these concerns, including the development of international and local standards, guidelines, and regulatory frameworks.

History

The main concept of a network of smart devices was discussed as early as 1982, with a modified Coca-Cola vending machine at Carnegie Mellon University becoming the first ARPANET-connected appliance, able to report its inventory and whether newly loaded drinks were cold or not. Mark Weiser's 1991 paper on ubiquitous computing, "The Computer of the 21st Century", as well as academic venues such as UbiComp and PerCom produced the contemporary vision of the IOT. In 1994, Reza Raji described the concept in IEEE Spectrum as "[moving] small packets of data to a large set of nodes, so as to integrate and automate everything from home appliances to entire factories". Between 1993 and 1997, several companies proposed solutions like Microsoft's at Work or Novell's NEST. The field gained momentum when Bill Joy envisioned device-to-device communication as a part of his "Six Webs" framework, presented at the World Economic Forum at Davos in 1999.

The concept of the "Internet of things" and the term itself, first appeared in a speech by Peter T. Lewis, to the Congressional Black Caucus Foundation 15th Annual Legislative Weekend in Washington, D.C., published in September 1985. According to Lewis, "The Internet of Things, or IoT, is the integration of people, processes and technology with connectable devices and sensors to enable remote monitoring, status, manipulation and evaluation of trends of such devices."

The term "Internet of things" was coined independently by Kevin Ashton of Procter & Gamble, later of MIT's Auto-ID Center, in 1999, though he prefers the phrase "Internet for things". At that point, he viewed radio-frequency identification (RFID) as essential to the Internet of things, which would allow computers to manage all individual things. The main theme of the Internet of things is to embed short-range mobile transceivers in various gadgets and daily necessities to enable new forms of communication between people and things, and between things themselves.

In 2004 Cornelius "Pete" Peterson, CEO of NetSilicon, predicted that, "The next era of information technology will be dominated by [IoT] devices, and networked devices will ultimately gain in popularity and significance to the extent that they will far exceed the number of networked computers and workstations." Peterson believed that medical devices and industrial controls would become dominant applications of the technology.

Defining the Internet of things as "simply the point in time when more 'things or objects' were connected to the Internet than people", Cisco Systems estimated that the IoT was "born" between 2008 and 2009, with the things/people ratio growing from 0.08 in 2003 to 1.84 in 2010.

Applications

The extensive set of applications for IoT devices is often divided into consumer, commercial, industrial, and infrastructure spaces.

Consumers

A growing portion of IoT devices is created for consumer use, including connected vehicles, home automation, wearable technology, connected health, and appliances with remote monitoring capabilities.

Home Automation

IoT devices are a part of the larger concept of home automation, which can include lighting, heating and air conditioning, media and security systems and camera systems. Long-term benefits could include energy savings by automatically ensuring lights and electronics are turned off or by making the residents in the home aware of usage.

A smart home or automated home could be based on a platform or hubs that control smart devices and appliances. For instance, using Apple's HomeKit, manufacturers can have their home products and accessories controlled by an application in iOS devices such as the iPhone and the Apple Watch. This could be a dedicated app or iOS native applications such as Siri. This can be demonstrated in the case of Lenovo's Smart Home Essentials, which is a line of smart home devices that are controlled through Apple's Home app or Siri without the need for a Wi-Fi bridge. There are also dedicated smart home hubs that are offered as standalone platforms to connect different smart home products. These include the Amazon Echo, Google Home, Apple's HomePod, and Samsung's SmartThings Hub. In addition to the commercial systems, there are many non-proprietary, open source ecosystems, including Home Assistant, OpenHAB and Domoticz.

Elder Care

One key application of a smart home is to assist the elderly and disabled. These home systems use assistive technology to accommodate an owner's specific disabilities. Voice control can assist users with sight and mobility limitations while alert systems can be connected directly to cochlear implants worn by hearing-impaired users. They can also be equipped with additional safety features, including sensors that monitor for medical emergencies such as falls or seizures. Smart home technology applied in this way can provide users with more freedom and a higher quality of life.

Organizations

The term "Enterprise IoT" refers to devices used in business and corporate settings. By 2019, it is estimated that the EIoT will account for 9.1 billion devices.

Medical and Healthcare

The Internet of Medical Things (IoMT) is an application of the IoT for medical and health-related purposes, data collection and analysis for research, and monitoring. The IoMT has been referenced as "Smart Healthcare", as the technology for creating a digitized healthcare system, connecting available medical resources and healthcare services.

IoT devices can be used to enable remote health monitoring and emergency notification systems. These health monitoring devices can range from blood pressure and heart rate monitors to advanced devices capable of monitoring specialized implants, such as pacemakers, Fitbit electronic wristbands, or advanced hearing aids. Some hospitals have begun implementing "smart beds" that can detect when they are occupied and when a patient is attempting to get up. It can also adjust itself to ensure appropriate pressure and support are applied to the patient without the manual interaction of nurses. A 2015 Goldman Sachs report indicated that healthcare IoT devices "can save the United States more than $300 billion in annual healthcare expenditures by increasing revenue and decreasing cost." Moreover, the use of mobile devices to support medical follow-up led to the creation of 'm-health', used analyzed health statistics."

Specialized sensors can also be equipped within living spaces to monitor the health and general well-being of senior citizens, while also ensuring that proper treatment is being administered and assisting people to regain lost mobility via therapy as well. These sensors create a network of intelligent sensors that are able to collect, process, transfer, and analyze valuable information in different environments, such as connecting in-home monitoring devices to hospital-based systems. Other consumer devices to encourage healthy living, such as connected scales or wearable heart monitors, are also a possibility with the IoT. End-to-end health monitoring IoT platforms are also available for antenatal and chronic patients, helping one manage health vitals and recurring medication requirements.

Advances in plastic and fabric electronics fabrication methods have enabled ultra-low cost, use-and-throw IoMT sensors. These sensors, along with the required RFID electronics, can be fabricated on paper or e-textiles for wireless powered disposable sensing devices. Applications have been established for point-of-care medical diagnostics, where portability and low system-complexity is essential.

As of 2018 IoMT was not only being applied in the clinical laboratory industry, but also in the healthcare and health insurance industries. IoMT in the healthcare industry is now permitting doctors, patients, and others, such as guardians of patients, nurses, families, and similar, to be part of a system, where patient records are saved in a database, allowing doctors and the rest of the medical staff to have access to patient information. IoMT in the insurance industry provides access to better and new types of dynamic information. This includes sensor-based solutions such as biosensors, wearables, connected health devices, and mobile apps to track customer behavior. This can lead to more accurate underwriting and new pricing models.

The application of the IoT in healthcare plays a fundamental role in managing chronic diseases and in disease prevention and control. Remote monitoring is made possible through the connection of powerful wireless solutions. The connectivity enables health practitioners to capture patient's data and apply complex algorithms in health data analysis.

Transportation

The IoT can assist in the integration of communications, control, and information processing across various transportation systems. Application of the IoT extends to all aspects of transportation systems (i.e., the vehicle, the infrastructure, and the driver or user). Dynamic interaction between these components of a transport system enables inter- and intra-vehicular communication, smart traffic control, smart parking, electronic toll collection systems, logistics and fleet management, vehicle control, safety, and road assistance.

V2X Communications

In vehicular communication systems, vehicle-to-everything communication (V2X), consists of three main components: vehicle-to-vehicle communication (V2V), vehicle-to-infrastructure communication (V2I) and vehicle to pedestrian communications (V2P). V2X is the first step to autonomous driving and connected road infrastructure.

Home Automation

IoT devices can be used to monitor and control the mechanical, electrical and electronic systems used in various types of buildings (e.g., public and private, industrial, institutions, or residential) in home automation and building automation systems. In this context, three main areas are being covered in literature:

- The integration of the Internet with building energy management systems to create energy-efficient and IOT-driven "smart buildings".
- The possible means of real-time monitoring for reducing energy consumption and monitoring occupant behaviors.
- The integration of smart devices in the built environment and how they might be used in future applications.

Industrial

Also known as IIoT, industrial IoT devices acquire and analyze data from connected equipment, operational technology (OT), locations, and people. Combined with operational technology (OT) monitoring devices, IIoT helps regulate and monitor industrial systems. Also, the same implementation can be carried out for automated record updates of asset placement in industrial storage units as the size of the assets can vary from a small screw to the whole motor spare part, and misplacement of such assets can cause a loss of manpower time and money.

Manufacturing

The IoT can connect various manufacturing devices equipped with sensing, identification, processing, communication, actuation, and networking capabilities. Network control and management of manufacturing equipment, asset and situation management, or manufacturing process control allow IoT to be used for industrial applications and smart manufacturing. IoT intelligent systems enable rapid manufacturing and optimization of new products and rapid response to product demands.

Digital control systems to automate process controls, operator tools and service information systems to optimize plant safety and security are within the purview of the IIoT. IoT can also be applied to asset management via predictive maintenance, statistical evaluation, and measurements to maximize reliability. Industrial management systems can be integrated with smart grids, enabling energy optimization. Measurements, automated controls, plant optimization, health and safety management, and other functions are provided by networked sensors.

In addition to general manufacturing, IoT is also used for processes in the industrialization of construction.

Agriculture

There are numerous IoT applications in farming such as collecting data on temperature, rainfall, humidity, wind speed, pest infestation, and soil content. This data can be used to automate farming techniques, take informed decisions to improve quality and quantity, minimize risk and waste, and reduce the effort required to manage crops. For example, farmers can now monitor soil temperature and moisture from afar and even apply IoT-acquired data to precision fertilization programs. The overall goal is that data from sensors, coupled with the farmer's knowledge and intuition about his or her farm, can help increase farm productivity, and also help reduce costs.

In August 2018, Toyota Tsusho began a partnership with Microsoft to create fish farming tools using the Microsoft Azure application suite for IoT technologies related to water management. Developed in part by researchers from Kindai University, the water pump mechanisms use artificial intelligence to count the number of fish on a conveyor belt, analyze the number of fish, and deduce the effectiveness of water flow from the data the fish provide. The FarmBeats project from Microsoft Research that uses TV white space to connect farms is also a part of the Azure Marketplace now.

Maritime

IoT devices are in use to monitor the environments and systems of boats and yachts. Many pleasure boats are left unattended for days in summer, and months in winter so such devices provide valuable early alerts of boat flooding, fire, and deep discharge of batteries. The use of global internet data networks such as Sigfox, combined with long-life batteries, and microelectronics allows the engine rooms, bilge, and batteries to be constantly monitored and reported to connected Android & Apple applications for example.

Infrastructure

Monitoring and controlling operations of sustainable urban and rural infrastructures like bridges, railway tracks and on- and offshore wind farms is a key application of the IoT. The IoT infrastructure can be used for monitoring any events or changes in structural conditions that can compromise safety and increase risk. The IoT can benefit the construction industry by cost-saving, time reduction, better quality workday, paperless workflow and increase in productivity. It can help in taking faster decisions and saving money in Real-Time Data Analytics. It can also be used for scheduling repair and maintenance activities efficiently, by coordinating tasks between different service providers and users of these facilities. IoT devices can also be used to control critical infrastructure like bridges to provide access to ships. The usage of IoT devices for monitoring and operating infrastructure is likely to improve incident management and emergency response coordination, and quality of service, up-times and reduce costs of operation in all infrastructure-related areas. Even areas such as waste management can benefit from automation and optimization that could be brought in by the IoT.

Metropolitan Scale Deployments

There are several planned or ongoing large-scale deployments of the IoT, to enable better management of cities and systems. For example, Songdo, South Korea, the first of its kind fully equipped and wired smart city, is gradually being built, with approximately 70 percent of the business district completed as of June 2018. Much of the city is planned to be wired and automated, with little or no human intervention.

Another application is currently undergoing a project in Santander, Spain. For this deployment, two approaches have been adopted. This city of 180,000 inhabitants has already seen 18,000 downloads of its city smartphone app. The app is connected to 10,000 sensors that enable services like parking search, environmental monitoring, digital city agenda, and more. City context information is used in this deployment so as to benefit merchants through a spark deals mechanism based on city behavior that aims at maximizing the impact of each notification.

Other examples of large-scale deployments underway include the Sino-Singapore Guangzhou Knowledge City; work on improving air and water quality, reducing noise pollution, and increasing transportation efficiency in San Jose, California; and smart traffic management in western Singapore. Using its RPMA (Random Phase Multiple Access) technology, San Diego-based Ingenu has built a nationwide public network for low-bandwidth data transmissions using the same unlicensed 2.4 gigahertz spectrum as Wi-Fi. Ingenu's "Machine Network" covers more than a third of the US population across 35 major cities including San Diego and Dallas. French company, Sigfox, commenced building an Ultra Narrowband wireless data network in the San Francisco Bay Area in 2014, the first business to achieve such a deployment in the U.S. It subsequently announced it would set up a total of 4000 base stations to cover a total of 30 cities in the U.S. by the end of 2016, making it the largest IoT network coverage provider in the country thus far. Cisco also participates in smart cities projects. Cisco has started deploying technologies for Smart Wi-Fi, Smart Safety & Security, Smart Lighting, Smart Parking, Smart Transports, Smart Bus Stops, Smart Kiosks, Remote Expert for Government Services (REGS) and Smart Education in the five km area in the city of Vijaywada, India.

Another example of a large deployment is the one completed by New York Waterways in New York City to connect all the city's vessels and be able to monitor them live 24/7. The network was designed and engineered by Fluidmesh Networks, a Chicago-based company developing wireless networks for critical applications. The NYWW network is currently providing coverage on the Hudson River, East River, and Upper New York Bay. With the wireless network in place, NY Waterway is able to take control of its fleet and passengers in a way that was not previously possible. New applications can include security, energy and fleet management, digital signage, public Wi-Fi, paperless ticketing and others.

Energy Management

Significant numbers of energy-consuming devices (e.g., lamps, household appliances, motors, pumps, etc.) already integrate Internet connectivity, which can allow them to communicate with utilities not only to balance power generation but also helps optimize the energy consumption as a whole. These devices allow for remote control by users, or central management via a cloud-based interface, and enable functions like scheduling (e.g., remotely powering on or off heating systems, controlling ovens, changing lighting conditions etc.). The smart grid is a utility-side IoT application; systems gather and act on energy and power-related information to improve the efficiency of the production and distribution of electricity. Using advanced metering infrastructure (AMI) Internet-connected devices, electric utilities not only collect data from end-users, but also manage distribution automation devices like transformers.

Environmental Monitoring

Environmental monitoring applications of the IoT typically use sensors to assist in environmental protection by monitoring air or water quality, atmospheric or soil conditions, and can even include areas like monitoring the movements of wildlife and their habitats. Development of resource-constrained devices connected to the Internet also means that other applications like earthquake or tsunami early-warning systems can also be used by emergency services to provide more effective aid. IoT devices in this application typically span a large geographic area and can also be mobile. It has been argued that the standardization that IoT brings to wireless sensing will revolutionize this area.

Living Lab

Another example of integrating the IoT is Living Lab which integrates and combines research and innovation processes, establishing within a public-private-people-partnership. Between 2006 and January 2024, there were over 440 Living Labs (though not all are currently active) that use the IoT to collaborate and share knowledge between stakeholders to co-create innovative and technological products. For companies to implement and develop IoT services for smart cities, they need to have incentives. The governments play key roles in smart city projects as changes in policies will help cities to implement the IoT which provides effectiveness, efficiency, and accuracy of the resources that are being used. For instance, the government provides tax incentives and cheap rent, improves public transports, and offers an environment where start-up companies, creative industries, and multinationals may co-create, share a common infrastructure and labor markets, and take advantage of locally embedded technologies, production process, and transaction costs. The relationship between the technology developers and governments who manage the city's assets, is key to provide open access to resources to users in an efficient way.

Trends and Characteristics

The IoT's major significant trend in recent years is the explosive growth of devices connected and controlled via the Internet. The wide range of applications for IoT technology mean that the specifics can be very different from one device to the next but there are basic characteristics shared by most.

The IoT creates opportunities for more direct integration of the physical world into computer-based systems, resulting in efficiency improvements, economic benefits, and reduced human exertions.

The number of IoT devices increased 31% year-over-year to 8.4 billion in the year 2017 and it is estimated that there will be 30 billion devices by 2020.

Intelligence

Ambient intelligence and autonomous control are not part of the original concept of the Internet of things. Ambient intelligence and autonomous control do not necessarily require Internet structures, either. However, there is a shift in research (by companies such as Intel) to integrate the concepts of the IoT and autonomous control, with initial outcomes towards this direction considering objects as the driving force for autonomous IoT. An approach in this context is deep reinforcement learning where most of IoT systems provide a dynamic and interactive environment. Training an agent (i.e., IoT device) to behave smartly in such an environment cannot be addressed by conventional machine learning algorithms such as supervised learning. By reinforcement learning approach, a learning agent can sense the environment's state (e.g., sensing home temperature), perform actions (e.g., turn HVAC on or off) and learn through the maximizing accumulated rewards it receives in long term.

IoT intelligence can be offered at three levels: IoT devices, Edge/Fog nodes, and cloud computing. The need for intelligent control and decision at each level depends on the time sensitiveness of the IoT application. For example, an autonomous vehicle's camera needs to make real-time obstacle detection to avoid an accident. This fast decision making would not be possible through transferring data from the vehicle to cloud instances and return the predictions back to the vehicle. Instead, all the operation should be performed locally in the vehicle. Integrating advanced machine learning algorithms including deep learning into IoT devices is an active research area to make smart objects closer to reality. Moreover, it is possible to get the most value out of IoT deployments through analyzing IoT data, extracting hidden information, and predicting control decisions. A wide variety of machine learning techniques have been used in IoT domain ranging from traditional methods such as regression, support vector machine, and random forest to advanced ones such as convolutional neural networks, LSTM, and variational autoencoder.

In the future, the Internet of things may be a non-deterministic and open network in which auto-organized or intelligent entities (web services, SOA components) and virtual objects (avatars) will be interoperable and able to act independently (pursuing their own objectives or shared ones) depending on the context, circumstances or environments. Autonomous behavior through the collection and reasoning of context information as well as the object's ability to detect changes in the environment (faults affecting sensors) and introduce suitable mitigation measures constitutes a major research trend, clearly needed to provide credibility to the IoT technology. Modern IoT products and solutions in the marketplace use a variety of different technologies to support such context-aware automation, but more sophisticated forms of intelligence are requested to permit sensor units and intelligent cyber-physical systems to be deployed in real environments.

Architecture

IoT system architecture, in its simplistic view, consists of three tiers: Tier 1: Devices, Tier 2: the Edge Gateway, and Tier 3: the Cloud. Devices include networked things, such as the sensors and actuators found in IoT equipment, particularly those that use protocols such as Modbus, Bluetooth, Zigbee, or proprietary protocols, to connect to an Edge Gateway. The Edge Gateway layer consists of sensor data aggregation systems called Edge Gateways that provide functionality, such as pre-processing of the data, securing connectivity to cloud, using systems such as WebSockets, the event hub, and, even in some cases, edge analytics or fog computing. Edge Gateway layer is also required to give a common view of the devices to the upper layers to facilitate in easier management. The final tier includes the cloud application built for IoT using the microservices architecture, which are usually polyglot and inherently secure in nature using HTTPS/OAuth. It includes various database systems that store sensor data, such as time series databases or asset stores using backend data storage systems (e.g. Cassandra, PostgreSQL). The cloud tier in most cloud-based IoT system features event queuing and messaging system that handles communication that transpires in all tiers. Some experts classified the three-tiers in the IoT system as edge, platform, and enterprise and these are connected by proximity network, access network, and service network, respectively.

Building on the Internet of things, the web of things is an architecture for the application layer of the Internet of things looking at the convergence of data from IoT devices into Web applications to create innovative use-cases. In order to program and control the flow of information in the Internet of things, a predicted architectural direction is being called BPM Everywhere which is a blending of traditional process management with process mining and special capabilities to automate the control of large numbers of coordinated devices.

Network Architecture

The Internet of things requires huge scalability in the network space to handle the surge of devices. IETF 6LoWPAN can be used to connect devices to IP networks. With billions of devices being added to the Internet space, IPv6 will play a major role in handling the network layer scalability. IETF's Constrained Application Protocol, ZeroMQ, and MQTT can provide lightweight data transport. In practice many groups of IoT devices are hidden behind gateway nodes and may not have unique addresses. Also the vision of everything-interconnected is not needed for most applications as it is mainly the data which need interconnecting at a higher layer.

Fog computing is a viable alternative to prevent such a large burst of data flow through the Internet. The edge devices' computation power to analyze and process data is extremely limited. Limited processing power is a key attribute of IoT devices as their purpose is to supply data about physical objects while remaining autonomous. Heavy processing requirements use more battery power harming IoT's ability to operate. Scalability is easy because IoT devices simply supply data through the internet to a server with sufficient processing power.

Decentralized IoT:

- Decentralized Internet of things, or decentralized IoT, is a modified IoT which utilizes fog computing to handle and balance requests of connected IoT devices in order to reduce loading on the cloud servers and improve responsiveness for latency-sensitive IoT applications like vital signs monitoring of patients, vehicle-to-vehicle communication of autonomous driving, and critical failure detection of industrial devices. Performance is improved, especially for huge IoT systems with millions of nodes.
- Conventional IoT is connected via a mesh network and led by a major head node (centralized controller). The head node decides how a data is created, stored, and transmitted. In contrast, decentralized IoT attempts to divide IoT systems into smaller divisions. The head node authorizes partial decision-making power to lower level sub-nodes under mutual agreed policy.
- Some approached to decentralized IoT attempts to address the limited bandwidth and hashing capacity of battery powered or wireless IoT devices via blockchain.

Complexity

In semi-open or closed loops (i.e., value chains, whenever a global finality can be settled) the IoT will often be considered and studied as a complex system due to the huge number of different links, interactions between autonomous actors, and its capacity to integrate new actors. At the overall stage (full open loop) it will likely be seen as a chaotic environment (since systems always have finality). As a practical approach, not all elements on the Internet of things run in a global, public space. Subsystems are often implemented to mitigate the risks of privacy, control and reliability. For example, domestic robotics (domotics) running inside a smart home might only share data within and be available via a local network. Managing and controlling a high dynamic ad hoc IoT things/devices network is a tough task with the traditional networks architecture, Software Defined Networking (SDN) provides the agile dynamic solution that can cope with the special requirements of the diversity of innovative IoT applications.

Space Considerations

In the Internet of things, the precise geographic location of a thing—and also the precise geographic dimensions of a thing—can be critical. Therefore, facts about a thing, such as its location in time and space, have been less critical to track because the person processing the information can decide whether or not that information was important to the action being taken, and if so, add the missing information (or decide to not take the action).

(Note that some things on the Internet of things will be sensors, and sensor location is usually important.) The GeoWeb and Digital Earth are applications that become possible when things can become organized and connected by location. However, the challenges that remain include the constraints of variable spatial scales, the need to handle massive amounts of data, and an indexing for fast search and neighbour operations. On the Internet of things, if things are able to take actions on their own initiative, this human-centric mediation role is eliminated. Thus, the time-space context that we as humans take for granted must be given a central role in this information ecosystem. Just as standards play a key role on the Internet and the Web, geo-spatial standards will play a key role on the Internet of things.

A Solution to "Basket of Remotes"

Many IoT devices have the potential to take a piece of this market. Jean-Louis Gassée (Apple initial alumni team, and BeOS co-founder) has addressed this topic in an article on Monday Note, where he predicts that the most likely problem will be what he calls the "basket of remotes" problem, where we'll have hundreds of applications to interface with hundreds of devices that don't share protocols for speaking with one another. For improved user interaction, some technology leaders are joining forces to create standards for communication between devices to solve this problem. Others are turning to the concept of predictive interaction of devices, "where collected data is used to predict and trigger actions on the specific devices" while making them work together.

Social Internet of Things

Social Internet of things (SIoT) is a new kind of IoT that focuses the importance of social interaction and relationship between IoT devices. SIoT is a pattern of how cross-domain IoT devices enabling application to application communication and collaboration without human intervention in order to serve their owners with autonomous services, and this only can be realized when gained low-level architecture support from both IoT software and hardware engineering.

Social Network for IoT Devices (Not Human)

IoT defines a device with an identity like a citizen in a community and connect them to the internet to provide services to its users. SIoT defines a social network for IoT devices only to interact with each other for different goals that to serve human.

How is SIoT different from IoT?

SIoT is different from the original IoT in terms of the collaboration characteristics. IoT is passive, it was set to serve for dedicated purposes with existing IoT devices in predetermined system. SIoT is active, it was programmed and managed by AI to serve for unplanned purposes with mix and match of potential IoT devices from different systems that benefit its users.

How does SIoT Work?

IoT devices built-in with sociability will broadcast their abilities or functionalities, and at the same time discovers, navigates and groups with other IoT devices in the same or nearby network for useful service compositions in order to help its users proactively in every day's life especially during emergency.

Social IoT Examples

1. IoT-based smart home technology monitors health data of patients or aging adults by analyzing their physiological parameters and prompt the nearby health facilities when emergency medical services needed. In case emergency, automatically, ambulance of a nearest available hospital will be called with pickup location provided, ward assigned, patient's health data will be transmitted to the emergency department, and display on the doctor's computer immediately for further action.
2. IoT sensors on the vehicles, road and traffic lights monitor the conditions of the vehicles and drivers and alert when attention needed and also coordinate themselves automatically to ensure autonomous driving is working normally. Unfortunately if an accident happens, IoT camera will inform the nearest hospital and police station for help.

Social IoT Challenges

1. Internet of things is multifaceted and complicated. One of the main factors that hindering people from adopting and use Internet of things (IoT) based products and services is its complexity. Installation and setup is a challenge to people, therefore, there is a need for IoT devices to mix match and configure themselves automatically to provide different services at different situation.
2. System security always a concern for any technology, and it is more crucial for SIoT as not only security of oneself need to be considered but also the mutual trust mechanism between collaborative IoT devices from time to time, from place to place.
3. Another critical challenge for SIoT is the accuracy and reliability of the sensors. At most of the circumstances, IoT sensors would need to respond in nanoseconds to avoid accidents, injury, and loss of life.

Enabling Technologies

There are many technologies that enable the IoT. Crucial to the field is the network used to communicate between devices of an IoT installation, a role that several wireless or wired technologies may fulfill:

Addressability

The original idea of the Auto-ID Center is based on RFID-tags and distinct identification through the Electronic Product Code. This has evolved into objects having an IP address or URI. An alternative view, from the world of the Semantic Web focuses instead on making all things (not just those electronic, smart, or RFID-enabled) addressable by the existing naming protocols, such as URI. The objects themselves do not converse, but they may now be referred to by other agents, such as powerful centralised servers acting for their human owners. Integration with the Internet implies that devices will use an IP address as a distinct identifier. Due to the limited address space of IPv4 (which allows for 4.3 billion different addresses), objects in the IoT will have to use the next generation of the Internet protocol (IPv6) to scale to the extremely large address space required. Internet-of-things devices additionally will benefit from the stateless address auto-configuration present in IPv6, as it reduces the configuration overhead on the hosts, and the IETF 6LoWPAN header compression. To a large extent, the future of the Internet of things will not be possible without the support of IPv6; and consequently, the global adoption of IPv6 in the coming years will be critical for the successful development of the IoT in the future.

Application Layer

- ADRC defines an application layer protocol and supporting framework for implementing IoT applications.

Short-range Wireless

- Bluetooth mesh networking: Specification providing a mesh networking variant to Bluetooth Low Energy (BLE) with an increased number of nodes and standardized application layer (Models).
- Li-Fi (light fidelity): Wireless communication technology similar to the Wi-Fi standard, but using visible-light communication for increased bandwidth.
- Near-field communication (NFC): Communication protocols enabling two electronic devices to communicate within a 4 cm range.
- Radio-frequency identification (RFID): Technology using electromagnetic fields to read data stored in tags embedded in other items.
- Wi-Fi: Technology for local area networking based on the IEEE 802.11 standard, where devices may communicate through a shared access point or directly between individual devices.

- Zigbee: Communication protocols for personal area networking based on the IEEE 802.15.4 standard, providing low power consumption, low data rate, low cost, and high throughput.
- Z-Wave: Wireless communications protocol used primarily for home automation and security applications

Medium-range Wireless

- LTE-Advanced: High-speed communication specification for mobile networks. Provides enhancements to the LTE standard with extended coverage, higher throughput, and lower latency.
- 5G: 5G wireless networks can be used to achieve the high communication requirements of the IoT and connect a large number of IoT devices, even when they are on the move. There are three features of 5G that are each considered to be useful for supporting particular elements of IoT: enhanced mobile broadband (eMBB), massive machine type communications (mMTC) and ultra-reliable low latency communications (URLLC).

Long-range Wireless

- Low-power wide-area networking (LPWAN): Wireless networks designed to allow long-range communication at a low data rate, reducing power and cost for transmission. Available LPWAN technologies and protocols: LoRaWan, Sigfox, NB-IoT, Weightless, RPMA, MIoTy.
- Very-small-aperture terminal (VSAT): Satellite communication technology using small dish antennas for narrowband and broadband data.

Wired

- Ethernet: General purpose networking standard using twisted pair and fiber optic links in conjunction with hubs or switches.
- Power-line communication (PLC): Communication technology using electrical wiring to carry power and data. Specifications such as HomePlug or G.hn utilize PLC for networking IoT devices.

Politics and Civic Engagement

Some scholars and activists argue that the IoT can be used to create new models of civic engagement if device networks can be open to user control and interoperable platforms. Philip N. Howard, a professor and author, writes that political life in both democracies and authoritarian regimes will be shaped by the way the IoT will be used for civic engagement. For that to happen, he argues that any connected device should be able to divulge a list of the "ultimate beneficiaries" of its sensor data and that individual citizens should be able to add new organisations to the beneficiary list. In addition, he argues that civil society groups need to start developing their IoT strategy for making use of data and engaging with the public.

Government Regulation

One of the key drivers of the IoT is data. The success of the idea of connecting devices to make them more efficient is dependent upon access to and storage & processing of data. For this purpose, companies working on the IoT collect data from multiple sources and store it in their cloud network for further processing. This leaves the door wide open for privacy and security dangers and single point vulnerability of multiple systems. The other issues pertain to consumer choice and ownership of data and how it is used.

Though still in their infancy, regulations and governance regarding these issues of privacy, security, and data ownership continue to develop. IoT regulation depends on the country. Some examples of legislation that is relevant to privacy and data collection are: the US Privacy Act of 1974, OECD Guidelines on the Protection of Privacy and Transborder Flows of Personal Data of 1980, and the EU Directive 95/46/EC of 1995.

Current Regulatory Environment

A report published by the Federal Trade Commission (FTC) in January 2015 made the following three recommendations:

- Data security: At the time of designing IoT companies should ensure that data collection, storage and processing would be secure at all times. Companies should adopt a "defense in depth" approach and encrypt data at each stage.
- Data consent: Users should have a choice as to what data they share with IoT companies and the users must be informed if their data gets exposed.
- Data minimisation: IoT companies should collect only the data they need and retain the collected information only for a limited time.

However, the FTC stopped at just making recommendations for now. According to an FTC analysis, the existing framework, consisting of the FTC Act, the Fair Credit Reporting Act, and the Children's Online Privacy Protection Act, along with developing consumer education and business guidance, participation in multi-stakeholder efforts and advocacy to other agencies at the federal, state and local level, is sufficient to protect consumer rights.

A resolution passed by the Senate in March 2015, is already being considered by the Congress. This resolution recognized the need for formulating a National Policy on IoT and the matter of privacy, security and spectrum. Furthermore, to provide an impetus to the IoT ecosystem, in March 2016, a bipartisan group of four Senators proposed a bill, The Developing Innovation and Growing the Internet of Things

(DIGIT) Act, to direct the Federal Communications Commission to assess the need for more spectrum to connect IoT devices.

Approved on 28 September 2018, California Senate Bill No. 327 goes into effect on 1 January 2020. The bill requires "a manufacturer of a connected device, as those terms are defined, to equip the device with a reasonable security feature or features that are appropriate to the nature and function of the device, appropriate to the information it may collect, contain, or transmit, and designed to protect the device and any information contained therein from unauthorized access, destruction, use, modification, or disclosure,"

Several standards for the IoT industry are actually being established relating to automobiles because most concerns arising from use of connected cars apply to healthcare devices as well. In fact, the National Highway Traffic Safety Administration (NHTSA) is preparing cybersecurity guidelines and a database of best practices to make automotive computer systems more secure.

A recent report from the World Bank examines the challenges and opportunities in government adoption of IoT. These include –

- Still early days for the IoT in government
- Underdeveloped policy and regulatory frameworks
- Unclear business models, despite strong value proposition
- Clear institutional and capacity gap in government AND the private sector
- Inconsistent data valuation and management
- Infrastructure a major barrier
- Government as an enabler
- Most successful pilots share common characteristics (public-private partnership, local, leadership)

In early December 2021, the U.K. government introduced the Product Security and Telecommunications Infrastructure bill (PST), an effort to legislate IoT distributors, manufacturers, and importers to meet certain cybersecurity standards. The bill also seeks to improve the security credentials of consumer IoT devices.

Criticism, Problems and Controversies

Platform Fragmentation

The IoT suffers from platform fragmentation, lack of interoperability and common technical standards a situation where the variety of IoT devices, in terms of both hardware variations and differences in the software running on them, makes the task of developing applications that work consistently between different inconsistent technology ecosystems hard. For example, wireless connectivity for IoT devices can be done using Bluetooth, Wi-Fi, Wi-Fi HaLow, Zigbee, Z-Wave,

LoRa, NB-IoT, Cat M1 as well as completely custom proprietary radios – each with its own advantages and disadvantages; and unique support ecosystem. The IoT's amorphous computing nature is also a problem for security, since patches to bugs found in the core operating system often do not reach users of older and lower-price devices. One set of researchers says that the failure of vendors to support older devices with patches and updates leaves more than 87% of active Android devices vulnerable.

Privacy, Autonomy and Control

Philip N. Howard, a professor and author, writes that the Internet of things offers immense potential for empowering citizens, making government transparent, and broadening information access. Howard cautions, however, that privacy threats are enormous, as is the potential for social control and political manipulation.

Concerns about privacy have led many to consider the possibility that big data infrastructures such as the Internet of things and data mining are inherently incompatible with privacy. Key challenges of increased digitalization in the water, transport or energy sector are related to privacy and cybersecurity which necessitate an adequate response from research and policymakers alike.

Writer Adam Greenfield claims that IoT technologies are not only an invasion of public space but are also being used to perpetuate normative behavior, citing an instance of billboards with hidden cameras that tracked the demographics of passersby who stopped to read the advertisement.

The Internet of Things Council compared the increased prevalence of digital surveillance due to the Internet of things to the conceptual panopticon described by Jeremy Bentham in the 18th century. The assertion was defended by the works of French philosophers Michel Foucault and Gilles Deleuze. In Discipline and Punish: The Birth of the Prison, Foucault asserts that the panopticon was a central element of the discipline society developed during the Industrial Era. Foucault also argued that the discipline systems established in factories and school reflected Bentham's vision of panopticism. In his 1992 paper "Postscripts on the Societies of Control", Deleuze wrote that the discipline society had transitioned into a control society, with the computer replacing the panopticon as an instrument of discipline and control while still maintaining the qualities similar to that of panopticism.

Peter-Paul Verbeek, a professor of philosophy of technology at the University of Twente, Netherlands, writes that technology already influences our moral decision making, which in turn affects human agency, privacy and autonomy. He cautions against viewing technology merely as a human tool and advocates instead to consider it as an active agent.

Justin Brookman, of the Center for Democracy and Technology, expressed concern regarding the impact of the IoT on consumer privacy, saying that "There are some people in the commercial space who say, 'Oh, big data – well, let's collect everything, keep it around forever, we'll pay for somebody to think about security later.' The question is whether we want to have some sort of policy framework in place to limit that."

Tim O'Reilly believes that the way companies sell the IoT devices on consumers are misplaced, disputing the notion that the IoT is about gaining efficiency from putting all kinds of devices online and postulating that the "IoT is really about human augmentation. The applications are profoundly different when you have sensors and data driving the decision-making."

Editorials at WIRED have also expressed concern, one stating "What you're about to lose is your privacy. Actually, it's worse than that. You aren't just going to lose your privacy, you're going to have to watch the very concept of privacy be rewritten under your nose."

The American Civil Liberties Union (ACLU) expressed concern regarding the ability of IoT to erode people's control over their own lives. The ACLU wrote that "There's simply no way to forecast how these immense powers – disproportionately accumulating in the hands of corporations seeking financial advantage and governments craving ever more control – will be used. Chances are big data and the Internet of Things will make it harder for us to control our own lives, as we grow increasingly transparent to powerful corporations and government institutions that are becoming more opaque to us."

In response to rising concerns about privacy and smart technology, in 2007 the British Government stated it would follow formal Privacy by Design principles when implementing their smart metering program. The program would lead to replacement of traditional power meters with smart power meters, which could track and manage energy usage more accurately. However the British Computer Society is doubtful these principles were ever actually implemented. In 2009 the Dutch Parliament rejected a similar smart metering program, basing their decision on privacy concerns. The Dutch program later revised and passed in 2011.

Data Storage

A challenge for producers of IoT applications is to clean, process and interpret the vast amount of data which is gathered by the sensors. There is a solution proposed for the analytics of the information referred to as Wireless Sensor Networks. These networks share data among sensor nodes that are sent to a distributed system for the analytics of the sensory data.

Another challenge is the storage of this bulk data. Depending on the application, there could be high data acquisition requirements, which in turn lead to high storage requirements. In 2013, the Internet was estimated to be responsible for consuming 5% of the total energy produced, and a "daunting challenge to power" IoT devices to collect and even store data still remains.

Data silos, although a common challenge of legacy systems, still commonly occur with the implementation of IoT devices, particularly within manufacturing. As there are a lot of benefits to be gained from IoT and IIoT devices, the means in which the data is stored can present serious challenges without the principles of autonomy, transparency, and interoperability being considered. The challenges do not occur by the device itself, but the means in which databases and data warehouses are set-up. These challenges were commonly identified in manufactures and enterprises which have begun upon digital transformation, and are part of the digital foundation, indicating that in order to receive the optimal benefits from IoT devices and for decision making, enterprises will have to first re-align their data storing methods. These challenges were identified by Keller (2021) when investigating the IT and application landscape of I4.0 implementation within German M&E manufactures.

Security

Security is the biggest concern in adopting Internet of things technology, with concerns that rapid development is happening without appropriate consideration of the profound security challenges involved and the regulatory changes that might be necessary. The rapid development of the Internet of Things (IoT) has allowed billions of devices to connect to the network. Due to too many connected devices and the limitation of communication security technology, various security issues gradually appear in the IoT.

Most of the technical security concerns are similar to those of conventional servers, workstations and smartphones. These concerns include using weak authentication, forgetting to change default credentials, unencrypted messages sent between devices, SQL injections, man-in-the-middle attacks, and poor handling of security updates. However, many IoT devices have severe operational limitations on the computational power available to them. These constraints often make them unable to directly use basic security measures such as implementing firewalls or using strong cryptosystems to encrypt their communications with other devices - and the low price and consumer focus of many devices makes a robust security patching system uncommon.

Rather than conventional security vulnerabilities, fault injection attacks are on the rise and targeting IoT devices. A fault injection attack is a physical attack on a device to purposefully introduce faults in the system to change the intended behavior. Faults might happen unintentionally by environmental noises and electromagnetic fields. There are ideas stemmed from control-flow integrity (CFI) to prevent fault injection attacks and system recovery to a healthy state before the fault.

Internet of things devices also have access to new areas of data, and can often control physical devices, so that even by 2014 it was possible to say that many Internet-connected appliances could already "spy on people in their own homes" including televisions, kitchen appliances, cameras, and thermostats. Computer-controlled devices in automobiles such as brakes, engine, locks, hood and trunk releases, horn, heat, and dashboard have been shown to be vulnerable to attackers who have access to the on-board network. In some cases, vehicle computer systems are Internet-connected, allowing them to be exploited remotely. By 2008 security researchers had shown the ability to remotely control pacemakers without authority. Later hackers demonstrated remote control of insulin pumps and implantable cardioverter defibrillators.

Poorly secured Internet-accessible IoT devices can also be subverted to attack others. In 2016, a distributed denial of service attack powered by Internet of things devices running the Mirai malware took down a DNS provider and major web sites. The Mirai Botnet had infected roughly 65,000 IoT devices within the first 20 hours. Eventually the infections increased to around 200,000 to 300,000 infections. Brazil, Colombia and Vietnam made up of 41.5% of the infections. The Mirai Botnet had singled out specific IoT devices that consisted of DVRs, IP cameras, routers and printers. Top vendors that contained the most infected devices were identified as Dahua, Huawei, ZTE, Cisco, ZyXEL and MikroTik. In May 2017, Junade Ali, a Computer Scientist at Cloudflare noted that native DDoS vulnerabilities exist in IoT devices due to a poor implementation of the Publish–subscribe pattern. These sorts of attacks have caused security experts to view IoT as a real threat to Internet services.

The U.S. National Intelligence Council in an unclassified report maintains that it would be hard to deny "access to networks of sensors and remotely-controlled objects by enemies of the United States, criminals, and mischief makers... An open market for aggregated sensor data could serve the interests of commerce and security no less than it helps criminals and spies identify vulnerable targets. Thus, massively parallel sensor fusion may undermine social cohesion, if it proves to be fundamentally incompatible with Fourth-Amendment guarantees against unreasonable search." In general, the intelligence community views the Internet of things as a rich source of data.

On 31 January 2019, the Washington Post wrote an article regarding the security and ethical challenges that can occur with IoT doorbells and cameras: "Last month, Ring got caught allowing its team in Ukraine to view and annotate certain user videos; the company says it only looks at publicly shared videos and those from Ring owners who provide consent. Just last week, a California family's Nest camera let a hacker take over and broadcast fake audio warnings about a missile attack, not to mention peer in on them, when they used a weak password."

There have been a range of responses to concerns over security. The Internet of Things Security Foundation (IoTSF) was launched on 23 September 2015 with a mission to secure the Internet of things by promoting knowledge and best practice. Its founding board is made from technology providers and telecommunications companies. In addition, large IT companies are continually developing innovative solutions to ensure the security of IoT devices. In 2017, Mozilla launched Project Things, which allows to route IoT devices through a safe Web of Things gateway. As per the estimates from KBV Research, the overall IoT security market would grow at 27.9% rate during 2016–2022 as a result of growing infrastructural concerns and diversified usage of Internet of things.

Governmental regulation is argued by some to be necessary to secure IoT devices and the wider Internet – as market incentives to secure IoT devices is insufficient. It was found that due to the nature of most of the IoT development boards, they generate predictable and weak keys which make it easy to be utilized by man-in-the-middle attack. However, various hardening approaches were proposed by many researchers to resolve the issue of SSH weak implementation and weak keys.

IoT security within the field of manufacturing presents different challenges, and varying perspectives. Within the EU and Germany, data protection is constantly referenced throughout manufacturing and digital policy particularly that of I4.0. However, the attitude towards data security differs from the enterprise perspective whereas there is an emphasis on less data protection in the form of GDPR as the data being collected from IoT devices in the manufacturing sector does not display personal details. Yet, research has indicated that manufacturing experts are concerned about "data security for protecting machine technology from international competitors with the ever-greater push for interconnectivity".

Safety

IoT systems are typically controlled by event-driven smart apps that take as input either sensed data, user inputs, or other external triggers (from the Internet) and command one or more actuators towards providing different forms of automation. Examples of sensors include smoke detectors, motion sensors, and contact sensors. Examples of actuators include smart locks, smart power outlets, and door controls. Popular control platforms on which third-party developers can build smart apps that interact wirelessly with these sensors and actuators include Samsung's SmartThings, Apple's HomeKit, and Amazon's Alexa, among others.

A problem specific to IoT systems is that buggy apps, unforeseen bad app interactions, or device/communication failures, can cause unsafe and dangerous physical states, e.g., "unlock the entrance door when no one is at home" or "turn off the heater when the temperature is below 0 degrees Celsius and people are sleeping at night". Detecting flaws that lead to such states, requires a holistic view of installed apps, component devices, their configurations, and more importantly, how they interact. Recently, researchers from the University of California Riverside have proposed IotSan, a novel practical system that uses model checking as a building block to reveal "interaction-level" flaws by identifying events that can lead the system to unsafe states. They have evaluated IotSan on the Samsung SmartThings platform. From 76 manually configured systems, IotSan detects 147 vulnerabilities (i.e., violations of safe physical states/properties).

Design

Given widespread recognition of the evolving nature of the design and management of the Internet of things, sustainable and secure deployment of IoT solutions must design for "anarchic scalability". Application of the concept of anarchic scalability can be extended to physical systems (i.e., controlled real-world objects), by virtue of those systems being designed to account for uncertain management futures. This hard anarchic scalability thus provides a pathway forward to fully realize the potential of Internet-of-things solutions by selectively constraining physical systems to allow for all management regimes without risking physical failure.

Brown University computer scientist Michael Littman has argued that successful execution of the Internet of things requires consideration of the interface's usability as well as the technology itself. These interfaces need to be not only more user-friendly but also better integrated: "If users need to learn different interfaces for their vacuums, their locks, their sprinklers, their lights, and their coffeemakers, it's tough to say that their lives have been made any easier."

Environmental Sustainability Impact

A concern regarding Internet-of-things technologies pertains to the environmental impacts of the manufacture, use, and eventual disposal of all these semiconductor-rich devices. Modern electronics are replete with a wide variety of heavy metals and rare-earth metals, as well as highly toxic synthetic chemicals. This makes them extremely difficult to properly recycle. Electronic components are often incinerated or placed in regular landfills. Furthermore, the human and environmental cost of mining the rare-earth metals that are integral to modern electronic components continues to grow. This leads to societal questions concerning the environmental impacts of IoT devices over their lifetime.

Intentional Obsolescence of Devices

The Electronic Frontier Foundation has raised concerns that companies can use the technologies necessary to support connected devices to intentionally disable or "brick" their customers' devices via a remote software update or by disabling a service necessary to the operation of the device. In one example, home automation devices sold with the promise of a "Lifetime Subscription" were rendered useless after Nest Labs acquired Revolv and made the decision to shut down the central servers the Revolv devices had used to operate. As Nest is a company owned by Alphabet (Google's parent company), the EFF argues this sets a "terrible precedent for a company with ambitions to sell self-driving cars, medical devices, and other high-end gadgets that may be essential to a person's livelihood or physical safety."

Owners should be free to point their devices to a different server or collaborate on improved software. But such action violates the United States DMCA section 1201, which only has an exemption for "local use". This forces tinkerers who want to keep using their own equipment into a legal grey area. EFF thinks buyers should refuse electronics and software that prioritize the manufacturer's wishes above their own. Examples of post-sale manipulations include Google Nest Revolv, disabled privacy settings on Android, Sony disabling Linux on PlayStation 3, enforced EULA on Wii U.

Confusing Terminology

Kevin Lonergan at Information Age, a business technology magazine, has referred to the terms surrounding the IoT as a "terminology zoo". The lack of clear terminology is not "useful from a practical point of view" and a "source of confusion for the end user". A company operating in the IoT space could be working in anything related to sensor technology, networking, embedded systems, or analytics. According to Lonergan, the term IoT was coined before smart phones, tablets, and devices as we know them today existed, and there is a long list of terms with varying degrees of overlap and technological convergence: Internet of things, Internet of everything (IoE), Internet of goods (supply chain), industrial Internet, pervasive computing, pervasive sensing, ubiquitous computing, cyber-physical systems (CPS), wireless sensor networks (WSN), smart objects, digital twin, cyberobjects or avatars, cooperating objects, machine to machine (M2M), ambient intelligence (AmI), Operational technology (OT), and information technology (IT). Regarding IIoT, an industrial sub-field of IoT, the Industrial Internet Consortium's Vocabulary Task Group has created a "common and reusable vocabulary of terms" to ensure "consistent terminology" across publications issued by the Industrial Internet Consortium. IoT One has created an IoT Terms Database including a New Term Alert to be notified when a new term is published. As of March 2020, this database aggregates 807 IoT-related terms, while keeping material "transparent and comprehensive".

Adoption Barriers

Lack of Interoperability and Unclear Value Propositions

Despite a shared belief in the potential of the IoT, industry leaders and consumers are facing barriers to adopt IoT technology more widely. Mike Farley argued in Forbes that while IoT solutions appeal to early adopters, they either lack interoperability or a clear use case for end-users. A study by Ericsson regarding the adoption of IoT among Danish companies suggests that many struggle "to pinpoint exactly where the value of IoT lies for them".

Privacy and Security Concerns

As for IoT, especially in regards to consumer IoT, information about a user's daily routine is collected so that the "things" around the user can cooperate to provide better services that fulfill personal preference. When the collected information which describes a user in detail travels through multiple hops in a network, due to a diverse integration of services, devices and network, the information stored on a device is vulnerable to privacy violation by compromising nodes existing in an IoT network.

For example, on 21 October 2016, a multiple distributed denial of service (DDoS) attacks systems operated by domain name system provider Dyn, which caused the inaccessibility of several websites, such as GitHub, Twitter, and others. This attack is executed through a botnet consisting of a large number of IoT devices including IP cameras, gateways, and even baby monitors.

Fundamentally there are 4 security objectives that the IoT system requires: (1) data confidentiality: unauthorised parties cannot have access to the transmitted and stored data; (2) data integrity: intentional and unintentional corruption of transmitted and stored data must be detected; (3) non-repudiation: the sender cannot deny having sent a given message; (4) data availability: the transmitted and stored data should be available to authorised parties even with the denial-of-service (DOS) attacks.

Information privacy regulations also require organisations to practice "reasonable security". California's SB-327 Information privacy: connected devices "would require a manufacturer of a connected device, as those terms are defined, to equip the device with a reasonable security feature or features that are appropriate to the nature and function of the device, appropriate to the information it may collect, contain, or transmit, and designed to protect the device and any information contained therein from unauthorised access, destruction, use, modification, or disclosure, as specified". As each organisation's environment is unique, it can prove challenging to demonstrate what "reasonable security" is and what potential risks could be involved for the business. Oregon's HB 2395 Archived 30 September 2020 at the Wayback Machine also "requires [a] person that manufactures, sells or offers to sell connected device] manufacturer to equip connected device with reasonable security features that protect connected device and information that connected device collects, contains, stores or transmits] stores from access, destruction, modification, use or disclosure that consumer does not authorise."

According to antivirus provider Kaspersky, there were 639 million data breaches of IoT devices in 2020 and 1.5 billion breaches in the first six months of 2021.

Traditional Governance Structure

A study issued by Ericsson regarding the adoption of Internet of things among Danish companies identified a "clash between IoT and companies' traditional governance structures, as IoT still presents both uncertainties and a lack of historical precedence." Among the respondents interviewed, 60 percent stated that they "do not believe they have the organizational capabilities, and three of four do not believe they have the processes needed, to capture the IoT opportunity." This has led to a need to understand organizational culture in order to facilitate organizational design processes and to test new innovation management practices. A lack of digital leadership in the age of digital transformation has also stifled innovation and IoT adoption to a degree that many companies, in the face of uncertainty, "were waiting for the market dynamics to play out", or further action in regards to IoT "was pending competitor moves, customer pull, or regulatory requirements". Some of these companies risk being "kodaked" – "Kodak was a market leader until digital disruption eclipsed film photography with digital photos" – failing to "see the disruptive forces affecting their industry" and "to truly embrace the new business models the disruptive change opens up". Scott Anthony has written in Harvard Business Review that Kodak "created a digital camera, invested in the technology, and even understood that photos would be shared online" but ultimately failed to realize that "online photo sharing was the new business, not just a way to expand the printing business."

Business Planning and Project Management

According to 2018 study, 70–75% of IoT deployments were stuck in the pilot or prototype stage, unable to reach scale due in part to a lack of business planning.

Even though scientists, engineers, and managers across the world are continuously working to create and exploit the benefits of IoT products, there are some flaws in the governance, management and implementation of such projects. Despite tremendous forward momentum in the field of information and other underlying technologies, IoT still remains a complex area and the problem of how IoT projects are managed still needs to be addressed. IoT projects must be run differently than simple and traditional IT, manufacturing or construction projects. Because IoT projects have longer project timelines, a lack of skilled resources and several security/legal issues, there is a need for new and specifically designed project processes. The following management techniques should improve the success rate of IoT projects:

- A separate research and development phase
- A Proof-of-Concept/Prototype before the actual project begins
- Project managers with interdisciplinary technical knowledge
- Universally defined business and technical jargon

5.4.2 Fundamentals of IoT in 5G

IoT in 5G refers to the integration of IoT devices and sensors with 5G networks, enabling seamless communication and data exchange between billions of interconnected devices and applications. Unlike previous generations of wireless technology, which may have struggled to support the massive scale and density of IoT deployments, 5G offers several key features that make it ideally suited for IoT applications:

1. High-Speed Connectivity: 5G networks offer significantly faster speeds compared to previous generations of wireless technology, enabling IoT devices and sensors to transmit and receive data more quickly and efficiently. This is essential for applications such as real-time monitoring, video surveillance, and autonomous vehicles, which require high-speed connectivity to operate effectively.
2. Low Latency: 5G networks provide ultra-low latency, reducing the delay between data transmission and reception to milliseconds or even microseconds. This enables real-time communication and control for critical IoT applications such as industrial automation, healthcare, and public safety, where even the slightest delay can have serious consequences.
3. Massive Connectivity: 5G networks support massive connectivity, allowing billions of devices and sensors to connect to the internet simultaneously. This scalability is essential for IoT deployments in smart cities, smart homes, smart grids, and other environments with large numbers of interconnected devices and sensors.
4. Reliability and Security: 5G networks offer enhanced reliability and security features, protecting IoT devices and sensors from threats such as cyberattacks, malware, and unauthorized access. This is critical for ensuring the integrity, confidentiality, and availability of IoT data and systems, particularly in sensitive and mission-critical applications.

5.4.3 Benefits of IoT in 5G

IoT in 5G offers several benefits over previous generations of wireless technology, including:

1. Improved Efficiency: IoT in 5G enables organizations to optimize operations, reduce costs, and improve efficiency by leveraging real-time data insights and analytics to make informed decisions and automate processes.
2. Enhanced Productivity: IoT in 5G enables workers to access information and collaborate more effectively, whether they are in the office, in the field, or working remotely. This improves productivity and flexibility, enabling organizations to adapt to changing business requirements and market conditions more quickly and efficiently.
3. Greater Innovation: IoT in 5G unlocks new possibilities for innovation and creativity, enabling organizations to develop new products, services, and business models that leverage the power of connected devices and sensors to address customer needs and market opportunities.

4. Sustainable Growth: IoT in 5G enables organizations to reduce resource consumption, minimize waste, and optimize energy usage, leading to more sustainable and environmentally friendly operations and practices.

5.4.4 Applications of IoT in 5G

IoT in 5G enables a wide range of applications and services across various industries and sectors, including:

1. Smart Cities: IoT in 5G enables smart city initiatives such as intelligent transportation systems, environmental monitoring, smart lighting, and waste management, allowing cities to become more efficient, sustainable, and livable.
2. Smart Homes: IoT in 5G enables smart home devices such as thermostats, security cameras, and appliances to communicate and collaborate seamlessly, providing homeowners with greater convenience, comfort, and security.
3. Industrial Automation: IoT in 5G supports industrial automation and smart manufacturing applications such as asset tracking, predictive maintenance, and remote monitoring and control of machinery and equipment, improving productivity, safety, and efficiency in factories and manufacturing plants.
4. Healthcare: IoT in 5G enables remote patient monitoring, telemedicine, and personalized healthcare applications, allowing healthcare providers to deliver better care, improve patient outcomes, and reduce healthcare costs.

5.4.5 Challenges and Implications for the Future

Despite its promising benefits and applications, IoT in 5G poses several challenges and considerations that must be addressed to realize its full potential:

1. Interoperability: IoT in 5G deployments may require interoperability across different devices, networks, and platforms, to ensure seamless integration and compatibility.
2. Security and Privacy: IoT in 5G devices and sensors may be vulnerable to security threats and privacy breaches, which can compromise the integrity, confidentiality, and availability of critical data and systems.
3. Regulatory and Compliance: IoT in 5G applications and services may be subject to regulatory requirements and compliance standards, particularly in highly regulated industries such as healthcare, transportation, and public safety, which may impose additional constraints and considerations on deployment and operation.

4. Resource Management: IoT in 5G deployments may require efficient resource management and allocation mechanisms to ensure optimal performance and reliability, particularly in environments with high levels of interference, congestion, and mobility.

CHAPTER 6

SECURITY AND PRIVACY IN 5G

6.1 SECURITY CHALLENGES IN 5G NETWORKS

As 5G technology continues to proliferate, promising faster speeds, lower latency, and greater reliability, the need to address security challenges becomes paramount. 5G networks are poised to transform industries, enable innovative applications, and connect billions of devices in the Internet of Things (IoT). However, with these opportunities come significant security risks, ranging from increased attack surfaces to new vulnerabilities introduced by the adoption of novel technologies. Security challenges in 5G networks pose significant risks to the integrity, confidentiality, and availability of network resources and services. Addressing these challenges requires a holistic approach that encompasses technical solutions, organizational policies, and user awareness. By implementing robust security measures, adopting best practices, and staying vigilant against emerging threats, organizations can mitigate the risks associated with 5G security and safeguard the next generation of connectivity against cyberattacks and vulnerabilities.

6.1.1 Security Challenges

1. Increased Attack Surface: 5G networks introduce a significantly expanded attack surface due to the proliferation of connected devices, the deployment of edge computing, and the integration of diverse technologies such as IoT, cloud computing, and artificial intelligence (AI). This broadens the potential vectors for cyberattacks, making it more challenging to defend against threats.
2. Virtualization and Software-Defined Networking (SDN): 5G networks rely heavily on virtualization and SDN to enable flexible, dynamic, and efficient resource allocation. While these technologies offer numerous benefits, they also introduce new security vulnerabilities, such as hypervisor attacks, software exploits, and unauthorized access to network functions.
3. Edge Computing and Mobile Edge Computing (MEC): Edge computing and MEC are integral components of 5G networks, enabling low-latency processing and data offloading at the network edge. However, the distributed nature of edge computing introduces security challenges related to data integrity, confidentiality, and access control, particularly in multi-tenant environments.

4. Network Slicing: Network slicing allows operators to partition a single physical network into multiple virtual networks, each tailored to specific use cases and applications. While network slicing offers enhanced flexibility and customization, it also introduces security concerns related to isolation, traffic management, and vulnerability propagation between slices.
5. Supply Chain Risks: The global nature of 5G supply chains introduces inherent risks related to the sourcing, manufacturing, and deployment of network equipment and components. Supply chain attacks, such as hardware tampering, counterfeit components, and supply chain compromise, pose significant threats to the integrity and security of 5G networks.

6.1.2 Potential Threats and Attacks

1. Denial-of-Service (DoS) Attacks: DoS attacks remain a significant threat to 5G networks, targeting network infrastructure, services, and IoT devices with overwhelming traffic or resource exhaustion. With the increased bandwidth and capacity of 5G networks, DoS attacks can cause widespread disruption and downtime, affecting critical services and operations.
2. Man-in-the-Middle (MitM) Attacks: MitM attacks intercept and manipulate communication between devices or systems, allowing attackers to eavesdrop on sensitive information, modify data packets, or impersonate legitimate entities. In 5G networks, MitM attacks can exploit vulnerabilities in protocols, encryption algorithms, and authentication mechanisms to compromise network integrity and confidentiality.
3. IoT Botnets: The proliferation of IoT devices in 5G networks introduces new opportunities for botnet attacks, where compromised devices are recruited into a network of malicious nodes controlled by an attacker. IoT botnets can be used to launch large-scale attacks, such as distributed denial-of-service (DDoS) attacks, spam campaigns, and credential stuffing attacks, posing significant risks to network availability and security.
4. Data Breaches and Privacy Violations: 5G networks carry vast amounts of sensitive data, including personal, financial, and business information, making them attractive targets for data breaches and privacy violations. Unauthorized access to data, data leaks, and data exfiltration can have serious consequences for individuals, organizations, and regulatory compliance.
5. Identity and Authentication Attacks: Identity and authentication attacks target weaknesses in user authentication mechanisms, such as weak passwords, stolen credentials, or compromised authentication tokens. In 5G networks, identity and authentication attacks can exploit vulnerabilities

in subscriber identity modules (SIMs), authentication protocols, and user authentication databases to gain unauthorized access to network resources and services.

6.1.3 Strategies for Mitigation

1. Network Segmentation and Isolation: Implementing network segmentation and isolation techniques to compartmentalize network traffic, segregate critical assets, and minimize the impact of security breaches or compromises.
2. Encryption and Authentication: Deploying strong encryption algorithms and authentication mechanisms to protect data in transit and verify the identity of users, devices, and applications accessing the network.
3. Intrusion Detection and Prevention Systems (IDPS): Deploying IDPS solutions to monitor network traffic, detect anomalies, and block malicious activities in real time, helping to identify and mitigate security threats before they can cause harm.
4. Patch Management and Vulnerability Scanning: Implementing robust patch management processes and vulnerability scanning procedures to identify and remediate security vulnerabilities in network infrastructure, software applications, and IoT devices.
5. Security Awareness and Training: Providing security awareness training and education to network administrators, employees, and end users to raise awareness of common security threats, best practices, and procedures for protecting sensitive information and assets.

6.2 AUTHENTICATION AND ENCRYPTION IN 5G

Authentication and encryption are essential components of 5G networks, providing mechanisms to verify the identity of users and devices and protect data privacy and confidentiality. As 5G technology continues to evolve and expand, the need for robust authentication and encryption mechanisms becomes increasingly critical to safeguard communication and ensure the integrity and security of network resources and services. Authentication and encryption are fundamental aspects of 5G networks, providing mechanisms to verify the identity of users/devices and protect data privacy and confidentiality. By implementing robust authentication and encryption mechanisms, 5G networks can ensure the integrity and security of communication and data transmission, safeguarding network resources and services against unauthorized access, interception, and tampering. As 5G technology continues to evolve and expand, addressing the challenges and considerations associated with authentication and encryption becomes increasingly critical to ensure the reliability, security, and resilience of 5G networks in the face of emerging threats and vulnerabilities.

6.2.1 Authentication in 5G

Authentication in 5G refers to the process of verifying the identity of users, devices, and applications attempting to access the network or services. Authentication ensures that only authorized entities are granted access to network resources and services, while unauthorized entities are denied access or blocked from accessing sensitive information or functionalities.

The key principles of authentication in 5G include:

1. Mutual Authentication: Mutual authentication requires both the user/device and the network to authenticate each other, ensuring mutual trust and verification of identities. This prevents unauthorized access and impersonation attacks, where malicious entities attempt to masquerade as legitimate users or devices.
2. Identity Management: Identity management involves the registration, provisioning, and maintenance of user/device identities within the network, including user credentials, device certificates, and access privileges. This ensures that identities are properly managed and authenticated throughout the lifecycle of the user/device.
3. Strong Authentication Mechanisms: 5G networks employ strong authentication mechanisms, such as digital certificates, biometric authentication, and multi-factor authentication (MFA), to enhance security and protect against unauthorized access and identity theft. These mechanisms require users/devices to provide multiple forms of verification, such as passwords, tokens, or biometric data, to prove their identity and gain access to network resources.
4. Secure Key Exchange: Secure key exchange protocols, such as the Transport Layer Security (TLS) protocol and the Internet Key Exchange (IKE) protocol, are used to establish secure communication channels between users/devices and the network, ensuring confidentiality and integrity of data transmission.

6.2.2 Encryption in 5G

Encryption in 5G refers to the process of encoding data in such a way that only authorized parties can access and decipher it, ensuring data privacy and confidentiality. Encryption protects sensitive information from eavesdropping, interception, and tampering during transmission over the network, thereby safeguarding the integrity and security of communication.

The key principles of encryption in 5G include:

1. End-to-End Encryption: End-to-end encryption ensures that data is encrypted at the source (sender) and decrypted at the destination (receiver), preventing intermediaries, including network operators and

service providers, from accessing or intercepting the plaintext data. This ensures that data remains confidential and secure throughout the entire transmission process.

2. Strong Encryption Algorithms: 5G networks employ strong encryption algorithms, such as Advanced Encryption Standard (AES), Rivest–Shamir–Adleman (RSA), and Elliptic Curve Cryptography (ECC), to protect data confidentiality and integrity. These algorithms use complex mathematical functions and cryptographic techniques to scramble data into ciphertext, making it unreadable to unauthorized parties.
3. Key Management: Key management involves the generation, distribution, and storage of encryption keys used to encrypt and decrypt data. 5G networks employ robust key management systems and protocols to securely generate, exchange, and store encryption keys, ensuring that only authorized parties have access to the keys needed to decipher encrypted data.
4. Secure Communication Protocols: Secure communication protocols, such as IPsec (Internet Protocol Security), SSL/TLS (Secure Sockets Layer/Transport Layer Security), and DTLS (Datagram Transport Layer Security), are used to establish encrypted communication channels between users/devices and the network, protecting data transmission from eavesdropping, tampering, and interception.

6.2.3 Challenges and Considerations

Despite their importance, authentication and encryption in 5G networks face several challenges and considerations, including:

1. Performance Overhead: Strong authentication and encryption mechanisms can introduce performance overhead, such as increased latency and processing overhead, which may impact network performance and user experience, particularly in resource-constrained environments or high-traffic scenarios.
2. Scalability and Complexity: Managing authentication and encryption for a large number of users/devices in 5G networks can be challenging due to scalability and complexity issues. As the number of connected devices continues to grow, network operators must deploy scalable and efficient authentication and encryption solutions to accommodate the increasing demand.
3. Interoperability and Standards: Ensuring interoperability and compliance with international standards and protocols is essential for seamless authentication and encryption across heterogeneous networks and devices. Interoperability challenges may arise when integrating different

authentication and encryption mechanisms or when interoperating with legacy systems and protocols.

4. Security Risks and Threats: Authentication and encryption mechanisms are susceptible to security risks and threats, such as brute-force attacks, key compromise, and cryptographic vulnerabilities. Network operators must continuously monitor and update authentication and encryption protocols to address emerging threats and vulnerabilities and ensure the security and integrity of 5G networks.

6.3 PRIVACY CONCERNS AND DATA PROTECTION

With the advent of 5G technology, the promise of faster speeds, lower latency, and greater connectivity brings with it significant privacy concerns and data protection challenges. As 5G networks enable a plethora of innovative applications and services, ranging from IoT devices to smart cities, the collection, processing, and sharing of personal information become more prevalent than ever before. Privacy concerns and data protection challenges in 5G networks pose significant risks to user privacy and data security, requiring proactive measures to safeguard personal information and ensure compliance with privacy regulations and standards. By implementing privacy by design principles, establishing robust data governance frameworks, educating users about their privacy rights, and ensuring regulatory compliance, organizations can mitigate privacy risks and protect personal data in 5G networks. As 5G technology continues to evolve and expand, addressing privacy concerns and data protection challenges remains essential to building trust, preserving privacy, and promoting responsible data stewardship in the age of connectivity.

6.3.1 Privacy Concerns in 5G

Privacy concerns in 5G revolve around the collection, use, and disclosure of personal information by network operators, service providers, and third-party entities. With the proliferation of connected devices, sensors, and applications, users face increased risks of privacy violations and unauthorized access to their sensitive information. Some key privacy concerns in 5G include:

1. Data Collection and Tracking: 5G networks enable the collection of vast amounts of data from connected devices and sensors, including location data, browsing history, and behavioral patterns. This data collection raises concerns about user privacy and the potential for intrusive tracking and profiling by network operators and service providers.
2. Data Processing and Profiling: The processing of personal data in 5G networks raises concerns about automated decision-making and profiling, where algorithms analyze user data to make predictions or decisions without human intervention. This can lead to discriminatory or unfair treatment based on factors such as race, gender, or socioeconomic status, raising ethical and legal concerns about data use and transparency.

3. Data Sharing and Disclosure: 5G networks facilitate the sharing and disclosure of personal data between network operators, service providers, and third-party entities, raising concerns about data breaches, unauthorized access, and misuse of personal information. This can lead to identity theft, fraud, or other malicious activities, compromising user privacy and security.
4. IoT Security and Vulnerabilities: The proliferation of IoT devices in 5G networks introduces new security vulnerabilities and privacy risks, as many devices lack robust security features and are susceptible to hacking, malware, and unauthorized access. This can result in unauthorized surveillance, data tampering, or remote exploitation of IoT devices for malicious purposes, posing significant risks to user privacy and data protection.

6.3.2 Data Protection Challenges in 5G

Data protection challenges in 5G stem from the need to safeguard personal information against unauthorized access, disclosure, or misuse, while ensuring compliance with privacy regulations and standards. Some key data protection challenges in 5G include:

1. Encryption and Authentication: Ensuring the confidentiality and integrity of data transmission in 5G networks requires robust encryption and authentication mechanisms to protect against eavesdropping, interception, and tampering. Deploying strong encryption algorithms and authentication protocols is essential to safeguard sensitive information and prevent unauthorized access to network resources.
2. Data Minimization and Purpose Limitation: Implementing data minimization and purpose limitation principles in 5G networks is essential to reduce the collection and retention of unnecessary personal data and limit its use to specific purposes authorized by the user. This helps to mitigate privacy risks and prevent the misuse or exploitation of personal information for unrelated purposes.
3. Transparency and Consent: Ensuring transparency and obtaining informed consent from users for the collection, processing, and sharing of their personal data is essential to build trust and accountability in 5G networks. Providing clear and concise privacy notices, consent forms, and user controls empowers users to make informed decisions about their data and privacy preferences.
4. Data Security and Breach Response: Implementing robust data security measures and incident response procedures is essential to protect against data breaches and unauthorized access to personal information in 5G networks. This includes encrypting sensitive data, implementing access

controls, and monitoring network traffic for suspicious activities to detect and respond to security incidents in a timely manner.

6.3.3 Strategies for Mitigation

Addressing privacy concerns and data protection challenges in 5G requires a holistic approach that encompasses technical solutions, organizational policies, and regulatory compliance. Some strategies for mitigating privacy risks and protecting personal information in 5G networks include:

1. Privacy by Design: Integrating privacy considerations into the design and development of 5G networks, applications, and services from the outset ensures that privacy features and controls are built-in by design, rather than added as an afterthought. This includes implementing privacy-enhancing technologies, such as anonymization, pseudonymization, and differential privacy, to minimize the collection and retention of personal data and protect user privacy.
2. Data Governance and Accountability: Establishing robust data governance frameworks and accountability mechanisms helps to ensure that personal data is managed and protected in accordance with privacy regulations and best practices. This includes appointing a data protection officer (DPO) responsible for overseeing data protection compliance, conducting privacy impact assessments (PIAs) to assess privacy risks, and implementing privacy policies and procedures to govern data handling practices.
3. User Education and Awareness: Educating users about their privacy rights, risks, and responsibilities in 5G networks empowers them to make informed decisions about their data and privacy preferences. Providing user-friendly privacy notices, consent forms, and privacy settings helps to enhance transparency and build trust between users and service providers.
4. Regulatory Compliance: Ensuring compliance with privacy regulations and standards, such as the General Data Protection Regulation (GDPR) in the European Union or the California Consumer Privacy Act (CCPA) in the United States, helps to mitigate legal and regulatory risks associated with data protection in 5G networks. This includes implementing technical and organizational measures to protect personal data, conducting regular audits and assessments to monitor compliance, and responding promptly to data breaches or privacy incidents in accordance with legal requirements.

6.4 SECURITY MEASURES FOR IOT DEVICES

The proliferation of IoT devices has revolutionized industries, homes, and cities, enabling innovative applications and services that enhance convenience, efficiency, and connectivity. However, the rapid adoption of IoT devices also brings significant security challenges, as these devices often lack robust security features and are susceptible to hacking, malware, and unauthorized access. Securing IoT devices is essential to protect against security threats and safeguard sensitive information, critical infrastructure, and user privacy. By implementing robust security measures, such as device authentication, data encryption, secure communication protocols, firmware updates, physical security measures, network segmentation, and security monitoring, organizations can mitigate security risks and build trust in IoT deployments. As the IoT ecosystem continues to evolve and expand, addressing security concerns and adopting best practices for IoT device security remains paramount to ensure the integrity, confidentiality, and availability of connected systems and services.

1. Device Authentication and Access Control:
   - Implementing strong device authentication mechanisms, such as digital certificates, secure tokens, or biometric authentication, helps to verify the identity of IoT devices and prevent unauthorized access.
   - Enforcing access control policies to restrict access to sensitive resources and functionalities based on user roles, permissions, and privileges helps to mitigate the risk of unauthorized activities and data breaches.
2. Data Encryption and Integrity:
   - Encrypting data in transit and at rest using strong encryption algorithms, such as AES (Advanced Encryption Standard) or RSA (Rivest-Shamir-Adleman), helps to protect sensitive information from eavesdropping, interception, and tampering.
   - Implementing data integrity checks, such as digital signatures or hash functions, helps to detect unauthorized modifications to data and ensure its authenticity and integrity.
3. Secure Communication Protocols:
   - Using secure communication protocols, such as TLS (Transport Layer Security) or MQTT (Message Queuing Telemetry Transport), helps to establish encrypted communication channels between IoT devices and servers, protecting data transmission from interception and tampering.
   - Implementing mutual authentication between IoT devices and servers helps to verify the identity of both parties and ensure mutual trust and confidentiality in communication.
4. Firmware and Software Updates:
   - Regularly updating firmware and software on IoT devices helps to patch known vulnerabilities, fix security flaws, and improve overall device security.
   - Implementing secure over-the-air (OTA) update mechanisms ensures

that firmware and software updates are delivered securely and authenticated to prevent tampering or unauthorized modifications.

5. Secure Boot and Device Integrity:
   - Implementing secure boot mechanisms helps to ensure the integrity of device firmware and software during the boot process, preventing unauthorized code execution or tampering.
   - Using trusted platform modules (TPMs) or hardware-based security features helps to protect device integrity and prevent unauthorized access or modifications to critical system components.
6. Physical Security Measures:
   - Implementing physical security measures, such as tamper-evident seals, locks, or enclosures, helps to protect IoT devices from physical tampering, theft, or unauthorized access.
   - Deploying devices in secure locations and implementing access controls, surveillance cameras, and alarm systems helps to deter intruders and protect against physical attacks.
7. Network Segmentation and Firewalls:
   - Segmenting IoT devices into separate network segments or VLANs (Virtual Local Area Networks) helps to isolate them from other devices and reduce the impact of security breaches or compromises.
   - Deploying firewalls and intrusion detection/prevention systems (IDPS) helps to monitor and filter network traffic, detect malicious activities, and block unauthorized access to IoT devices and networks.
8. Security Monitoring and Incident Response:
   - Implementing security monitoring tools and techniques, such as log monitoring, network traffic analysis, and anomaly detection, helps to detect and respond to security incidents in real time.
   - Establishing incident response procedures and protocols helps to quickly mitigate security breaches, contain the impact of incidents, and restore normal operations.

CHAPTER 7

APPLICATIONS OF 5G TECHNOLOGY

7.1 SMART CITIES AND INFRASTRUCTURE

In an increasingly urbanized world, the concept of smart cities has emerged as a transformative approach to addressing the complex challenges of urbanization, such as traffic congestion, air pollution, energy consumption, and resource management. Smart cities leverage advanced technologies, including Internet of Things (IoT), big data analytics, artificial intelligence (AI), and 5G technology, to enhance the efficiency, sustainability, and livability of urban environments. 5G technology plays a pivotal role in the development and deployment of smart cities and infrastructure, enabling innovative solutions that address urban challenges and improve quality of life for residents. By harnessing the power of 5G, cities can optimize infrastructure, enhance sustainability, promote economic growth, and create more resilient and livable urban environments. However, realizing the full potential of 5G-enabled smart cities requires collaboration, investment, and commitment from stakeholders across government, industry, academia, and the community to overcome challenges, foster innovation, and create a brighter future for urban development.

7.1.1 Foundations of Smart Cities

A smart city is a technologically modern urban area that uses different types of electronic methods and sensors to collect specific data. Information gained from that data is used to manage assets, resources and services efficiently; in return, that data is used to improve operations across the city. This includes data collected from citizens, devices, buildings and assets that is processed and analyzed to monitor and manage traffic and transportation systems, power plants, utilities, urban forestry, water supply networks, waste, criminal investigations, information systems, schools, libraries, hospitals, and other community services. Smart cities are defined as smart both in the ways in which their governments harness technology as well as in how they monitor, analyze, plan, and govern the city. In smart cities, the sharing of data is not limited to the city itself but also includes businesses, citizens and other third parties that can benefit from various uses of that data. Sharing data from different systems and sectors creates opportunities for increased understanding and economic benefits.

The smart city concept integrates information and communication technology (ICT), and various physical devices connected to the Internet of things (IOT) network to optimize the efficiency of city operations and services and connect to citizens. Smart city technology allows city officials to interact directly with both community and city infrastructure and to monitor what is happening in the city and how the city is evolving. ICT is used to enhance quality, performance and interactivity of urban services, to reduce costs and resource consumption and to increase contact between citizens and government. Smart city applications are developed to manage urban flows and allow for real-time responses. A smart city may therefore be more prepared to respond to challenges than one with a conventional "transactional" relationship with its citizens. Yet, the term itself remains unclear in its specifics and therefore, open to many interpretations. Many cities have already adopted some sort of smart city technology.

Smart city initiatives have been criticized as a marketing fad, poorly adapted to residents' needs, as largely unsuccessful, and as a dangerous move toward totalitarian surveillance. It has been suggested that a smart city (also community, business cluster, urban agglomeration or region) uses information technologies to:

1. Make more efficient use of physical infrastructure (roads, built environment and other physical assets) through artificial intelligence and data analytics in order to support a strong and healthy economic, social, cultural development.
2. Engage effectively with local governance by use of open innovation processes and e-participation, improving the collective intelligence of the city's institutions through e-governance, with emphasis placed on citizen participation and co-design.
3. Learn, adapt and innovate and thereby respond more effectively and promptly to changing circumstances by improving the intelligence of the city.

They evolve towards a strong integration of all dimensions of human intelligence, collective intelligence, and also artificial intelligence within the city. The intelligence of cities "resides in the increasingly effective combination of digital telecommunication networks (the nerves), ubiquitously embedded intelligence (the brains), sensors and tags (the sensory organs), and software (the knowledge and cognitive competence)". These forms of intelligence in smart cities have been demonstrated in three ways

1. Orchestration intelligence: Where cities establish institutions and community-based problem solving and collaborations, such as in Bletchley Park, where the Nazi Enigma cipher was decoded by a team led by Alan Turing. This has been referred to as the first example of a smart city or an intelligent community.
2. Empowerment intelligence: Cities provide open platforms, experimental facilities and smart city infrastructure in order to cluster innovation in

certain districts. These are seen in the Kista Science City in Stockholm and the Cyberport Zone in Hong Kong. Similar facilities have also been established in Melbourne and Kyiv.

3. Instrumentation intelligence: Where city infrastructure is made smart through real-time data collection, with analysis and predictive modelling across city districts. There is much controversy surrounding this, particularly with regards to surveillance issues in smart cities. Examples of Instrumentation intelligence are those implemented in Amsterdam.

This is realized through:

1. A common IP infrastructure that is open to researchers to develop applications.
2. Wireless meters and devices transmit information at the point in time.
3. A number of homes being provided with smart energy meters to become aware of energy consumption and reduce energy usage.
4. Solar power garbage compactors, car recharging stations and energy saving lamps.

Smart cities have been conceptualized using the OSI model of 'layer' abstractions. Smart cities are constructed by connecting the city's public infrastructure with city application systems and passing collected data through three layers, the perception layer, the network layer and the application layer. City application systems then use data to make better decisions when controlling different city infrastructures. The perception layer is where data is collected across the smart city using sensors. This data could be collected through sensors such as cameras, RFID, or GPS positioning. The perception layer sends data it collects using wireless transmissions to the network layer. The network layer is responsible for transporting collected data from the perception layer to the application layer. The network layer utilizes a city's communication infrastructure to send data meaning it can be intercepted by attackers and must be held responsible for keeping collected data and information private. The application layer is responsible for processing the data received from network layer. The application layer uses the data it processes to make decisions on how to control the city infrastructure based on the data it receives.

A smart city relies heavily on the deployment of technology. Different combinations of technological infrastructure interact to form the array of smart city technologies with varying levels of interaction between human and technological systems.

- Digital: A service oriented infrastructure is required to connect individuals and devices in a smart city. These include innovation services and communication infrastructure. Yovanof, G. S. & Hazapis, G. N. define a digital city as "a connected community that combines broadband communications infrastructure; a flexible, service-oriented computing infrastructure based on open industry standards; and, innovative services to meet the needs of governments and their employees, citizens and businesses."

- Intelligent: Cognitive technologies, such as artificial intelligence and machine learning, can be trained on the data generated by connected city devices to identify patterns. The efficacy and impact of particular policy decisions can be quantified by cognitive systems studying the continuous interactions of humans with their urban surroundings.
- Ubiquitous: A ubiquitous city provides access to public services through any connected device. U-city is an extension of the digital city concept because of the facility in terms of accessibility to every infrastructure.
- Wired: The physical components of IT systems are crucial to early-stage smart city development. Wired infrastructure is required to support the IoT and wireless technologies central to more interconnected living. A wired city environment provides general access to continually updated digital and physical infrastructure. The latest in telecommunications, robotics, IoT, and various connected technologies can then be deployed to support human capital and productivity.
- Hybrid: A hybrid city is the combination of a physical conurbation and a virtual city related to the physical space. This relationship can be one of virtual design or the presence of a critical mass of virtual community participants in a physical urban space. Hybrid spaces can serve to actualize future-state projects for smart city services and integration.
- Information city: The multiplicity of interactive devices in a smart city generates a large quantity of data. How that information is interpreted and stored is critical to Smart city growth and security.

Smart city initiatives have measurable positive impacts on the quality of life of its citizens and visitors. The human framework of a smart city – its economy, knowledge networks, and human support systems – is an important indicator of its success.

- Creativity: Arts and culture initiatives are common focus areas in smart city planning. Innovation is associated with intellectual curiosity and creativeness, and various projects have demonstrated that knowledge workers participate in a diverse mix of cultural and artistic activities.
- Learning: Since mobility is a key area of Smart city development, building a capable workforce through education initiatives is necessary. A city's learning capacity includes its education system, including available workforce training and support, and its cultural development and exchange.
- Humanity: Numerous Smart city programs focus on soft infrastructure development, like increasing access to voluntary organizations and

designated safe zones. This focus on social and relational capital means diversity, inclusion, and ubiquitous access to public services is worked in to city planning.

- Knowledge: The development of a knowledge economy is central to Smart city projects. Smart cities seeking to be hubs of economic activity in emerging tech and service sectors stress the value of innovation in city development.

According to Mary Anne Moser since the 1990s, the smart communities movement took shape as a strategy to broaden the base of users involved in IT. Members of these Communities are people that share their interest and work in a partnership with government and other institutional organizations to push the use of IT to improve the quality of daily life as a consequence of different worsening in daily actions. John M. Eger said that a smart community makes a conscious and agreed-upon decision to deploy technology as a catalyst to solving its social and business needs. It is very important to understand that this use of IT and the consequent improvement could be more demanding without the institutional help; indeed institutional involvement is essential to the success of smart community initiatives. Again Moser explained that "building and planning a smart community seeks for smart growth"; smart growth is essential for the partnership between citizen and institutional organizations to react to worsening trends in daily issues like traffic congestion, school overcrowding and air pollution.

Technological propagation is not an end in itself, but a means to reinventing cities for a new economy and society. Smart city initiatives require co-ordination and support from the city government and other governing bodies for their success. As has been noted by Fleur Johns, the increasing and evolving use of data has significant implications at multiple levels of governance. Data and infrastructure include digital platforms, algorithms, and the embedding of information technology in the physical infrastructure of smart cities. Digital technology has the potential to be used in negative as well as positive ways, and its use is inherently political. Care needs to be taken to ensure that the development of smart cities does not perpetuate inequalities and exclude marginalized groups in relation to gender, age, race, and other human characteristics.

The importance of these three different dimensions is that only a link among them can make possible the development of a real smart city concept. According to the definition of smart city given by Andrea Caragliu et al., a city is smart when investments in human/social capital and IT infrastructure fuel sustainable growth and enhance quality of life, through participatory governance.

Smart cities use data and technology to create efficiencies, improve sustainability, create economic development, and enhance quality of life factors for people living and working in the city. A variety of different datasets may need to be integrated to create a smart energy infrastructure. More formally, a smart city is: "An urban area that has securely integrated technology across the information... and Internet of Things (IoT) sectors to better manage a city's assets." Employment of smart technologies enables the more efficient application of integrated energy technologies in the city allowing the development of more self-sustaining areas or even Positive Energy Districts that produce more energy than consume.

A smart city is powered by "smart connections" for various items such as street lighting, smart buildings, distributed energy resources (DER), data analytics, and smart transportation. Amongst these things, energy is paramount; this is why utility companies play a key role in smart cities. Electric companies, working partnership with city officials, technology companies and a number of other institutions, are among the major players that helped accelerate the growth of America's smart cities.

Smart cities employ a combination of data collection, processing, and disseminating technologies in conjunction with networking and computing technologies and data security and privacy measures encouraging the application of innovation to promote the overall quality of life for its citizens and covering dimensions that include: utilities, health, transportation, entertainment and government services.

Technologies:

- Smart grids are an important technology in smart cities. The improved flexibility of the smart grid permits greater penetration of highly variable renewable energy sources such as solar power and wind power. The modern smart city policy also focuses on online monitoring of real time energy consumption of households and businesses, identification of problems with energy efficiency, adjusting tariffs to achieve resource saving and ecology goals, stimulating sustainable buildings.
- Mobile devices (such as smartphones and tablets) are another key technology allowing citizens to connect to the smart city services.
- Smart cities also rely on smart homes and specifically, the technology used in them.
- Bicycle-sharing systems are an important element in smart cities.
- Smart mobility is also important to smart cities.
- Intelligent transportation systems and CCTV systems are also being developed.
- Digital libraries have been established in several smart cities.
- Online collaborative sensor data management platforms are on-line database services that allow sensor owners to register and connect their devices to feed data into an on-line database for storage and allow developers to connect to the database and build their own applications based on that data.

- Additional supporting technology and trends include remote work, telehealth, the blockchain, online banking technology,
- Electronic cards (known as smart cards) are another common component in smart city contexts. These cards possess a unique encrypted identifier that allows the owner to log into a range of government provided services (or e-services) without setting up multiple accounts. The single identifier allows governments to aggregate data about citizens and their preferences to improve the provision of services and to determine common interests of groups. This technology has been implemented in Southampton.
- In 2022, the Russian corporation Rostec developed the SmartAirKey. This is an electronic key that gives access to doors, barriers, elevators and turnstiles. Registration takes place through the "Gosuslugi"
- Retractable bollards allow to restrict access inside city centers (i.e., to delivery trucks resupplying outlet stores). Opening and closing of such barriers is traditionally done manually, through an electronic pass but can even be done by means of ANPR cameras connected to the bollard system.
- Energy Data Management Systems (EDMS) can help to save cities energy by recording data and using it to increase efficiency.
- Cost-benefit analysis has been done into smart cities and the individual technologies. These can help to assess whether it is economically and ecologically beneficial to implement some technologies at all, and also compare the cost-effectiveness of each technology among each other

7.1.2 Role of 5G Technology

- 5G technology serves as a foundational enabler for smart cities, providing high-speed, low-latency connectivity that supports a wide range of IoT devices and applications.
- Compared to previous generations of wireless technology, 5G offers significantly faster speeds, lower latency, and greater reliability, making it ideal for real-time data transmission, edge computing, and mission-critical applications.

7.1.3 Applications of 5G in Smart Cities

- Intelligent Transportation Systems (ITS): 5G enables connected vehicles, smart traffic management, and real-time monitoring of transportation networks, improving traffic flow, reducing congestion, and enhancing road safety.
- Smart Grids and Energy Management: 5G facilitates smart meters, distributed energy resources, and demand-response systems, enabling

more efficient energy distribution, consumption, and optimization in urban areas.

- Environmental Monitoring: 5G supports IoT sensors and remote monitoring devices for air quality, water quality, and waste management, enabling proactive environmental management and sustainability initiatives.
- Public Safety and Security: 5G enables real-time video surveillance, emergency response systems, and situational awareness platforms, enhancing public safety and security in urban environments.
- Healthcare and Telemedicine: 5G facilitates remote patient monitoring, telehealth services, and medical diagnostics, expanding access to healthcare and improving health outcomes for urban populations.

7.1.4 Challenges and Considerations

- Infrastructure Deployment: Deploying 5G infrastructure, such as small cells and base stations, requires collaboration between government agencies, telecommunications providers, and urban planners to address regulatory, zoning, and aesthetic considerations.
- Data Privacy and Security: Collecting and analyzing vast amounts of data in smart cities raises concerns about data privacy, security, and ethical use, requiring robust data protection measures and transparency mechanisms to safeguard personal information and mitigate privacy risks.
- Digital Inclusion: Ensuring equitable access to 5G technology and digital services is essential to prevent the exacerbation of existing socioeconomic disparities and bridge the digital divide in urban communities.
- Interoperability and Standards: Ensuring interoperability and compatibility between different IoT devices, platforms, and networks is crucial to enable seamless communication and integration of smart city solutions, requiring the development of common standards and protocols.

7.1.5 Case Studies and Success Stories

- Barcelona, Spain: Barcelona has implemented smart city initiatives, such as the CityOS platform, which integrates data from various sources to optimize urban services, enhance sustainability, and improve quality of life for residents.
- Singapore: Singapore has deployed smart transportation systems, including autonomous vehicles and predictive maintenance for public transit, to improve mobility, reduce congestion, and enhance urban resilience.
- Songdo, South Korea: Songdo is a planned smart city that leverages advanced technologies, including 5G, IoT, and AI, to create a sustainable

and interconnected urban environment with efficient energy management, smart buildings, and integrated transportation systems.

7.2 HEALTHCARE AND REMOTE MEDICAL SERVICES

The integration of 5G technology into healthcare systems is ushering in a new era of medical services, offering transformative opportunities to improve patient care, enhance medical diagnostics, and revolutionize healthcare delivery. From remote consultations to real-time monitoring and surgical robotics, 5G technology is poised to reshape the healthcare landscape by enabling faster, more reliable, and more immersive connectivity. 5G technology holds immense promise for revolutionizing healthcare and remote medical services, offering unprecedented opportunities to improve patient access, enhance clinical outcomes, and transform the delivery of healthcare. By leveraging the high-speed, low-latency connectivity of 5G, healthcare providers can deliver personalized, efficient, and cost-effective medical care to patients, regardless of their location. However, realizing the full potential of 5G-enabled healthcare requires collaboration, investment, and regulatory support from stakeholders across the healthcare ecosystem to overcome challenges, ensure interoperability, and build a sustainable and resilient healthcare infrastructure for the future.

The Promise of 5G Technology in Healthcare:

- 5G technology offers several key advantages for healthcare applications, including ultra-fast data transmission, low latency, high reliability, and increased network capacity.
- These characteristics make 5G well-suited for real-time communication, remote monitoring, telemedicine, augmented reality (AR), virtual reality (VR), and the Internet of Medical Things (IoMT).

Remote Consultations and Telemedicine:

- 5G enables high-definition video conferencing, remote consultations, and telemedicine services, allowing healthcare providers to deliver medical care and advice to patients in remote or underserved areas.
- Patients can consult with specialists, receive diagnoses, and access medical treatment without the need for physical travel, reducing healthcare costs, improving access to care, and enhancing patient convenience.

Remote Patient Monitoring:

- 5G facilitates remote patient monitoring through wearable devices, sensors, and connected medical devices that continuously collect and transmit patient data, such as vital signs, activity levels, and medication adherence.
- Healthcare providers can remotely monitor patients' health status, detect early warning signs of deterioration, and intervene proactively to prevent complications, reducing hospital readmissions and improving patient outcomes.

Emergency Response and Disaster Management:

- 5G enables real-time communication and coordination among emergency responders, healthcare professionals, and disaster relief organizations during natural disasters, mass casualty incidents, or public health emergencies.
- High-speed data transmission and low latency enable faster response times, more accurate situational awareness, and better coordination of resources, helping to save lives and mitigate the impact of emergencies.

Augmented Reality (AR) and Virtual Reality (VR) in Healthcare:

- 5G technology enhances the capabilities of AR and VR applications in healthcare, enabling immersive medical training, surgical simulation, patient education, and remote assistance for complex procedures.
- Surgeons can use AR and VR technologies to visualize patient anatomy, plan surgeries, and perform minimally invasive procedures with greater precision and accuracy, leading to better surgical outcomes and reduced patient risk.

Remote Surgery and Robotic Assisted Surgery:

- 5G enables remote surgery and robotic-assisted surgery by providing high-speed, low-latency connectivity between surgeons and robotic systems in different locations.
- Surgeons can remotely control surgical robots, perform procedures with sub-millimeter precision, and collaborate with colleagues in real time, expanding access to specialized surgical expertise and improving patient care.

Data Security and Privacy Considerations:

- As healthcare data becomes increasingly digital and interconnected, ensuring the security and privacy of patient information is paramount.
- Healthcare organizations must implement robust cybersecurity measures, encryption protocols, access controls, and compliance frameworks to protect sensitive medical data and comply with regulations such as the Health Insurance Portability and Accountability Act (HIPAA).

7.3 AUTOMOTIVE AND INTELLIGENT TRANSPORTATION SYSTEMS

The automotive industry is undergoing a transformation, driven by advancements in technology and the emergence of connected and autonomous vehicles. 5G technology is poised to play a pivotal role in shaping the future of automotive and intelligent transportation systems (ITS), offering unprecedented opportunities to enhance safety, efficiency, and mobility on the roads. 5G technology holds immense promise for transforming the automotive industry and intelligent transportation systems, offering unprecedented opportunities to enhance safety, efficiency, and mobility on the roads. By leveraging the high-speed, low-latency connectivity of 5G, automotive manufacturers, transportation authorities, and service providers can unlock new capabilities, services, and business models that revolutionize the way we move people and goods. However, realizing the full potential of 5G-enabled automotive and ITS applications requires collaboration, investment, and regulatory support from stakeholders across the automotive ecosystem to overcome challenges, ensure interoperability, and create a safer, smarter, and more sustainable transportation future.

The Evolution of Automotive Technology:

- The automotive industry is experiencing a paradigm shift, with vehicles becoming increasingly connected, autonomous, and electrified.
- Advancements in sensors, communication technologies, artificial intelligence (AI), and 5G connectivity are driving innovation in automotive design, manufacturing, and transportation services.

Enabling Technologies of 5G:

- 5G technology offers several key features that are essential for automotive and ITS applications, including high-speed data transmission, ultra-low latency, massive connectivity, and network reliability.
- These characteristics enable real-time communication, sensor fusion, vehicle-to-everything (V2X) connectivity, and cooperative driving functionalities that are critical for safe and efficient transportation systems.

Vehicle Connectivity and Telematics:

- 5G enables seamless connectivity between vehicles, infrastructure, and the cloud, facilitating the exchange of data, information, and commands in real time.
- Connected vehicles can access real-time traffic updates, weather forecasts, navigation services, and vehicle diagnostics, enhancing driver awareness, safety, and convenience on the road.

Cooperative and Autonomous Driving:

- 5G technology enables cooperative and autonomous driving functionalities, allowing vehicles to communicate with each other and with the surrounding infrastructure to coordinate maneuvers, avoid collisions, and optimize traffic flow.
- Cooperative driving applications, such as platooning, intersection coordination, and lane merging, leverage V2X communication and sensor fusion to enhance safety, efficiency, and throughput on the roads.

Smart Traffic Management and Infrastructure:

- 5G enables smart traffic management systems that use real-time data analytics, predictive modeling, and AI algorithms to optimize traffic flow, reduce congestion, and improve road safety.
- Traffic signals, road signs, and infrastructure elements can be equipped with sensors and connected to the cloud, allowing for dynamic control and adaptive optimization of traffic patterns based on changing conditions and demand.

Enhanced Safety and Collision Avoidance:

- 5G technology enables advanced driver assistance systems (ADAS) and collision avoidance mechanisms that use V2X communication, sensor fusion, and AI algorithms to detect and respond to potential hazards in real time.
- Vehicles can exchange information about their speed, position, and trajectory with nearby vehicles, pedestrians, and infrastructure, enabling cooperative collision avoidance maneuvers and preemptive braking to prevent accidents.

Vehicle-to-Grid (V2G) and Energy Management:

- 5G facilitates vehicle-to-grid (V2G) communication, allowing electric vehicles to interact with the power grid and participate in demand response programs, energy trading, and grid stabilization.
- Electric vehicles can charge, discharge, and exchange energy with the grid based on real-time electricity prices, grid conditions, and user preferences, optimizing energy usage and reducing the overall carbon footprint of transportation.

Challenges and Considerations:

- Deployment of Infrastructure: Deploying 5G infrastructure, such as small cells and base stations, to support automotive and ITS applications requires collaboration between telecommunications providers, government agencies, and transportation authorities.
- Spectrum Allocation: Allocating sufficient spectrum for automotive and ITS applications is essential to ensure reliable and interference-free communication between vehicles, infrastructure, and the cloud.
- Standardization and Interoperability: Developing common standards and protocols for V2X communication, sensor interfaces, and data exchange is critical to enable interoperability and compatibility between different automotive systems and manufacturers.
- Security and Privacy: Ensuring the security and privacy of V2X communication and connected vehicles is paramount to protect against

cyber threats, data breaches, and unauthorized access to vehicle systems and sensitive information.

7.4 AUGMENTED REALITY (AR) AND VIRTUAL REALITY (VR)

The advent of 5G technology has ushered in a new era of connectivity, one that promises ultra-fast speeds, low latency, and massive connectivity. Among the myriad of potential applications, Augmented Reality (AR) and Virtual Reality (VR) stand out as transformative technologies that are poised to leverage the capabilities of 5G to revolutionize various industries and everyday experiences. Augmented Reality (AR) and Virtual Reality (VR) represent compelling applications of 5G technology, offering immersive, interactive, and transformative experiences across various domains. By leveraging the high-speed connectivity, low latency, and massive connectivity enabled by 5G networks, AR and VR unlock new possibilities for communication, collaboration, entertainment, and education. However, realizing the full potential of AR and VR requires addressing infrastructure challenges, ensuring privacy and security, fostering content creation and accessibility, optimizing quality of service, and navigating regulatory and ethical considerations. With continued innovation and collaboration, AR and VR powered by 5G technology have the potential to reshape how we interact with the world around us, ushering in a future where virtual and physical realities seamlessly converge.

7.4.1 Integration with 5G Technology

The integration of AR and VR with 5G technology unlocks a host of new possibilities, thanks to the unique capabilities of fifth-generation networks. Here are several ways in which AR and VR benefit from the deployment of 5G:

1. High-Speed Data Transfer: 5G networks boast significantly higher data transfer speeds compared to their predecessors, enabling seamless streaming and rendering of high-resolution AR and VR content. This ensures smoother and more immersive experiences for users without the lag or buffering often associated with slower networks.
2. Low Latency: One of the most significant advantages of 5G technology is its ultra-low latency, reducing the delay between user actions and system responses to milliseconds. In the context of AR and VR, this translates to near-instantaneous interactions, enhancing realism and user engagement. Whether it's manipulating virtual objects or collaborating with remote users in shared virtual spaces, low latency is crucial for a truly immersive experience.
3. Massive Connectivity: 5G networks are designed to support a vast number of connected devices simultaneously, paving the way for multi-user AR and VR experiences on a massive scale. From live events and virtual conferences to collaborative work environments and multiplayer gaming,

5G enables seamless interactions among numerous users in shared virtual environments.

4. Edge Computing: Edge computing brings processing power closer to the end-user, reducing latency and enabling real-time data processing. This is particularly advantageous for AR and VR applications, where split-second responsiveness is critical for a seamless user experience. By leveraging edge computing capabilities facilitated by 5G networks, AR and VR applications can offload intensive computational tasks to edge servers, resulting in smoother performance and reduced dependence on local hardware.
5. Remote Assistance and Telepresence: With 5G-enabled AR, remote experts can provide real-time guidance and support to field technicians or medical professionals. By overlaying instructions, diagrams, or annotations onto the user's field of view, AR enhances situational awareness and facilitates more efficient problem-solving. Similarly, VR-powered telepresence enables users to interact with distant environments or individuals as if they were physically present, fostering collaboration and reducing the need for travel.
6. Immersive Entertainment and Retail Experiences: 5G-powered AR and VR technologies revolutionize entertainment and retail experiences by offering immersive storytelling, interactive product demonstrations, and personalized shopping experiences. From virtual try-on solutions for fashion retailers to immersive previews of movies and live events, AR and VR enhance engagement and drive customer satisfaction.
7. Training and Simulation: In sectors such as healthcare, manufacturing, and defense, AR and VR provide cost-effective training and simulation solutions that replicate real-world scenarios with high fidelity. With 5G technology, these training environments can be accessed remotely, enabling distributed teams to collaborate on complex tasks and simulations in real-time.

7.4.2 Challenges and Considerations

While the integration of AR and VR with 5G technology holds tremendous promise, several challenges and considerations must be addressed:

1. Infrastructure Requirements: The widespread deployment of 5G infrastructure, including small cells and mmWave technology, is necessary to realize the full potential of AR and VR applications. This requires substantial investments from network operators and regulatory support to overcome logistical and regulatory hurdles.
2. Privacy and Security: AR and VR applications raise concerns regarding user privacy and data security, particularly in scenarios where personal

information is collected or shared. Robust privacy policies, data encryption, and secure authentication mechanisms are essential to mitigate these risks and foster trust among users.

3. Content Creation and Accessibility: Developing compelling AR and VR experiences requires specialized skills and tools, posing challenges for content creators and developers. Moreover, ensuring accessibility for users with diverse needs and abilities remains a priority to promote inclusivity and reach a broader audience.
4. Quality of Service (QoS): Maintaining consistent QoS is critical for delivering high-quality AR and VR experiences over 5G networks. Factors such as network congestion, signal interference, and device compatibility can impact performance, necessitating proactive network management and optimization strategies.
5. Regulatory and Ethical Considerations: As AR and VR applications become more pervasive, regulatory frameworks must adapt to address emerging issues related to content moderation, digital rights management, and ethical use cases. Balancing innovation with responsible governance is essential to foster a sustainable ecosystem for AR and VR technologies.

CHAPTER 8

CHALLENGES AND FUTURE DEVELOPMENTS

8.1 SPECTRUM ALLOCATION AND REGULATION

In the modern era, wireless communication has become an indispensable part of everyday life, powering everything from mobile phones and internet access to satellite navigation and smart devices. At the heart of wireless communication lies the electromagnetic spectrum, a finite resource that must be carefully managed and regulated to ensure optimal use and equitable access. Spectrum allocation and regulation play a crucial role in shaping the landscape of telecommunications, influencing technological innovation, economic development, and societal progress.

Spectrum allocation and regulation play a vital role in facilitating wireless communication, enabling connectivity, innovation, and economic growth. Effective spectrum management requires coordination among governments, regulatory agencies, industry stakeholders, and international organizations to maximize spectrum utilization, foster competition, and promote the public interest. Addressing the challenges posed by spectrum scarcity, fragmentation, and emerging technologies requires proactive policy interventions and collaborative efforts to ensure the efficient and equitable use of this finite resource.

8.1.1 Understanding the Electromagnetic Spectrum

The electromagnetic spectrum is the full range of electromagnetic radiation, organized by frequency or wavelength. The spectrum is divided into separate bands, with different names for the electromagnetic waves within each band. From low to high frequency these are: radio waves, microwaves, infrared, visible light, ultraviolet, X-rays, and gamma rays. The electromagnetic waves in each of these bands have different characteristics, such as how they are produced, how they interact with matter, and their practical applications.

Radio waves, at the low-frequency end of the spectrum, have the lowest photon energy and the longest wavelengths—thousands of kilometers, or more. They can be emitted and received by antennas, and pass through the atmosphere, foliage, and most building materials.

Gamma rays, at the high-frequency end of the spectrum, have the highest photon energies and the shortest wavelengths—much smaller than an atomic nucleus. Gamma rays, X-rays, and extreme ultraviolet rays are called ionizing radiation because their high photon energy is able to ionize atoms, causing chemical reactions. Visible light and radiation of longer wavelengths are nonionizing; their photons do not have sufficient energy to cause these effects.

Throughout most of the electromagnetic spectrum, spectroscopy can be used to separate waves of different frequencies, so that the intensity of the radiation can be measured as a function of frequency or wavelength. Spectroscopy is used to study the interactions of electromagnetic waves with matter.

History and Discovery

Humans have always been aware of visible light and radiant heat but for most of history it was not known that these phenomena were connected or were representatives of a more extensive principle. The ancient Greeks recognized that light traveled in straight lines and studied some of its properties, including reflection and refraction. Light was intensively studied from the beginning of the 17th century leading to the invention of important instruments like the telescope and microscope. Isaac Newton was the first to use the term spectrum for the range of colours that white light could be split into with a prism. Starting in 1666, Newton showed that these colours were intrinsic to light and could be recombined into white light. A debate arose over whether light had a wave nature or a particle nature with René Descartes, Robert Hooke and Christiaan Huygens favouring a wave description and Newton favouring a particle description. Huygens in particular had a well developed theory from which he was able to derive the laws of reflection and refraction. Around 1801, Thomas Young measured the wavelength of a light beam with his two-slit experiment thus conclusively demonstrating that light was a wave.

In 1800, William Herschel discovered infrared radiation. He was studying the temperature of different colours by moving a thermometer through light split by a prism. He noticed that the highest temperature was beyond red. He theorized that this temperature change was due to "calorific rays", a type of light ray that could not be seen. The next year, Johann Ritter, working at the other end of the spectrum, noticed what he called "chemical rays" (invisible light rays that induced certain chemical reactions). These behaved similarly to visible violet light rays, but were beyond them in the spectrum. They were later renamed ultraviolet radiation.

The study of electromagnetism began in 1820 when Hans Christian Ørsted discovered that electric currents produce magnetic fields (Oersted's law). Light was first linked to electromagnetism in 1845, when Michael Faraday noticed that the polarization of light traveling through a transparent material responded to a magnetic field. During the 1860s, James Clerk Maxwell developed four partial differential equations

(Maxwell's equations) for the electromagnetic field. Two of these equations predicted the possibility and behavior of waves in the field. Analyzing the speed of these theoretical waves, Maxwell realized that they must travel at a speed that was about the known speed of light. This startling coincidence in value led Maxwell to make the inference that light itself is a type of electromagnetic wave. Maxwell's equations predicted an infinite range of frequencies of electromagnetic waves, all traveling at the speed of light. This was the first indication of the existence of the entire electromagnetic spectrum.

Maxwell's predicted waves included waves at very low frequencies compared to infrared, which in theory might be created by oscillating charges in an ordinary electrical circuit of a certain type. Attempting to prove Maxwell's equations and detect such low frequency electromagnetic radiation, in 1886, the physicist Heinrich Hertz built an apparatus to generate and detect what are now called radio waves. Hertz found the waves and was able to infer (by measuring their wavelength and multiplying it by their frequency) that they traveled at the speed of light. Hertz also demonstrated that the new radiation could be both reflected and refracted by various dielectric media, in the same manner as light. For example, Hertz was able to focus the waves using a lens made of tree resin. In a later experiment, Hertz similarly produced and measured the properties of microwaves. These new types of waves paved the way for inventions such as the wireless telegraph and the radio.

In 1895, Wilhelm Röntgen noticed a new type of radiation emitted during an experiment with an evacuated tube subjected to a high voltage. He called this radiation "x-rays" and found that they were able to travel through parts of the human body but were reflected or stopped by denser matter such as bones. Before long, many uses were found for this radiography.

The last portion of the electromagnetic spectrum was filled in with the discovery of gamma rays. In 1900, Paul Villard was studying the radioactive emissions of radium when he identified a new type of radiation that he at first thought consisted of particles similar to known alpha and beta particles, but with the power of being far more penetrating than either. However, in 1910, British physicist William Henry Bragg demonstrated that gamma rays are electromagnetic radiation, not particles, and in 1914, Ernest Rutherford (who had named them gamma rays in 1903 when he realized that they were fundamentally different from charged alpha and beta particles) and Edward Andrade measured their wavelengths, and found that gamma rays were similar to X-rays, but with shorter wavelengths.

The wave-particle debate was rekindled in 1901 when Max Planck discovered that light is absorbed only in discrete "quanta", now called photons, implying that light has a particle nature. This idea was made explicit by Albert Einstein in 1905, but never accepted by Planck and many other contemporaries. The modern position of science is that electromagnetic radiation has both a wave and a particle nature, the wave-particle duality. The contradictions arising from this position are still being debated by scientists and philosophers.

Regions

The types of electromagnetic radiation are broadly classified into the following classes (regions, bands or types):

1. Gamma radiation
2. X-ray radiation
3. Ultraviolet radiation
4. Visible light (light that humans can see)
5. Infrared radiation
6. Microwave radiation
7. Radio waves

This classification goes in the increasing order of wavelength, which is characteristic of the type of radiation.

There are no precisely defined boundaries between the bands of the electromagnetic spectrum; rather they fade into each other like the bands in a rainbow (which is the sub-spectrum of visible light). Radiation of each frequency and wavelength (or in each band) has a mix of properties of the two regions of the spectrum that bound it. For example, red light resembles infrared radiation in that it can excite and add energy to some chemical bonds and indeed must do so to power the chemical mechanisms responsible for photosynthesis and the working of the visual system.

The distinction between X-rays and gamma rays is partly based on sources: the photons generated from nuclear decay or other nuclear and subnuclear/particle process are always termed gamma rays, whereas X-rays are generated by electronic transitions involving highly energetic inner atomic electrons. In general, nuclear transitions are much more energetic than electronic transitions, so gamma rays are more energetic than X-rays, but exceptions exist. By analogy to electronic transitions, muonic atom transitions are also said to produce X-rays, even though their energy may exceed 6 megaelectronvolts (0.96 pJ), whereas there are many (77 known to be less than 10 keV (1.6 fJ)) low-energy nuclear transitions (e.g., the 7.6 eV (1.22 aJ) nuclear transition of thorium-229m), and, despite being one million-fold less energetic than some muonic X-rays, the emitted photons are still called gamma rays due to their nuclear origin.

The convention that EM radiation that is known to come from the nucleus is always called "gamma ray" radiation is the only convention that is universally respected, however. Many astronomical gamma ray sources (such as gamma ray bursts) are known to be too energetic (in both intensity and wavelength) to be of nuclear origin. Quite often, in high-energy physics and in medical radiotherapy, very high energy EMR (in the > 10 MeV region)—which is of higher energy than any nuclear gamma ray—is not called X-ray or gamma ray, but instead by the generic term of "high-energy photons".

The region of the spectrum where a particular observed electromagnetic radiation falls is reference frame-dependent (due to the Doppler shift for light), so EM radiation that one observer would say is in one region of the spectrum could appear to an observer moving at a substantial fraction of the speed of light with respect to the first to be in another part of the spectrum. For example, consider the cosmic microwave background. It was produced when matter and radiation decoupled, by the de-excitation of hydrogen atoms to the ground state. These photons were from Lyman series transitions, putting them in the ultraviolet (UV) part of the electromagnetic spectrum. Now this radiation has undergone enough cosmological red shift to put it into the microwave region of the spectrum for observers moving slowly (compared to the speed of light) with respect to the cosmos.

Types of Radiation

Radio Waves

Radio waves are emitted and received by antennas, which consist of conductors such as metal rod resonators. In artificial generation of radio waves, an electronic device called a transmitter generates an alternating electric current which is applied to an antenna. The oscillating electrons in the antenna generate oscillating electric and magnetic fields that radiate away from the antenna as radio waves. In reception of radio waves, the oscillating electric and magnetic fields of a radio wave couple to the electrons in an antenna, pushing them back and forth, creating oscillating currents which are applied to a radio receiver. Earth's atmosphere is mainly transparent to radio waves, except for layers of charged particles in the ionosphere which can reflect certain frequencies.

Radio waves are extremely widely used to transmit information across distances in radio communication systems such as radio broadcasting, television, two way radios, mobile phones, communication satellites, and wireless networking. In a radio communication system, a radio frequency current is modulated with an information-bearing signal in a transmitter by varying either the amplitude, frequency or phase, and applied to an antenna. The radio waves carry the information across space to a receiver, where they are received by an antenna and the information extracted by demodulation in the receiver. Radio waves are also used for navigation in systems like Global Positioning System (GPS) and navigational beacons, and locating distant objects in radiolocation and radar. They are also used for remote control, and for industrial heating.

The use of the radio spectrum is strictly regulated by governments, coordinated by the International Telecommunication Union (ITU) which allocates frequencies to different users for different uses.

Microwaves

Microwaves are radio waves of short wavelength, from about 10 centimeters to one millimeter, in the SHF and EHF frequency bands. Microwave energy is produced with klystron and magnetron tubes, and with solid state devices such as Gunn and IMPATT diodes. Although they are emitted and absorbed by short antennas, they are also absorbed by polar molecules, coupling to vibrational and rotational modes, resulting in bulk heating. Unlike higher frequency waves such as infrared and visible light which are absorbed mainly at surfaces, microwaves can penetrate into materials and deposit their energy below the surface. This effect is used to heat food in microwave ovens, and for industrial heating and medical diathermy. Microwaves are the main wavelengths used in radar, and are used for satellite communication, and wireless networking technologies such as Wi-Fi. The copper cables (transmission lines) which are used to carry lower-frequency radio waves to antennas have excessive power losses at microwave frequencies, and metal pipes called waveguides are used to carry them. Although at the low end of the band the atmosphere is mainly transparent, at the upper end of the band absorption of microwaves by atmospheric gases limits practical propagation distances to a few kilometers.

Terahertz radiation or sub-millimeter radiation is a region of the spectrum from about 100 GHz to 30 terahertz (THz) between microwaves and far infrared which can be regarded as belonging to either band. Until recently, the range was rarely studied and few sources existed for microwave energy in the so-called terahertz gap, but applications such as imaging and communications are now appearing. Scientists are also looking to apply terahertz technology in the armed forces, where high-frequency waves might be directed at enemy troops to incapacitate their electronic equipment. Terahertz radiation is strongly absorbed by atmospheric gases, making this frequency range useless for long-distance communication.

Infrared Radiation

The infrared part of the electromagnetic spectrum covers the range from roughly 300 GHz to 400 THz (1 mm – 750 nm). It can be divided into three parts:

- Far-infrared, from 300 GHz to 30 THz (1 mm – 10 μm): The lower part of this range may also be called microwaves or terahertz waves. This radiation is typically absorbed by so-called rotational modes in gas-phase molecules, by molecular motions in liquids, and by phonons in solids. The water in Earth's atmosphere absorbs so strongly in this range that it renders the atmosphere in effect opaque. However, there are certain wavelength ranges ("windows") within the opaque range that allow partial transmission, and can be used for astronomy. The wavelength range from approximately 200 μm up to a few mm is often referred to as Submillimetre astronomy, reserving far infrared for wavelengths below 200 μm.

- Mid-infrared, from 30 THz to 120 THz (10–2.5 ìm): Hot objects (black-body radiators) can radiate strongly in this range, and human skin at normal body temperature radiates strongly at the lower end of this region. This radiation is absorbed by molecular vibrations, where the different atoms in a molecule vibrate around their equilibrium positions. This range is sometimes called the fingerprint region, since the mid-infrared absorption spectrum of a compound is very specific for that compound.
- Near-infrared, from 120 THz to 400 THz (2,500–750 nm): Physical processes that are relevant for this range are similar to those for visible light. The highest frequencies in this region can be detected directly by some types of photographic film, and by many types of solid state image sensors for infrared photography and videography.

Visible Light

Above infrared in frequency comes visible light. The Sun emits its peak power in the visible region, although integrating the entire emission power spectrum through all wavelengths shows that the Sun emits slightly more infrared than visible light. By definition, visible light is the part of the EM spectrum the human eye is the most sensitive to. Visible light (and near-infrared light) is typically absorbed and emitted by electrons in molecules and atoms that move from one energy level to another. This action allows the chemical mechanisms that underlie human vision and plant photosynthesis. The light that excites the human visual system is a very small portion of the electromagnetic spectrum. A rainbow shows the optical (visible) part of the electromagnetic spectrum; infrared (if it could be seen) would be located just beyond the red side of the rainbow whilst ultraviolet would appear just beyond the opposite violet end.

Electromagnetic radiation with a wavelength between 380 nm and 760 nm (400–790 terahertz) is detected by the human eye and perceived as visible light. Other wavelengths, especially near infrared (longer than 760 nm) and ultraviolet (shorter than 380 nm) are also sometimes referred to as light, especially when the visibility to humans is not relevant. White light is a combination of lights of different wavelengths in the visible spectrum. Passing white light through a prism splits it up into the several colours of light observed in the visible spectrum between 400 nm and 780 nm.

If radiation having a frequency in the visible region of the EM spectrum reflects off an object, say, a bowl of fruit, and then strikes the eyes, this results in visual perception of the scene. The brain's visual system processes the multitude of reflected frequencies into different shades and hues, and through this insufficiently understood psychophysical phenomenon, most people perceive a bowl of fruit.

At most wavelengths, however, the information carried by electromagnetic radiation is not directly detected by human senses. Natural sources produce EM radiation across the spectrum, and technology can also manipulate a broad range of wavelengths. Optical fiber transmits light that, although not necessarily in the visible part of the spectrum (it is usually infrared), can carry information. The modulation is similar to that used with radio waves.

Ultraviolet Radiation

Next in frequency comes ultraviolet (UV). In frequency (and thus energy), UV rays sit between the violet end of the visible spectrum and the X-ray range. The UV wavelength spectrum ranges from 399 nm to 10 nm and is divided into 3 sections: UVA, UVB, and UVC.

UV is the lowest energy range energetic enough to ionize atoms, separating electrons from them, and thus causing chemical reactions. UV, X-rays, and gamma rays are thus collectively called ionizing radiation; exposure to them can damage living tissue. UV can also cause substances to glow with visible light; this is called fluorescence. UV fluorescence is used by forensics to detect any evidence like blood and urine, that is produced by a crime scene. Also UV fluorescence is used to detect counterfeit money and IDs, as they are laced with material that can glow under UV.

At the middle range of UV, UV rays cannot ionize but can break chemical bonds, making molecules unusually reactive. Sunburn, for example, is caused by the disruptive effects of middle range UV radiation on skin cells, which is the main cause of skin cancer.

UV rays in the middle range can irreparably damage the complex DNA molecules in the cells producing thymine dimers making it a very potent mutagen. Due to skin cancer caused by UV, the sunscreen industry was invented to combat UV damage. Mid UV wavelengths are called UVB and UVB lights such as germicidal lamps are used to kill germs and also to sterilize water.

The Sun emits UV radiation (about 10% of its total power), including extremely short wavelength UV that could potentially destroy most life on land (ocean water would provide some protection for life there). However, most of the Sun's damaging UV wavelengths are absorbed by the atmosphere before they reach the surface. The higher energy (shortest wavelength) ranges of UV (called "vacuum UV") are absorbed by nitrogen and, at longer wavelengths, by simple diatomic oxygen in the air. Most of the UV in the mid-range of energy is blocked by the ozone layer, which absorbs strongly in the important 200–315 nm range, the lower energy part of which is too long for ordinary dioxygen in air to absorb. This leaves less than 3% of sunlight at sea level in UV, with all of this remainder at the lower energies. The remainder is UV-A, along with some UV-B. The very lowest energy range of UV between 315 nm and visible light (called UV-A) is not blocked well by the atmosphere, but does not cause sunburn and does less biological damage. However, it is not harmless and does create oxygen radicals, mutations and skin damage.

X-rays

After UV come X-rays, which, like the upper ranges of UV are also ionizing. However, due to their higher energies, X-rays can also interact with matter by means of the Compton effect. Hard X-rays have shorter wavelengths than soft X-rays and as they can pass through many substances with little absorption, they can be used to 'see through' objects with 'thicknesses' less than that equivalent to a few meters of water. One notable use is diagnostic X-ray imaging in medicine (a process known as radiography). X-rays are useful as probes in high-energy physics. In astronomy, the accretion disks around neutron stars and black holes emit X-rays, enabling studies of these phenomena. X-rays are also emitted by stellar corona and are strongly emitted by some types of nebulae. However, X-ray telescopes must be placed outside the Earth's atmosphere to see astronomical X-rays, since the great depth of the atmosphere of Earth is opaque to X-rays (with areal density of 1000 g/cm), equivalent to 10 meters thickness of water. This is an amount sufficient to block almost all astronomical X-rays.

Gamma Rays

After hard X-rays come gamma rays, which were discovered by Paul Ulrich Villard in 1900. These are the most energetic photons, having no defined lower limit to their wavelength. In astronomy they are valuable for studying high-energy objects or regions, however as with X-rays this can only be done with telescopes outside the Earth's atmosphere. Gamma rays are used experimentally by physicists for their penetrating ability and are produced by a number of radioisotopes. They are used for irradiation of foods and seeds for sterilization, and in medicine they are occasionally used in radiation cancer therapy. More commonly, gamma rays are used for diagnostic imaging in nuclear medicine, an example being PET scans. The wavelength of gamma rays can be measured with high accuracy through the effects of Compton scattering.

8.1.2 Spectrum Allocation and Management

Spectrum management is the process of regulating the use of radio frequencies to promote efficient use and gain a net social benefit. The term radio spectrum typically refers to the full frequency range from 1 Hz to 3000 GHz (3 THz) that may be used for wireless communication. Increasing demand for services such as mobile telephones and many others has required changes in the philosophy of spectrum management. Demand for wireless broadband has soared due to technological innovation, such as 3G and 4G mobile services, and the rapid expansion of wireless internet services.

Since the 1930s, spectrum was assigned through administrative licensing. Limited by technology, signal interference was once considered as a major problem of spectrum use. Therefore, exclusive licensing was established to protect licensees' signals. This former practice of discrete bands licensed to groups of similar services is giving way, in many countries, to a "spectrum auction" model that is intended to speed technological innovation and improve the efficiency of spectrum use. During the experimental process of spectrum assignment, other approaches have also been carried out, namely, lotteries, unlicensed access, and privatization of spectrum.

Most recently, America has been moving toward a shared spectrum policy, whereas Europe has been pursuing an authorized shared access (ASA) licensing model. President Obama made shared spectrum the policy of the United States on 14 June 2013, following recommendations from the President's Council of Advisors for Science and Technology (PCAST) which advocated the sharing of (uncleared) federal radio spectrum when unused at a place and time provided it does not pose undue risks. In line with this guidance, as of Dec 2014 the FCC was extending the limited success of television band spectrum sharing (TV white space) into other bands, significantly into the 3550–3700 MHz US Navy radar band via a three tier licensing model (incumbent, priority, and general access).

Governments and Spectrum Management

Most countries consider RF spectrum as an exclusive property of the state. The RF spectrum is a national resource, much like water, land, gas and minerals. Unlike these, however, RF is reusable. The purpose of spectrum management is to mitigate radio spectrum pollution, and maximize the benefit of usable radio spectrum.

The first sentence of the International Telecommunication Union (ITU) constitution fully recognises "the sovereign right of each State to regulate its telecommunication". Effective spectrum management requires regulation at national, regional, and global levels.

Goals of spectrum management include: rationalize and optimize the use of the RF spectrum; avoid and solve interference; design short and long range frequency allocations; advance the introduction of new wireless technologies; coordinate wireless communications with neighbours and other administrations. Radio spectrum items which need to be nationally regulated: frequency allocation for various radio services, assignment of license and RF to transmitting stations, type approval of equipment (for countries out of the European Union), fee collection, notifying ITU for the Master International Frequency Register (MIFR), coordination with neighbour countries (as there are no borders to the radio waves), external relations toward regional commissions (such as CEPT in Europe, CITEL in America) and toward ITU.

Spectrum Use

Spectrum management is a growing problem due to the growing number of spectrum uses. Uses include: over-the-air broadcasting, (which started in 1920); government and research uses (which include defense, public safety—maritime, air, police—resource management, transport, and radio astronomy); commercial services to the public (including voice, data, home networking); and industrial, scientific and medical services (which include Telemedicine, and remote control).

In the 1980s, the only concern was about radio and television broadcasting; but today mobile phones and wireless computer networks are more and more important as fewer than 15% of US households rely on over-the-air broadcasting to receive their TV signals.

The US spectrum is managed either by the Federal Communications Commission (FCC) for non-governmental applications or by the National Telecommunications and Information Administration (NTIA) for governmental applications. For shared application, both entities should agree.

The spectrum is divided into different frequency bands, each having a specific application. For instance, the frequency band that covers 300 kHz to 535 kHz is reserved for aeronautical and maritime communications and the spectrum from 520 kHz to 1700 kHz for AM radio. This process is called "allocation".

The next step is to assign frequencies to specific users or classes of users. Each frequency band has a specific assignment that depends on the nature of the application and the numbers of users. Indeed, some applications require a wider band than others (AM radio uses blocks of 10 kHz where FM radio uses blocks of 200 kHz). In addition, "guard bands" are needed to keep the interference between applications to a minimum.

Status Quo: The Command and Control Approach

The Command and Control management approach is the one currently employed by most regulators around the globe. This approach advocates that the regulators be the centralized authorities for spectrum allocation and usage decisions. In the US example, the regulator (FCC) determines the use cases for specified spectrum portions, as well as the parties who will have access to them. The Federal Communications Commission (FCC) also regulates the physical layer technologies to be employed.

The allocation decisions are often static in temporal and spatial dimensions, meaning that they are valid for extended periods of time (usually decades) and for large geographical regions (country wide). The usage is often set to be exclusive; each band is dedicated to a single provider, thus maintaining interference free communication. The command and control management model dates back to initial days of wireless communications, when the technologies employed required interference-free mediums for achieving acceptable quality. Thus, it is often argued that the exclusive nature of the command and control approach is an artifact of outdated technologies.

The apparent advantages of this model is that services related to public interest could be sustained. In terms of profitability, public interest programs, for example, over-the-air television, may not be as attractive as commercial ones in the provider perspective, but they are nevertheless beneficial for the society. Therefore, these services are often implicitly enforced by the regulator through the license agreements. Another advantage is the standardization that results from such a centralized approach.

Such standardization is critical in networked industries, for which the telecommunication industry is a text-book example. One scholar has published a paper that shows how the development of new technologies promises to bring considerably more spectrum to the public, but would require that society embrace a new paradigm of spectrum use.

GAO Report on Spectrum Management (2004)

Excerpt:

- The current structure and management of spectrum use in the United States does not encourage the development and use of some spectrum efficient technologies. Because the spectrum allocation framework largely compartmentalizes spectrum by types of services (such as aeronautical radio navigation) and users (federal, non-federal, and shared), the capability of emerging technologies designed to use spectrum in different ways is often diminished. For example, software-defined cognitive radios — radios that adapt their use of the spectrum to the real-time conditions of their operating environments — could be used to sense unused frequencies, or "white spaces," and automatically make use of those frequencies. It may also be possible to use software-defined cognitive radios to exploit "gray spaces" in the spectrum — areas where emissions exist yet could still accommodate additional users without creating a level of interference that is unacceptable to incumbent users — to increase spectrum efficiency. Currently, however, the spectrum allocation system may not provide the freedom needed for these technologies to operate across existing spectrum designations, and defining new rules requires knowledge about spectrum that spectrum leaders do not have. At the same time, there are few federal regulatory requirements and incentives to use spectrum more efficiently. While the National Telecommunications and Information Administration (NTIA) is responsible for managing the federal government's use of spectrum and ensuring spectrum efficiency, NTIA primarily relies on individual agencies to ensure that the systems they develop are as spectrum efficient as possible. Agencies' guidance and policies, however, do not require systematic consideration of spectrum efficiency in their acquisitions. The lack of economic consequence associated with the manner in which spectrum is used has also provided little incentive to agencies to pursue opportunities proactively to develop and use technologies that would improve spectrum efficiency government-wide.

Alternative Spectrum Governance Regimes and the Spectrum Debate

With the digital transition, spectrum management entered a new age. Full conversion to digital TV by 17 February 2009 (Digital Transition and Public Safety Act of 2005) allows broadcasters to use spectrum more efficiently and save space for the possibility of sharing spectrum.

Spectrum sharing is the subject of heated discussion. Exponential growth of commercial wireless calls for additional spectrum to accommodate more traffic. As a regulator, the FCC responded to these needs by making more spectrum available. A secondary market has been allowed to emerge and licensees are encouraged to lease use of the spectrum to third parties temporarily. Making licenses transferable is an important attempt by the FCC to create incentives for broadcasters to share unused spectrum. Another proposed solution to the spectrum scarcity problem is to enable communications systems to occupy spectrum that was previously allocated for radar use and to cooperatively share spectrum. This approach has received increased attention recently with several research programs, including DARPA projects, investigating several methods of cooperative radar-communications spectrum sharing. More alternatives are underway such as spectrum sharing in cellular networks.

Spectrum scarcity has emerged as a primary problem encountered when trying to launch new wireless services. The effects of this scarcity are most noticeable in spectrum auctions where the operators often need to invest billions of dollars to secure access to specified bands in the available spectrum. In spite of this scarcity, recent spectrum utilization measurements have shown that the available spectrum opportunities are severely underutilized, i.e., left unused. This artificial "access limitation"-based scarcity is often considered to result from the static and rigid nature of the command and control governance regime. Interested parties have started to consider possible improvements in the governance regime by relaxing the constraints on spectrum access. Two prevailing models are the "spectrum commons" and the "spectrum property rights" approaches.

Spectrum Commons Theory

Under US law, the spectrum is not considered to be the property of the private sector nor of the government except insofar as the term "government" is used to be synonymous with "the people".

The original use of the term "the commons" was the practice by which the public at large had limited rights to use the commons; each person then had an interest in their own usage rights, but the commons themselves were not property, nor were the rights "property" since they could not be traded. The term "tragedy of the commons" was popularized by Garrett Hardin in a 1968 article which appeared in Science. The tragedy of the commons illustrates the philosophy that destructive use of public reservations ("the commons") by private interests can result when the best strategy for individuals conflicts with the "common good". In such a scenario, it asserts that even though the contribution of each "bad actor" may be minute, when the results of these actions are combined the resource could be degraded to the point of uselessness. This concern has led to the regulation of the spectrum.

Spectrum Property Rights Model

The spectrum property rights model advocates that the spectrum resources should be treated like land, i.e., private ownership of spectrum portions should be permitted. The allocation of these portions should be implemented by means of market forces. The spectrum owners should be able to trade these portions in secondary markets. Alternatively, the spectrum owners would be able to use their bands in any way they want through any technology they prefer (service and technology neutrality). Although the spectrum property rights model advocates exclusive allocation of transmission rights, it is not the same as a licensed regime. The main difference is the service and technology neutrality advocated in the spectrum property rights approach, as opposed to strict requirements on services and communications technologies inherent in licensed governance regimes.

The basic idea of spectrum property rights was first proposed by Leo Herzel in 1951, who was a law student at the time, preparing a critique of the US FCC policies in spectrum management. Ronald Coase, a Nobel Prize–winning economist, championed the idea of auctioning off spectrum rights as a superior alternative to the status quo in 1959. Coase argued that, though initial distributions may affect matters, property rights in a frequency will lead to the most efficient usage thereof. When he first presented his vision to the FCC, he was asked whether he was making a joke.

The supporters of the spectrum property rights model argue that such a management scheme would potentially promote innovation and more efficient use of spectrum resources, as the spectrum owners would potentially want to economize on their resources.

The spectrum property rights model is often critiqued for potentially leading to artificial scarcity and the hold-up problem. The hold-up problem refers to the difficulty in aggregation of the spectrum resources (which would be required for high bandwidth applications), as the individual spectrum owners could ask for very high compensation in return for their contribution. Since spectrum is a scarce finite good, there is a perverse incentive to not use it at all. Participants and existing spectrum owners in the spectrum market can preemptively buy spectrum, then warehouse it to prevent existing or newcomer competitors from utilizing it. The existing spectrum owner's official plans for this warehoused spectrum would be save it for an unknown future use, and therefore not utilize it at all for the foreseeable future.

In a partial or incomplete "spectrum as property" regulatory regime, incumbent and grandfathered owners who obtained spectrum under the old cause and merit policy, can obtain windfalls in selling the spectrum they obtained for no cost under the earlier regulatory regime. When a regulatory regime changes to the property model, the original merit and cause guidelines for incumbent and grandfathered users are often removed. No regulatory review mechanism exists to check if the merit guidelines are still being followed, and if not, to then revoke the spectrum license from the incumbent spectrum owner and reissue the spectrum to a new user under old merit guidelines, or sell the spectrum inline with the new "spectrum as property" policy.

U.S. Regulatory Agencies

The Communications Act of 1934 grants authority for spectrum management to the President for all federal use (47 USC 305). The National Telecommunications and Information Administration (NTIA) manages the spectrum for the Federal Government. Its rules are found in the NTIA Manual of Regulations and Procedures for Federal Radio Frequency Management".

The Federal Communications Commission (FCC) manages and regulates all domestic non-federal spectrum use (47 USC 301).

International Spectrum Management

The International Telecommunication Union (ITU) is the part of the United Nations (UN) that manages the use of both the RF Spectrum and space satellites among nation states. The Plenipotentiary Conference is the top policy-making body of the ITU, meeting every four years in order to set the Union's general policies. The ITU is divided into three Sectors: the Radiocommunication Sector (ITU-R) determines the technical characteristics and operational procedures for wireless services, and plays a vital role in the Spectrum Management of the radio-frequency; ITU-R Study Group 1 is the Spectrum Management study group; the Telecommunication Standardization Sector (ITU-T) develops internationally agreed technical and operating standards; and the Telecommunication Development Sector (ITU-D) fosters the expansion of telecommunications infrastructure in developing nations throughout the world, that make up two-thirds of the ITU's 191 Member States. The ITU Radio Regulations set a binding international treaty governing the use of the radio spectrum by some 40 different services.

Frequency Administration

In telecommunication, frequency assignment authority is the power granted for the administration, designation or delegation to an agency or administrator via treaty or law, to specify frequencies, frequency channels or frequency bands, in the electromagnetic spectrum for use in radiocommunication services, radio stations or ISM applications.

Frequency administration is – according to Article 1.2 of the International Telecommunication Union's (ITU) Radio Regulations (RR) – defined as «Any governmental department or service responsible for discharging the obligations undertaken in the Constitution of the International Telecommunication Union, in the Convention of the International Telecommunication Union and in the Administrative Regulations (CS 1002).» Definitions identical to those contained in the Annex to the Constitution or the Annex to the Convention of the International Telecommunication Union (Geneva, 1992) are marked "(CS)" or "(CV)" respectively.

International frequency assignment authority is vested in the Radiocommunication Bureau of the International Telecommunication Union (ITU).

Europe

- In Europe each country has regulatory input into the progress of European and international policy, standards, and legislation governing these sectors through their respective frequency administration.
- European frequency administrations might receive military advice by the appropriate National Radio Frequency Agency (NRFA). Pertaining to NATO-Europe, this expertise is within the Spectrum Consultation Command and Control & Infrastructure Branch (SC3IB). However, the decision making body, pertaining to military access to the radio frequency spectrum, is the NATO Civ/Mil Spectrum Capability Panel 3 (CaP3), on behalf of the NATO Consultation, Command and Control Board (C3B), with participation of competent, authorised and mandated representatives of national frequency administrations.
- Civil frequency management for Europe is driven by a number of organisations. These include the:
    - European Union (EU)
    - Independent Regulator's Group (IRG)
    - European Radiocommunications Office (ERO)

In July 2002, the European Commission also established the European Regulators Group for Electronic Communications Networks and Services; creating, for the first time, a formal structure for interaction and coordination between the European Commission and regulators in all EU Member States to ensure consistent application of European legislation.

United States

In the United States, primary frequency assignment authority is exercised by the National Telecommunications and Information Administration (NTIA) for the

Federal Government and by the Federal Communications Commission (FCC) for non-Federal Government organizations.

8.1.3 Regulatory Frameworks and Policy Considerations

Effective spectrum management relies on robust regulatory frameworks and policy interventions that promote efficient spectrum utilization, foster competition, and protect the public interest. Key regulatory tools and policy considerations include:

1. Spectrum Auctions: Auctioning spectrum licenses to telecommunications companies generates revenue for governments and allocates scarce resources to the highest-value uses. Auction mechanisms may vary, including ascending bid auctions, sealed bid auctions, and combinatorial auctions.
2. Spectrum Sharing: Spectrum sharing allows multiple users to access the same frequency band, increasing spectrum efficiency and accommodating diverse use cases. Dynamic spectrum access (DSA) and cognitive radio technologies enable opportunistic spectrum access while minimizing interference.
3. License Exemptions: Some spectrum bands may be designated for license-exempt use, allowing unlicensed devices to operate within predefined technical parameters. Wi-Fi, Bluetooth, and other short-range communication technologies often operate in license-exempt bands, fostering innovation and consumer choice.
4. Spectrum Management Tools: Regulatory agencies employ various tools and techniques to manage spectrum effectively, including spectrum caps, interference limits, spectrum trading, and spectrum rebanding. These tools help balance competing interests and ensure the orderly development of wireless communication networks.
5. International Coordination: Spectrum allocation is often subject to international agreements and coordination efforts to harmonize frequency assignments and facilitate cross-border communication. The ITU plays a central role in coordinating global spectrum allocations through international treaty frameworks and spectrum management conferences.

8.1.4 Challenges and Future Directions

Despite the significant progress in spectrum allocation and regulation, several challenges and opportunities lie ahead:

1. Spectrum Scarcity: The growing demand for wireless communication services, fueled by the proliferation of mobile devices, IoT devices, and emerging technologies, exacerbates spectrum scarcity. Addressing this challenge requires innovative spectrum management approaches, such as dynamic spectrum sharing and spectrum refarming.

2. Spectrum Fragmentation: Fragmentation of spectrum allocations across different frequency bands and regulatory jurisdictions can hinder interoperability and hinder the deployment of new technologies. Harmonization efforts at the regional and international levels are essential to mitigate fragmentation and promote global compatibility.
3. Spectrum for 5G and Beyond: The rollout of 5G networks requires substantial spectrum allocations in both sub-6 GHz and millimeter wave bands. Furthermore, future generations of wireless technology, such as 6G, will demand even larger swaths of spectrum to support ultra-high-speed and low-latency applications.
4. Spectrum Sharing and Interference Management: Dynamic spectrum sharing and cognitive radio technologies hold promise for maximizing spectrum efficiency but pose challenges in terms of interference management and spectrum coordination. Developing robust interference mitigation techniques and regulatory frameworks is essential to realize the full potential of spectrum sharing.
5. Emerging Policy Issues: Emerging policy issues, such as spectrum security, spectrum pricing, and spectrum for public safety and critical infrastructure, require careful consideration to address evolving threats and societal needs. Balancing commercial interests with public interest considerations is paramount in shaping future spectrum policies.

8.2 INTEGRATION WITH EXISTING TECHNOLOGIES

In today's rapidly evolving technological landscape, the integration of new and existing technologies is essential for driving innovation, enhancing efficiency, and unlocking new opportunities across various industries. From artificial intelligence (AI) and cloud computing to the Internet of Things (IoT) and blockchain, integration with existing technologies enables synergies that amplify the capabilities and impact of individual components. Integration with existing technologies is essential for driving innovation, efficiency, and competitiveness in today's digital economy. By seamlessly incorporating new technologies into established systems and workflows, organizations can enhance functionality, improve efficiency, and deliver superior experiences for customers, employees, and stakeholders. Despite the challenges and complexities involved, strategic integration initiatives hold the key to unlocking the full potential of emerging technologies and achieving sustainable growth in the digital age.

8.2.1 The Significance of Integration

Integration with existing technologies refers to the seamless incorporation of new technologies into established systems, workflows, or infrastructures. Rather than operating in isolation, new technologies are integrated into existing frameworks to complement, enhance, or extend their functionalities. This approach enables organizations to leverage their existing investments, infrastructure, and expertise while harnessing the transformative potential of emerging technologies.

The significance of integration with existing technologies can be observed across various domains:

1. Business and Enterprise: In the business world, integration with existing technologies is essential for digital transformation initiatives aimed at improving operational efficiency, customer engagement, and competitive advantage. For example, integrating AI-driven chatbots with existing customer relationship management (CRM) systems enables personalized interactions and automated customer support.
2. Healthcare: Integration of electronic health records (EHR) systems with AI-powered diagnostic tools enhances clinical decision-making, patient care, and medical research. By analyzing vast amounts of patient data and medical literature, AI algorithms can assist healthcare professionals in diagnosing diseases, predicting outcomes, and recommending personalized treatment plans.
3. Manufacturing: In the manufacturing sector, integration with IoT devices, sensors, and analytics platforms enables real-time monitoring, predictive maintenance, and process optimization. By connecting machinery and production systems to the Internet, manufacturers can collect, analyze, and act on data to improve quality, efficiency, and resource utilization.
4. Smart Cities: Integration with existing infrastructure and sensor networks is key to building smart cities that leverage technology to enhance urban livability, sustainability, and resilience. By integrating IoT devices for traffic management, energy monitoring, and waste management, cities can optimize resource allocation, reduce environmental impact, and improve the quality of life for residents.
5. Finance and Banking: Integration with blockchain technology enables secure, transparent, and efficient transactions, reducing costs and risks associated with traditional financial systems. By leveraging blockchain for payments, settlements, and asset tokenization, financial institutions can streamline processes, enhance security, and unlock new business models.

8.2.2 Benefits of Integration

The integration of new technologies with existing systems offers a multitude of benefits:

1. Enhanced Functionality: Integration expands the capabilities of existing systems, enabling them to perform new tasks, handle larger volumes of data, or deliver improved user experiences. For example, integrating voice

recognition technology with mobile banking apps enables hands-free transactions and accessibility for users with disabilities.

2. Improved Efficiency: Integration streamlines workflows, automates repetitive tasks, and eliminates silos between disparate systems, resulting in increased efficiency and productivity. By integrating project management software with collaboration tools, teams can coordinate tasks, share documents, and track progress in real-time, regardless of location or device.
3. Cost Savings: Integration reduces duplication of efforts, eliminates manual interventions, and optimizes resource allocation, leading to cost savings for organizations. For instance, integrating inventory management systems with supply chain analytics tools enables predictive inventory planning, reducing excess inventory and stockouts.
4. Better Decision-Making: Integration provides access to richer data sources, advanced analytics, and real-time insights, empowering organizations to make data-driven decisions with greater confidence and accuracy. By integrating business intelligence (BI) tools with data visualization platforms, executives can visualize trends, identify patterns, and uncover actionable insights to drive strategic initiatives.
5. Enhanced Customer Experience: Integration enables organizations to deliver seamless, personalized, and omnichannel experiences to customers across multiple touchpoints. By integrating customer data platforms (CDP) with marketing automation tools, businesses can orchestrate targeted campaigns, personalized offers, and timely interactions based on customer preferences and behaviors.

8.2.3 Challenges and Considerations

Despite the numerous benefits, integration with existing technologies presents several challenges and considerations:

1. Compatibility Issues: Integrating new technologies with legacy systems or heterogeneous environments may encounter compatibility issues, requiring custom development, middleware, or adapters to bridge the gap between different platforms, protocols, or data formats.
2. Data Security and Privacy: Integration increases the complexity and attack surface of IT systems, raising concerns about data security, privacy, and regulatory compliance. Organizations must implement robust authentication, encryption, and access controls to protect sensitive information and mitigate cyber threats.
3. Interoperability: Ensuring interoperability between disparate systems, devices, and protocols is essential for seamless communication and data

exchange. Standards-based approaches, open APIs, and interoperability testing can facilitate integration and promote ecosystem compatibility.

4. Scalability and Performance: Integration may impact system scalability, performance, and reliability, particularly as data volumes and user loads increase over time. Proper capacity planning, performance tuning, and scalability testing are necessary to ensure that integrated systems can meet evolving demands and maintain optimal performance.
5. Organizational Change Management: Integration initiatives often require organizational changes, process redesign, and cultural shifts to align with new technologies and workflows. Effective change management, stakeholder engagement, and training programs are essential to overcome resistance, build buy-in, and drive adoption across the organization.

8.2.4 Future Directions

Looking ahead, integration with existing technologies will continue to play a critical role in shaping the digital landscape and driving innovation across industries. Several trends and emerging technologies are poised to influence the future of integration:

1. Hybrid Cloud and Multi-Cloud: Integration of on-premises systems with hybrid cloud and multi-cloud environments enables organizations to leverage the scalability, flexibility, and agility of cloud computing while maintaining control over sensitive data and workloads.
2. Edge Computing: Integration with edge computing platforms brings processing power closer to the point of data generation, enabling real-time analytics, low-latency applications, and distributed intelligence for IoT, AI, and immersive technologies.
3. AI and Machine Learning: Integration of AI and machine learning capabilities into existing systems enables predictive analytics, natural language processing, and computer vision applications that enhance automation, decision-making, and personalized experiences.
4. 5G and IoT: Integration with 5G networks and IoT devices unlocks new opportunities for real-time data collection, analysis, and automation across industries such as manufacturing, transportation, healthcare, and smart cities.
5. Blockchain and Distributed Ledger Technology: Integration with blockchain and distributed ledger technology enables secure, transparent, and auditable transactions, contracts, and supply chain processes, reducing fraud, disputes, and inefficiencies.

8.3 ENERGY EFFICIENCY AND SUSTAINABILITY

8.3.1 Energy Conservation

Energy conservation is the effort to reduce wasteful energy consumption by using fewer energy services. This can be done by using energy more effectively (using less energy for continuous service) or changing one's behavior to use less service (for example, by driving less). Energy conservation can be achieved through efficient energy use, which has some advantages, including a reduction in greenhouse gas emissions and a smaller carbon footprint, as well as cost, water, and energy savings.

Green engineering practices improve the life cycle of the components of machines which convert energy from one form into another.

Energy can be conserved by reducing waste and losses, improving efficiency through technological upgrades, improving operations and maintenance, changing users' behaviors through user profiling or user activities, monitoring appliances, shifting load to off-peak hours, and providing energy-saving recommendations. Observing appliance usage, establishing an energy usage profile, and revealing energy consumption patterns in circumstances where energy is used poorly, can pinpoint user habits and behaviors in energy consumption. Appliance energy profiling helps identify inefficient appliances with high energy consumption and energy load. Seasonal variations also greatly influence energy load, as more air-conditioning is used in warmer seasons and heating in colder seasons. Achieving a balance between energy load and user comfort is complex yet essential for energy preservation. On a large scale, a few factors affect energy consumption trends, including political issues, technological developments, economic growth, and environmental concerns.

User-oriented Energy Conservation

User behavior has a significant effect on energy conservation. It involves user activity detection, profiling, and appliance interaction behaviors. User profiling consists of the identification of energy usage patterns of the user and replacing required system settings with automated settings that can be initiated on request. Within user profiling, personal characteristics are instrumental in affecting energy conservation behavior. These characteristics include household income, education, gender, age, and social norms.

User behavior also relies on the impact of personality traits, social norms, and attitudes on energy conservation behavior. Beliefs and attitudes toward a convenient lifestyle, environmentally friendly transport, energy security, and residential location choices affect energy conservation behavior. As a result, energy conservation can be made possible by adopting pro-environmental behavior and energy-efficient systems. Education on approaches to energy conservation can result in wise energy use. The choices made by the users yield energy usage patterns. Rigorous analysis of these usage patterns identifies waste energy patterns, and improving those patterns may reduce significant energy load. Therefore, human behavior is critical to determining the implications of energy conservation measures and solving environmental problems. Substantial energy conservation may be achieved if users' habit loops are modified.

User Habits

User habits significantly impact energy demand; thus, providing recommendations for improving user habits contributes to energy conservation. Micro-moments are essential in realizing energy consumption patterns and are identified using a variety of sensing units positioned in prominent areas across the home. The micro-moment is an event that changes the state of the appliance from inactive to active and helps in building users' energy consumption profiles according to their activities. Energy conservation can be achieved through user habits by following energy-saving recommendations at micro-moments. Unnecessary energy usage can be decreased by selecting a suitable schedule for appliance operation. Creating an effective scheduling system requires an understanding of user habits regarding appliances.

Off-peak Scheduling

Many techniques for energy conservation comprise off-peak scheduling, which means operating an appliance in a low-price energy hour. This schedule can be achieved after user habits regarding appliance use are understood. Most energy providers divide the energy tariff into high and low-price hours; therefore, scheduling an appliance to work an off-peak hour will significantly reduce electricity bills.

User Activity Detection

User activity detection leads to the precise detection of appliances required for an activity. If an appliance is active but not required for a user's current activity, it wastes energy and can be turned off to conserve energy. The precise identification of user activities is necessary to achieve this method of energy conservation.

Energy Conservation Opportunities by Sector

Buildings

Existing Buildings

Energy conservation measures have primarily focused on technological innovations to improve efficiencies and financial incentives with theoretical explanations obtained from the mentioned analytical traditions. Existing buildings can improve energy efficiency by changing structural maintenance materials, adjusting the composition of air conditioning systems, selecting energy-saving equipment, and formulating subsidy policies. These measures can improve users' thermal comfort and reduce buildings' environmental impact. The selection of combinatorial optimization schemes that contain measures to guide and restrict users' behavior in addition to carrying out demand-side management can dynamically adjust energy consumption. At the same time, economic means should enable users to change their behavior and achieve a low-carbon life. Combination optimization and pricing incentives reduce building energy consumption and carbon emissions and reduce users' costs.

Energy monitoring through energy audits can achieve energy efficiency in existing buildings. An energy audit is an inspection and analysis of energy use and flows for energy conservation in a structure, process, or system intending to reduce energy input without negatively affecting output. Energy audits can determine specific opportunities for energy conservation and efficiency measures as well as determine cost-effective strategies. The recent development of smartphone apps enables homeowners to complete relatively sophisticated energy audits themselves. For instance, smart thermostats can connect to standard HVAC systems to maintain energy-efficient indoor temperatures. In addition, data loggers can also be installed to monitor the interior temperature and humidity levels to provide a more precise understanding of the conditions. If the data gathered is compared with the users' perceptions of comfort, more fine-tuning of the interiors can be implemented (e.g., increasing the temperature where A.C. is used to prevent over-cooling). Building technologies and smart meters can allow commercial and residential energy users to visualize the impact their energy use can have in their workplaces or homes. Advanced real-time energy metering can help people save energy through their actions.

Another approach towards energy conservation is the implementation of E.C.M.s in commercial buildings, which often employ Energy Service Companies (ESCOs) experienced in energy performance contracting. This industry has been around since the 1970s and is more prevalent than ever today. The US-based organization E.V.O. (Efficiency Valuation Organization) has created a set of guidelines for ESCOs to adhere to in evaluating the savings achieved by E.C.M.s. These guidelines are called the International Performance Measurement and Verification Protocol(IPMVP).

Energy efficiency can also be achieved by upgrading certain aspects of existing buildings. Firstly, making thermal improvements by adding insulation to crawl spaces and ensuring no leaks achieves an efficient building envelope, reducing the need for mechanical systems to heat and cool the space. High-performance insulation is also supported by adding double/triple-glazed windows to minimize thermal heat transmission. Minor upgrades in existing buildings include changing mixers to low flow greatly aids in water conservation, changing light bulbs to LED lights results in 70-90% less energy consumption than a standard incandescent or

C.F.L. bulb, changing inefficient appliances with Energy Star-rated appliances will consume less energy, and finally adding vegetation in the landscape surrounding the building to function as a shading element. A window windcatcher can reduce the total energy use of a building by 23.3%.

Energy conservation through users' behaviors requires understanding household occupants' lifestyle, social, and behavioral factors in analyzing energy consumption. This involves one-time investments in energy efficiency, such as purchasing new energy-efficient appliances or upgrading the building insulation without curtailing economic utility or the level of energy services, and energy curtailment behaviors which are theorized to be driven more by social-psychological factors and environmental concerns in comparison to the energy efficiency behaviors. Replacing existing appliances with newer and more efficient ones leads to energy efficiency as less energy is wasted throughout. Overall, energy efficiency behaviors are identified more with one-time, cost-incurring investments in efficient appliances and retrofits, while energy curtailment behaviors include repetitive, low-cost energy-saving efforts.

To identify and optimize residential energy use, conventional and behavioral economics, technology adoption theory and attitude-based decision-making, social and environmental psychology, and sociology must be analyzed. The techno-economic and psychological literature analysis focuses on the individual attitude, behavior, and choice/context/external conditions. In contrast, the sociological literature relies more on the energy consumption practices shaped by the social, cultural, and economic factors in a dynamic setting.

New Buildings

Many steps can be taken toward energy conservation and efficiency when designing new buildings. Firstly, the building can be designed to optimize building performance by having an efficient building envelope with high-performing insulation and window glazing systems, window facades strategically oriented to optimize daylighting, shading elements to mitigate unwanted glare, and passive energy systems for appliances. In passive solar building designs, windows, walls, and floors are made to collect, store, and distribute solar energy in the form of heat in the winter and reject solar heat in the summer.

The key to designing a passive solar building is to best take advantage of the local climate. Elements to be considered include window placement and glazing type, thermal insulation, thermal mass, and shading. Optimizing daylighting can decrease energy waste from incandescent bulbs, windows, and balconies, allow natural ventilation, reduce the need for heating and cooling, low flow mixers aid in water conservation, and upgrade to Energy star rated appliances consume less energy. Designing a building according to LEED guidelines while incorporating smart home technology can help save a lot of energy and money in the long run.

Passive solar design techniques can be applied most easily to new buildings, but existing buildings can be retrofitted.

Mainly, energy conservation is achieved by modifying user habits or providing an energy-saving recommendation of curtailing an appliance or scheduling it to low-price energy tariff hours. Besides changing user habits and appliance control, identifying irrelevant appliances concerning user activities in smart homes saves energy. Smart home technology can advise users on energy-saving strategies according to their behavior, encouraging behavioral change that leads to energy conservation. This guidance includes reminders to turn off lights, leakage sensors to prevent plumbing issues, running appliances on off-peak hours, and smart sensors that save energy. Such technology learns user-appliance activity patterns, gives a complete overview of various energy-consuming appliances, and can provide guidance to improve these patterns to contribute to energy conservation. As a result, they can strategically schedule appliances by monitoring the energy consumption profiles of the appliances, schedule devices to the energy-efficient mode, or plan to work during off-peak hours.

Appliance-oriented approaches emphasize appliance profiling, curtailing, and scheduling to off-peak hours, as supervision of appliances is key to energy preservation. It usually leads to appliance curtailment in which an appliance is either scheduled to work another time or is turned off. Appliance curtailment involves appliance recognition, activity-appliances model, unattended appliance detection, and energy conservation service. The appliance recognition module detects active appliances to identify the activities of smart home users. After identifying users' activities, the association between the functional appliances and user activities is established. The unattended appliance detection module looks for active appliances but is unrelated to user activity. These functional appliances waste energy and can be turned off by providing recommendations to the user.

Based on the smart home recommendations, users can give weight to certain appliances that increase user comfort and satisfaction while conserving energy. Energy consumption models of energy consumption of appliances and the level of comfort they create can balance priorities among smart home comfort levels and energy consumption. According to Kashimoto, Ogura, Yamamoto, Yasumoto, and Ito, the energy supply reduces based on the historical state of the appliance and increases according to the comfort level requirement of the user, leading to a targeted energy-saving ratio. Scenarios-based energy consumption can be employed as a strategy for energy conservation, with each scenario encompassing a specific set of rules for energy consumption.

Transportation

Transporting people, goods, and services represented 29% of U.S. energy consumption in 2007. The transportation sector also accounted for about 33% of U.S. carbon dioxide emissions in 2006, with highway vehicles accounting for about

84% of that, making transportation an essential target for addressing global climate change (E.I.A., 2008). Suburban infrastructure evolved during an age of relatively easy access to fossil fuels, leading to transportation-dependent living systems. The amount of energy used to transport people to and from a facility, whether they are commuters, customers, vendors, or homeowners, is known as the transportation energy intensity of the building. Land is developing at a faster rate than population growth, leading to urban sprawl and, therefore, high transportation energy intensity as more people need to commute longer distances to jobs. As a result, the location of a building is essential in decreasing embodied emissions.

In transportation, state and local efforts in energy conservation and efficiency measures tend to be more targeted and smaller in scale. However, with more robust fuel economy standards, new targets for the use of alternative transportation fuels, and new efforts in electric and hybrid electric vehicles, EPAct05 and EISA provide a new set of national policy signals and financial incentives to the private sector and state and local governments for the transportation sector. Zoning reforms that allow greater urban density and designs for walking and bicycling can greatly reduce energy consumed for transportation. Many Americans work in jobs that allow for remote work instead of commuting daily, which is a significant opportunity to conserve energy. Intelligent transportation systems (ITS) provide a solution to traffic congestion and C.E.s caused by increased vehicles. ITS combines improvements in information technology and systems, communications, sensors, controllers, and advanced mathematical methods with the traditional world of transportation infrastructure. It improves traffic safety and mobility, reduces environmental impact, promotes sustainable transportation, and increases productivity. The ITS strengthens the connection and cooperation between people, vehicles, roads, and the environment while improving road capacity, reducing traffic accidents, and improving transportation efficiency and safety by alleviating traffic congestion and reducing pollution. It makes full use of traffic information as an application service, which can enhance the operational efficiency of existing traffic facilities.

The most significant energy-saving potential is that there are the most problems in urban transportation in various countries, such as management systems, policies and regulations, planning, technology, operation, and management mechanism. Improvements in one or several aspects will improve road transportation. Efficiency has a positive impact, which leads to the improvement of the urban traffic environment and efficiency.

In addition to ITS, transit-oriented development (T.O.D.) significantly improves transportation in urban areas by emphasizing density, proximity to transit, diversity of uses, and streetscape design. Density is important for optimizing location and is a way to cut down on driving. Planners can regulate development rights by exchanging them from ecologically sensitive areas to growth-friendly zones according to density transfer procedures. Distance is defined as the accessibility of rail and bus transits, which serve as deterrents for driving. For transit-oriented development to be feasible, transportation stops must be close to where people live. Diversity refers to mixed-use areas that offer essential services close to homes and offices and include residential spaces for different socioeconomic categories, commercial and retail. This creates a pedestrian shed where one area can meet people's everyday needs on foot. Lastly, the streetscapes design involves minimal parking and walkable areas that calm traffic. Generous parking incentivizes people to use cars, whereas minimal and expensive parking deters commuters. At the same time, streetscapes can be designed to incorporate bicycling lanes and designated bicycle paths and trails. People may commute by bicycle to work without being concerned about their bicycles becoming wet because of covered bicycle storage. This encourages commuters to use bicycles rather than other modes of transportation and contributes to energy saving. People will be happy to walk a few blocks from a train stop if there are attractive, pedestrian-friendly outdoor spaces nearby with good lighting, park benches, outdoor tables at cafés, shade tree plantings, pedestrian courts that are blocked off to cars, and public internet connection. Additionally, this strategy calms traffic, improving the intended pedestrian environment.

New urban planning schemes can be designed to improve connectivity in cities through networks of interconnected streets that spread out traffic flow, slow down vehicles, and make walking more pleasant. By dividing the number of road links by the number of road nodes, the connectivity index is calculated. The higher the connectivity index, the greater the route choices and the better the pedestrian access. Realizing the transportation impacts associated with buildings allows commuters to take steps toward energy conservation. Connectivity encourages energy-conserving behaviors as commuters use fewer cars, walk and bike more, and use public transportation. For commuters that do not have the option of public transportation, smaller vehicles that are hybrid or have better mileage can be used.

Consumer Products

Homeowners implementing ECMs in their residential buildings often start with an energy audit. This is a way homeowners look at what areas of their homes are using, and possibly losing energy. Residential energy auditors are accredited by the Building Performance Institute (BPI) or the Residential Energy Services Network (RESNET). Homeowners can hire a professional or do it themselves or use a smartphone to help do an audit.

Energy conservation measures are often combined into larger guaranteed Energy Savings Performance Contracts to maximize energy savings while minimizing disruption to building occupants by coordinating renovations. Some ECMs cost less to implement yet return higher energy savings. Traditionally, lighting projects were a good example of "low hanging fruit" that could be used to drive implementation of more substantial upgrades to HVAC systems in large facilities. Smaller buildings might combine window replacement with modern insulation using advanced building foams to improve energy for performance. Energy dashboard projects are a new kind of ECM that relies on the behavioral change of building occupants to save energy. When implemented as part of a program, case studies, such as that for the DC Schools, report energy savings up 30%. Under the right circumstances, open energy dashboards can even be implemented for free to improve upon these savings even more.

Consumers are often poorly informed of the savings of energy-efficient products. A prominent example of this is the energy savings that can be made by replacing an incandescent light bulb with a more modern alternative. When purchasing light bulbs, many consumers opt for cheap incandescent bulbs, failing to take into account their higher energy costs and lower lifespans when compared to modern compact fluorescent and LED bulbs. Although these energy-efficient alternatives have a higher upfront cost, their long lifespan and low energy use can save consumers a considerable amount of money. The price of LED bulbs has also been steadily decreasing in the past five years due to improvements in semiconductor technology. Many LED bulbs on the market qualify for utility rebates that further reduce the price of the purchase to the consumer. Estimates by the U.S. Department of Energy state that widespread adoption of LED lighting over the next 20 years could result in about $265 billion worth of savings in United States energy costs.

The research one must put into conserving energy is often too time-consuming and costly for the average consumer when there are cheaper products and technology available using today's fossil fuels. Some governments and NGOs are attempting to reduce this complexity with Eco-labels that make differences in energy efficiency easy to research while shopping.

To provide the kind of information and support people need to invest money, time and effort in energy conservation, it is important to understand and link to people's topical concerns. For instance, some retailers argue that bright lighting stimulates purchasing. However, health studies have demonstrated that headache, stress, blood pressure, fatigue and worker error all generally increase with the common over-illumination present in many workplace and retail settings. It has been shown that natural daylighting increases productivity levels of workers, while reducing energy consumption.

In warm climates where air conditioning is used, any household device that gives off heat will result in a larger load on the cooling system. Items such as stoves, dishwashers, clothes dryers, hot water, and incandescent lighting all add heat to the home. Low-power or insulated versions of these devices give off less heat for the air conditioning to remove. The air conditioning system can also improve efficiency by using a heat sink that is cooler than the standard air heat exchanger, such as geothermal or water.

In cold climates, heating air and water is a major demand for household energy use. Significant energy reductions are possible by using different technologies. Heat pumps are a more efficient alternative to electrical resistance heaters for warming air or water. A variety of efficient clothes dryers are available, and the clothes lines requires no energy- only time. Natural-gas (or bio-gas) condensing boilers and hot-air furnaces increase efficiency over standard hot-flue models. Standard electric boilers can be made to run only at hours of the day when they are needed by means of a time switch. This decreases energy use vastly. In showers, a semi-closed-loop system could be used. New construction implementing heat exchangers can capture heat from wastewater or exhaust air in bathrooms, laundry, and kitchens.

In both warm and cold climate extremes, airtight thermal insulated construction is the largest factor determining the efficiency of a home. Insulation is added to minimize the flow of heat to or from the home, but can be labor-intensive to retrofit to an existing home.

Asia: Energy Conservation

Although energy efficiency is expected to play a vital role in cost-effectively cutting energy demand, only a small part of its economic potential is exploited in Asia. Governments have implemented a range of subsidies such as cash grants, cheap credit, tax exemptions, and co-financing with public-sector funds to encourage energy-efficiency initiatives across several sectors. Governments in the Asia-Pacific region have implemented a range of information provision and labeling programs for buildings, appliances, and the transportation and industrial sectors. Information programs can simply provide data, such as fuel-economy labels, or actively seek to encourage behavioral changes, such as Japan's Cool Biz campaign that encourages setting air conditioners at 28-degrees Celsius and allowing employees to dress casually in the summer.

China's government has launched a series of policies since 2005 to effectively promote the goal of reducing energy-saving emissions; however, road transportation, the fastest-growing energy-consuming sector in the transportation industry, lacks specific, operational, and systematic energy-saving plans. Road transportation is the highest priority to achieve energy conservation effectively and reduce emissions, particularly since social and economic development has entered the "new norm" period. Generally speaking, the government should make comprehensive plans for conservation and emissions reduction in the road transportation industry within the three dimensions of demand, structure, and technology. For example, encouraging trips using public transportation and new transportation modes such as car-sharing and increasing investment in new energy vehicles in structure reform, etc.

European Union: Energy Conservation

At the end of 2006, the European Union (EU) pledged to cut its annual consumption of primary energy by 20% by 2020. The EU Energy Efficiency Directive 2012 mandates energy efficiency improvements within the EU.

As part of the EU's SAVE program, aimed at promoting energy efficiency and encouraging energy-saving behavior, the Boiler Efficiency Directive specifies minimum levels of efficiency for boilers using liquid or gaseous fuels.

There is steady progress on energy regulation implementation in Europe, North America, and Asia, with the highest number of building energy standards being adopted and implemented. Moreover, the performance of Europe is highly encouraging concerning energy standard activities. They recorded the highest percentage of mandatory energy standards compared to the other five regions.

In 2050, energy savings in Europe can reach 67% of the 2019 baseline scenario, amounting to a demand of 361 Mtoe in an "energy efficiency first" societal trend scenario. A condition is that there be no rebound effect, for otherwise the savings are 32% only or energy use may even increase by 42% if techno-economic potentials are not realized.

Germany has reduced its primary energy consumption by 11% from 1990 to 2015 and set itself goals of reducing it by 30% by the year 2030 and by 50% by the year 2050 in comparison to the level of 2008.

Iran: Energy Conservation

Supreme leader of Iran Ali Khamenei had regularly criticized energy administration and high fuel consumption.

Japan: Energy Conservation

Since the 1973 oil crisis, energy conservation has been an issue in Japan. All oil-based fuel is imported, so domestic sustainable energy is being developed.

The Energy Conservation Center promotes energy efficiency in every aspect of Japan. Public entities are implementing the efficient use of energy for industries and research. It includes projects such as the Top Runner Program. In this project, new appliances are regularly tested on efficiency, and the most efficient ones are made the standard.

Middle East: Energy Conservation

The Middle East holds 40% of the world's crude oil reserves and 23% of its natural gas reserves. Conservation of domestic fossil fuels is, therefore, a legitimate priority for the Gulf countries, given domestic needs as well as the global market for these products. Energy subsidies are the chief barrier to conservation in the Gulf. Residential electricity prices can be a tenth of U.S. rates. As a result, increased tariff revenues from gas, electricity, and water sales would encourage investment in natural gas exploration and production and generation capacity, helping to alleviate future shortages.

Households in the MENA region are responsible for 53% of energy use in Saudi Arabia and 57% of the UAE's ecological footprint. This is partially due to poorly designed and constructed buildings, mainly under a cheap energy model that has left them without contemporary control technology or even proper insulation and efficient appliances. Building energy consumption can be cut by 20% under a combination of insulation, efficient windows and appliances, shading, reflective roofing, and a host of automated controls that adjust energy use.

Governments could also set minimum energy efficiency and water use standards on importing appliances sold inside their countries, effectively banning the sale of inefficient air conditioners, dishwashers, and washing machines. Administration of the laws would essentially be a function of national customs services. Governments could go further, offering incentives - or mandates - that air conditioners of a certain age be replaced.

Lebanon

In Lebanon and since 2002 The Lebanese Center for Energy Conservation (LCEC) has been promoting the development of efficient and rational uses of energy and the use of renewable energy at the consumer level. It was created as a project financed by the International Environment Facility (GEF) and the Ministry of Energy Water (MEW) under the management of the United Nations Development Programme (UNDP) and gradually established itself as an independent technical national center although it continues to be supported by the United Nations Development Programme (UNDP) as indicated in the Memorandum of Understanding (MoU) signed between MEW and UNDP on 18 June 2007.

Nepal: Energy Conservation

Until recently, Nepal has been focusing on the exploitation of its huge water resources to produce hydropower. Demand-side management and energy conservation were not in the focus of government action. In 2009, bilateral Development Cooperation between Nepal and the Federal Republic of Germany has agreed upon the joint implementation of the "Nepal Energy Efficiency Programme". The lead executing agencies for the implementation are the Water and Energy Commission Secretariat (WECS). The aim of the program is the promotion of energy efficiency in policymaking, in rural and urban households as well as in the industry.

Due to the lack of a government organization that promotes energy efficiency in the country, the Federation of Nepalese Chambers of Commerce and Industry (FNCCI) has established the Energy Efficiency Centre under his roof to promote energy conservation in the private sector. The Energy Efficiency Centre is a non-profit initiative that is offering energy auditing services to the industries. The centre is also supported by Nepal Energy Efficiency Programme of Deutsche Gesellschaft für Internationale Zusammenarbeit. A study conducted in 2012 found out that Nepalese industries could save 160,000-megawatt hours of electricity and 8,000 terajoules of thermal energy (like diesel, furnace oil, and coal) every year. These savings are equivalent to annual energy cost cut of up to 6.4 Billion Nepalese Rupees. As a result of Nepal Economic Forum 2014, an economic reform agenda in the priority sectors was declared focusing on energy conservation among others. In the energy reform agenda, the government of Nepal gave the commitment to introduce incentive packages in the budget of the fiscal year 2015/16 for industries that practices energy efficiency or use efficient technologies (incl. cogeneration).

New Zealand: Energy Conservation

In New Zealand the Energy Efficiency and Conservation Authority is the Government Agency responsible for promoting energy efficiency and conservation. The Energy Management Association of New Zealand is a membership-based organization representing the New Zealand energy services sector, providing training and accreditation services with the aim of ensuring energy management services are credible and dependable.

Nigeria: Energy Conservation

In Nigeria, the Lagos State Government is encouraging Lagosians to imbibe an energy conservation culture. In 2013, the Lagos State Electricity Board (LSEB) ran an initiative tagged "Conserve Energy, Save Money" under the Ministry of Energy and Mineral Resources. The initiative is designed to sensitize Lagosians around the theme of energy conservation by influencing their behavior through do-it-yourself tips. In September 2013, Governor Babatunde Raji Fashola of Lagos State and the campaign ambassador, rapper Jude "MI" Abaga participated in the Governor's conference video call on the topic of energy conservation. In addition to this, during the month of October (the official energy conservation month in the state), LSEB hosted experience centers in malls around Lagos State where members of the public were encouraged to calculate their household energy consumption and discover ways to save money using a consumer-focused energy app. To get Lagosians started on energy conservation, solar lamps and energy-saving bulbs were also handed out. In Kaduna State, the Kaduna Power Supply Company (KAPSCO) ran a program to replace all light bulbs in Public Offices; fitting energy-saving bulbs in place of incandescent bulbs. KAPSCO is also embarking on an initiative to retrofit all conventional streetlights in the Kaduna Metropolis to LEDs which consume much less energy.

Sri Lanka: Energy Conservation

Sri Lanka currently consumes fossil fuels, hydro power, wind power, solar power and dendro power for their day to day power generation. The Sri Lanka Sustainable

Energy Authority is playing a major role regarding energy management and energy conservation. Today, most industries are requested to reduce their energy consumption by using renewable energy sources and optimizing their energy usage.

Turkey: Energy Conservation

Turkey aims to decrease by at least 20% the amount of energy consumed per GDP of Turkey by 2023 (energy intensity).

United Kingdom: Energy Conservation

The Department for Business, Energy and Industrial Strategy is responsible for promoting energy efficiency in the United Kingdom.

United States: Energy Conservation

The United States is currently the second-largest single consumer of energy, following China. The U.S. Department of Energy categorizes national energy use in four broad sectors: transportation, residential, commercial, and industrial.

About half of U.S. energy consumption in the transportation and residential sectors is primarily controlled by individual consumers. In the typical American home, space heating is the most significant energy use, followed by electrical technology (appliances, lighting, and electronics) and water heating. Commercial and industrial energy expenditures are determined by businesses entities and other facility managers. National energy policy has a significant effect on energy usage across all four sectors.

Since the oil embargoes and price spikes of the 1970s, energy efficiency and conservation have been fundamental tenets of U.S. energy policy. The scope of energy conservation and efficiency measures has been broadened throughout time by U.S. energy policies and programs, including federal and state legislation and regulatory actions, to include all economic sectors and all geographical areas of the nation. Measurable energy conservation and efficiency gains in the 1980s led to the 1987 Energy Security Report to the President (DOE, 1987) that "the United States uses about 29 quads less energy in a year today than it would have if our economic growth since 1972 had been accompanied by the less- efficient trends in energy use we were following at that time" The DOE Strategy and the legislation included new strategies for strengthening conservation and efficiency in buildings, industry, and electric power, such as integrated resource planning for electric and natural gas utilities and efficiency and labeling standards for 13 residential appliances and equipment categories. Lack of a national consensus on how to proceed interfered with developing a consistent and comprehensive approach. Nevertheless, the Energy Policy Act of 2005 (EPAct05; 109th U.S. Congress, 2005) contained many new energy conservation and efficiency provisions in the transportation, buildings, and electric power sectors.

The most recent federal law to increase and broaden U.S. energy conservation and efficiency laws, programs, and practices is the Energy Independence and Security Act of 2007 (EISA). Over the next few decades, it is anticipated that EISA will significantly reduce energy use because it has more standards and targets than previous legislation. Both acts reinforce the importance of lighting and appliance efficiency programs, targeting an additional 70% lighting efficiency by 2020, introducing 45 new standards for appliances, and setting up new standards for vehicle fuel economy. The Federal Government is also promoting a new 30% model code for efficient building practices in the construction industry. Additionally, according to the American Council for an Energy-Efficient Economy (ACEEE), the EISA's energy efficiency and conservation initiatives will cut carbon dioxide emissions by 9% in 2030. These requirements cover appliance and lighting efficiency, energy savings in homes, businesses, and public buildings, the effectiveness of industrial manufacturing facilities, and the efficiency of electricity supply and end use. Expectations are high for increased energy savings due to these initiatives, which have already started contributing to new federal, state, and local laws, programs, and practices across the U.S.

The development and use of alternative transportation fuels (whose supply is expected to expand by 15% by 2022), renewable energy sources, and other clean energy technologies have also received more attention and financial incentives. Recent policies also emphasize growing the use of coal with carbon capture and sequestration, solar, wind, nuclear, and other clean energy sources.

In February 2023 the United States Department of Energy proposed a set of new energy efficiency standards that, if implemented, will save to users of different electric machines in the United States around $3,500,000,000 per year and will reduce by the year 2050 carbon emissions by the same amount as emitted by 29,000,000 houses.

Mechanisms to Promote Conservation

Governmental Mechanisms

Governments at the national, regional, and local levels may implement policies to promote energy efficiency. Building energy rules can cover the energy consumption of an entire structure or specific building components, like heating and cooling systems. They represent some of the most frequently used instruments for energy efficiency improvements in buildings and can play an essential role in improving energy conservation in buildings. There are multiple reasons for the growth of these policies and programs since the 2000s, including cost savings as energy prices increased, growing concern about the environmental impacts of energy use, and public health concerns. The policies and programs related to energy conservation are critical to establishing safety and performance levels, assisting in consumer decision-making, and explicitly identifying energy-conserving and energy-efficient products. Recent policies include new programs and regulatory incentives that call for electric and natural gas utilities to increase their involvement in delivering energy-efficiency products and services to their customers. For example, the National Action Plan for Energy Efficiency (NAPEE) is a public-private partnership created in response to EPAct05 that brings together senior executives from electric and natural gas utilities, state public utility commissions, other state agencies, and environmental and consumer groups representing every region of the country. The success of building energy regulation in effectively controlling energy consumption in the building sector will be, to a great extent, associated with the adopted energy performance indicator and the promoted energy assessment tools. It can help overcome significant market barriers and ensure cost-effective energy efficiency opportunities are incorporated into new buildings. This is crucial in emerging nations where new constructions are rapidly developing, and market and energy prices sometimes discourage efficient technologies. The building energy standards development and adoption showed that 42% of emerging developing countries surveyed have no energy standard in place, 20% have mandatory, 22% have mixed, and 16% proposed.

The major impediments to implementing building energy regulations for energy conservation and efficiency in the building sector are institutional barriers and market failures rather than technical problems, as pointed out by Nature Publishing Group (2008). Among these, Santamouris (2005) includes a lack of owners' awareness of energy conservation benefits, building energy regulations benefits, insufficient awareness and training of property managers, builders, and engineers, and a lack of specialized professionals to ensure compliance. The development and adoption of building energy regulations, such as energy standards in developing countries, are still far behind compared to building energy regulation adoption and implementation in developed countries.

Building energy standards are starting to appear in Africa, Latin America, and Middle East regions, even though this is a new development going to the result obtained in this study. The level of progress on energy regulation activities in Africa, Latin America, and the Middle East is increasing, given the higher number of energy standard proposals recorded in these regions. According to the Royal Institute of Chartered Surveyors, several codes are being developed in developing countries with UNDP and GEF support. These typically include elemental and integrated routes to compliance, such as a fundamental method defining the performance requirements of specific building elements. However, they are still far behind in building energy regulation development, implementation, and compliance compared to developed nations. Also, decision-making regarding energy regulations is still from the government only, with little or no input from non-governmental entities. As a result, lower energy regulation development is recorded in these regions compared to regions with integrated and consensus approaches.

Additionally, there is growing government involvement in the development and implementation of energy standards; 62% of Middle Eastern respondents, 45% of African respondents, and 43% of Latin American respondents indicated that existing government agencies, such as building agencies and energy agencies, are involved in implementing building energy standards in their respective nations, as opposed to 20% of European respondents, 38% of Asian respondents, and 0% of North American respondents, who indicated the involvement of existing agencies. Several North African nations, like Tunisia and Egypt, have programs relating to building energy standards, while Algeria and Morocco are now seeking to establish building energy standards, according to the Royal Institute of Chartered Surveyors. Similarly, Egypt's residential energy standard became law in 2005, and their commercial standard was anticipated to follow. The standards provide minimal performance requirements for applications involving air conditioners and other appliances and elemental and integrated pathways. However, it was claimed that enforcement legislation was still required in 2005. Additionally, Morocco launched a program in 2005 to create thermal energy requirements for construction, concentrating on the hospitality, healthcare, and communal housing industries.

Mandatory Energy Standards

Energy standards are the primary way governments foster energy efficiency as a public good. A recognized standard-setting organization prepares a standard. Standards developed by recognized organizations are often used as the basis for the development and updating of building codes. They allow innovative approaches and techniques to achieve effective energy use and optimum building performance. Besides, it encourages cost-effective energy use of building components, including building envelope, lighting, HVAC, electrical installations, lift and escalator, and other equipment. Energy-efficiency standards have been expanded and strengthened for appliances, building equipment, and lighting. For example, appliances and equipment standards are being developed for a new range of devices, including reduction goals for "standby" power that keeps consumer electronic products in a ready-to-use mode. Some devices require certain levels of energy performance from a car, building, appliance, or other technical equipment. If the vehicle, building, appliance, or equipment does not meet these standards, there may be restrictions on its sale or rent. In the U.K., these are called "minimum energy efficiency standards" or MEES and were applied to privately rented accommodation in 2019.

Energy codes and standards are vital in setting minimum energy-efficient design and construction requirements. Buildings should be developed following energy standards to save energy efficiently. They specify uniform requirements for new buildings, additions, and modifications. National organizations like the American Society of Heating, Refrigerating, and Air-Conditioning Engineers publish the standards (ASHRAE). State and municipal governments frequently use energy standards as the technical foundation for creating their energy regulations. Some energy standards are written in a mandatory and enforceable language, making it simple for governments to add the standards' provisions directly to their laws or regulations.

The American Society of Heating, Refrigeration, and Air-Conditioning Engineers (ASHRAE) is a well-known example of a standard-making organization. This organization dates to the nineteenth century and is international in its membership (About ASHRAE 2018). Examples of ASHRAE standards that relate to energy conservation in the built environment are:

- Standard 62.1-2016 Ventilation for Acceptable Indoor Air Quality.
- Standard 90.2-2007 Energy Efficient Design of Low-Rise Residential Buildings.
- Standard 100-2018 Energy Efficiency in Existing Buildings.
- Standard 189.1-2014 Standard for the Design of High-Performance Green Buildings.

The Residential Energy Services Network is a crucial benchmark for energy reduction (RESNET). The Home Energy Rating System (HERS) of RESNET, which is based on the International Code Council's (ICC) energy code, is used to rate home energy consumption with a standard numerical scale that examines factors in home energy use (About HERS 2018). The American National Standards Institute (ANSI) has acknowledged the HERS assessment system as a national benchmark for evaluating energy efficiency. The International Energy Conservation Code (IECC) of the ICC requires an energy rating index, and the main index used in the residential building sector is HERS. The mortgage financing sector makes substantial use of the HERS index. A home's expected energy usage may impact the available mortgage funds based on the HERS score, with more energy-efficient, lower energy-using homes potentially qualifying for a better mortgage rate or amount.

Mandatory Energy Labels

Many governments require that a car, building, or piece of equipment be labeled with its energy performance. This allows consumers and customers to see the energy implications of their choices, but does not restrict their choices or regulate which products are available to choose from.

It also does not enable easily comparing options (such as being able to filter by energy-efficiency in online stores) or have the best energy-conserving options accessible (such as energy-conserving options being available in the frequented local store). (An analogy would be nutritional labeling on food.) A trial of estimated financial energy cost of refrigerators alongside EU energy-efficiency class (EEEC) labels online found that the approach of labels involves a trade-off between financial considerations and higher cost requirements in effort or time for the product-selection from the many available options which are often unlabelled and don't have any EEEC-requirement for being bought, used or sold within the EU. Moreover, in this one trial the labeling was ineffective in shifting purchases towards more sustainable options.

Energy Taxes

Some countries employ energy or carbon taxes to motivate energy users to reduce their consumption. Carbon taxes can motivate consumption to shift to energy sources with fewer emissions of carbon dioxide, such as solar power, wind power, hydroelectricity or nuclear power while avoiding cars with combustion engines, jet fuel, oil, fossil gas and coal. On the other hand, taxes on all energy consumption can reduce energy use across the board while reducing a broader array of environmental consequences arising from energy production. The state of California employs a tiered energy tax whereby every consumer receives a baseline energy allowance that carries a low tax. The tax increases drastically. Such programs aim to protect poorer households while creating a larger tax burden for high energy consumers.

Developing countries specifically are less likely to impose policy measures that slow carbon emissions as this would slow their economic development. These growing countries may be more likely to support their own economic growth and support their citizens rather than decreasing their carbon emissions.

Pros of Carbon Tax include:

- Making polluters pay the external cost of carbon emissions.
- Enables greater social efficiency as all citizens pay the full social cost.
- Raises revenue which can, in turn, be spent on mitigating the effects of pollution.
- Encourages firms and consumers to search for non-carbon producing alternatives (ex. solar power, wind power, hydroelectricity, or nuclear power).
- Reduces environmental costs associated with excess carbon pollution.

Cons of Carbon Tax include:

- Businesses claim higher taxes which can discourage investment and economic growth.
- A carbon tax may encourage tax evasion as firms may pollute in secret to avoid a carbon tax.
- It may be difficult to measure external costs and how much the carbon tax should truly be.
- There are administration costs in measuring pollution and collecting the associated tax.
- Firms may move production to countries in which there is no carbon tax.

Non-governmental Mechanisms

Voluntary Energy Standards

Another aspect of promoting energy efficiency is using the Leadership in Energy and Environmental Design (LEED) voluntary building design standards. This program is supported by the US Green Building Council. The "Energy and Atmosphere" Prerequisite applies to energy issues, it focuses on energy performance, renewable energy, and other.

8.3.2 Sustainability

Sustainability is a social goal for people to co-exist on Earth over a long time. Specific definitions of this term are disputed and have varied with literature, context, and time. Experts often describe sustainability as having three dimensions (or pillars): environmental, economic, and social, and many publications emphasize the environmental dimension. In everyday use, sustainability often focuses on countering major environmental problems, including climate change, loss of biodiversity, loss of ecosystem services, land degradation, and air and water pollution. The idea of sustainability can guide decisions at the global, national, and individual levels (e.g., sustainable living). A related concept is sustainable development, and the terms are often used to mean the same thing. UNESCO distinguishes the two like this: "Sustainability is often thought of as a long-term goal (i.e., a more sustainable world), while sustainable development refers to the many processes and pathways to achieve it."

The economic dimension of sustainability is controversial. Scholars have discussed this under the concept of "weak and strong sustainability"; for example, there will always be tension between the ideas of "welfare and prosperity for all" and environmental conservation, so trade-offs are necessary. Approaches that decouple economic growth from environmental deterioration would be desirable. But they are difficult to carry out.

Measuring sustainability is difficult. Indicators consider environmental, social and economic domains. The metrics are evolving. Currently, they include certification systems, types of corporate accounting, and types of index.

It is necessary to address many barriers to sustainability to make a sustainability transition possible. Some barriers arise from nature and its complexity. Other barriers are extrinsic to the concept of sustainability. For example they can result from the dominant institutional frameworks in countries.

There are many approaches people can take to transition to environmental sustainability. These include maintaining ecosystem services, reducing food waste, and promoting dietary shifts towards plant-based foods. Another is reducing population growth by cutting fertility rates. Others are promoting new green technologies, and adopting renewable energy sources while phasing out subsidies to fossil fuels. The United Nations agreed the Sustainable Development Goals (SDGs) in 2015. These set a global agenda for sustainable development, with a deadline of 2030.

One of many ways to overcome barriers to sustainable development is to decouple economic growth from environmental conservation. This means using fewer resources per unit of output even while growing the economy. This reduces the environmental impact of economic growth such as pollution. Doing this is difficult. Some experts say there is no evidence that it is happening at the required scale. Global issues are difficult to tackle as they need global solutions. Existing global organizations such as the UN and WTO are inefficient in enforcing current global regulations. One reason for this is the lack of suitable sanctioning mechanisms. Governments are not the only sources of action for sustainability. Business groups have tried to integrate ecological concerns with economic activity. Religious leaders have stressed the need for caring for nature and environmental stability. Individuals can also live in a more sustainable way.

The concept of sustainability has faced various criticisms. One is that the concept is vague and only a buzzword. Another is that sustainability might be an impossible goal. Some experts have pointed out that "no country is delivering what its citizens need without transgressing the biophysical planetary boundaries".

Definitions

Current Usage

Sustainability is regarded as a "normative concept". This means it is based on what people value or find desirable: "The quest for sustainability involves connecting what is known through scientific study to applications in pursuit of what people want for the future."

The 1983 UN Commission on Environment and Development (Brundtland Commission) had a big influence on how we use the term sustainability today. The commission's 1987 Brundtland Report provided a definition of sustainable development. The report, Our Common Future, defines it as development that "meets the needs of the present without compromising the ability of future generations to meet their own needs". The report helped bring sustainability into the mainstream of policy discussions. It also popularized the concept of sustainable development.

Some other key concepts to illustrate the meaning of sustainability include:

- It may be a fuzzy concept but in a positive sense: the goals are more important than the approaches or means applied;
- It connects with other essential concepts such as resilience, adaptive capacity, and vulnerability.

- Choices matter: "it is not possible to sustain everything, everywhere, forever";
- Scale matters in both space and time, and place matters;
- Limits exist.

Specific Definitions

Scholars say that a single specific definition of sustainability may never be possible. But the concept is still useful. There have been attempts to define it, for example:

- "Sustainability can be defined as the capacity to maintain or improve the state and availability of desirable materials or conditions over the long term."
- "Sustainability [is] the long-term viability of a community, set of social institutions, or societal practice. In general, sustainability is understood as a form of intergenerational ethics in which the environmental and economic actions taken by present persons do not diminish the opportunities of future persons to enjoy similar levels of wealth, utility, or welfare."
- "Sustainability means meeting our own needs without compromising the ability of future generations to meet their own needs. In addition to natural resources, we also need social and economic resources. Sustainability is not just environmentalism. Embedded in most definitions of sustainability we also find concerns for social equity and economic development."

Some definitions focus on the environmental dimension. The Oxford Dictionary of English defines sustainability as: "the property of being environmentally sustainable; the degree to which a process or enterprise is able to be maintained or continued while avoiding the long-term depletion of natural resources".

Historical Usage

The term sustainability is derived from the Latin word sustinere. "To sustain" can mean to maintain, support, uphold, or endure. So sustainability is the ability to continue over a long period of time.

In the past, sustainability referred to environmental sustainability. It meant using natural resources so that people in the future could continue to rely on them in the long term. The concept of sustainability, or Nachhaltigkeit in German, goes back to Hans Carl von Carlowitz (1645–1714), and applied to forestry. We would now call this sustainable forest management. He used this term to mean the long-term responsible use of a natural resource. In his 1713 work Silvicultura oeconomica, he wrote that "the highest art/science/industriousness [...] will consist in such a conservation and replanting of timber that there can be a continuous, ongoing and sustainable use". The shift in use of "sustainability" from preservation of forests (for future wood production) to broader preservation of environmental resources (to sustain the world for future generations) traces to a 1972 book by Ernst Basler, based on a series of lectures at M.I.T.

The idea itself goes back a very long time: Communities have always worried about the capacity of their environment to sustain them in the long term. Many ancient cultures, traditional societies, and indigenous peoples have restricted the use of natural resources.

Comparison to Sustainable Development

The terms sustainability and sustainable development are closely related. In fact, they are often used to mean the same thing. Both terms are linked with the "three dimensions of sustainability" concept. One distinction is that sustainability is a general concept, while sustainable development can be a policy or organizing principle. Scholars say sustainability is a broader concept because sustainable development focuses mainly on human well-being.

Sustainable development has two linked goals. It aims to meet human development goals. It also aims to enable natural systems to provide the natural resources and ecosystem services needed for economies and society. The concept of sustainable development has come to focus on economic development, social development and environmental protection for future generations.

Dimensions

Development of Three Dimensions

Scholars usually distinguish three different areas of sustainability. These are the environmental, the social, and the economic. Several terms are in use for this concept. Authors may speak of three pillars, dimensions, components, aspects, perspectives, factors, or goals. All mean the same thing in this context. The three dimensions paradigm has few theoretical foundations. It emerged without a single point of origin. Scholars rarely question the distinction itself. The idea of sustainability with three dimensions is a dominant interpretation in the literature.

In the Brundtland Report, the environment and development are inseparable and go together in the search for sustainability. It described sustainable development as a global concept linking environmental and social issues. It added sustainable development is important for both developing countries and industrialized countries:

- The 'environment' is where we all live; and 'development' is what we all do in attempting to improve our lot within that abode. The two are inseparable. [...] We came to see that a new development path was required, one that sustained human progress not just in a few pieces

> for a few years, but for the entire planet into the distant future. Thus 'sustainable development' becomes a goal not just for the 'developing' nations, but for industrial ones as well.— Our Common Future (also known as the Brundtland Report),

The Rio Declaration from 1992 is seen as "the foundational instrument in the move towards sustainability". It includes specific references to ecosystem integrity. The plan associated with carrying out the Rio Declaration also discusses sustainability in this way. The plan, Agenda 21, talks about economic, social, and environmental dimensions:

- Countries could develop systems for monitoring and evaluation of progress towards achieving sustainable development by adopting indicators that measure changes across economic, social and environmental dimensions.— United Nations Conference on Environment & Development - Earth Summit (1992),

Agenda 2030 from 2015 also viewed sustainability in this way. It sees the 17 Sustainable Development Goals (SDGs) with their 169 targets as balancing "the three dimensions of sustainable development, the economic, social and environmental".

Hierarchy

Scholars have discussed how to rank the three dimensions of sustainability. Many publications state that the environmental dimension is the most important. (Planetary integrity or ecological integrity are other terms for the environmental dimension.)

Protecting ecological integrity is the core of sustainability according to many experts. If this is the case then its environmental dimension sets limits to economic and social development.

The diagram with three nested ellipses is one way of showing the three dimensions of sustainability together with a hierarchy: It gives the environmental dimension a special status. In this diagram, the environment includes society, and society includes economic conditions. Thus it stresses a hierarchy.

Another model shows the three dimensions in a similar way: In this SDG wedding cake model, the economy is a smaller subset of the societal system. And the societal system in turn is a smaller subset of the biosphere system.

In 2022 an assessment examined the political impacts of the Sustainable Development Goals. The assessment found that the "integrity of the earth's life-support systems" was essential for sustainability. The authors said that "the SDGs fail to recognize that planetary, people and prosperity concerns are all part of one earth system, and that the protection of planetary integrity should not be a means to an end, but an end in itself". The aspect of environmental protection is not an explicit priority for the SDGs. This causes problems as it could encourage countries to give the environment less weight in their developmental plans. The authors state that "sustainability on a planetary scale is only achievable under an overarching Planetary Integrity Goal that recognizes the biophysical limits of the planet".

Other frameworks bypass the compartmentalization of sustainability into separate dimensions completely.

Environmental Sustainability

The environmental dimension is central to the overall concept of sustainability. People became more and more aware of environmental pollution in the 1960s and 1970s. This led to discussions of sustainability and sustainable development. This process began in the 1970s with concern for environmental issues. These included natural ecosystems or natural resources and the human environment. It later extended to all systems that support life on Earth, including human society. Reducing these negative impacts on the environment would improve environmental sustainability.

Environmental pollution is not a new phenomenon. But it has been only a local or regional concern for most of human history. Awareness of global environmental issues increased in the 20th century. The harmful effects and global spread of pesticides like DDT came under scrutiny in the 1960s. In the 1970s it emerged that chlorofluorocarbons (CFCs) were depleting the ozone layer. This led to the de facto ban of CFCs with the Montreal Protocol in 1987.

In the early 20th century, Arrhenius discussed the effect of greenhouse gases on the climate. Climate change due to human activity became an academic and political topic several decades later. This led to the establishment of the IPCC in 1988 and the UNFCCC in 1992.

In 1972, the UN Conference on the Human Environment took place. It was the first UN conference on environmental issues. It stated it was important to protect and improve the human environment.It emphasized the need to protect wildlife and natural habitats:

- The natural resources of the earth, including the air, water, land, flora and fauna and [...] natural ecosystems must be safeguarded for the benefit of present and future generations through careful planning or management, as appropriate.— UN Conference on the Human Environment,

In 2000, the UN launched eight Millennium Development Goals. The aim was for the global community to achieve them by 2015. Goal 7 was to "ensure environmental sustainability". But this goal did not mention the concepts of social or economic sustainability.

Specific problems often dominate public discussion of the environmental dimension of sustainability: In the 21st century these problems have included climate change, biodiversity and pollution. Other global problems are loss of ecosystem services, land degradation, environmental impacts of animal agriculture and air and water pollution, including marine plastic pollution and ocean acidification. Many people worry about human impacts on the environment. These include impacts on the atmosphere, land, and water resources.

Human activities now have an impact on Earth's geology and ecosystems. This led Paul Crutzen to call the current geological epoch the Anthropocene. For example, the impact of human activity on ecosystems can reach tipping points in the climate system.

Economic Sustainability

The economic dimension of sustainability is controversial. This is because the term development within sustainable development can be interpreted in different ways. Some may take it to mean only economic development and growth. This can promote an economic system that is bad for the environment. Others focus more on the trade-offs between environmental conservation and achieving welfare goals for basic needs (food, water, health, and shelter).

Economic development can indeed reduce hunger or energy poverty. This is especially the case in the least developed countries. That is why Sustainable Development Goal 8 calls for economic growth to drive social progress and well-being. Its first target is for: "at least 7 per cent GDP growth per annum in the least developed countries". However, the challenge is to expand economic activities while reducing their environmental impact. In other words, humanity will have to find ways how societal progress (potentially by economic development) can be reached without excess strain on the environment.

The Brundtland report says poverty causes environmental problems. Poverty also results from them. So addressing environmental problems requires understanding the factors behind world poverty and inequality. The report demands a new development path for sustained human progress. It highlights that this is a goal for both developing and industrialized nations.

UNEP and UNDP launched the Poverty-Environment Initiative in 2005 which has three goals. These are reducing extreme poverty, greenhouse gas emissions, and net natural asset loss. This guide to structural reform will enable countries to achieve the SDGs. It should also show how to address the trade-offs between ecological footprint and economic development.

Social Sustainability

The social dimension of sustainability is not well defined. One definition states that a society is sustainable in social terms if people do not face structural obstacles in key areas. These key areas are health, influence, competence, impartiality and meaning-making. Some scholars place social issues at the very center of discussions. They suggest that all the domains of sustainability are social. These include ecological, economic, political, and cultural sustainability. These domains all depend on the relationship between the social and the natural. The ecological domain is defined as human embeddedness in the environment. From this perspective, social sustainability encompasses all human activities. It goes beyond the intersection of economics, the environment, and the social.

There are many broad strategies for more sustainable social systems. They include improved education and the political empowerment of women. This is especially the case in developing countries. They include greater regard for social justice. This involves equity between rich and poor both within and between countries. And it includes intergenerational equity. Providing more social safety nets to vulnerable populations would contribute to social sustainability.

A society with a high degree of social sustainability would lead to livable communities with a good quality of life (being fair, diverse, connected and democratic).

Indigenous communities might have a focus on particular aspects of sustainability, for example spiritual aspects, community-based governance and an emphasis on place and locality.

Proposed Additional Dimensions

Some experts have proposed further dimensions. These could cover institutional, cultural, political, and technical dimensions.

Cultural Sustainability

Some scholars have argued for a fourth dimension. They say the traditional three dimensions do not reflect the complexity of contemporary society. For example, Agenda 21 for culture and the United Cities and Local Governments argue that sustainable development should include a solid cultural policy. They also advocate for a cultural dimension in all public policies. Another example was the Circles of Sustainability approach, which included cultural sustainability.

Interactions between Dimensions

Environmental and Economic Dimensions

People often debate the relationship between the environmental and economic dimensions of sustainability. In academia, this is discussed under the term weak and strong sustainability. In that model, the weak sustainability concept states that capital made by humans could replace most of the natural capital. Natural capital is a way of describing environmental resources. People may refer to it as nature. An example for this is the use of environmental technologies to reduce pollution.

The opposite concept in that model is strong sustainability. This assumes that nature provides functions that technology cannot replace. Thus, strong sustainability acknowledges the need to preserve ecological integrity. Once we lose those functions we cannot recover or repair many resources and ecosystem services. Biodiversity, along with pollination and fertile soils, are examples. Others are clean air, clean water, and regulation of climate systems.

Weak sustainability has come under criticism. It may be popular with governments and business but does not ensure the preservation of the earth's ecological integrity. This is why the environmental dimension is so important.

The World Economic Forum illustrated this in 2020. It found that $44 trillion of economic value generation depends on nature. This value, more than half of the world's GDP, is thus vulnerable to nature loss. Three large economic sectors are highly dependent on nature: construction, agriculture, and food and beverages. Nature loss results from many factors. They include land use change, sea use change and climate change. Other examples are natural resource use, pollution, and invasive alien species.

Trade-offs

Trade-offs between different dimensions of sustainability are a common topic for debate. Balancing the environmental, social, and economic dimensions of sustainability is difficult. This is because there is often disagreement about the relative importance of each. To resolve this, there is a need to integrate, balance, and reconcile the dimensions. For example, humans can choose to make ecological integrity a priority or to compromise it.

Some even argue the Sustainable Development Goals are unrealistic. Their aim of universal human well-being conflicts with the physical limits of Earth and its ecosystems.

Measurement Tools

Sustainability measurement is a set of frameworks or indicators to measure how sustainable something is. This includes processes, products, services and businesses. Sustainability is difficult to quantify. It may even be impossible to measure. To measure sustainability, the indicators consider environmental, social and economic domains. The metrics are still evolving. They include indicators, benchmarks and audits. They include sustainability standards and certification systems like Fairtrade and Organic. They also involve indices and accounting. And they can include assessment, appraisal and other reporting systems. These metrics are used over a wide range of spatial and temporal scales. Sustainability measures include corporate sustainability reporting, Triple Bottom Line accounting. They include estimates of the quality of sustainability governance for individual countries. These use the Environmental Sustainability Index and Environmental Performance Index. Some methods let us track sustainable development. These include the UN Human Development Index and ecological footprints.

Environmental Impacts of Humans

There are several methods to measure or describe human impacts on Earth. They include the ecological footprint, ecological debt, carrying capacity, and sustainable yield. The idea of planetary boundaries is that there are limits to the carrying capacity of the Earth. We should not cross these thresholds to prevent irreversible harm to the Earth. These planetary boundaries involve several environmental issues. These include climate change and biodiversity loss. They also include types of pollution. These are biogeochemical (nitrogen and phosphorus), ocean acidification, land use, freshwater, ozone depletion, atmospheric aerosols, and chemical pollution. (Since 2015 some experts refer to biodiversity loss as change in biosphere integrity. They refer to chemical pollution as introduction of novel entities.)

The IPAT formula measures the environmental impact of humans. It emerged in the 1970s. It states this impact is proportional to human population, affluence and technology. This implies various ways to increase environmental sustainability. One would be human population control. Another would be to reduce consumption and affluence such as energy consumption. Another would be to develop innovative or green technologies such as renewable energy. In other words, there are two broad aims. The first would be to have fewer consumers. The second would be to have less environmental footprint per consumer.

The Millennium Ecosystem Assessment from 2005 measured 24 ecosystem services. It concluded that only four have improved over the last 50 years. It found 15 are in serious decline and five are in a precarious condition.

Economic Costs

Experts in environmental economics have calculated the cost of using public natural resources. One project calculated the damage to ecosystems and biodiversity loss. This was the Economics of Ecosystems and Biodiversity project from 2007 to 2011.

An entity that creates environmental and social costs often does not pay for them. The market price also does not reflect those costs. In the end, government policy is usually required to resolve this problem.

We can take future costs and benefits into account when we make decisions. To do this we use the social discount rate. The bigger our concern for future generations, the lower the social discount rate should be. Another approach is to put an economic value on ecosystem services. This allows us to assess environmental damage against perceived short-term welfare benefits. One calculation is that, "for every dollar spent on ecosystem restoration, between three and 75 dollars of economic benefits from ecosystem goods and services can be expected".

In recent years, economist Kate Raworth has developed the concept of doughnut economics. This aims to integrate social and environmental sustainability into economic thinking. The social dimension acts as a minimum standard to which a society should aspire. The carrying capacity of the planet acts an outer limit.

Barriers

There are many reasons why sustainability is so difficult to achieve. These reasons have the name sustainability barriers. Before we address these barriers we must analyze and understand them. Some barriers arise from nature and its complexity ("everything is related"). Others arise from the human condition. One example is the value-action gap. This reflects the fact that we often do not act according to our convictions. Experts describe these barriers as intrinsic to the concept of sustainability.

Other barriers are extrinsic to the concept of sustainability. This means it is possible to overcome them. One way would be to put a price tag on the consumption of public goods. Some extrinsic barriers relate to the nature of dominant institutional frameworks. Examples would be where market mechanisms fail for public goods. Existing societies, economies, and cultures encourage increased consumption. There is a structural imperative for growth in competitive market economies. This inhibits necessary societal change.

Furthermore, there are several barriers related to the difficulties of implementing sustainability policies. There are trade-offs between the goals of environmental policies and economic development. Environmental goals include nature conservation. Development may focus on poverty reduction. There are also trade-offs between short-term profit and long-term viability. Political pressures generally favor the short term over the long term. So they form a barrier to actions oriented toward improving sustainability. Barriers to sustainability may also reflect current trends. These could include consumerism and short-termism.

Transitions

Components and Characteristics

The European Environment Agency defines a sustainability transition as "a fundamental and wide-ranging transformation of a socio-technical system towards a more sustainable configuration that helps alleviate persistent problems such as climate change, pollution, biodiversity loss or resource scarcities." The concept of sustainability transitions is like the concept of energy transitions. One expert argues a sustainability transition must be "supported by a new kind of culture, a new kind of collaboration, [and] a new kind of leadership". It requires a large investment in "new and greener capital goods, while simultaneously shifting capital away from unsustainable systems". It prefers these to unsustainable options.

A sustainability transition requires major change in societies. They must change their fundamental values and organizing principles. These new values would emphasize "the quality of life and material sufficiency, human solidarity and global equity, and affinity with nature and environmental sustainability". A transition may only work if far-reaching lifestyle changes accompany technological advances.

Scientists have pointed out that: "Sustainability transitions come about in diverse ways, and all require civil-society pressure and evidence-based advocacy, political leadership, and a solid understanding of policy instruments, markets, and other drivers." We can propose four overlapping processes of transformation. They each have different political dynamics. Technology, markets, government, or citizens can lead these processes.

Action Principles

We can divide action principles that people can use to make societies more sustainable into four types. These are nature-related, personal, society-related and systems-related principles.

- Nature-related principles: Decarbonize; reduce human environmental impact by efficiency, sufficiency and consistency; be net-positive - build up environmental and societal capital; prefer local, seasonal, plant-based and labor-intensive; polluter-pays principle; precautionary principle; and appreciate and celebrate the beauty of nature.
- Personal principles: Practise contemplation, apply policies with caution, celebrate frugality.
- Society-related principles: Grant the least privileged the greatest support; seek mutual understanding, trust and many wins; strengthen social cohesion and collaboration; engage stakeholders; foster education - share knowledge and collaborate.
- Systems-related principles: Apply systems thinking; foster diversity; make what is relevant to the public more transparent; maintain or increase option diversity.

Example Steps

In 2017 scientists published an update to the 1992 World Scientists' Warning to Humanity. It showed how to move towards environmental sustainability. It proposed steps in three areas:

- Reduced consumption: Reducing food waste, promoting dietary shifts towards mostly plant-based foods.
- Reducing the number of consumers: Further reducing fertility rates and thus population growth.
- Technology and nature conservation: There are several related approaches. One is to maintain nature's ecosystem services. Another is promote new green technologies. Another is changing our energy use. One aspect of this is to adopt renewable energy sources. At the same time it is necessary to end subsidies to energy production through fossil fuels.

Agenda 2030 for the Sustainable Development Goals

In 2015, the United Nations agreed the Sustainable Development Goals (SDGs). Their official name is Agenda 2030 for the Sustainable Development Goals. The UN described this programme as a very ambitious and transformational vision. It said the SDGs were of unprecedented scope and significance.

- The UN said: "We are determined to take the bold and transformative steps which are urgently needed to shift the world on to a sustainable and resilient path."

The 17 goals and targets lay out transformative steps. For example, the SDGs aim to protect the future of planet Earth. Here the UN pledged to "protect the planet from degradation, including through sustainable consumption and production, sustainably managing its natural resources and taking urgent action on climate change, so that it can support the needs of the present and future generations".

Options for Overcoming Barriers

Issues around Economic Growth

Eco-economic decoupling is an idea to resolve tradeoffs between economic growth and environmental conservation. The idea is to "decouple environmental bads from economic goods as a path towards sustainability". This would mean "using less resources per unit of economic output and reducing the environmental impact of any resources that are used or economic activities that are undertaken". We can measure pressure on the environment by the intensity of pollutants emitted.

We can then measure decoupling. To do this we follow changes in the emission intensity associated with economic output. Examples of absolute long-term decoupling are rare. But some industrialized countries have decoupled GDP growth from production- and consumption-based CO_2 emissions. Yet, even in this example, decoupling alone is not enough. We need to accompany it with "sufficiency-oriented strategies and strict enforcement of absolute reduction targets".

One study in 2020 found no evidence of necessary decoupling. This was a meta-analysis of 180 scientific studies. It found that there is "no evidence of the kind of decoupling needed for ecological sustainability" and that "in the absence of robust evidence, the goal of decoupling rests partly on faith". Some experts have questioned the possibilities for decoupling and thus the feasibility of green growth.

Some have argued that decoupling on its own will not be enough to reduce environmental pressures. They say it would need to include the issue of economic growth. There are several reasons why adequate decoupling is currently not taking place. These are rising energy expenditure, rebound effects, problem shifting, the underestimated impact of services, the limited potential of recycling, insufficient and inappropriate technological change, and cost-shifting.

The decoupling of economic growth from environmental deterioration is difficult. This is because the entity that causes environmental and social costs does not generally pay for them.

So the market price does not express such costs. For example, we can factor the cost of packaging into the price of a product. But we may omit the cost of disposing of that packaging. Economics describes such factors as externalities, in this case a negative externality. Usually, it is up to government action or local governance to deal with externalities.

There are various ways to incorporate environmental and social costs and benefits into economic activities. Examples include: taxing the activity (the polluter pays); subsidizing activities with positive effects (rewarding stewardship); and outlawing particular levels of damaging practices (legal limits on pollution).

Government Action and Local Governance

A textbook on natural resources and environmental economics stated in 2011: "Nobody who has seriously studied the issues believes that the economy's relationship to the natural environment can be left entirely to market forces." This means natural resources will be over-exploited and destroyed in the long run without government action.

Elinor Ostrom (winner of the 2009 Nobel economics prize) expanded on this. She stated that local governance (or self-governance) can be a third option besides the market or the national government. She studied how people in small, local communities manage shared natural resources. She showed that communities using natural resources can establish rules their for use and maintenance. These are resources such as pastures, fishing waters, and forests. This leads to both economic and ecological sustainability. Successful self-governance needs groups with frequent communication among participants. In this case, groups can manage the usage of common goods without overexploitation. Based on Ostrom's work, some have argued that: "Common-pool resources today are overcultivated because the different agents do not know each other and cannot directly communicate with one another."

Global Governance

Questions of global concern are difficult to tackle. That is because global issues need global solutions. But existing global organizations (UN, WTO, and others) do not have sufficient means. For example, they lack sanctioning mechanisms to enforce existing global regulations. Some institutions do not enjoy universal acceptance. An example is the International Criminal Court. Their agendas are not aligned (for example UNEP, UNDP, and WTO) And some accuse them of nepotism and mismanagement.

Multilateral international agreements, treaties, and intergovernmental organizations (IGOs) face further challenges. These result in barriers to sustainability. Often these arrangements rely on voluntary commitments. An example is Nationally Determined Contributions for climate action. There can be a lack of enforcement of existing national or international regulation. And there can be gaps in regulation for international actors such as multi-national enterprises.Critics of some global organizations say they lack legitimacy and democracy. Institutions facing such criticism include the WTO, IMF, World Bank, UNFCCC, G7, G8 and OECD.

Responses by Nongovernmental Stakeholders

Businesses

Sustainable business practices integrate ecological concerns with social and economic ones. One accounting framework for this approach uses the phrase "people, planet, and profit". The name of this approach is the triple bottom line. The circular economy is a related concept. Its goal is to decouple environmental pressure from economic growth.

Growing attention towards sustainability has led to the formation of many organizations. These include the Sustainability Consortium of the Society for Organizational Learning, the Sustainable Business Institute, and the World Business Council for Sustainable Development. Supply chain sustainability looks at the environmental and human impacts of products in the supply chain. It considers how they move from raw materials sourcing to production, storage, and delivery, and every transportation link on the way.

Religious Communities

Religious leaders have stressed the importance of caring for nature and environmental sustainability. In 2015 over 150 leaders from various faiths issued a joint statement to the UN Climate Summit in Paris 2015. They reiterated a statement made in the Interfaith Summit in New York in 2014:

- As representatives from different faith and religious traditions, we stand together to express deep concern for the consequences of climate change on the earth and its people, all entrusted, as our faiths reveal, to our common care. Climate change is indeed a threat to life, a precious gift we have received and that we need to care for.

Individuals

Individuals can also live in a more sustainable way. They can change their lifestyles, practise ethical consumerism, and embrace frugality. These sustainable living approaches can also make cities more sustainable. They do this by altering the built environment. Such approaches include sustainable transport, sustainable architecture, and zero emission housing. Research can identify the main issues to focus on. These include flying, meat and dairy products, car driving, and household sufficiency. Research can show how to create cultures of sufficiency, care, solidarity, and simplicity. Some young people are using activism, litigation, and on-the-ground efforts to advance sustainability. This is particularly the case in the area of climate action.

8.3.3 The Promise of 5G Technology

5G technology holds immense promise for driving innovation, economic growth, and societal progress. With its ultra-fast data rates, low latency, and high reliability, 5G enables a wide range of applications, including augmented reality (AR), virtual reality (VR), autonomous vehicles, smart cities, and the Internet of Things (IoT). By connecting billions of devices and enabling real-time communication and data exchange, 5G has the potential to transform industries, enhance productivity, and improve quality of life for people around the world.

8.3.4 Energy Consumption in 5G Networks

Despite its transformative potential, 5G technology poses challenges in terms of energy consumption and environmental sustainability. The deployment of 5G networks requires a massive infrastructure of base stations, small cells, antennas, and data centers, all of which consume significant amounts of energy. Moreover, the increased data traffic and complexity of 5G networks may further exacerbate energy consumption, particularly in densely populated urban areas with high demand for connectivity.

8.3.5 Strategies for Energy Efficiency in 5G

Addressing the energy consumption of 5G networks requires a multi-faceted approach that encompasses both hardware and software optimizations, as well as innovative network design and management strategies. Some key strategies for improving energy efficiency in 5G technology include:

1. Network Optimization: Optimizing network design and configuration to minimize energy consumption while ensuring coverage, capacity, and quality of service. This includes intelligent deployment of base stations, dynamic spectrum allocation, and load balancing algorithms to reduce energy waste and improve network performance.
2. Energy-Efficient Hardware: Developing energy-efficient hardware components, such as power-efficient antennas, low-power radio frequency (RF) transceivers, and energy-saving processors, for base stations and user devices. Advances in semiconductor technology and power management techniques can help reduce energy consumption without compromising performance.

3. Software Optimization: Implementing software optimizations, such as energy-aware scheduling algorithms, sleep mode policies, and traffic optimization techniques, to reduce idle power consumption and optimize resource utilization in 5G networks. Software-defined networking (SDN) and network function virtualization (NFV) enable dynamic resource allocation and energy management based on real-time traffic and demand.
4. Renewable Energy Integration: Leveraging renewable energy sources, such as solar, wind, and hydroelectric power, to power 5G infrastructure and data centers. By integrating renewable energy generation with energy storage systems and smart grid technologies, operators can reduce reliance on fossil fuels and mitigate the environmental impact of 5G networks.
5. Heat Recovery and Cooling Efficiency: Implementing heat recovery systems and efficient cooling technologies, such as liquid cooling and free-air cooling, to reduce energy consumption and environmental impact associated with cooling data centers and network equipment. By capturing waste heat and reusing it for heating or other purposes, operators can improve overall energy efficiency and reduce carbon emissions.

8.3.6 Benefits of Energy Efficiency in 5G

Improving energy efficiency in 5G technology offers several benefits for operators, users, and the environment:

1. Cost Savings: Energy-efficient network design and operation reduce operating expenses associated with electricity consumption, cooling, and infrastructure maintenance, resulting in cost savings for network operators and service providers.
2. Environmental Impact Reduction: Lower energy consumption and reliance on fossil fuels help reduce carbon emissions and mitigate the environmental impact of 5G networks, contributing to global efforts to combat climate change and promote sustainability.
3. Resource Conservation: Energy efficiency measures in 5G networks help conserve natural resources, such as fossil fuels and water, by reducing the demand for electricity and cooling resources required to power network infrastructure and data centers.
4. Improved Reliability and Resilience: Energy-efficient network designs and technologies enhance the reliability, resilience, and scalability of 5G networks, enabling operators to deliver high-quality services and maintain operational continuity in diverse environmental conditions.
5. Enhanced Corporate Social Responsibility: Demonstrating a commitment to energy efficiency and sustainability enhances the corporate social responsibility (CSR) profile of network operators and service providers, fostering goodwill among customers, investors, and stakeholders.

8.3.7 Challenges and Considerations

Despite the benefits, improving energy efficiency in 5G technology poses several challenges and considerations:

1. Cost and Investment: Implementing energy-efficient technologies and infrastructure upgrades may require significant upfront investment and operational costs, particularly for renewable energy integration and hardware optimization.
2. Complexity and Trade-Offs: Balancing energy efficiency with performance, coverage, and quality of service considerations requires careful trade-offs and optimization strategies. Overly aggressive energy-saving measures may compromise network performance or user experience.
3. Regulatory Compliance: Meeting regulatory requirements and environmental standards related to energy efficiency, carbon emissions, and sustainable practices may pose challenges for network operators, particularly in regions with stringent environmental regulations.
4. Technological Innovation: Continual technological innovation and research are necessary to develop and deploy energy-efficient solutions for 5G networks, including advancements in hardware design, software optimization, renewable energy integration, and cooling technologies.
5. Collaboration and Stakeholder Engagement: Addressing energy efficiency challenges in 5G technology requires collaboration and engagement among stakeholders, including network operators, equipment vendors, policymakers, environmental organizations, and the public.

8.3.8 Future Directions

Looking ahead, energy efficiency and sustainability will continue to be critical priorities for the evolution of 5G technology and the telecommunications industry as a whole. Several trends and future directions are likely to shape the development of energy-efficient 5G networks:

1. Advanced Technologies: Continued advancements in semiconductor technology, energy-efficient hardware components, and software optimization techniques will drive improvements in energy efficiency and performance for 5G networks.
2. Renewable Energy Integration: Greater integration of renewable energy sources, energy storage systems, and smart grid technologies will enable network operators to reduce carbon emissions and reliance on fossil fuels while enhancing energy resilience and sustainability.
3. Regulatory Policies and Incentives: Regulatory policies, incentives, and mandates aimed at promoting energy efficiency, carbon reduction, and

sustainable practices will drive investment and innovation in energy-efficient 5G technologies and infrastructure.

4. International Collaboration: International collaboration and cooperation among governments, industry stakeholders, and environmental organizations will play a key role in addressing global challenges related to energy efficiency, climate change, and sustainable development in the telecommunications sector.
5. Public Awareness and Education: Increasing public awareness and education about the environmental impact of telecommunications technologies and the importance of energy efficiency and sustainability will foster greater demand for green products and services and drive industry-wide efforts to reduce carbon footprint.

8.4 BEYOND 5G: 6G AND FUTURE INNOVATIONS

As the world eagerly embraces the transformative potential of fifth-generation (5G) wireless technology, researchers and innovators are already looking ahead to the next frontier of connectivity: sixth-generation (6G) and beyond. While 5G promises unprecedented speed, low latency, and massive connectivity, the evolution towards 6G opens up new possibilities for innovation, pushing the boundaries of what is possible in wireless communication. The journey beyond 5G represents a frontier of innovation, exploration, and possibility in the field of wireless communication. From terahertz communication and AI-driven networks to holographic communication and quantum encryption, 6G technology and future innovations promise to revolutionize connectivity, ushering in a new era of speed, intelligence, and connectivity. While significant technical, regulatory, and societal challenges lie ahead, the vision of 6G presents boundless opportunities for creating a more connected, intelligent, and sustainable future for humanity. As researchers, innovators, and stakeholders continue to push the boundaries of what is possible, the journey towards 6G holds the potential to transform the way we live, work, communicate, and interact with the world around us.

8.4.1 The Promise of 6G and Future Innovations

As the deployment of 5G networks accelerates, attention is already turning towards the development of 6G technology and beyond. While 5G represents a significant leap forward in wireless communication, 6G promises to further revolutionize connectivity with even faster speeds, lower latency, and more advanced capabilities. Some key areas of focus for 6G and future innovations include:

1. Terahertz Communication: 6G is expected to leverage terahertz (THz) frequencies, which offer significantly higher bandwidths than the microwave frequencies used in 5G. Terahertz communication enables ultra-high-speed data transmission, enabling applications such as real-time

holographic communication, high-definition 3D imaging, and ultra-high-definition video streaming.

2. AI-driven Networks: Artificial intelligence (AI) will play a crucial role in shaping the future of wireless communication, enabling autonomous network management, adaptive resource allocation, and intelligent optimization. AI-driven networks can dynamically adapt to changing traffic patterns, environmental conditions, and user demands, maximizing efficiency and performance.
3. Holographic Communication: Holographic communication represents a futuristic concept where users can interact with realistic holographic projections of remote individuals or objects in real-time. 6G technology may enable seamless holographic communication, blurring the boundaries between physical and virtual worlds and revolutionizing remote collaboration, telepresence, and entertainment.
4. Quantum Communication: Quantum communication harnesses the principles of quantum mechanics to enable ultra-secure, unbreakable communication channels. 6G networks may incorporate quantum encryption techniques, quantum key distribution (QKD), and quantum teleportation protocols to ensure privacy, confidentiality, and integrity of data transmission, particularly for sensitive applications such as government communications, financial transactions, and healthcare.
5. Bio-inspired Networks: Inspired by biological systems, bio-inspired networks mimic the self-organizing, adaptive, and resilient properties of natural ecosystems. 6G technology may leverage concepts from biology, such as swarm intelligence, neural networks, and genetic algorithms, to create self-organizing networks that can autonomously adapt to changing conditions, mitigate interference, and optimize resource allocation.
6. Satellite Communication: Satellite communication will play an increasingly important role in extending connectivity to remote and underserved areas, enabling global coverage and seamless mobility. 6G networks may incorporate low-earth orbit (LEO) satellite constellations, high-altitude platforms (HAPs), and airborne platforms to provide ubiquitous, high-speed connectivity for terrestrial and aerial applications.

8.4.2 Challenges and Considerations

While the vision of 6G and future innovations holds great promise, several challenges and considerations must be addressed to realize this vision:

1. Technical Complexity: Developing and deploying 6G technology and future innovations will require overcoming technical challenges related to spectrum allocation, signal propagation, hardware design, and software optimization.

Innovations such as terahertz communication, quantum encryption, and bio-inspired networks present unique technical hurdles that must be addressed through research, experimentation, and collaboration.

2. Standardization and Interoperability: Achieving global standardization and interoperability is essential for ensuring compatibility, scalability, and seamless integration of 6G technologies and services. Collaborative efforts among industry stakeholders, standards organizations, and regulatory bodies are needed to develop common specifications, protocols, and frameworks for 6G deployment.
3. Privacy and Security: Addressing privacy and security concerns is paramount for ensuring trust, adoption, and acceptance of 6G technology and future innovations. Advanced encryption techniques, secure authentication mechanisms, and robust privacy-preserving technologies must be implemented to protect sensitive data and communications from cyber threats, surveillance, and unauthorized access.
4. Socio-economic Impact: The deployment of 6G technology and future innovations will have far-reaching socio-economic implications, influencing job markets, industries, education, healthcare, and society as a whole. Proactive measures, such as workforce training, digital inclusion initiatives, and policy frameworks, are needed to mitigate potential disruptions and ensure equitable access to the benefits of connectivity.
5. Environmental Sustainability: As with previous generations of technology, ensuring environmental sustainability is essential for minimizing the carbon footprint and ecological impact of 6G networks and future innovations. Energy-efficient design, renewable energy integration, and eco-friendly manufacturing practices can help reduce energy consumption, carbon emissions, and electronic waste associated with wireless communication infrastructure.

CHAPTER 9

GLOBAL DEPLOYMENT AND ADOPTION

9.1 CURRENT STATUS OF 5G ROLLOUT WORLDWIDE

1. United States: Major carriers such as Verizon, AT&T, and T-Mobile have been aggressively expanding their 5G networks across the country. Urban areas and densely populated regions have seen widespread coverage, with emphasis on high-speed mmWave deployments in urban cores and mid-band deployments for broader coverage.
2. China: China has emerged as a global leader in 5G deployment, with extensive coverage in major cities and urban areas. Chinese telecom giants like Huawei, ZTE, and China Mobile have been instrumental in building out the country's 5G infrastructure, focusing on both standalone (SA) and non-standalone (NSA) deployments.
3. South Korea: South Korea was one of the first countries to launch commercial 5G services, with nationwide coverage in major cities. SK Telecom, KT Corporation, and LG Uplus have been leading the rollout, leveraging both sub-6 GHz and mmWave spectrum for high-speed connectivity.
4. Japan: Japanese telecom operators, including NTT Docomo, KDDI, and SoftBank, have been steadily expanding their 5G networks, with a focus on urban areas and key transport routes. Japan aims to accelerate 5G adoption in preparation for major events like the Tokyo Olympics.
5. Europe: 5G deployment in Europe varies by country, with some nations leading the way in coverage and adoption while others lag behind. Countries like the United Kingdom, Germany, and Spain have made significant progress in rolling out 5G networks, while others are still in the early stages of deployment.
6. Middle East and Africa: Several countries in the Middle East, such as the United Arab Emirates, Saudi Arabia, and Qatar, have launched commercial 5G services, focusing on urban centers and key economic hubs. In Africa, 5G deployment is still limited, with only a few countries beginning to explore the technology's potential.

7. Asia-Pacific: Countries like Australia, Singapore, and Taiwan have been actively deploying 5G networks, with a focus on enhancing connectivity, driving innovation, and fostering economic growth. Australia, in particular, has seen significant investment in 5G infrastructure by major telecom operators.
8. Latin America: 5G deployment in Latin America varies by country, with some nations making progress while others face challenges related to spectrum allocation, infrastructure investment, and regulatory hurdles. Brazil, Mexico, and Argentina are among the countries that have initiated 5G trials and deployments.

9.2 CASE STUDIES OF SUCCESSFUL DEPLOYMENTS

The implementation of any new technology or strategy can be daunting, but examining successful deployments provides valuable insights and lessons for organizations looking to embark on similar initiatives. These case studies of successful deployments illustrate the diverse strategies, approaches, and best practices employed by organizations across different industries to achieve their goals and drive positive outcomes.

Whether it's customer obsession, innovation, community engagement, or digital transformation, the common thread among these success stories is a relentless focus on delivering value, meeting customer needs, and embracing change in pursuit of excellence. By studying these examples and extracting valuable lessons, organizations can gain insights and inspiration to inform their own strategies and initiatives, positioning themselves for success in an increasingly competitive and dynamic business environment.

9.2.1 Amazon Web Services (AWS)

Amazon Web Services (AWS) has become a global leader in cloud computing services, powering millions of businesses and organizations worldwide. One of the key factors behind AWS's success is its relentless focus on customer obsession. By prioritizing customer needs and continuously innovating to address them, AWS has built a reputation for reliability, scalability, and flexibility.

Case Study: Netflix

Netflix, the world's leading streaming entertainment service, relies on AWS to deliver high-quality video content to millions of subscribers around the globe. By leveraging AWS's cloud infrastructure, Netflix can scale its streaming platform dynamically to meet fluctuating demand, deliver personalized recommendations, and optimize content delivery for a seamless viewing experience.

Key Takeaways:

- Customer obsession: AWS's customer-centric approach has enabled it to build long-term partnerships with organizations like Netflix, delivering value and driving mutual success.

- Scalability and flexibility: AWS's cloud infrastructure provides Netflix with the scalability and flexibility to accommodate rapid growth, handle peak traffic loads, and adapt to changing market conditions.
- Continuous innovation: AWS continually introduces new features, services, and optimizations to enhance its platform's performance, reliability, and security, ensuring that customers like Netflix have access to the latest technologies and capabilities.

9.2.2 Tesla

Tesla has revolutionized the automotive industry with its electric vehicles (EVs), innovative technologies, and visionary leadership. From electric cars and solar energy to energy storage solutions and autonomous driving systems, Tesla's holistic approach to sustainable transportation has reshaped the automotive landscape.

Case Study: Gigafactory

Tesla's Gigafactory in Nevada is a prime example of successful deployment, enabling the mass production of lithium-ion batteries for electric vehicles and energy storage systems.

By vertically integrating battery production, Tesla has achieved economies of scale, cost efficiencies, and supply chain resilience, driving down the cost of EVs and accelerating the transition to sustainable energy.

Key Takeaways:

- Vertical integration: Tesla's vertically integrated approach to battery production allows it to control quality, optimize performance, and drive down costs, positioning the company for long-term growth and profitability.
- Scale and efficiency: The Gigafactory's massive scale and advanced manufacturing processes enable Tesla to produce batteries at a lower cost per kilowatt-hour, making EVs more affordable and accessible to consumers.
- Sustainability and innovation: Tesla's commitment to sustainability and innovation extends beyond its products to its manufacturing processes, with initiatives such as renewable energy generation, waste reduction, and recycling, demonstrating the company's environmental stewardship and corporate responsibility.

9.2.3 Airbnb

Airbnb has disrupted the hospitality industry by offering a platform that connects travelers with unique accommodations and experiences worldwide. Through its peer-to-peer marketplace, Airbnb has democratized travel, empowered hosts, and enriched communities, transforming the way people book lodging and explore destinations.

Case Study: Community Engagement

Airbnb's success is built on its community-centric approach, which emphasizes trust, authenticity, and belonging. By fostering meaningful connections between hosts and guests, Airbnb creates value beyond accommodation, enabling cultural exchange, economic empowerment, and sustainable tourism.

Key Takeaways:

- Trust and safety: Airbnb prioritizes trust and safety through identity verification, guest screening, and review systems, creating a secure and reliable platform for hosts and guests to engage with confidence.
- Authentic experiences: Airbnb celebrates diversity, creativity, and local culture, offering travelers the opportunity to discover unique accommodations, meet interesting hosts, and immerse themselves in authentic experiences that traditional hotels cannot replicate.
- Social impact: Airbnb's community-driven model has positive social and economic impacts, empowering hosts to earn income, support local businesses, and preserve cultural heritage, while also fostering empathy, understanding, and connection among travelers from diverse backgrounds.

9.2.4 Procter & Gamble (P&G)

Procter & Gamble (P&G) is a multinational consumer goods company that manufactures and markets a wide range of household and personal care products. P&G's success is attributed to its focus on innovation, brand building, and consumer insights, driving growth and market leadership in the fast-moving consumer goods (FMCG) sector.

Case Study: Digital Transformation

P&G's digital transformation journey is a testament to its agility, adaptability, and resilience in a rapidly changing business landscape. By embracing digital technologies and data-driven insights, P&G has enhanced its marketing effectiveness, supply chain efficiency, and customer engagement, gaining a competitive edge in the digital age.

Key Takeaways:

- Data-driven decision-making: P&G leverages data analytics, machine learning, and artificial intelligence (AI) to gain actionable insights into consumer behavior, market trends, and product performance, enabling more informed decision-making and strategic planning.
- Agile and adaptive culture: P&G fosters a culture of innovation, experimentation, and continuous improvement, encouraging employees to embrace change, challenge the status quo, and adapt to evolving market dynamics.
- Customer-centric approach: P&G places the customer at the center of its business strategy, focusing on delivering superior value, convenience, and satisfaction through personalized products, services, and experiences that resonate with consumers' needs and preferences.

9.3 CHALLENGES IN GLOBAL STANDARDIZATION

9.3.1 Diverse Stakeholder Interests

One of the primary challenges in global standardization is reconciling the diverse interests and priorities of stakeholders with competing agendas. Standardization efforts often involve a wide range of participants, including industry associations, government agencies, regulatory bodies, academia, and multinational corporations, each with their own objectives, perspectives, and incentives. Balancing these interests and reaching consensus on standards can be challenging, especially when stakeholders have conflicting priorities or vested interests.

9.3.2 Technological Complexity and Rapid Innovation

The rapid pace of technological innovation presents another challenge in global standardization. Emerging technologies such as artificial intelligence (AI), blockchain, Internet of Things (IoT), and 5G introduce new complexities and uncertainties that can complicate standardization efforts. As these technologies evolve and mature, standards must adapt to accommodate new use cases, requirements, and capabilities, posing challenges for standard-setting organizations and stakeholders tasked with developing and maintaining standards.

9.3.3 Fragmentation and Duplication

Fragmentation and duplication of standards pose significant challenges to global standardization efforts. In some cases, competing standards bodies may develop overlapping or incompatible standards, leading to confusion, inefficiencies, and increased costs for industry stakeholders. Fragmentation can also hinder interoperability and innovation, as organizations must navigate a complex landscape of conflicting standards and specifications.

9.3.4 Geographic and Cultural Differences

Geographic and cultural differences present additional challenges in global standardization. Standards that work well in one region or market may not be suitable for others due to differences in infrastructure, regulatory frameworks, business practices, and cultural norms. Bridging these differences and developing standards that are globally applicable and culturally sensitive requires collaboration, flexibility, and an understanding of local contexts and needs.

9.3.5 Intellectual Property Rights (IPR) Issues

Intellectual property rights (IPR) issues can complicate global standardization efforts, particularly when proprietary technologies or patented inventions are involved. Standard-setting organizations must navigate complex legal and regulatory frameworks governing patents, copyrights, and trademarks, ensuring that standards are developed in a manner that respects intellectual property rights while promoting innovation, competition, and interoperability.

9.3.6 Evolving Regulatory Landscape

The evolving regulatory landscape presents challenges and uncertainties for global standardization efforts. Regulatory requirements and compliance obligations may vary across jurisdictions, creating compliance burdens and barriers to market entry for organizations operating in multiple regions. Standard-setting organizations must stay abreast of regulatory developments and engage with policymakers to ensure that standards align with regulatory requirements and promote public interest objectives.

9.3.7 Lack of Resources and Expertise

A lack of resources and expertise can hinder global standardization efforts, particularly for smaller organizations or developing countries with limited capacity to participate in standard-setting activities. Standardization requires significant investments of time, money, and human capital, as well as access to specialized knowledge, technical expertise, and infrastructure. Ensuring broad participation and inclusivity in standardization processes requires overcoming barriers to entry and providing support for capacity building and skills development.

9.3.8 Addressing the Challenges: Strategies and Solutions

While the challenges in global standardization are significant, there are several strategies and solutions that can help overcome them:

1. Collaboration and Stakeholder Engagement: Foster collaboration and engagement among stakeholders from diverse backgrounds, industries, and regions to build consensus, share knowledge, and leverage collective expertise in standard-setting processes.

2. Transparency and Openness: Promote transparency and openness in standardization processes by making standards development activities, meetings, and decisions accessible to all interested parties, allowing for greater visibility, accountability, and inclusivity.
3. Alignment with Market Needs: Ensure that standards are aligned with market needs, user requirements, and industry trends by conducting thorough market research, stakeholder consultations, and needs assessments to identify priorities and gaps in existing standards.
4. Harmonization and Convergence: Encourage harmonization and convergence of standards by fostering cooperation and coordination among standards bodies, industry consortia, and regulatory authorities to avoid duplication, minimize conflicts, and streamline standardization efforts.
5. Education and Capacity Building: Provide education, training, and capacity building initiatives to empower stakeholders with the knowledge, skills, and resources needed to participate effectively in standardization activities, particularly in regions or sectors with limited capacity.
6. Adaptability and Flexibility: Embrace adaptability and flexibility in standardization processes to accommodate evolving technologies, market dynamics, and regulatory requirements, allowing standards to evolve over time to address emerging challenges and opportunities.
7. Public-Private Partnerships: Foster public-private partnerships and collaborations to leverage the strengths and resources of both the public and private sectors in advancing global standardization goals, promoting innovation, and driving economic growth.

9.4 REGIONAL DIFFERENCES AND CONSIDERATION

In our interconnected world, businesses, organizations, and policymakers must navigate a complex landscape of regional differences and considerations. From cultural norms and regulatory frameworks to economic conditions and geopolitical factors, regional variations can significantly impact operations, strategies, and outcomes.

Navigating regional differences requires organizations to embrace diversity, adaptability, and collaboration in their operations, strategies, and relationships.

By understanding and addressing cultural, regulatory, economic, political, social, and technological differences, organizations can effectively navigate regional complexities and capitalize on global opportunities. By fostering inclusive, resilient, and sustainable approaches to business, organizations can thrive in diverse markets and contribute to positive social and economic development on a global scale.

9.4.1 Cultural Diversity

Cultural diversity is one of the most significant regional differences that organizations must consider when operating in diverse markets. Cultural norms, values, beliefs, and behaviors vary widely across regions, influencing consumer preferences, business practices, and interpersonal interactions. Understanding and respecting cultural differences is essential for building trust, fostering meaningful relationships, and avoiding misunderstandings or cultural faux pas.

9.4.2 Regulatory Frameworks

Regulatory frameworks vary from one region to another, reflecting differences in legal systems, governance structures, and policy priorities. Regulations related to taxation, trade, intellectual property, data privacy, labor, and environmental protection can have significant implications for businesses operating across borders. Navigating complex regulatory landscapes requires careful compliance, risk management, and engagement with regulatory authorities and stakeholders.

9.4.3 Economic Conditions

Economic conditions, including GDP growth, inflation rates, unemployment levels, and currency fluctuations, vary across regions and impact business operations, investment decisions, and market opportunities. Differences in consumer purchasing power, disposable income, and spending habits also influence demand patterns and market dynamics. Adapting to diverse economic conditions requires agility, flexibility, and market intelligence to capitalize on opportunities and mitigate risks effectively.

9.4.4 Infrastructure and Technology

Infrastructure and technology capabilities vary widely across regions, affecting access to essential services, digital connectivity, and innovation ecosystems. Disparities in transportation networks, energy resources, telecommunications infrastructure, and internet penetration levels can create barriers to market entry and hinder business expansion. Leveraging local infrastructure and technology assets while investing in capacity building and digital transformation initiatives can help organizations overcome these challenges and unlock growth opportunities.

9.4.5 Political and Geopolitical Factors

Political stability, geopolitical tensions, and government policies can have profound effects on regional dynamics and business environments. Factors such as trade agreements, diplomatic relations, security threats, and regulatory reforms can impact market access, supply chain resilience, and business continuity. Monitoring geopolitical developments and engaging with relevant stakeholders to anticipate and manage risks are critical for organizations operating in volatile or high-risk regions.

9.4.6 Social and Demographic Trends

Social and demographic trends, including population growth, urbanization, aging populations, and migration patterns, shape consumer markets, labor pools, and societal dynamics. Understanding these trends and their implications for consumer behavior, workforce demographics, and market demand is essential for developing targeted strategies and tailored solutions that resonate with local populations.

9.4.7 Strategies for Navigating Regional Differences

While regional differences present challenges, organizations can adopt several strategies to navigate them effectively:

1. Localized Market Research: Conduct localized market research to gain insights into consumer preferences, market trends, competitive landscapes, and regulatory environments in target regions. Tailor products, services, and marketing strategies to meet the specific needs and preferences of local customers.
2. Cross-Cultural Training: Provide cross-cultural training and education to employees and stakeholders to enhance cultural awareness, sensitivity, and competence. Encourage open dialogue, mutual respect, and empathy to bridge cultural gaps and build effective cross-cultural relationships.
3. Partnerships and Alliances: Forge strategic partnerships and alliances with local partners, suppliers, distributors, and stakeholders to leverage their expertise, networks, and market knowledge. Collaborate with local communities, organizations, and authorities to build trust, credibility, and goodwill.
4. Adaptive Business Models: Develop adaptive business models that can flexibly respond to regional differences and market conditions. Adopt agile, iterative approaches to product development, marketing campaigns, and business strategies to accommodate diverse customer needs and preferences.
5. Compliance and Risk Management: Establish robust compliance and risk management processes to ensure adherence to regional regulations, standards, and ethical practices. Monitor regulatory developments, assess compliance risks, and implement mitigation strategies to minimize legal and reputational liabilities.
6. Technology Enablement: Leverage technology and digital solutions to overcome infrastructure limitations, enhance operational efficiency, and improve access to markets and resources. Invest in digital infrastructure, e-commerce platforms, and data analytics capabilities to support cross-border operations and decision-making.

7. Long-Term Perspective: Adopt a long-term perspective and commitment to sustainable growth, recognizing that building successful businesses in diverse regions requires patience, perseverance, and continuous learning. Cultivate relationships, invest in local communities, and demonstrate corporate social responsibility to earn trust and loyalty over time.

CHAPTER 10

5G AND SOCIETY

10.1 IMPACT ON BUSINESSES AND INDUSTRIES

5G technology is expected to have a significant impact on businesses, especially those that rely on real-time communication.

- Faster and More Efficient Communication: One of the primary benefits of 5G technology for businesses is faster and more efficient communication. With 5G, businesses will be able to transmit large amounts of data quickly and efficiently, which will improve collaboration and productivity. This is especially important for businesses that operate in real-time, such as those in the finance and healthcare industries.
- Increased Efficiency: 5G technology can significantly increase efficiency in businesses. With faster data transfer rates, businesses will be able to process and analyze data in real-time, which will help them make informed decisions quickly. This will also help businesses automate more tasks, leading to increased productivity and reduced costs.
- Improved Customer Experience: 5G technology will also improve the customer experience for businesses. With faster data transfer rates, businesses will be able to offer better and faster services, leading to increased customer satisfaction. This is especially important for businesses in the retail and hospitality industries, where customers expect quick and efficient service.
- New Business Opportunities: 5G technology will also create new business opportunities for businesses. With faster and more efficient communication, businesses will be able to expand their operations to new markets, which will lead to increased revenue and growth. This is especially important for businesses that operate globally, as 5G technology will allow them to operate in real-time across multiple locations.
- Improved Healthcare: 5G technology will significantly improve healthcare. With faster and more efficient data transfer, healthcare providers will be able to diagnose and treat patients more quickly and efficiently, leading to improved outcomes. This is especially important for patients in rural areas, where access to healthcare is limited.

- Improved Transportation: 5G technology will also improve transportation. With faster and more efficient data transfer, transportation companies will be able to optimize their routes and schedules, leading to reduced congestion and improved safety. This will also lead to reduced emissions, which will help to reduce the impact of transportation on the environment.
- Increased Accessibility: 5G technology will also increase accessibility. With faster and more efficient data transfer, people in remote and rural areas will be able to access services and resources that were previously unavailable to them. This will help to reduce the digital divide, which is a significant issue in many countries.
- New Technologies: 5G technology will also lead to the development of new technologies. With faster and more efficient data transfer, businesses and researchers will be able to develop and implement new technologies, such as augmented reality and virtual reality.

10.2 SOCIO-ECONOMICS IMPLICATIONS OF 5G

The advent of fifth-generation (5G) wireless technology promises to usher in a new era of connectivity, innovation, and economic growth. With its potential to deliver ultra-fast speeds, low latency, and massive connectivity, 5G has far-reaching socio-economic implications that extend across various sectors and industries. The socio-economic implications of 5G technology are vast and multifaceted, with the potential to drive economic development, industry transformation, societal empowerment, and sustainable development. By leveraging 5G's transformative capabilities, businesses, governments, and communities can unlock new opportunities for innovation, growth, and prosperity. However, realizing the full potential of 5G requires addressing challenges such as digital inclusion, privacy, security, job displacement, and skills development to ensure that the benefits of 5G technology are shared equitably and sustainably across society. By embracing collaboration, innovation, and inclusive growth strategies, we can harness the power of 5G to create a more connected, prosperous, and inclusive future for all.

10.2.1 Economic Development and Growth

Economic Development

In the economics study of the public sector, economic and social development is the process by which the economic well-being and quality of life of a nation, region, local community, or an individual are improved according to targeted goals and objectives. The term has been used frequently in the 20th and 21st centuries, but the concept has existed in the West for far longer. "Modernization", "Westernization", and especially "industrialization" are other terms often used while discussing economic development. Historically, economic development policies focused on industrialization and infrastructure; since the 1960s, it has increasingly focused on poverty reduction.

Whereas economic development is a policy intervention aiming to improve the well-being of people, economic growth is a phenomenon of market productivity and increases in GDP; economist Amartya Sen describes economic growth as but "one aspect of the process of economic development".

Definition and Terminology

The precise definition of economic development has been contested: while economists in the 20th century viewed development primarily in terms of economic growth, sociologists instead emphasized broader processes of change and modernization. Development and urban studies scholar Karl Seidman summarizes economic development as "a process of creating and utilizing physical, human, financial, and social assets to generate improved and broadly shared economic well-being and quality of life for a community or region". Daphne Greenwood and Richard Holt distinguish economic development from economic growth on the basis that economic development is a "broadly based and sustainable increase in the overall standard of living for individuals within a community", and measures of growth such as per capita income do not necessarily correlate with improvements in quality of life. The United Nations Development Programme in 1997 defined development as increasing people s choices. Choices depend on the people in question and their nation. The UNDP indicates four chief factors in development, specially human development, which are empowerment, equity, productivity and sustainability.

Mansell and Wehn state that economic development has been understood by non-practitioners since the World War II to involve economic growth, namely the increases in per capita income, and (if currently absent) the attainment of a standard of living equivalent to that of industrialized countries. Economic development can also be considered as a static theory that documents the state of an economy at a certain time. According to Schumpeter and Backhaus (2003), the changes in this equilibrium state documented in economic theory can only be caused by intervening factors coming from the outside.

History

Economic development originated in the post-war period of reconstruction initiated by the United States. In 1949, during his inaugural speech, President Harry Truman identified the development of undeveloped areas as a priority for the west:

- "More than half the people of the world are living in conditions approaching misery. Their food is inadequate, they are victims of the disease. Their economic life is primitive and stagnant. Their poverty is a handicap and a threat both to them and to more prosperous areas. For the first time in history, humanity possesses the knowledge and the skill

> to relieve the suffering of these people... I believe that we should make available to peace-loving people the benefits of our store of technical knowledge in order to help them realize their aspirations for a better life... What we envisage is a program of development based on the concepts of democratic fair dealing... Greater production is the key to prosperity and peace. And the key to greater production is a wider and more vigorous application of modem scientific and technical knowledge."

There have been several major phases of development theory since 1945. Alexander Gerschenkron argued that the less developed the country is at the outset of economic development (relative to others), the more likely certain conditions are to occur.

Hence, all countries do not progress similarly. From the 1940s to the 1960s the state played a large role in promoting industrialization in developing countries, following the idea of modernization theory. This period was followed by a brief period of basic needs development focusing on human capital development and redistribution in the 1970s. Neoliberalism emerged in the 1980s pushing an agenda of free trade and removal of import substitution industrialization policies.

In economics, the study of economic development was born out of an extension to traditional economics that focused entirely on the national product, or the aggregate output of goods and services. Economic development was concerned with the expansion of people's entitlements and their corresponding capabilities, such as morbidity, nourishment, literacy, education, and other socio-economic indicators.

Borne out of the backdrop of Keynesian economics (advocating government intervention), and neoclassical economics (stressing reduced intervention), with the rise of high-growth countries (Singapore, South Korea, Hong Kong) and planned governments (Argentina, Chile, Sudan, Uganda), economic development and more generally development economics emerged amidst these mid-20th century theoretical interpretations of how economies prosper. Also, economist Albert O. Hirschman, a major contributor to development economics, asserted that economic development grew to concentrate on the poor regions of the world, primarily in Africa, Asia and Latin America yet on the outpouring of fundamental ideas and models.

It has also been argued, notably by Asian and European proponents of infrastructure-based development, that systematic, long-term government investments in transportation, housing, education, and healthcare are necessary to ensure sustainable economic growth in emerging countries.

During Robert McNamara's 13 years at the World Bank, he introduced key changes, most notably, shifting the Bank's economic development policies toward targeted poverty reduction.

Prior to his tenure at the World Bank, poverty did not receive substantial attention as part of international and national economic development; the focus of development had been on industrialization and infrastructure. Poverty also came to be redefined as a condition faced by people rather than countries. According to Martha Finnemore, the World Bank under McNamara's tenure "sold" states poverty reduction "through a mixture of persuasion and coercion."

Economic Development Goals

The development of a country has been associated with different concepts but generally encompasses economic growth through higher productivity, political systems that represent as accurately as possible the preferences of its citizens, the extension of rights to all social groups and the opportunities to get them and the proper functionality of institutions and organizations that are able to attend more technically and logistically complex tasks (i.e., raise taxes and deliver public services). These processes describe the State's capabilities to manage its economy, polity, society and public administration. Generally, economic development policies attempt to solve issues in these topics.

With this in mind, economic development is typically associated with improvements in a variety of areas or indicators (such as literacy rates, life expectancy, and poverty rates), that may be causes of economic development rather than consequences of specific economic development programs.

For example, health and education improvements have been closely related to economic growth, but the causality with economic development may not be obvious. In any case, it is important to not expect that particular economic development programs be able to fix many problems at once as that would be establishing unsurmountable goals for them that are highly unlikely they can achieve. Any development policy should set limited goals and a gradual approach to avoid falling victim to something Prittchet, Woolcock and Andrews call 'premature load bearing'.

Many times the economic development goals of specific countries cannot be reached because they lack the State's capabilities to do so. For example, if a nation has little capacity to carry out basic functions like security and policing or core service delivery it is unlikely that a program that wants to foster a free-trade zone (special economic zones) or distribute vaccinations to vulnerable populations can accomplish their goals.

This has been something overlooked by multiple international organizations, aid programs and even participating governments who attempt to carry out 'best practices' from other places in a carbon-copy manner with little success. This isomorphic mimicry –adopting organizational forms that have been successful elsewhere but that only hide institutional dysfunction without solving it on the home country –can contribute to getting countries stuck in 'capability traps' where the country does not advance in its development goals. An example of this can be seen through some of the criticisms of foreign aid and its success rate at helping countries develop.

Beyond the incentive compatibility problems that can happen to foreign aid donations –that foreign aid granting countries continue to give it to countries with little results of economic growth but with corrupt leaders that are aligned with the granting countries' geopolitical interests and agenda –there are problems of fiscal fragility associated to receiving an important amount of government revenues through foreign aid. Governments that can raise a significant amount of revenue from this source are less accountable to their citizens (they are more autonomous) as they have less pressure to legitimately use those resources. Just as it has been documented for countries with an abundant supply of natural resources such as oil, countries whose government budget consists largely of foreign aid donations and not regular taxes are less likely to have incentives to develop effective public institutions. This in turn can undermine the country's efforts to develop.

Economic Development Policies

In its broadest sense, policies of economic development encompass three major areas:

- Governments undertaking to meet broad economic objectives such as price stability, high employment, and sustainable growth. Such efforts include monetary and fiscal policies, regulation of financial institutions, trade, and tax policies.
- Programs that provide infrastructure and services such as highways, parks, affordable housing, crime prevention, and K–12 education.
- Job creation and retention through specific efforts in business finance, marketing, neighborhood development, workforce development, small business development, business retention and expansion, technology transfer, and real estate development. This third category is a primary focus of economic development professionals.

Contractionary monetary policy is a tool used by central banks to slow down a country's economic growth. An example would be raising interest rates to decrease lending. In the United States, the use of contractionary monetary policy has increased women's unemployment. Seguino and Heintz uses a panel dataset for each 50 states with unemployment, labor force participation by race, and annual labor market statistics. In addition, for contractionary monetary policy, they utilize the federal funds rate, the short-term interest rates charged to banks. Seguino and Heintz Seguino concludes that the impact of a one percentage point increase in the federal funds rate relative to white and black women's unemployment is 0.015 and 0.043, respectively

One growing understanding in economic development is the promotion of regional clusters and a thriving metropolitan economy. In today's global landscape, location is vitally important and becomes a key in competitive advantage.

International trade and exchange rates are key issues in economic development. Currencies are often either under-valued or over-valued, resulting in trade surpluses or deficits. Furthermore, the growth of globalization has linked economic development with trends on international trade and participation in global value chains (GVCs) and international financial markets. The last financial crisis had a huge effect on economies in developing countries. Economist Jayati Ghosh states that it is necessary to make financial markets in developing countries more resilient by providing a variety of financial institutions. This could also add to financial security for small-scale producers.

Economic development has evolved into a professional industry of highly specialized practitioners. The practitioners have two key roles: one is to provide leadership in policy-making, and the other is to administer policy, programs, and projects.

Economic development practitioners generally work in public offices on the state, regional, or municipal level, or in public-private partnerships organizations that may be partially funded by local, regional, state, or federal tax money. These economic development organizations function as individual entities and in some cases as departments of local governments. Their role is to seek out new economic opportunities and retain their existing business wealth.

There are numerous other organizations whose primary function is not economic development that work in partnership with economic developers. They include the news media, foundations, utilities, schools, health care providers, faith-based organizations, and colleges, universities, and other education or research institutions.

Development Indicators and Indices

There are various types of macroeconomic and sociocultural indicators or "metrics" used by economists and geographers to assess the relative economic advancement of a given region or nation.

The World Bank's "World Development Indicators" are compiled annually from officially recognized international sources and include national, regional and global estimates. GDP per capita is gross domestic product divided by mid-year population. GDP is the sum of gross value added by all resident producers in the economy plus any product taxes and minus any subsidizes not included in the value of the products. It is calculated without making deductions for depreciation of fabricated assets or for depletion and degradation of natural resources.

European development economists have argued that the existence of modern transportation networks- such as high-speed rail infrastructure constitutes a significant indicator of a country's economic advancement: this perspective is illustrated notably through the Basic Rail Transportation Infrastructure Index (known as BRTI Index) and related models such as the (Modified) Rail Transportation Infrastructure Index (RTI).

In an effort to create an indicator that would help measure gender equality, the United Nations has created two measures: the Gender-Related Development Index (GDI) and the Gender Empowerment Measure (GEM). These indicators were first introduced in the 1995 UNDP Human Development Report.

Other factors include the inflation rate, investment level and national debt, birth and death rates, morbidity, education levels (measured through literacy and numeracy rates, life skills, housing, social services like hospitals, health facilities, clean and safe drinking water, schools (measured by the distance learners must travel to reach them), ability to use hard infrastructure (railways, roads, ports, airports, harbours and telecommunication, soft infrastructure, like Internet and life expectancy.

The Gender Empowerment Measure (GEM) focuses on aggregating various indicators that focus on capturing the economic, political, and professional gains made by women. The GEM is composed of just three variables: income earning power, share in professional and managerial jobs, and share of parliamentary seats.

The Gender Development Index (GDI) measures the gender gap in human development achievements. It takes the disparity between men and women into account through three variables, health, knowledge, and living standards.

Economic Growth

Economic growth can be defined as the increase or improvement in the inflation-adjusted market value of the goods and services produced by an economy in a financial year. Statisticians conventionally measure such growth as the percent rate of increase in the real and nominal gross domestic product (GDP).

Growth is usually calculated in real terms – i.e., inflation-adjusted terms – to eliminate the distorting effect of inflation on the prices of goods produced. Measurement of economic growth uses national income accounting. Since economic growth is measured as the annual percent change of gross domestic product (GDP), it has all the advantages and drawbacks of that measure. The economic growth-rates of countries are commonly compared using the ratio of the GDP to population (per-capita income).

The "rate of economic growth" refers to the geometric annual rate of growth in GDP between the first and the last year over a period of time. This growth rate represents the trend in the average level of GDP over the period, and ignores any fluctuations in the GDP around this trend.

Economists refer to economic growth caused by more efficient use of inputs (increased productivity of labor, of physical capital, of energy or of materials) as intensive growth. In contrast, GDP growth caused only by increases in the amount of inputs available for use (increased population, for example, or new territory) counts as extensive growth.

Development of new goods and services also generates economic growth. As it so happens, in the U.S. about 60% of consumer spending in 2013 went on goods and services that did not exist in 1869.

Measurement

The economic growth rate is calculated from data on GDP estimated by countries' statistical agencies. The rate of growth of GDP per capita is calculated from data on GDP and people for the initial and final periods included in the analysis of the analyst.

Determinants of Per Capita GDP Growth

In national income accounting, per capita output can be calculated using the following factors: output per unit of labor input (labor productivity), hours worked (intensity), the percentage of the working-age population actually working (participation rate) and the proportion of the working-age population to the total population (demographics). "The rate of change of GDP/population is the sum of the rates of change of these four variables plus their cross products."

Economists distinguish between long-run economic growth and short-run economic changes in production. Short-run variation in economic growth is termed the business cycle. Generally, according to economists, the ups and downs in the business cycle can be attributed to fluctuations in aggregate demand. In contrast, economic growth is concerned with the long-run trend in production due to structural causes such as technological growth and factor accumulation.

Increases in labor productivity (the ratio of the value of output to labor input) have historically been the most important source of real per capita economic growth. In a famous estimate, MIT Professor Robert Solow concluded that technological progress has accounted for 80 percent of the long-term rise in U.S. per capita income, with increased investment in capital explaining only the remaining 20 percent.

Increases in productivity lower the real cost of goods. Over the 20th century, the real price of many goods fell by over 90%.

Economic growth has traditionally been attributed to the accumulation of human and physical capital and the increase in productivity and creation of new goods arising from technological innovation. Further division of labour (specialization) is also fundamental to rising productivity.

Before industrialization technological progress resulted in an increase in the population, which was kept in check by food supply and other resources, which acted to limit per capita income, a condition known as the Malthusian trap. The rapid economic growth that occurred during the Industrial Revolution was remarkable because it was in excess of population growth, providing an escape from the Malthusian trap. Countries that industrialized eventually saw their population growth slow down, a phenomenon known as the demographic transition.

Increases in productivity are the major factor responsible for per capita economic growth—this has been especially evident since the mid-19th century. Most of the economic growth in the 20th century was due to increased output per unit of labor, materials, energy, and land (less input per widget). The balance of the growth in output has come from using more inputs. Both of these changes increase output. The increased output included more of the same goods produced previously and new goods and services.

During the Industrial Revolution, mechanization began to replace hand methods in manufacturing, and new processes streamlined production of chemicals, iron, steel, and other products. Machine tools made the economical production of metal parts possible, so that parts could be interchangeable.

During the Second Industrial Revolution, a major factor of productivity growth was the substitution of inanimate power for human and animal labor. Also there was a great increase in power as steam-powered electricity generation and internal combustion supplanted limited wind and water power. Since that replacement, the great expansion of total power was driven by continuous improvements in energy conversion efficiency. Other major historical sources of productivity were automation, transportation infrastructures (canals, railroads, and highways), new materials (steel) and power, which includes steam and internal combustion engines and electricity. Other productivity improvements included mechanized agriculture and scientific agriculture including chemical fertilizers and livestock and poultry management, and the Green Revolution. Interchangeable parts made with machine tools powered by electric motors evolved into mass production, which is universally used today.

Great sources of productivity improvement in the late 19th century were railroads, steam ships, horse-pulled reapers and combine harvesters, and steam-powered factories. The invention of processes for making cheap steel were important for many forms of mechanization and transportation. By the late 19th century both prices and weekly work hours fell because less labor, materials, and energy were required to produce and transport goods. However, real wages rose, allowing workers to improve their diet, buy consumer goods and afford better housing.

Mass production of the 1920s created overproduction, which was arguably one of several causes of the Great Depression of the 1930s. Following the Great Depression, economic growth resumed, aided in part by increased demand for existing goods and services, such as automobiles, telephones, radios, electricity and household appliances. New goods and services included television, air conditioning and commercial aviation (after 1950), creating enough new demand to stabilize the work week. The building of highway infrastructures also contributed to post-World War II growth, as did capital investments in manufacturing and chemical industries. The post-World War II economy also benefited from the discovery of vast amounts of oil around the world, particularly in the Middle East. By John W. Kendrick's estimate, three-quarters of increase in U.S. per capita GDP from 1889 to 1957 was due to increased productivity.

Economic growth in the United States slowed down after 1973. In contrast, growth in Asia has been strong since then, starting with Japan and spreading to Four Asian Tigers, China, Southeast Asia, the Indian subcontinent and Asia Pacific. In 1957 South Korea had a lower per capita GDP than Ghana, and by 2008 it was 17 times as high as Ghana's. The Japanese economic growth has slackened considerably since the late 1980s.

Productivity in the United States grew at an increasing rate throughout the 19th century and was most rapid in the early to middle decades of the 20th century. U.S. productivity growth spiked towards the end of the century in 1996–2004, due to an acceleration in the rate of technological innovation known as Moore's law. After 2004 U.S. productivity growth returned to the low levels of 1972–96.

Capital in economics ordinarily refers to physical capital, which consists of structures (largest component of physical capital) and equipment used in business (machinery, factory equipment, computers and office equipment, construction equipment, business vehicles, medical equipment, etc.). Up to a point increases in the amount of capital per worker are an important cause of economic output growth. Capital is subject to diminishing returns because of the amount that can be effectively invested and because of the growing burden of depreciation. In the development of economic theory, the distribution of income was considered to be between labor and the owners of land and capital. In recent decades there have been several Asian countries with high rates of economic growth driven by capital investment.

The work week declined considerably over the 19th century. By the 1920s the average work week in the U.S. was 49 hours, but the work week was reduced to 40 hours (after which overtime premium was applied) as part of the National Industrial Recovery Act of 1933.

Demographic factors may influence growth by changing the employment to population ratio and the labor force participation rate. Industrialization creates a demographic transition in which birth rates decline and the average age of the population increases.

Women with fewer children and better access to market employment tend to join the labor force in higher percentages. There is a reduced demand for child labor and children spend more years in school. The increase in the percentage of women in the labor force in the U.S. contributed to economic growth, as did the entrance of the baby boomers into the workforce.

Growth Theories

Adam Smith

Adam Smith pioneered modern economic growth and performance theory in his book The Wealth of Nations, first published in 1776. For Smith, the main factors of economic growth are division of labour and capital accumulation. However, these are conditioned by what he calls "the extent of the market". This is conditioned notably by geographic factors but also institutional ones such as the political-legal environment.

Malthusian Theory

Malthusianism is the idea that population growth is potentially exponential while the growth of the food supply or other resources is linear, which eventually reduces living standards to the point of triggering a population die off. The Malthusian theory also proposes that over most of human history technological progress caused larger population growth but had no impact on income per capita in the long run. According to the theory, while technologically advanced economies over this epoch were characterized by higher population density, their level of income per capita was not different from those among technologically regressed society.

The conceptual foundations of the Malthusian theory were formed by Thomas Malthus, and a modern representation of these approach is provided by Ashraf and Galor. In line with the predictions of the Malthusian theory, a cross-country analysis finds a significant positive effect of the technological level on population density and an insignificant effect on income per capita significantly over the years 1–1500.

Classical Growth Theory

In classical (Ricardian) economics, the theory of production and the theory of growth are based on the theory of sustainability and law of variable proportions, whereby increasing either of the factors of production (labor or capital), while holding the other constant and assuming no technological change, will increase output, but at a diminishing rate that eventually will approach zero. These concepts have their origins in Thomas Malthus's theorizing about agriculture. Malthus's examples included the number of seeds harvested relative to the number of seeds planted (capital) on a plot of land and the size of the harvest from a plot of land versus the number of workers employed.

Criticisms of classical growth theory are that technology, an important factor in economic growth, is held constant and that economies of scale are ignored. One popular theory in the 1940s was the big push model, which suggested that countries needed to jump from one stage of development to another through a virtuous cycle, in which large investments in infrastructure and education coupled with private investments would move the economy to a more productive stage, breaking free from economic paradigms appropriate to a lower productivity stage. The idea was revived and formulated rigorously, in the late 1980s by Kevin Murphy, Andrei Shleifer and Robert Vishny.

Solow–Swan Model

Robert Solow and Trevor Swan developed what eventually became the main model used in growth economics in the 1950s. This model assumes that there are diminishing returns to capital and labor. Capital accumulates through investment, but its level or stock continually decreases due to depreciation. Due to the diminishing returns to capital, with increases in capital/worker and absent technological progress, economic output/worker eventually reaches a point where capital per worker and economic output/worker remain constant because annual investment in capital equals annual depreciation. This condition is called the 'steady state'.

In the Solow–Swan model if productivity increases through technological progress, then output/worker increases even when the economy is in the steady state. If productivity increases at a constant rate, output/worker also increases at a related steady-state rate. As a consequence, growth in the model can occur either by increasing the share of GDP invested or through technological progress. But at whatever share of GDP invested, capital/worker eventually converges on the steady state, leaving the growth rate of output/worker determined only by the rate of technological progress.

As a consequence, with world technology available to all and progressing at a constant rate, all countries have the same steady state rate of growth. Each country has a different level of GDP/worker determined by the share of GDP it invests, but all countries have the same rate of economic growth.

Implicitly in this model rich countries are those that have invested a high share of GDP for a long time. Poor countries can become rich by increasing the share of GDP they invest. One important prediction of the model, mostly borne out by the data, is that of conditional convergence; the idea that poor countries will grow faster and catch up with rich countries as long as they have similar investment (and saving) rates and access to the same technology.

The Solow–Swan model is considered an "exogenous" growth model because it does not explain why countries invest different shares of GDP in capital nor why technology improves over time. Instead, the rate of investment and the rate of technological progress are exogenous. The value of the model is that it predicts the pattern of economic growth once these two rates are specified. Its failure to explain the determinants of these rates is one of its limitations.

Although the rate of investment in the model is exogenous, under certain conditions the model implicitly predicts convergence in the rates of investment across countries. In a global economy with a global financial capital market, financial capital flows to the countries with the highest return on investment. In the Solow-Swan model countries with less capital/worker (poor countries) have a higher return on investment due to the diminishing returns to capital.

As a consequence, capital/worker and output/worker in a global financial capital market should converge to the same level in all countries. Since historically financial capital has not flowed to the countries with less capital/worker, the basic Solow–Swan model has a conceptual flaw. Beginning in the 1990s, this flaw has been addressed by adding additional variables to the model that can explain why some countries are less productive than others and, therefore, do not attract flows of global financial capital even though they have less (physical) capital/worker.

In practice, convergence was rarely achieved. In 1957, Solow applied his model to data from the U.S. gross national product to estimate contributions. This showed that the increase in capital and labor stock only accounted for about half of the output, while the population increase adjustments to capital explained eighth. This remaining unaccounted growth output is known as the Solow Residual.

Here the A of (t) "technical progress" was the reason for increased output. Nevertheless, the model still had flaws. It gave no room for policy to influence the growth rate. Few attempts were also made by the RAND Corporation the non-profit think tank and frequently visiting economist Kenneth Arrow to work out the kinks in the model. They suggested that new knowledge was indivisible and that it is endogenous with a certain fixed cost. Arrow's further explained that new knowledge obtained by firms comes from practice and built a model that "knowledge" accumulated through experience.

According to Harrod, the natural growth rate is the maximum rate of growth allowed by the increase of variables like population growth, technological improvement and growth in natural resources.

In fact, the natural growth rate is the highest attainable growth rate which would bring about the fullest possible employment of the resources existing in the economy.

Endogenous Growth Theory

Unsatisfied with the assumption of exogenous technological progress in the Solow–Swan model, economists worked to "endogenize" (i.e., explain it "from within" the models) productivity growth in the 1980s.

The resulting endogenous growth theory, most notably advanced by Robert Lucas, Jr. and his student Paul Romer, includes a mathematical explanation of technological advancement. This model was notable for its incorporation of human capital, which is interpreted from changes to investment patterns in education, training, and healthcare by private sector firms or governments. Notwithstanding the implications this component has for policy, the endogenous perspective on human capital investment emphasizes the possibility for broad-based effects which can be realized by other firms in the economy.

Accordingly, human capital is theorized to deliver increasing rates of return unlike physical capital. Research done in this area has focused on what increases human capital (e.g., education) or technological change (e.g., innovation). The quantity theory of endogenous productivity growth was proposed by Russian economist Vladimir Pokrovskii. It explains growth as a consequence of the dynamics of three factors, including the technological characteristics of production equipment. Without any arbitrary parameters, historical rates of economic growth can be predicted with considerable precision.

On Memorial Day weekend in 1988, a conference in Buffalo brought together influential thinkers to evaluate the conflicting theories of growth. Romer, Krugman, Barro, and Becker were in attendance along with many other high profiled economists of the time. Amongst many papers that day the one that stood out was Romer's "Micro Foundations for Aggregate Technological Change." The Micro Foundation claimed that endogenous technological change had the concept of Intellectual Property imbedded and that knowledge is an input and output of production.

Romer argued that outcomes to the national growth rates were significantly affected by public policy, trade activity, and intellectual property. He stressed that cumulative capital and specialization were key, and that not only population growth can increase capital of knowledge, it was human capital that is specifically trained in harvesting new ideas.

While intellectual property may be important, Baker (2016) cites multiple sources claiming that "stronger patent protection seems to be associated with slower growth". That's particularly true for patents in the ethical health care industry. In effect taxpayers pay twice for new drugs and diagnostic procedures: First in tax subsidies and second for the high prices of diagnostic procedures treatments.

If the results of research paid by taxpayers were placed in the public domain, Baker claims that people everywhere would be healthier, because better diagnoses and treatment would be more affordable the world over.

One branch of endogenous growth theory was developed on the foundations of the Schumpeterian theory, named after the 20th-century Austrian economist Joseph Schumpeter.

The approach explains growth as a consequence of innovation and a process of creative destruction that captures the dual nature of technological progress: in terms of creation, entrepreneurs introduce new products or processes in the hope that they will enjoy temporary monopoly-like profits as they capture markets. In doing so, they make old technologies or products obsolete. This can be seen as an annulment of previous technologies, which makes them obsolete, and "destroys the rents generated by previous innovations". A major model that illustrates Schumpeterian growth is the Aghion–Howitt model [ru].

Unified Growth Theory

Unified growth theory was developed by Oded Galor and his co-authors to address the inability of endogenous growth theory to explain key empirical regularities in the growth processes of individual economies and the world economy as a whole. Unlike endogenous growth theory that focuses entirely on the modern growth regime and is therefore unable to explain the roots of inequality across nations, unified growth theory captures in a single framework the fundamental phases of the process of development in the course of human history:

- the Malthusian epoch that was prevalent over most of human history,
- the escape from the Malthusian trap,
- the emergence of human capital as a central element in the growth process,
- the onset of the fertility decline,
- the origins of the modern era of sustained economic growth, and
- the roots of divergence in income per capita across nations in the past two centuries.

The theory suggests that during most of human existence, technological progress was offset by population growth, and living standards were near subsistence across time and space. However, the reinforcing interaction between the rate of technological progress and the size and composition of the population has gradually increased the pace of technological progress, enhancing the importance of education in the ability of individuals to adapt to the changing technological environment.

The rise in the allocation of resources towards education triggered a fertility decline enabling economies to allocate a larger share of the fruits of technological progress to a steady increase in income per capita, rather than towards the growth of population, paving the way for the emergence of sustained economic growth. The theory further suggests that variations in biogeographical characteristics, as well as cultural and institutional characteristics, have generated a differential pace of transition from stagnation to growth across countries and consequently divergence in their income per capita over the past two centuries.

Inequality and Growth

Theories

The prevailing views about the role of inequality in the growth process has radically shifted in the past century. The classical perspective, as expressed by Adam Smith, and others, suggests that inequality fosters the growth process. Specifically, since the aggregate saving increases with inequality due to higher property to save among the wealthy, the classical viewpoint suggests that inequality stimulates capital accumulation and therefore economic growth.

The Neoclassical perspective that is based on representative agent approach denies the role of inequality in the growth process. It suggests that while the growth process may affect inequality, income distribution has no impact on the growth process.

The modern perspective which has emerged in the late 1980s suggests, in contrast, that income distribution has a significant impact on the growth process. The modern perspective, originated by Galor and Zeira, highlights the important role of heterogeneity in the determination of aggregate economic activity, and economic growth. In particular, Galor and Zeira argue that since credit markets are imperfect, inequality has an enduring impact on human capital formation, the level of income per capita, and the growth process. In contrast to the classical paradigm, which underlined the positive implications of inequality for capital formation and economic growth, Galor and Zeira argue that inequality has an adverse effect on human capital formation and the development process, in all but the very poor economies.

Later theoretical developments have reinforced the view that inequality has an adverse effect on the growth process. Specifically, Alesina and Rodrik and Persson and Tabellini advance a political economy mechanism and argue that inequality has a negative impact on economic development since it creates a pressure for distortionary redistributive policies that have an adverse effect on investment and economic growth.

In accordance with the credit market imperfection approach, a study by Roberto Perotti showed that inequality is associated with lower level of human capital formation (education, experience, apprenticeship) and higher level of fertility, while lower level of human capital is associated with lower growth and lower levels of economic growth. In contrast, his examination of the political economy channel found no support for the political economy mechanism. Consequently, the political economy perspective on the relationship between inequality and growth have been revised and later studies have established that inequality may provide an incentive for the elite to block redistributive policies and institutional changes. In particular, inequality in the distribution of land ownership provides the landed elite with an incentive to limit the mobility of rural workers by depriving them from education and by blocking the development of the industrial sector.

A unified theory of inequality and growth that captures that changing role of inequality in the growth process offers a reconciliation between the conflicting predictions of classical viewpoint that maintained that inequality is beneficial for growth and the modern viewpoint that suggests that in the presence of credit market imperfections, inequality predominantly results in underinvestment in human capital and lower economic growth. This unified theory of inequality and growth, developed by Oded Galor and Omer Moav, suggests that the effect of inequality on the growth process has been reversed as human capital has replaced physical capital as the main engine of economic growth. In the initial phases of industrialization, when physical capital accumulation was the dominating source of economic growth, inequality boosted the development process by directing resources toward individuals with higher propensity to save. However, in later phases, as human capital become the main engine of economic growth, more equal distribution of income, in the presence of credit constraints, stimulated investment in human capital and economic growth.

In 2013, French economist Thomas Piketty postulated that in periods when the average annual rate on return on investment in capital (r) exceeds the average annual growth in economic output (g), the rate of inequality will increase. According to Piketty, this is the case because wealth that is already held or inherited, which is expected to grow at the rate r, will grow at a rate faster than wealth accumulated through labor, which is more closely tied to g. An advocate of reducing inequality levels, Piketty suggests levying a global wealth tax in order to reduce the divergence in wealth caused by inequality.

Evidence: Reduced Form

The reduced form empirical relationship between inequality and growth was studied by Alberto Alesina and Dani Rodrik, and Torsten Persson and Guido Tabellini. They find that inequality is negatively associated with economic growth in a cross-country analysis.

Robert Barro reexamined the reduced form relationship between inequality on economic growth in a panel of countries. He argues that there is "little overall relation between income inequality and rates of growth and investment". However, his empirical strategy limits its applicability to the understanding of the relationship between inequality and growth for several reasons. First, his regression analysis control for education, fertility, investment, and it therefore excludes, by construction, the important effect of inequality on growth via education, fertility, and investment. His findings simply imply that inequality has no direct effect on growth beyond the important indirect effects through the main channels proposed in the literature. Second, his study analyzes the effect of inequality on the average growth rate in the following 10 years. However, existing theories suggest that the effect of inequality will be observed much later, as is the case in human capital formation, for instance. Third, the empirical analysis does not account for biases that are generated by reverse causality and omitted variables.

Recent papers based on superior data, find negative relationship between inequality and growth. Andrew Berg and Jonathan Ostry of the International Monetary Fund, find that "lower net inequality is robustly correlated with faster and more durable growth, controlling for the level of redistribution". Likewise, Dierk Herzer and Sebastian Vollmer find that increased income inequality reduces economic growth.

Evidence: Mechanisms

The Galor and Zeira's model predicts that the effect of rising inequality on GDP per capita is negative in relatively rich countries but positive in poor countries. These testable predictions have been examined and confirmed empirically in recent studies. In particular, Brückner and Lederman test the prediction of the model by in the panel of countries during the period 1970–2010, by considering the impact of the interaction between the level of income inequality and the initial level of GDP per capita. In line with the predictions of the model, they find that at the 25th percentile of initial income in the world sample, a 1 percentage point increase in the Gini coefficient increases income per capita by 2.3%, whereas at the 75th percentile of initial income a 1 percentage point increase in the Gini coefficient decreases income per capita by -5.3%. Moreover, the proposed human capital mechanism that mediates the effect of inequality on growth in the Galor-Zeira model is also confirmed. Increases in income inequality increase human capital in poor countries but reduce it in high and middle-income countries.

This recent support for the predictions of the Galor-Zeira model is in line with earlier findings. Roberto Perotti showed that in accordance with the credit market imperfection approach, developed by Galor and Zeira, inequality is associated with lower level of human capital formation (education, experience, apprenticeship) and higher level of fertility, while lower level of human capital is associated with lower levels of economic growth. Princeton economist Roland Benabou's finds that the growth process of Korea and the Philippines "are broadly consistent with the credit-constrained human-capital accumulation hypothesis". In addition, Andrew Berg and Jonathan Ostry suggest that inequality seems to affect growth through human capital accumulation and fertility channels.

In contrast, Perotti argues that the political economy mechanism is not supported empirically. Inequality is associated with lower redistribution, and lower redistribution (under-investment in education and infrastructure) is associated with lower economic growth.

Importance of Long-run Growth

Over long periods of time, even small rates of growth, such as a 2% annual increase, have large effects. For example, the United Kingdom experienced a 1.97% average annual increase in its inflation-adjusted GDP between 1830 and 2008. In 1830, the GDP was 41,373 million pounds. It grew to 1,330,088 million pounds by 2008. A growth rate that averaged 1.97% over 178 years resulted in a 32-fold increase in GDP by 2008.

The large impact of a relatively small growth rate over a long period of time is due to the power of exponential growth. The rule of 72, a mathematical result, states that if something grows at the rate of x% per year, then its level will double every 72/x years.

For example, a growth rate of 2.5% per annum leads to a doubling of the GDP within 28.8 years, whilst a growth rate of 8% per year leads to a doubling of GDP within nine years. Thus, a small difference in economic growth rates between countries can result in very different standards of living for their populations if this small difference continues for many years.

Quality of Life

One theory that relates economic growth with quality of life is the "Threshold Hypothesis", which states that economic growth up to a point brings with it an increase in quality of life. But at that point – called the threshold point – further economic growth can bring with it a deterioration in quality of life. This results in an upside-down-U-shaped curve, where the vertex of the curve represents the level of growth that should be targeted. Happiness has been shown to increase with GDP per capita, at least up to a level of $15,000 per person.

Economic growth has the indirect potential to alleviate poverty, as a result of a simultaneous increase in employment opportunities and increased labor productivity. A study by researchers at the Overseas Development Institute (ODI) of 24 countries that experienced growth found that in 18 cases, poverty was alleviated.

In some instances, quality of life factors such as healthcare outcomes and educational attainment, as well as social and political liberties, do not improve as economic growth occurs.

Productivity increases do not always lead to increased wages, as can be seen in the United States, where the gap between productivity and wages has been rising since the 1980s.

Equitable Growth

While acknowledging the central role economic growth can potentially play in human development, poverty reduction and the achievement of the Millennium Development Goals, it is becoming widely understood amongst the development community that special efforts must be made to ensure poorer sections of society are able to participate in economic growth. The effect of economic growth on poverty reduction – the growth elasticity of poverty – can depend on the existing level of inequality. For instance, with low inequality a country with a growth rate of 2% per head and 40% of its population living in poverty, can halve poverty in ten years, but a country with high inequality would take nearly 60 years to achieve the same reduction. In the words of the Secretary-General of the United Nations Ban Ki-moon: "While economic growth is necessary, it is not sufficient for progress on reducing poverty."

Environmental Impact

Critics such as the Club of Rome argue that a narrow view of economic growth, combined with globalization, is creating a scenario where we could see a systemic collapse of our planet's natural resources.

Concerns about negative environmental effects of growth have prompted some people to advocate lower levels of growth, or the abandoning of growth altogether. In academia, concepts like uneconomic growth, steady-state economy, eco-taxes, green investments, basic income guarantees, along with more radical approaches associated with degrowth, eco-socialism and eco-anarchism have been developed in order to achieve this and to overcome possible growth imperatives. In politics, green parties embrace the Global Greens Charter, recognising that "... the dogma of economic growth at any cost and the excessive and wasteful use of natural resources without considering Earth's carrying capacity, are causing extreme deterioration in the environment and a massive extinction of species."

The 2019 Global Assessment Report on Biodiversity and Ecosystem Services published by the United Nations' Intergovernmental Science-Policy Platform on Biodiversity and Ecosystem Services warned that given the substantial loss of biodiversity, society should not focus solely on economic growth. Anthropologist Eduardo S. Brondizio, one of the co-chairs of the report, said "We need to change our narratives. Both our individual narratives that associate wasteful consumption with quality of life and with status, and the narratives of the economic systems that still consider that environmental degradation and social inequality are inevitable outcomes of economic growth. Economic growth is a means and not an end. We need to look for the quality of life of the planet."

Those more optimistic about the environmental impacts of growth believe that, though localized environmental effects may occur, large-scale ecological effects are minor. The argument, as posited by commentator Julian Lincoln Simon, stated in 1981 that if these global-scale ecological effects exist, human ingenuity will find ways to adapt to them. Conversely Partha Dasgupta, in a 2021 report on the economics of biodiversity commissioned by the British Treasury, argued that biodiversity is collapsing faster than at any time in human history as a result of the demands of contemporary human civilization, which "far exceed nature's capacity to supply us with the goods and services we all rely on. We would require 1.6 Earths to maintain the world's current living standards." He says that major transformative changes will be needed "akin to, or even greater than, those of the Marshall Plan," including abandoning GDP as a measure of economic success and societal progress. Philip Cafaro, professor of philosophy at the School of Global Environmental Sustainability at Colorado State University, wrote in 2022 that a scientific consensus has emerged which demonstrates that humanity is on the precipice of unleashing a major extinction event, and that "the cause of global biodiversity loss is clear: other species are being displaced by a rapidly growing human economy."

In 2019, a warning on climate change signed by 11,000 scientists from over 150 nations said economic growth is the driving force behind the "excessive extraction of materials and overexploitation of ecosystems" and that this "must be quickly curtailed to maintain long-term sustainability of the biosphere." They add that "our goals need to shift from GDP growth and the pursuit of affluence toward sustaining ecosystems and improving human well-being by prioritizing basic needs and reducing inequality." A 2021 paper authored by top scientists in Frontiers in Conservation Science posited that given the environmental crises including biodiversity loss and climate change, and possible "ghastly future" facing humanity, there must be "fundamental changes to global capitalism," including the "abolition of perpetual economic growth."

Global Warming

Up to the present, there is a close correlation between economic growth and the rate of carbon dioxide emissions across nations, although there is also a considerable divergence in carbon intensity (carbon emissions per GDP). Up to the present, there is also a direct relation between global economic wealth and the rate of global emissions. The Stern Review notes that the prediction that, "Under business as usual, global emissions will be sufficient to propel greenhouse gas concentrations to over 550 ppm CO_2 by 2050 and over 650–700 ppm by the end of this century is robust to a wide range of changes in model assumptions." The scientific consensus is that planetary ecosystem functioning without incurring dangerous risks requires stabilization at 450–550 ppm.

As a consequence, growth-oriented environmental economists propose government intervention into switching sources of energy production, favouring wind, solar, hydroelectric, and nuclear. This would largely confine use of fossil fuels to either domestic cooking needs (such as for kerosene burners) or where carbon capture and storage technology can be cost-effective and reliable. The Stern Review, published by the United Kingdom Government in 2006, concluded that an investment of 1% of GDP (later changed to 2%) would be sufficient to avoid the worst effects of climate change, and that failure to do so could risk climate-related costs equal to 20% of GDP. Because carbon capture and storage are as yet widely unproven, and its long term effectiveness (such as in containing carbon dioxide 'leaks') unknown, and because of current costs of alternative fuels, these policy responses largely rest on faith of technological change.

British conservative politician and journalist Nigel Lawson has deemed carbon emission trading an 'inefficient system of rationing'. Instead, he favours carbon taxes to make full use of the efficiency of the market. However, in order to avoid the migration of energy-intensive industries, the whole world should impose such a tax, not just Britain, Lawson pointed out. There is no point in taking the lead if nobody follows suit.

Resource Constraint

Many earlier predictions of resource depletion, such as Thomas Malthus' 1798 predictions about approaching famines in Europe, The Population Bomb, and the Simon–Ehrlich wager (1980) have not materialized. Diminished production of most resources has not occurred so far, one reason being that advancements in technology and science have allowed some previously unavailable resources to be produced. In some cases, substitution of more abundant materials, such as plastics for cast metals, lowered growth of usage for some metals. In the case of the limited resource of land, famine was relieved firstly by the revolution in transportation caused by railroads and steam ships, and later by the Green Revolution and chemical fertilizers, especially the Haber process for ammonia synthesis.

Resource quality is composed of a variety of factors including ore grades, location, altitude above or below sea level, proximity to railroads, highways, water supply and climate. These factors affect the capital and operating cost of extracting resources. In the case of minerals, lower grades of mineral resources are being extracted, requiring higher inputs of capital and energy for both extraction and processing. Copper ore grades have declined significantly over the last century. Another example is natural gas from shale and other low permeability rock, whose extraction requires much higher inputs of energy, capital, and materials than conventional gas in previous decades. Offshore oil and gas have exponentially increased cost as water depth increases.

Some physical scientists like Sanyam Mittal regard continuous economic growth as unsustainable. Several factors may constrain economic growth – for example: finite, peaked, or depleted resources.

In 1972, The Limits to Growth study modeled limitations to infinite growth; originally ridiculed, some of the predicted trends have materialized, raising concerns of an impending collapse or decline due to resource constraints.

Malthusians such as William R. Catton, Jr. are skeptical of technological advances that improve resource availability. Such advances and increases in efficiency, they suggest, merely accelerate the drawing down of finite resources. Catton claims that increasing rates of resource extraction are "...stealing ravenously from the future".

Energy

Energy economic theories hold that rates of energy consumption and energy efficiency are linked causally to economic growth. The Garrett Relation holds that there has been a fixed relationship between current rates of global energy consumption and the historical accumulation of world GDP, independent of the year considered. It follows that economic growth, as represented by GDP growth, requires higher rates of energy consumption growth. Seemingly paradoxically, these are sustained through increases in energy efficiency. Increases in energy efficiency were a portion of the increase in Total factor productivity. Some of the most technologically important innovations in history involved increases in energy efficiency. These include the great improvements in efficiency of conversion of heat to work, the reuse of heat, the reduction in friction and the transmission of power, especially through electrification. There is a strong correlation between per capita electricity consumption and economic development.

Possibility of Infinite Economic Growth

Ecological economics criticizes the possibility of infinite economic growth on a finite planet. Current economic models ignore physical constraints and thus suggest the economy can grow continuously as a perpetual motion machine. However, according to the laws of thermodynamics, perpetual motion machines do not exist. Thus, no system can continue without inputs of new energy that exit as high entropy waste. Just as no animal can live on its own waste, no economy can recycle the waste it produces without the input of new energy to reproduce itself.

Matter and energy enter the economy in the form of low entropy natural capital, such as solar energy, oil wells, fisheries, and mines. These materials and energy are used by households and firms alike to create products and wealth. After the materials are used up, the energy and matter leaves the economy in the form of high entropy waste that is no longer valuable to the economy. The natural materials that power the motion of the economic system from the environment, and the waste must be absorbed by the larger ecosystem in which the economy exists.

It cannot be ignored that the economy intrinsically requires natural resources and the creation of waste that must be absorbed in some manner. The economy can only continue churning if it has matter and energy to power it and the ability to absorb the waste it creates. This matter and low entropy energy and the ability to absorb waste exists in a finite amount, and thus there is a finite amount of inputs to the flow and outputs of the flow that the environment can handle, implying there is a sustainable limit to motion, and therefore growth, of the economy. The Limits to Growth states that, due to those limits caused by thermodynamical laws, the availability of resources will decrease in a context of everlasting growth, leading to the increase of the prices of those resources, therefore to a decrease of the investment in industry. This decrease of industry will eventually lead to scarcity of goods and services that could eventually lead to a decrease of the living conditions and an increase of death rates all over the world.

5G Technology and Socio-Economic Implications

5G technology is expected to drive economic development and growth by enabling new business models, industries, and revenue streams. The deployment of 5G networks will stimulate investment in digital infrastructure, create jobs in telecommunications, construction, and technology sectors, and catalyze innovation and entrepreneurship. Industries such as manufacturing, healthcare, transportation, agriculture, and entertainment stand to benefit from 5G's transformative capabilities, unlocking productivity gains, cost efficiencies, and competitive advantages.

10.2.2 Industry Transformation and Innovation

5G technology has the potential to revolutionize industries and business processes by enabling advanced applications such as Internet of Things (IoT), artificial intelligence (AI), augmented reality (AR), and virtual reality (VR). In manufacturing, for example, 5G-powered IoT sensors and robotics can optimize production processes, improve quality control, and enable predictive maintenance, leading to higher productivity and lower costs. In healthcare, remote patient monitoring, telemedicine, and AI-driven diagnostics facilitated by 5G can enhance access to healthcare services, improve patient outcomes, and reduce healthcare costs.

10.2.3 Societal Empowerment and Digital Inclusion

5G technology has the potential to empower individuals, communities, and marginalized groups by providing access to high-speed internet connectivity and digital services. Bridging the digital divide and promoting digital inclusion are critical for ensuring equitable access to opportunities, resources, and information in the digital age. 5G networks can extend broadband coverage to underserved areas, enable distance learning, remote work, and telecommuting, and facilitate access to e-government services, financial inclusion, and online healthcare, empowering individuals and communities to participate in the digital economy and society.

10.2.4 Smart Cities and Sustainable Development

5G technology can accelerate the development of smart cities and sustainable urbanization by enabling connected infrastructure, intelligent transportation systems, and efficient resource management. Smart city initiatives leveraging 5G can improve public safety, reduce traffic congestion, optimize energy consumption, and enhance environmental sustainability. By leveraging real-time data and analytics, cities can make informed decisions, optimize service delivery, and improve quality of life for residents while minimizing environmental impact and resource consumption.

10.2.5 Privacy, Security, and Ethical Considerations

While 5G technology offers tremendous potential for socio-economic development, it also raises concerns about privacy, security, and ethical considerations. As 5G networks enable the proliferation of connected devices and data-intensive applications, concerns about data privacy, cybersecurity, surveillance, and algorithmic bias become more pronounced. It is essential for policymakers, industry stakeholders, and civil society to collaborate in developing robust regulatory frameworks, standards, and best practices to safeguard individuals' privacy rights, protect against cyber threats, and ensure ethical use of 5G technology.

10.2.6 Job Displacement and Skills Gap

The adoption of 5G technology may lead to job displacement and skills gaps as automation, AI, and digitalization reshape labor markets and workforce requirements. While 5G-driven innovation creates new job opportunities in technology, digital media, and telecommunications sectors, traditional roles may become obsolete, requiring workers to acquire new skills and competencies to remain relevant in the digital economy.

Addressing the skills gap and promoting lifelong learning are essential for ensuring that individuals can adapt to changing job market demands and thrive in the 5G-powered future.

10.3 DIGITAL INCLUSION AND ACCESSIBILITY

In an increasingly digital world, access to technology and the internet is essential for full participation in society, education, employment, and civic engagement. However, many individuals and communities face barriers to accessing and utilizing digital technologies, creating disparities in opportunity and inclusion. Digital inclusion and accessibility are essential for promoting equity, opportunity, and empowerment in the digital age.

By addressing barriers to access, promoting digital literacy, and designing inclusive digital technologies, we can bridge the digital divide and ensure that all individuals and communities have the opportunity to participate fully in the digital economy and society. Embracing digital inclusion as a fundamental principle of social justice and economic development can foster a more equitable, connected, and inclusive future for all.

10.3.1 Understanding Digital Inclusion

Digital inclusion involves the activities necessary to ensure equitable access to and use of information and communication technologies for participation in social and economic life including for education, social services, health, social and community participation. Digital inclusion includes access to affordable broadband Internet services, Internet-enabled devices, access to digital literacy training, quality technical support, and applications and online content designed to enable and encourage self-sufficiency, participation, and collaboration. Related concepts include digital divide, digital exclusion and digital inequality however digital inclusion focuses more on the strategies, policies and programs required to address the digital divide.

As many services have moved online and with the increasing use of telehealth to deliver primary care, particularly during the COVID-19 pandemic in 2020, digital inclusion, including digital literacy and internet access is increasingly regarded as a social determinant of health.

Background

With the increasing use of computers and the Internet in the 1990s and early 2000s concerns rose around digital equality, however this primarily focused on the physical access to technology. This gave rise to the concept of the digital divide which was originally developed to describe the growing disparity in Internet access between rural and urban areas of the United States of America. This gradually expanded to considerations of digital access between countries in what is termed the global digital divide, which mirrors many of the disparities seen within countries but on an international scale. However with the adoption of digital technologies across most sectors of society, and the increasing diversity of technologies and programs, access and use of ICT became more complex and essential for many aspects of daily life. This led to new terminology and a second wave of research on digital inequality which has been identified as the (1) usage gap, (2) second level digital divide, (3) emerging digital differentiation, and (4) digital inclusion.

Strategies for Digital Inclusion

A review of the literature in 2019 found that while physical access to digital technologies and the internet continues to be a barrier to digital inclusion, digital ability and attitude were also potential barriers. Key strategies identified for improving digital inclusion are social support, direct user experience and collaborative learning/design.

Education is a key aspect of digital inclusion as digital technologies have become a key means of engaging with all levels of the education system, requiring levels of digital competence for successful engagement with the curriculum. In addition lifelong learning is required as technologies, services and systems are changing constantly. Public libraries and community service providers play a key role in supporting digital inclusion through access to computers, internet connection and expertise and training. Designing for digital inclusion may also help with poor written literacy, which remains a barrier for 10% of the world's population. UNESCO has developed Guidelines for designing digital technologies in ways that could assist those who are illiterate.

Indigenous Digital Inclusion

Digital inclusion is a critical issue for many Indigenous communities across the globe, many of whom lack access to adequate resources. The Australian Government has set a National Closing the Gap target for Aboriginal and Torres Strait Islander people to have equal levels of digital inclusion by 2026.

Measuring Digital Inclusion

The Australian Digital Inclusion Index (ADII) is a research project which has been tracking digital inclusion throughout Australia since 2016. It uses survey data to measure digital inclusion across three dimensions of access, affordability and digital ability.

The Future of Digital Inclusion

On February 16, 2021, a global dialogue within the United Nations (UN) took a look at the future of digital inclusion. Through the adoption of the 2030 UN Agenda for Sustainable Development, Member States made a commitment. They pledged to "leave no one behind." By 2030, the UN's goal is to close the digital divide by providing access to the Internet and mobile technologies for all nations and peoples and for all segments of society. The UN sees the crisis of too many people in our global society still living unconnected and how the digital divide remains a challenge that must be addressed.

10.3.2 Web Accessibility

Web accessibility, or eAccessibility, is the inclusive practice of ensuring there are no barriers that prevent interaction with, or access to, websites on the World Wide Web by people with physical disabilities, situational disabilities, and socio-economic restrictions on bandwidth and speed. When sites are correctly designed, developed and edited, more users have equal access to information and functionality.

For example, when a site is coded with semantically meaningful HTML, with textual equivalents provided for images and with links named meaningfully, this helps blind users using text-to-speech software and/or text-to-Braille hardware. When text and images are large and/or enlargeable, it is easier for users with poor sight to read and understand the content.

When links are underlined (or otherwise differentiated) as well as colored, this ensures that color blind users will be able to notice them. When clickable links and areas are large, this helps users who cannot control a mouse with precision. When pages are not coded in a way that hinders navigation by means of the keyboard alone, or a single switch access device alone, this helps users who cannot use a mouse or even a standard keyboard.

When videos are closed captioned, chaptered, or a sign language version is available, deaf and hard-of-hearing users can understand the video. When flashing effects are avoided or made optional, users prone to seizures caused by these effects are not put at risk. And when content is written in plain language and illustrated with instructional diagrams and animations, users with dyslexia and learning difficulties are better able to understand the content. When sites are correctly built and maintained, all of these users can be accommodated without decreasing the usability of the site for non-disabled users.

The needs that web accessibility aims to address include:

- Visual: Visual impairments including blindness, various common types of low vision and poor eyesight, various types of color blindness;
- Motor/mobility: E.g., difficulty or inability to use the hands, including tremors, muscle slowness, loss of fine muscle control, etc., due to conditions such as Parkinson's disease, muscular dystrophy, cerebral palsy, stroke;
- Auditory: Deafness or hearing impairments, including individuals who are hard of hearing;
- Seizures: Photo epileptic seizures caused by visual strobe or flashing effects.
- Cognitive and intellectual: Developmental disabilities, learning difficulties (dyslexia, dyscalculia, etc.), and cognitive disabilities (PTSD, Alzheimer's) of various origins, affecting memory, attention, developmental "maturity", problem-solving and logic skills, etc.

Situational disability refers to someone who may be experiencing a boundary based on the current experience. For example, a person may be situationally one-handed if they are carrying a baby.

Web accessibility should be mindful of users experiencing a wide variety of barriers. According to a 2018 WebAIM global survey of web accessibility practitioners, close to 93% of survey respondents received no formal schooling on web accessibility.

Assistive Technologies Used for Web Browsing

Individuals living with a disability use assistive technologies such as the following to enable and assist web browsing:

- Screen reader software, which can read out, using synthesized speech, either selected elements of what is being displayed on the monitor (helpful for users with reading or learning difficulties), or which can read out everything that is happening on the computer (used by blind and vision impaired users).

- Braille terminals, consisting of a refreshable braille display which renders text as braille characters (usually by means of raising pegs through holes in a flat surface) and either a mainstream keyboard or a braille keyboard.
- Screen magnification software, which enlarges what is displayed on the computer monitor, making it easier to read for vision impaired users.
- Speech recognition software that can accept spoken commands to the computer, or turn dictation into grammatically correct text – useful for those who have difficulty using a mouse or a keyboard.
- Keyboard overlays, which can make typing easier or more accurate for those who have motor control difficulties.
- Access to subtitled or sign language videos for deaf people.

Guidelines on Accessible Web Design

Web Content Accessibility Guidelines

In 1999 the Web Accessibility Initiative, a project by the World Wide Web Consortium (W3C), published the Web Content Accessibility Guidelines WCAG 1.0. On 11 December 2008, the WAI released the WCAG 2.0 as a Recommendation. WCAG 2.0 aims to be up to date and more technology neutral. Though web designers can choose either standard to follow, the WCAG 2.0 have been widely accepted as the definitive guidelines on how to create accessible websites. Governments are steadily adopting the WCAG 2.0 as the accessibility standard for their own websites. In 2012, the Web Content Accessibility Guidelines were also published as an ISO/IEC standard: "ISO/IEC 40500:2012: Information technology – W3C Web Content Accessibility Guidelines (WCAG) 2.0". In 2018, the WAI released the WCAG 2.1 Recommendation that extends WCAG 2.0.

Criticism of WAI Guidelines

There has been some criticism of the W3C process, claiming that it does not sufficiently put the user at the heart of the process. There was a formal objection to WCAG's original claim that WCAG 2.0 will address requirements for people with learning disabilities and cognitive limitations headed by Lisa Seeman and signed by 40 organizations and people. In articles such as "WCAG 2.0: The new W3C guidelines evaluated", "To Hell with WCAG 2.0" and "Testability Costs Too Much", the WAI has been criticised for allowing WCAG 1.0 to get increasingly out of step with today's technologies and techniques for creating and consuming web content, for the slow pace of development of WCAG 2.0, for making the new guidelines difficult to navigate and understand, and other argued failings.

Essential Components of Web Accessibility

The accessibility of websites relies on the cooperation of several components:

1. content – the information in a web page or web application, including natural information (such as text, images, and sounds) and code or markup that defines structure, presentation, etc.
2. web browsers, media players, and other "user agents"
3. assistive technology, in some cases – screen readers, alternative keyboards, switches, scanning software, etc.
4. users' knowledge, experiences, and in some cases, adaptive strategies using the web
5. developers – designers, coders, authors, etc., including developers with disabilities and users who contribute content
6. authoring tools – software that creates websites
7. evaluation tools – web accessibility evaluation tools, HTML validators, CSS validators, etc.

Web developers usually use authoring tools and evaluation tools to create web content.

People ("users") use web browsers, media players, assistive technologies or other "user agents" to get and interact with the content.

Guidelines for Different Components

Authoring Tool Accessibility Guidelines (ATAG)

- ATAG contains 28 checkpoints that provide guidance on:
  - producing accessible output that meets standards and guidelines
  - promoting the content author for accessibility-related information
  - providing ways of checking and correcting inaccessible content
  - integrating accessibility in the overall look and feel
  - making the authoring tool itself accessible to people with disabilities

Web Content Accessibility Guidelines (WCAG)

- WCAG 1.0: 14 guidelines that are general principles of accessible design
- WCAG 2.0: 4 principles that form the foundation for web accessibility; 12 guidelines (untestable) that are goals for which authors should aim; and 65 testable success criteria. The W3C's Techniques for WCAG 2.0 is a list of techniques that support authors to meet the guidelines and success criteria. The techniques are periodically updated whereas the principles, guidelines and success criteria are stable and do not change.

User Agent Accessibility Guidelines (UAAG)

- UAAG contains a comprehensive set of checkpoints that cover:
  - access to all content
  - user control over how content is rendered
  - user control over the user interface
  - standard programming interfaces

Web Accessibility Legislation

Because of the growth in internet usage and its growing importance in everyday life, countries around the world are addressing digital access issues through legislation. One approach is to protect access to websites for people with disabilities by using existing human or civil rights legislation. Some countries, like the U.S., protect access for people with disabilities through the technology procurement process. It is common for nations to support and adopt the Web Content Accessibility Guidelines (WCAG) 2.0 by referring to the guidelines in their legislation. Compliance with web accessibility guidelines is a legal requirement primarily in North America, Europe, parts of South America and parts of Asia.

Australia

In 2000, an Australian blind man won a $20,000 court case against the Sydney Organising Committee of the Olympic Games (SOCOG). This was the first successful case under Disability Discrimination Act 1992 because SOCOG had failed to make their official website, Sydney Olympic Games, adequately accessible to blind users. The Human Rights and Equal Opportunity Commission (HREOC) also published World Wide Web Access: Disability Discrimination Act Advisory Notes. All Governments in Australia also have policies and guidelines that require accessible public websites.

Brazil

In Brazil, the federal government published a paper with guidelines for accessibility on 18 January 2005, for public reviewing. On 14 December of the same year, the second version was published, including suggestions made to the first version of the paper. On 7 May 2007, the accessibility guidelines of the paper became compulsory to all federal websites. The current version of the paper, which follows the WCAG 2.0 guidelines, is named e-MAG, Modelo de Acessibilidade de Governo Eletrônico (Electronic Government Accessibility Model), and is maintained by Brazilian Ministry of Planning, Budget, and Management.

Canada

In 2011, the Government of Canada began phasing in the implementation of a new set of web standards that are aimed at ensuring government websites are accessible, usable, interoperable and optimized for mobile devices. These standards replace Common Look and Feel 2.0 (CLF 2.0) Standards for the Internet.

The first of these four standards, Standard on Web Accessibility came into full effect on 31 July 2013. The Standard on Web Accessibility follows the Web Content Accessibility Guidelines (WCAG) 2.0 AA, and contains a list of exclusions that is updated annually. It is accompanied by an explicit Assessment Methodology that helps government departments comply. The government also developed the Web Experience Toolkit (WET), a set of reusable web components for building innovative websites. The WET helps government departments build innovative websites that are accessible, usable and interoperable and therefore comply with the government's standards. The WET toolkit is open source and available for anyone to use.

The three related web standards are: the Standard on Optimizing Websites and Applications for Mobile Devices, the Standard on Web Usability and the Standard on Web Interoperability.

In 2019 the Government of Canada passed the Accessible Canada Act. This builds on the on provincial legislation like the Accessibility for Ontarians with Disabilities Act, The Accessibility for Manitobans Act and the Nova Scotia Accessibility Act.

European Union

In February 2014 a draft law was endorsed by the European Parliament stating that all websites managed by public sector bodies have to be made accessible to everyone.

A European Commission Communication on eAccessibility was published on 13 September 2005. The commission's aim to "harmonise and facilitate the public procurement of accessible ICT products and services" was embedded in a mandate issued to CEN, CENELEC and ETSI in December 2005, reference M 376. A mandate is a request for the drafting and adoption of a European standard or European standardisation deliverables issued to one or more of the European standardisation organisations. Mandates are usually accepted by the standardisation organisation because they are based on preliminary consultation, although technically the organisation is independent and has a right to decline the mandate. The mandate also called for the development of an electronic toolkit for public procurers enabling them to have access to the resulting harmonised requirements. The commission also noted that the harmonised outcome, while intended for public procurement purposes, might also be useful for procurement in the private sector.

On 26 October 2016, the European Parliament approved the Web Accessibility Directive, which requires that the websites and mobile apps of public sector bodies be accessible. The relevant accessibility requirements are described in the European standard EN 301 549 V3.2.1 (published by ETSI). EU member states were expected to bring into force by 23 September 2018 laws and regulations that enforce the relevant accessibility requirements.

- websites of public sector bodies should comply by 23 September 2018;
- mobile apps by 23 June 2021.

Some categories of websites and apps are excepted from the directive, for example "websites and mobile applications of public service broadcasters and their subsidiaries".

The European Commission's "Rolling Plan for ICT Standardisation 2017" notes that ETSI standard EN 301 549 V1.1.2 will need to be updated to add accessibility requirements for mobile applications and evaluation methodologies to test compliance with the standard.

In 2019 the European Union introduced the European Accessibility Act, which is now seen as one of the leading pieces of legislation for digital accessibility.

Ireland

In Ireland, the Disability Act 2005 requires that where a public body communicates in electronic form with one or more persons, the contents of the communication must be, as far as practicable, "accessible to persons with a visual impairment to whom adaptive technology is available" (Section 28(2)). The National Disability Authority has produced a Code of Practice giving guidance to public bodies on how to meet the obligations of the Act. This is an approved code of practice and its provisions have the force of legally binding statutory obligations. It states that a public body can achieve compliance with Section 28(2) by "reviewing existing practices for electronic communications in terms of accessibility against relevant guidelines and standards", giving the example of "Double A conformance with the Web Accessibility Initiative's (WAI) Web Content Accessibility Guidelines (WCAG)".

Israel

The Israeli Ministry of Justice recently published regulations requiring Internet websites to comply with Israeli standard 5568, which is based on the W3C Web Content Accessibility Guidelines 2.0. The main differences between the Israeli standard and the W3C standard concern the requirements to provide captions and texts for audio and video media. The Israeli standards are somewhat more lenient, reflecting the current technical difficulties in providing such captions and texts in Hebrew.

Italy

In Italy, web accessibility is ruled by the so-called "Legge Stanca" (Stanca Act), formally Act n.4 of 9 January 2004, officially published on the Gazzetta Ufficiale on 17 January 2004. The original Stanca Act was based on the WCAG 1.0. On 20 March 2013 the standards required by the Stanca Act were updated to the WCAG 2.0.

Japan

Web Content Accessibility Guidelines in Japan were established in 2004 as JIS (Japanese Industrial Standards) X 8341-3. JIS X 8341-3 was revised in 2010 as JIS X 8341-3:2010 to encompass WCAG 2.0, and it was revised in 2016 as JIS X 8341-3:2016 to be identical standards with the international standard ISO/IEC 40500:2012. The Japanese organization WAIC (Web Accessibility Infrastructure Committee) has published the history and structure of JIS X 8341-3:2016.

Malta

In Malta Web Content Accessibility assessments were carried out by the Foundation for Information Technology Accessibility (FITA) since 2003. Until 2018, this was done in conformance with the requirements of the Equal Opportunities Act (2000) CAP 43 and applied WACG guidelines. With the advent of the EU Web Accessibility Directive the Malta Communications Authority was charged with ensuring the accessibility of online resources owned by Maltese public entities. FITA continues to provide ICT accessibility assessments to public and commercial entities, applying standard EN301549 and WCAG 2.1 as applicable. Therefore, both the Equal Opportunities Act anti-discrimination legislation and the transposed EU Web Accessibility Directive are applicable to the Maltese scenario.

Norway

In Norway, web accessibility is a legal obligation under the Act 20 June 2008 No 42 relating to a prohibition against discrimination on the basis of disability, also known as the Anti-discrimination Accessibility Act. The Act went into force in 2009, and the Ministry of Government Administration, Reform and Church Affairs [Fornyings-, administrasjons- og kirkedepartementet] published the Regulations for universal design of information and communication technology (ICT) solutions [Forskrift om universell utforming av informasjons- og kommunikasjonsteknologiske (IKT)-løsninger] in 2013. The regulations require compliance with Web Content Accessibility Guidelines 2.0 (WCAG 2.0) / NS / ISO / IEC 40500: 2012, level A and AA with some exceptions. The Norwegian Agency for Public Management and eGovernment (Difi) is responsible for overseeing that ICT solutions aimed at the general public are in compliance with the legislative and regulatory requirements.

Philippines

As part of the Web Accessibility Initiatives in the Philippines, the government through the National Council for the Welfare of Disabled Persons (NCWDP) board approved the recommendation of forming an ad hoc or core group of webmasters that will help in the implementation of the Biwako Millennium Framework set by the UNESCAP.

The Philippines was also the place where the Interregional Seminar and Regional Demonstration Workshop on Accessible Information and Communications

Technologies (ICT) to Persons with Disabilities was held where eleven countries from Asia - Pacific were represented. The Manila Accessible Information and Communications Technologies Design Recommendations was drafted and adopted in 2003.

Spain

In Spain, UNE 139803:2012 is the norm entrusted to regulate web accessibility. This standard is based on Web Content Accessibility Guidelines 2.0.

Sweden

In Sweden, Verva, the Swedish Administrative Development Agency is responsible for a set of guidelines for Swedish public sector web sites. Through the guidelines, web accessibility is presented as an integral part of the overall development process and not as a separate issue. The Swedish guidelines contain criteria which cover the entire life cycle of a website; from its conception to the publication of live web content. These criteria address several areas which should be considered, including:

- accessibility
- usability
- web standards
- privacy issues
- information architecture
- developing content for the web
- Content Management Systems (CMS) / authoring tools selection.
- development of web content for mobile devices.

An English translation was released in April 2008: Swedish National Guidelines for Public Sector Websites. The translation is based on the latest version of Guidelines which was released in 2006.

United Kingdom

In the UK, the Equality Act 2010 does not refer explicitly to website accessibility, but makes it illegal to discriminate against people with disabilities. The Act applies to anyone providing a service; public, private and voluntary sectors. The Code of Practice: Rights of Access - Goods, Facilities, Services and Premises document published by the government's Equality and Human Rights Commission to accompany the Act does refer explicitly to websites as one of the "services to the public" which should be considered covered by the Act.

In December 2010 the UK released the standard BS 8878:2010 Web accessibility. Code of practice. This standard effectively supersedes PAS 78 (pub. 2006). PAS 78, produced by the Disability Rights Commission and usable by disabled people. The standard has been designed to introduce non-technical professionals to improved accessibility, usability and user experience for disabled and older people. It will be especially beneficial to anyone new to this subject as it gives guidance on process, rather than on technical and design issues. BS 8878 is consistent with the Equality Act 2010 and is referenced in the UK government's e-Accessibility Action Plan as the basis of updated advice on developing accessible online services. It includes recommendations for:

- Involving disabled people in the development process and using automated tools to assist with accessibility testing
- The management of the guidance and process for upholding existing accessibility guidelines and specifications.

BS 8878 is intended for anyone responsible for the policies covering web product creation within their organization, and governance against those policies. It additionally assists people responsible for promoting and supporting equality and inclusion initiatives within organizations and people involved in the procurement, creation or training of web products and content. A summary of BS 8878 is available to help organisations better understand how the standard can help them embed accessibility and inclusive design in their business-as-usual processes.

On 28 May 2019, BS 8878 was superseded by ISO 30071-1, the international Standard that built on BS 8878 and expanded it for international use. A summary of how ISO 30071-1 relates to BS 8878 is available to help organisations understand the new Standard.

On April 9, National Rail replaced its blue and white aesthetic with a black and white theme, which was criticized for not conforming to the Web Content Accessibility Guidelines. The company restored the blue and white theme and said it is investing in modernising its website in accords to the latest accessibility guidelines.

In 2019 new accessibility regulations came into force setting a legal duty for public sector bodies to publish accessibility statements and make their websites accessible by 23 September 2020 Accessibility statements include information about how the website was tested and the organisation's plan to fix any accessibility problems. Statements should be published and linked to on every page on the website.

United States

In the United States, Section 508 Amendment to the Rehabilitation Act of 1973 requires all Federal agencies' electronic and information technology to be accessible to those with disabilities. Both members of the public and federal employees have the right to access this technology, such as computer hardware and software, websites, phone systems, and copiers. Also, Section 504 of the Rehabilitation Act prohibits discrimination on the basis of disability for entities receiving federal funds and has been cited in multiple lawsuits against organizations such as hospitals that receive federal funds through medicare/medicaid.

In addition, Title III of the Americans with Disabilities Act (ADA) prohibits discrimination on the basis of disability. There is some debate on the matter; multiple courts and the U.S. Department of Justice have taken the position that the ADA requires website and app operators and owners to take affirmative steps to make their websites and apps accessible to disabled persons and compatible with common assistive technologies such as the JAWS screen reader, while other courts have taken the position that the ADA does not apply online. The U.S. Department of Justice has endorsed the WCAG2.0AA standard as an appropriate standard for accessibility in multiple settlement agreements.

Numerous lawsuits challenging websites and mobile apps on the basis of the ADA have been filed since 2017. These cases appears spurred by a 2017 case, Gil v. Winn Dixie Stores, in which a federal court in Florida ruled that Winn Dixie's website must be accessible. Around 800 cases related to web accessibility were filed in 2017, and over 2,200 were filed in 2018. Additionally, though the Justice Department had stated in 2010 that they would publish guidelines for web accessibility, they reversed this plan in 2017, also spurring legal action against inaccessible sites.

A notable lawsuit related to the ADA was filed against Domino's Pizza by a blind user who could not use Domino's mobile app. At the federal district level, the court ruled in favor of Domino's as the Justice Department had not established the guidelines for accessibility, but this was appealed to the Ninth Circuit. The Ninth Circuit overruled the district court, ruling that because Domino's is a brick-and-mortar store, which must meet the ADA, and the mobile app an extension of their services, their app must also be compliant with the ADA. Domino's petitioned to the Supreme Court, backed by many other restaurants and retail chains, arguing that this decision impacts their Due Process since disabled customers have other, more accessible means to order. In October 2019, the Supreme Court declined to hear the case, which effectively upheld the decision of the 9th Circuit Court and requires the case to be heard as it stands.

The number and cost of federal accessibility lawsuits has risen dramatically in the last few years.

Website Accessibility Audits

A growing number of organizations, companies and consultants offer website accessibility audits. These audits, a type of system testing, identify accessibility problems that exist within a website, and provide advice and guidance on the steps that need to be taken to correct these problems.

A range of methods are used to audit websites for accessibility:

- Automated tools are available which can identify some of the problems that are present. Depending on the tool the result may vary widely making it difficult to compare test results.

- Expert technical reviewers, knowledgeable in web design technologies and accessibility, can review a representative selection of pages and provide detailed feedback and advice based on their findings.
- User testing, usually overseen by technical experts, involves setting tasks for ordinary users to carry out on the website, and reviewing the problems these users encounter as they try to carry out the tasks.

Each of these methods has its strengths and weaknesses:

- Automated tools can process many pages in a relatively short length of time, but can only identify a limited portion of the accessibility problems that might be present in the website.
- Technical expert review will identify many of the problems that exist, but the process is time-consuming, and many websites are too large to make it possible for a person to review every page.
- User testing combines elements of usability and accessibility testing, and is valuable for identifying problems that might otherwise be overlooked, but needs to be used knowledgeably to avoid the risk of basing design decisions on one user's preferences.

Ideally, a combination of methods should be used to assess the accessibility of a website.

Remediating Inaccessible Websites

Once an accessibility audit has been conducted, and accessibility errors have been identified, the errors will need to be remediated in order to ensure the site is compliant with accessibility errors. The traditional way of correcting an inaccessible site is to go back into the source code, reprogram the error, and then test to make sure the bug was fixed.

If the website is not scheduled to be revised in the near future, that error (and others) would remain on the site for a lengthy period of time, possibly violating accessibility guidelines. Because this is a complicated process, many website owners choose to build accessibility into a new site design or re-launch, as it can be more efficient to develop the site to comply with accessibility guidelines, rather than to remediate errors later.

With the progress in AI technology, web accessibility has become more accessible. With 3rd party addons that leverage AI and machine learning, it is possible to offer changes to the website design without altering the source code. This way, a website can be accessible to different types of users without the need to adjust the website for every accessibility equipment.

Accessible Web Applications and WAI-ARIA

For a web page to be accessible all important semantics about the page's functionality must be available so that assistive technology can understand and process the content and adapt it for the user. However, as content becomes more and more complex, the standard HTML tags and attributes become inadequate in providing semantics reliably.

Modern Web applications often apply scripts to elements to control their functionality and to enable them to act as a control or other dynamic component. These custom components or widgets do not provide a way to convey semantic information to the user agent.

WAI-ARIA (Accessible Rich Internet Applications) is a specification published by the World Wide Web Consortium that specifies how to increase the accessibility of dynamic content and user interface components developed with Ajax, HTML, JavaScript and related technologies. ARIA enables accessibility by enabling the author to provide all the semantics to fully describe its supported behaviour. It also allows each element to expose its current states and properties and its relationships between other elements. Accessibility problems with the focus and tab index are also corrected.

10.3.3 Addressing Barriers to Access

Several barriers contribute to digital exclusion, including:

- Lack of Infrastructure: Many rural and underserved areas lack access to high-speed internet infrastructure, limiting connectivity and digital opportunities for residents.
- Affordability: The cost of internet service and devices can be prohibitive for low-income individuals and families, preventing them from accessing essential online services and resources.
- Digital Literacy: Many individuals lack the skills and knowledge to navigate digital technologies effectively, hindering their ability to access information, communicate, and participate in online activities.
- Physical Disabilities: Individuals with disabilities may face barriers to accessing and using digital technologies due to inaccessible design, lack of assistive technologies, and limited awareness of accessibility features and accommodations.

Addressing these barriers requires a multi-faceted approach involving collaboration among governments, industry stakeholders, non-profit organizations, and communities to expand access, promote digital literacy, and ensure inclusivity in digital design and development.

10.3.4 Strategies for Digital Inclusion

Several strategies can promote digital inclusion and accessibility:

- Infrastructure Investment: Governments and telecommunications providers can invest in expanding broadband infrastructure to underserved areas, including rural communities, tribal lands, and urban neighborhoods, to improve connectivity and reduce the digital divide.
- Affordable Access Programs: Public-private partnerships can develop and implement affordable access programs, such as discounted internet service plans, subsidized devices, and digital literacy training, to make internet access more accessible to low-income individuals and families.
- Digital Literacy and Skills Training: Educational institutions, libraries, community centers, and non-profit organizations can offer digital literacy and skills training programs to empower individuals with the knowledge and confidence to use digital technologies effectively for education, employment, and personal development.
- Accessible Design and Technology: Businesses and developers can prioritize accessibility in the design and development of digital products and services, ensuring that they are usable by individuals with diverse abilities and disabilities. This includes incorporating accessibility features, providing alternative formats, and conducting usability testing with diverse user groups.
- Community Engagement and Collaboration: Engaging with communities and stakeholders to understand their unique needs, preferences, and challenges is essential for developing inclusive and responsive digital inclusion initiatives. Collaborating with local organizations, advocacy groups, and community leaders can help tailor solutions to meet the specific needs of diverse populations.

10.3.5 Benefits of Digital Inclusion

Digital inclusion brings numerous benefits to individuals, communities, and society as a whole:

- Empowerment: Digital inclusion empowers individuals to access information, education, employment opportunities, and essential services, enabling them to participate more fully in society and the economy.
- Economic Opportunity: Access to digital technologies and online resources can open up new economic opportunities, including remote work, freelance opportunities, entrepreneurship, and e-commerce, particularly for underserved and marginalized populations.

- Social Connection: Digital technologies facilitate social connection and community engagement, enabling individuals to communicate, collaborate, and connect with others, regardless of geographical barriers or physical limitations.
- Educational Access: Digital inclusion enhances access to educational resources, online learning platforms, and distance education programs, enabling students of all ages to pursue learning opportunities and acquire new skills.
- Civic Engagement: Digital inclusion promotes civic engagement and democratic participation by providing individuals with access to information, government services, and online platforms for advocacy, activism, and civic participation.

10.4 ETHICAL CONSIDERATIONS ON 5G DEVELOPMENT

As fifth-generation (5G) wireless technology continues to roll out, it brings with it promises of unprecedented connectivity, innovation, and economic growth. However, amidst the excitement surrounding its potential, there are ethical considerations that must be carefully navigated to ensure that 5G development and deployment prioritize societal well-being, privacy, security, and equity.

Navigating the ethical landscape of 5G development requires careful consideration of privacy, security, health, environmental impact, socio-economic equity, AI ethics, and responsible data governance.

By addressing these ethical considerations, stakeholders can promote trust, transparency, and accountability in 5G deployment and ensure that technology serves the common good and advances human well-being. Ethical decision-making, stakeholder engagement, and collaboration are essential for fostering a responsible and sustainable approach to 5G development that upholds ethical principles and values while harnessing the transformative potential of technology for positive social and economic impact.

10.4.1 Privacy and Data Protection

One of the primary ethical considerations in 5G development is the protection of privacy and personal data. 5G networks enable the collection of vast amounts of data from connected devices, sensors, and applications, raising concerns about data privacy, surveillance, and potential misuse.

It is essential to establish robust data protection regulations, encryption standards, and privacy-preserving technologies to safeguard individuals' privacy rights and ensure responsible data stewardship by network operators, service providers, and device manufacturers.

10.4.2 Security and Cybersecurity

Ensuring the security of 5G networks and infrastructure is paramount to prevent cyberattacks, data breaches, and disruptions to critical services. With the proliferation of connected devices and the expansion of the attack surface, 5G networks become more vulnerable to cyber threats such as malware, ransomware, and distributed denial-of-service (DDoS) attacks.

Ethical considerations in 5G development include implementing robust security protocols, authentication mechanisms, and intrusion detection systems to protect against cyber threats and ensure the integrity, confidentiality, and availability of network resources and services.

10.4.3 Health and Safety

Another ethical consideration in 5G development is the potential health and safety impacts of radiofrequency (RF) radiation emitted by wireless devices and infrastructure. While scientific research on the health effects of RF radiation is ongoing, concerns have been raised about potential risks, particularly with the deployment of small cells and mmWave frequencies in urban areas. It is essential to conduct rigorous, independent research to assess the health impacts of 5G technology, mitigate potential risks, and ensure transparency, informed consent, and public engagement in decision-making processes.

10.4.4 Environmental Impact

The environmental impact of 5G development is another ethical consideration, particularly in terms of energy consumption, electronic waste, and resource depletion.

As 5G networks require denser infrastructure, including small cells, antennas, and data centers, there are concerns about increased energy consumption and carbon emissions associated with network operation and maintenance. Ethical considerations include promoting energy-efficient technologies, renewable energy sources, and sustainable practices to minimize the environmental footprint of 5G deployment and ensure responsible stewardship of natural resources.

10.4.5 Socio-Economic Equity

Ensuring socio-economic equity and digital inclusion is a critical ethical consideration in 5G development. While 5G technology has the potential to drive economic growth and innovation, there is a risk of widening the digital divide and exacerbating existing inequalities if access to high-speed internet connectivity and digital services is not equitable.

Ethical considerations include promoting universal access to affordable, reliable broadband infrastructure, digital literacy programs, and inclusive design practices to ensure that 5G benefits are shared equitably and contribute to social cohesion and economic opportunity for all.

10.4.6 Ethical AI and Automation

The integration of artificial intelligence (AI) and automation in 5G networks raises ethical considerations related to transparency, accountability, and fairness. As AI algorithms make increasingly autonomous decisions in network management, traffic optimization, and service provisioning, there is a need to ensure ethical AI principles, such as transparency, accountability, fairness, and human oversight, are incorporated into AI systems to mitigate biases, errors, and unintended consequences.

Ethical considerations include developing ethical AI frameworks, guidelines, and regulations to govern the responsible use of AI in 5G networks and promote ethical decision-making and human-centric design.

10.4.7 Ethical Use of Data and Algorithms

The ethical use of data and algorithms in 5G development is essential to prevent discrimination, bias, and abuse of power. As 5G networks enable the collection, analysis, and utilization of vast amounts of data from diverse sources, there is a risk of algorithmic bias, privacy violations, and misuse of personal data.

Ethical considerations include promoting transparency, accountability, and fairness in data collection, processing, and decision-making, as well as establishing ethical guidelines, standards, and oversight mechanisms to ensure responsible data governance and algorithmic accountability.

CHAPTER 11

FUTURE PERSPECTIVES AND TRENDS

11.1 EVOLVING TECHNOLOGIES AND INNOVATIONS

In the dynamic landscape of technological advancements, innovation is the engine that propels us into the future. As we journey through the 21st century, the pace of technological evolution continues to accelerate, ushering in transformative changes across every aspect of human life.

From artificial intelligence and blockchain to quantum computing and biotechnology, evolving technologies are reshaping industries, societies, and economies in profound ways. The rapid evolution of technology and innovation is reshaping the world as we know it, driving progress, prosperity, and human advancement. By embracing emerging technologies and fostering a culture of innovation, we can harness the transformative power of technology to address global challenges, improve quality of life, and create a more sustainable and inclusive future for all. As we navigate the complexities and opportunities of the digital age, it is essential to prioritize ethical considerations, collaboration, and responsible stewardship to ensure that evolving technologies serve the common good and benefit humanity as a whole.

11.1.1 Artificial Intelligence (AI)

Artificial intelligence (AI) stands at the forefront of technological innovation, revolutionizing industries with its ability to analyze data, recognize patterns, and make autonomous decisions. Machine learning, deep learning, and natural language processing are just a few of the AI techniques that are powering intelligent systems and applications in areas such as healthcare, finance, transportation, and manufacturing. From virtual assistants and autonomous vehicles to personalized medicine and predictive analytics, AI is transforming how we work, live, and interact with the world around us.

11.1.2 Blockchain Technology

Blockchain technology has emerged as a disruptive force, revolutionizing the way we transact, communicate, and secure digital assets. Initially known as the underlying technology behind cryptocurrencies like Bitcoin, blockchain has evolved to enable decentralized applications, smart contracts, and digital identity solutions. With its transparent, immutable, and tamper-proof ledger, blockchain technology is being leveraged in diverse sectors, including finance, supply chain management, healthcare, and voting systems, to increase transparency, traceability, and security while reducing intermediaries and transaction costs.

11.1.3 Quantum Computing

Quantum computing represents a paradigm shift in computing power, promising to solve complex problems that are beyond the reach of classical computers. By harnessing the principles of quantum mechanics, quantum computers leverage quantum bits, or qubits, to perform calculations exponentially faster than traditional binary bits. While still in the early stages of development, quantum computing has the potential to revolutionize fields such as cryptography, material science, drug discovery, and optimization, unlocking new frontiers in scientific research, innovation, and problem-solving.

11.1.4 Biotechnology and Genetic Engineering

Advancements in biotechnology and genetic engineering are driving breakthroughs in healthcare, agriculture, and environmental sustainability. From gene editing techniques like CRISPR-Cas9 to synthetic biology and regenerative medicine, biotechnology is enabling precise manipulation of biological systems to cure diseases, improve crop yields, and mitigate environmental challenges. Personalized medicine, gene therapy, and biofuels are just a few examples of the transformative applications of biotechnology that are shaping the future of human health, food security, and environmental conservation.

11.1.5 Internet of Things (IoT)

The Internet of Things (IoT) is connecting billions of devices and sensors worldwide, creating a network of interconnected systems that can collect, analyze, and exchange data in real-time. From smart homes and wearable devices to industrial automation and smart cities, IoT technology is enabling a new era of connectivity, efficiency, and convenience. By embedding intelligence into everyday objects and environments, IoT is driving innovation in areas such as energy management, asset tracking, predictive maintenance, and urban planning, transforming industries and enhancing quality of life.

11.1.6 Renewable Energy and Sustainability

The transition to renewable energy sources such as solar, wind, and hydroelectric power is reshaping the global energy landscape and driving sustainability initiatives worldwide. Advances in renewable energy technologies, energy storage systems, and smart grid infrastructure are enabling the transition to a low-carbon economy and reducing dependence on fossil fuels. From decentralized energy generation and grid resilience to carbon capture and energy efficiency, renewable energy innovations are paving the way towards a more sustainable and resilient future for generations to come.

11.1.7 Augmented Reality (AR) and Virtual Reality (VR)

Augmented reality (AR) and virtual reality (VR) are transforming how we experience and interact with digital content, blurring the lines between the physical and virtual worlds. AR overlays digital information onto the real world, enhancing our perception and interaction with the environment, while VR immerses users in entirely virtual environments, providing immersive experiences and simulations.

From gaming and entertainment to education, healthcare, and training, AR and VR technologies are revolutionizing storytelling, learning, and collaboration, unlocking new possibilities for creativity, exploration, and human expression.

11.2 USER EXPERIENCE AND QUALITY OF SERVICE

In the ever-evolving landscape of telecommunications, fifth-generation (5G) wireless technology stands out as a game-changer, promising ultra-fast speeds, low latency, and massive connectivity. As 5G networks continue to roll out globally, ensuring an exceptional user experience and high-quality service delivery is paramount. 5G technology holds immense promise for enhancing connectivity, enabling innovative applications, and transforming the way we live, work, and communicate. By prioritizing user experience and quality of service, operators and service providers can unlock the full potential of 5G technology and deliver exceptional connectivity experiences that empower users, drive productivity, and enrich lives. As 5G networks continue to evolve and mature, ensuring a seamless and reliable user experience will remain paramount, driving innovation and value creation in the digital economy.

11.2.1 Enhanced Mobile Broadband

5G technology brings significant improvements to mobile broadband connectivity, offering higher data transfer rates and greater network capacity compared to previous generations. This translates to smoother and more responsive mobile internet experiences, allowing users to download large files, stream high-definition video, and access bandwidth-intensive applications with ease. Whether browsing the web, downloading content, or video conferencing on the go, 5G users can enjoy seamless connectivity and faster data speeds, enhancing productivity and convenience.

11.2.2 Massive Connectivity and IoT Capabilities

Another key feature of 5G technology is its ability to support massive connectivity and the Internet of Things (IoT) ecosystem. With its ability to connect a vast number of devices simultaneously, 5G networks enable the proliferation of IoT devices and sensors, powering smart cities, connected vehicles, industrial automation, and smart homes. This enables users to experience a wide range of innovative IoT applications and services, from smart meters and wearable devices to autonomous vehicles and smart appliances, enhancing efficiency, safety, and convenience in everyday life.

11.2.3 Network Reliability and Resilience

5G networks are designed to deliver high levels of reliability and resilience, ensuring consistent connectivity and quality of service even in challenging environments. Through advanced network management techniques, dynamic spectrum allocation, and self-healing capabilities, 5G networks can adapt to changing conditions, optimize performance, and mitigate network congestion and disruptions. This enhances the user experience by minimizing downtime, dropped calls, and service interruptions, particularly in densely populated areas and high-traffic environments.

11.2.4 Quality of Service (QoS) Guarantees

Quality of Service (QoS) guarantees are essential for ensuring a consistent and satisfactory user experience across diverse applications and use cases. 5G networks incorporate QoS mechanisms such as network slicing, traffic prioritization, and service level agreements (SLAs) to allocate resources effectively and meet the varying requirements of different applications and users. This enables operators to deliver differentiated services based on factors such as bandwidth, latency, reliability, and security, ensuring that critical applications receive the necessary resources and performance levels to operate optimally.

11.2.5 Security and Privacy Protections

Ensuring the security and privacy of user data and communications is paramount in 5G networks. With the proliferation of connected devices and the transmission of sensitive information over wireless networks, robust security measures are essential to protect against cyber threats, data breaches, and unauthorized access. 5G networks incorporate encryption, authentication, and access control mechanisms to safeguard user data, prevent eavesdropping, and ensure the integrity and confidentiality of communications, enhancing trust and confidence in the network infrastructure.

11.2.6 User-Centric Design and Accessibility

A user-centric approach to design and accessibility is critical for ensuring that 5G technology meets the diverse needs and preferences of users, including those with disabilities and special requirements. User experience (UX) design principles, usability testing, and accessibility standards can help ensure that 5G services and applications are intuitive, inclusive, and accessible to all users, regardless of age, ability, or technological proficiency. By prioritizing user needs and feedback, operators and service providers can deliver personalized and user-friendly experiences that enhance satisfaction and engagement.

11.3 COLLABORATION AND INTERCONNECTED TECHNOLOGIES

In the era of fifth-generation (5G) wireless technology, collaboration and interconnectedness are key drivers of innovation and progress. As 5G networks continue to expand globally, they are not just transforming connectivity but also fostering synergies with a myriad of interconnected technologies. From artificial intelligence (AI) and Internet of Things (IoT) to cloud computing and edge computing, the integration of these technologies with 5G is unlocking new opportunities for businesses, industries, and society as a whole. Collaboration and interconnected technologies are fundamental pillars of the 5G ecosystem, driving innovation, efficiency, and value creation across industries and society. By harnessing the synergies between AI, IoT, cloud computing, edge computing, and other technologies, organizations can unlock new capabilities, enhance connectivity, and deliver transformative experiences that shape the future of connectivity and innovation. As the 5G ecosystem continues to evolve, collaboration will remain essential for driving progress and unlocking the full potential of interconnected technologies to address global challenges and create a better, more connected world for generations to come.

11.3.1 Convergence of Technologies

One of the defining characteristics of the 5G era is the convergence of multiple technologies, each with its unique capabilities and applications. 5G networks serve as the backbone for integrating these technologies, providing high-speed, low-latency connectivity that enables seamless communication and data exchange among diverse devices and systems. From smartphones and wearables to smart sensors and autonomous vehicles, the convergence of AI, IoT, and other technologies with 5G is creating a highly interconnected and intelligent ecosystem that drives innovation across industries.

11.3.2 Artificial Intelligence (AI) and Machine Learning

Artificial intelligence (AI) and machine learning play a central role in maximizing the potential of 5G networks by enabling intelligent decision-making, automation, and optimization. AI-powered algorithms analyze vast amounts of data generated by 5G-connected devices and sensors, extracting valuable insights, predicting future trends, and optimizing network performance. From dynamic resource allocation and traffic management to predictive maintenance and anomaly detection, AI enhances the efficiency, reliability, and security of 5G networks, enabling operators to deliver superior quality of service and user experiences.

11.3.3 Internet of Things (IoT) and Sensor Networks

The Internet of Things (IoT) is another key enabler of the 5G ecosystem, connecting billions of devices and sensors to the internet and enabling real-time monitoring, control, and automation. 5G networks provide the high-bandwidth, low-latency connectivity required to support massive IoT deployments across diverse verticals, including smart cities, healthcare, agriculture, and manufacturing. By integrating IoT devices and sensor networks with 5G, organizations can collect and analyze data more efficiently, optimize processes, and create new business opportunities based on actionable insights.

11.3.4 Cloud Computing and Edge Computing

Cloud computing and edge computing complement 5G networks by providing scalable, distributed computing resources for processing and storing data closer to the point of origin or consumption. While cloud computing centralizes data processing and storage in remote data centers, edge computing decentralizes these functions, enabling real-time data processing and analysis at the network edge. By leveraging cloud and edge computing in conjunction with 5G, organizations can optimize workloads, reduce latency, and deliver low-latency applications and services such as augmented reality (AR), virtual reality (VR), and autonomous vehicles.

11.3.5 Cybersecurity and Network Resilience

As the number of interconnected devices and systems grows in the 5G era, cybersecurity and network resilience become critical considerations for ensuring the integrity, confidentiality, and availability of data and services. Collaborative efforts between 5G stakeholders, cybersecurity experts, and technology providers are essential to develop robust security solutions that protect against evolving cyber threats, vulnerabilities, and attacks. By implementing multi-layered security measures, encryption protocols, and threat intelligence capabilities, organizations can mitigate risks and build resilient 5G networks that inspire trust and confidence among users and stakeholders.

11.3.6 Industry Collaboration and Standards Development

Industry collaboration and standards development play a vital role in driving interoperability, compatibility, and innovation in the 5G ecosystem. Standardization bodies such as the 3rd Generation Partnership Project (3GPP) and the Institute of Electrical and Electronics Engineers (IEEE) facilitate collaboration among stakeholders, define technical specifications, and establish interoperable standards for 5G technologies and applications. By adhering to industry standards and best practices, organizations can ensure compatibility and seamless integration of interconnected technologies within the 5G ecosystem, fostering innovation and accelerating time-to-market for new products and services.

11.3.7 Cross-Sector Partnerships and Use Cases

Cross-sector partnerships and use cases demonstrate the transformative potential of collaboration and interconnected technologies in the 5G era. From smart cities and connected healthcare to industrial automation and intelligent transportation systems, collaborative initiatives leverage the combined expertise of diverse stakeholders to address complex challenges, drive innovation, and deliver tangible benefits to society. By fostering open innovation ecosystems and fostering cross-sector collaboration, organizations can unlock new opportunities for growth, competitiveness, and sustainability in the interconnected world of 5G.

11.4 ANTICIPATED DEVELOPMENTS BEYOND 5G

As the world eagerly embraces the transformative potential of fifth-generation (5G) wireless technology, researchers, innovators, and industry leaders are already looking ahead to the next frontier of connectivity. Anticipated developments beyond 5G promise to push the boundaries of speed, capacity, and efficiency, unlocking new possibilities for communication, collaboration, and innovation. The anticipated developments beyond 5G represent an exciting frontier of innovation and exploration in wireless communication and connectivity. From sixth-generation (6G) wireless technology to terahertz communication, quantum computing, and intelligent networks, these advancements hold the potential to revolutionize how we connect, communicate, and collaborate in the digital age. By embracing emerging technologies, fostering collaboration, and prioritizing sustainability, researchers and industry stakeholders can shape the future of wireless communication and unlock new possibilities for human progress and prosperity.

11.4.1 Sixth-Generation (6G) Wireless Technology

One of the most anticipated developments beyond 5G is the advent of sixth-generation (6G) wireless technology. Building on the foundation laid by 5G, 6G aims to further enhance connectivity by delivering even faster speeds, lower latency, and greater capacity. With anticipated data rates exceeding multiple terabits per second and latency reduced to microseconds, 6G promises to revolutionize communication and enable futuristic applications such as holographic telepresence, immersive virtual reality (VR), and ubiquitous connectivity for Internet of Things (IoT) devices.

11.4.2 Terahertz Communication

Terahertz communication is a promising area of research for future wireless networks, offering the potential for ultra-high-speed data transmission in the terahertz frequency band. Terahertz waves, which lie between microwaves and infrared light on the electromagnetic spectrum, have the ability to carry vast amounts of data due to their high frequency and bandwidth.

By harnessing terahertz communication technology, future networks could achieve data rates far surpassing those of current wireless technologies, opening up new possibilities for high-definition multimedia streaming, real-time remote surgery, and autonomous vehicles.

11.4.3 Quantum Communication and Computing

Quantum communication and computing represent another frontier of development beyond 5G, offering unprecedented levels of security and computational power. Quantum communication utilizes the principles of quantum mechanics to enable secure, unbreakable encryption through the generation and transmission of quantum keys.

Quantum computing, on the other hand, leverages quantum bits (qubits) to perform computations exponentially faster than classical computers, solving complex problems that are currently infeasible. By integrating quantum communication and computing technologies into future networks, researchers aim to address cybersecurity challenges, optimize network efficiency, and unlock new frontiers in computational science and cryptography.

11.4.4 Intelligent and Autonomous Networks

Future wireless networks are expected to become increasingly intelligent and autonomous, leveraging artificial intelligence (AI) and machine learning (ML) algorithms to optimize performance, adapt to changing conditions, and self-organize in real-time. Intelligent networks can dynamically allocate resources, predict network congestion, and prioritize traffic based on user requirements, enhancing quality of service and user experience. Autonomous networks, enabled by AI-driven automation and orchestration, can streamline network operations, reduce human intervention, and improve efficiency, scalability, and reliability.

11.4.5 Metamaterials and Reconfigurable Antennas

Metamaterials and reconfigurable antennas hold promise for enhancing the performance and flexibility of future wireless networks. Metamaterials are engineered materials with unique electromagnetic properties that can manipulate electromagnetic waves, enabling novel antenna designs and signal processing techniques. Reconfigurable antennas can dynamically adjust their radiation patterns, frequencies, and polarization states to adapt to changing network conditions and user requirements. By integrating metamaterials and reconfigurable antennas into future network infrastructure, researchers aim to improve signal quality, coverage, and spectral efficiency, enabling seamless connectivity and ubiquitous access to high-speed data services.

11.4.6 Space-Based Communication Networks

Space-based communication networks, including satellite constellations and low Earth orbit (LEO) satellites, are poised to play a significant role in future wireless communication. By deploying constellations of small satellites in low Earth orbit, companies like SpaceX, OneWeb, and Amazon aim to provide global broadband coverage with low latency and high reliability. Space-based communication networks have the potential to bridge the digital divide, connect remote and underserved regions, and enable seamless connectivity for maritime, aviation, and IoT applications.

11.4.7 Green and Sustainable Networks

As concerns about environmental sustainability continue to grow, future wireless networks are expected to prioritize energy efficiency and environmental sustainability. Green and sustainable networks leverage renewable energy sources, energy-efficient hardware, and intelligent power management techniques to minimize energy consumption and carbon emissions. By adopting green technologies and sustainable practices, future networks can reduce their environmental footprint, mitigate climate change, and contribute to a more sustainable and resilient future for generations to come.

CHAPTER 12

CONCLUSION

12.1 RECAPITULATION OF KEY CONCEPTS

- 5G Technology: Fifth-generation (5G) technology represents the latest evolution in wireless communication, promising to deliver faster speeds, lower latency, and greater connectivity than previous generations. With data rates potentially reaching multiple gigabits per second, 5G enables high-definition video streaming, real-time gaming, and immersive experiences like augmented reality (AR) and virtual reality (VR). Its ultra-low latency of milliseconds enables instantaneous communication for applications such as autonomous vehicles, remote surgery, and industrial automation. 5G technology is poised to revolutionize industries, transform economies, and empower individuals with unprecedented levels of connectivity and innovation.
- Wireless Communication: Wireless communication refers to the transmission of data over radio waves without the need for physical cables or wires. It enables mobility, flexibility, and ubiquitous connectivity, allowing users to access information and communicate from anywhere, anytime. Wireless communication technologies include cellular networks, Wi-Fi, Bluetooth, and satellite communication systems, each with its unique characteristics and applications. Wireless communication plays a vital role in modern society, powering mobile devices, IoT devices, smart appliances, and connected vehicles, and enabling seamless connectivity for individuals and businesses worldwide.
- 5G Architecture: 5G architecture comprises a network of interconnected components that enable the delivery of high-speed, low-latency wireless communication services. It includes radio access network (RAN), core network, and edge computing infrastructure. The RAN consists of base stations, antennas, and radio units that transmit and receive wireless signals. The core network manages data routing, authentication, and service delivery, while edge computing brings computational resources closer to end-users for faster processing and reduced latency. 5G architecture is designed to support diverse use cases and applications, from enhanced mobile broadband to mission-critical communications and massive IoT deployments.

- Network Components: 5G network components include base stations, antennas, radio units, routers, switches, servers, and software-defined networking (SDN) controllers. Base stations, also known as cell towers, transmit and receive wireless signals to and from user devices. Antennas capture and transmit radio waves, while radio units process signals and manage radio resources. Routers and switches route data between network nodes, while servers host applications and services. SDN controllers manage network resources and orchestrate traffic flows for optimal performance and efficiency.
- New Radio (NR): New Radio (NR) is the air interface standard for 5G wireless communication, defining the specifications for radio transmission and reception. NR supports a wide range of frequency bands, including sub-6 GHz and mmWave, and incorporates advanced technologies such as massive MIMO (Multiple Input Multiple Output), beamforming, and dynamic spectrum sharing. NR enables higher data rates, lower latency, and greater spectral efficiency compared to previous generations, making it well-suited for a wide range of applications, including enhanced mobile broadband, ultra-reliable low-latency communication (URLLC), and massive machine-type communication (mMTC).

12.2 FINAL THOUGHTS ON THE TRANSFORMATIVE IMPACT OF 5G

As we reflect on the transformative impact of fifth-generation (5G) wireless technology, it becomes evident that we stand on the brink of a new era of connectivity, innovation, and opportunity. From ultra-fast speeds and low latency to massive connectivity and intelligent networks, 5G has the potential to revolutionize industries, empower individuals, and reshape the fabric of society in profound ways. The transformative impact of 5G extends far beyond faster speeds and lower latency to encompass a wide range of societal, economic, and environmental implications. By embracing the opportunities and challenges of 5G technology, we can harness its transformative potential to create a more connected, inclusive, and sustainable future for generations to come. As we embark on this journey of innovation and progress, let us remain mindful of the ethical considerations, societal impacts, and global responsibilities that accompany the adoption of 5G, ensuring that technology serves as a force for good and advances human well-being in the digital age.

12.2.1 Ubiquitous Connectivity and Digital Transformation

One of the most significant implications of 5G is its ability to provide ubiquitous connectivity, bridging the digital divide and enabling access to high-speed internet services for individuals and communities worldwide. 5G has the potential to accelerate digital transformation across sectors, from healthcare and education to transportation and manufacturing, unlocking new opportunities for innovation, efficiency, and economic growth. By connecting billions of devices and sensors, 5G networks create a foundation for the Internet of Things (IoT) ecosystem, enabling smart cities, autonomous vehicles, and connected infrastructure that enhance quality of life and sustainability.

12.2.2 Innovation and Entrepreneurship

5G technology is a catalyst for innovation and entrepreneurship, fueling the development of new products, services, and business models that leverage its high-speed, low-latency connectivity. Startups and enterprises alike are exploring the potential of 5G-enabled applications such as augmented reality (AR), virtual reality (VR), telemedicine, and autonomous systems, driving advancements in areas such as gaming, entertainment, healthcare, and manufacturing.

By fostering a culture of innovation and collaboration, 5G empowers entrepreneurs to disrupt traditional industries, create value, and drive economic growth in the digital economy.

12.2.3 Resilience and Sustainability

5G networks are designed to be resilient, scalable, and energy-efficient, enabling operators to meet the growing demand for connectivity while minimizing their environmental footprint. By leveraging technologies such as network slicing, edge computing, and renewable energy sources, 5G networks can optimize resource allocation, reduce energy consumption, and mitigate carbon emissions, contributing to environmental sustainability and climate resilience. As organizations prioritize sustainability goals and corporate responsibility, 5G technology offers a pathway to greener, more sustainable business practices and operations.

12.2.4 Societal Impacts and Ethical Considerations

The transformative impact of 5G extends beyond technology and business to encompass broader societal implications and ethical considerations. As 5G networks enable unprecedented levels of connectivity and data exchange, concerns arise about privacy, security, and digital rights. It is essential to address these ethical considerations and ensure that 5G development and deployment prioritize principles such as transparency, accountability, and inclusivity. By fostering dialogue, collaboration, and stakeholder engagement, we can navigate the ethical landscape of 5G and ensure that technology serves the common good and benefits humanity as a whole.

12.2.5 Global Collaboration and Partnership

Realizing the full potential of 5G requires global collaboration and partnership among governments, industry stakeholders, academia, and civil society. By working together to develop interoperable standards, share best practices, and address regulatory challenges, we can unlock the transformative power of 5G and bridge the digital divide between nations and regions. International cooperation is essential for ensuring equitable access to 5G technology, promoting innovation and entrepreneurship, and addressing global challenges such as climate change, public health, and social inequality.

BIBLIOGRAPHY

- 5G and Satellite Spectrum, Standards and Scale by Mark Gibson and Luis M. Correia. Published by Academic Press in 2020.
- 5G Cellular Communications by Bernhard H. Walke and Stefan Mangold. Published by Springer in 2019.
- 5G Core Networks: Powering Digitalization by Stefan Rommer, Peter Hedman, and Magnus Olsson. Published by Academic Press in 2017.
- 5G Explained: Security and Deployment of Advanced Mobile Communications by Jyrki T. J. Penttinen. Published by John Wiley & Sons in 2017.
- 5G for Future Wireless Networks: An Introduction by Frederik Tilmans and Luciano Leonel Mendes. Published by Springer in 2020.
- 5G for the Connected World by Devaki Chandramouli and Rainer Liebhart. Published by Artech House in 2019.
- 5G for the Industrial Internet of Things by Anand R. Prasad and Niranth Amogh. Published by Springer in 2020.
- 5G Mobile and Wireless Communications Technology by Afif Osseiran, Josef F. Monserrat, and Patrick Marsch. Published by Cambridge University Press in 2016.
- 5G Mobile and Wireless Communications Technology by Erik Dahlman, Stefan Parkvall, and Johan Skold. Published by Academic Press in 2017.
- 5G Mobile and Wireless Communications Technology by Erik Dahlman, Stefan Parkvall, and Johan Skold. Published by Academic Press in 2018.
- 5G Mobile Communications by Afif Osseiran, Jose F. Monserrat, and Patrick Marsch. Published by Springer in 2017.
- 5G Mobile Communications by Woon Hau Chin and David J. Goodman. Published by Springer in 2020.
- 5G Networks: Fundamental Requirements, Enabling Technologies, and Operations Management by Mehdi Rasti and Marzieh Maleki. Published by Springer in 2019.

- 5G New Radio: 3GPP Release 15 by Sassan Ahmadi. Published by Wiley-IEEE Press in 2020.
- 5G New Radio: A Beam-based Air Interface by Sachin Abhyankar, Erik Dahlman, and Jianxin Wang. Published by Academic Press in 2019.
- 5G NR: The Next Generation Wireless Access Technology by Erik Dahlman, Stefan Parkvall, and Johan Skold. Published by Academic Press in 2018.
- 5G Radio Access Networks: Centralized RAN, Cloud-RAN, and Virtualization of Small Cells by Hadi Baligh. Published by Wiley-IEEE Press in 2017.
- 5G System Design: An End to End Perspective by Sadayuki Abeta, Jun Terada, and Koji Yamamoto. Published by John Wiley & Sons in 2019.
- 5G System Design: Architectural and Functional Considerations and Long Term Research by Patrick Marsch, Gerhard P. Fettweis, and Gerhard Fettweis. Published by Springer in 2017.
- 5G System Design: The Next Big Thing in Wireless Networks by Samarjit Chakraborty and Dipankar Raychaudhuri. Published by Springer in 2019.
- 5G Wireless Systems: Simulation and Evaluation Techniques by Federico Boccardi, Lorenzo Galati Giordano, and Chih-Lin I. Published by Cambridge University Press in 2017.
- 5G Wireless Technologies by Angeliki Alexiou and Maria-Nectaria Antonopoulou. Published by CRC Press in 2017.

INDEX

S

V

W

X

Z

www.ingramcontent.com/pod-product-compliance
Lightning Source LLC
LaVergne TN
LVHW062116200926
848484LV00007B/1681